Computational Social Sciences

Computational Social Sciences

A series of authored and edited monographs that utilize quantitative and computational methods to model, analyze and interpret large-scale social phenomena. Titles within the series contain methods and practices that test and develop theories of complex social processes through bottom-up modeling of social interactions. Of particular interest is the study of the co-evolution of modern communication technology and social behavior and norms, in connection with emerging issues such as trust, risk, security and privacy in novel socio-technical environments. Computational Social Sciences is explicitly transdisciplinary: quantitative methods from fields such as dynamical systems, artificial intelligence, network theory, agent-based modeling, and statistical mechanics are invoked and combined with state-of-the-art mining and analysis of large data sets to help us understand social agents, their interactions on and offline, and the effect of these interactions at the macro level. Topics include, but are not limited to social networks and media, dynamics of opinions, cultures and conflicts, socio-technical co-evolution and social psychology. Computational Social Sciences will also publish monographs and selected edited contributions from specialized conferences and workshops specifically aimed at communicating new findings to a large transdisciplinary audience. A fundamental goal of the series is to provide a single forum within which commonalities and differences in the workings of this field may be discerned, hence leading to deeper insight and understanding.

Marijn A. Keijzer · Jan Lorenz · Michał Bojanowski
Editors

Computational Social Science of Social Cohesion and Polarization

Springer

Editors
Marijn A. Keijzer
Toulouse School of Economics
Institute for Advanced Study in Toulouse
Toulouse, France

Jan Lorenz
Constructor University
Bremen, Germany

Michał Bojanowski
Kozminski University
Warsaw, Poland

Autonomous University of Barcelona
Barcelona, Spain

ISSN 2509-9574 ISSN 2509-9582 (electronic)
Computational Social Sciences
ISBN 978-3-032-01372-9 ISBN 978-3-032-01373-6 (eBook)
https://doi.org/10.1007/978-3-032-01373-6

The work was supported by by VolkswagenStiftung through a grant in their program "International Research in Computational Social Sciences"

This Springer imprint is published by the registered company Springer Nature Switzerland AG
The registered company address is: Gewerbestrasse 11, 6330 Cham, Switzerland

Preface

The erosion of social cohesion and looming political polarization sit at the heart of today's most pressing societal questions. As democratic institutions appear to waver in the absence of widespread social support, political discourse fragments among increasingly complex ideological groups and communities form along increasingly complex lines of identity and affiliation, the ability to understand what binds and drives societies apart is more crucial than ever before.

At the same time, social science is witnessing the rise of computational social science (CSS)—a scientific paradigm that blends observational data of unprecedented scale with the power of computationally driven statistical and formal modeling. Its tools—from machine learning to social network analysis, and from agent-based modeling to microsimulation—are well-suited to study social cohesion and polarization with exceptional precision and scale. The challenge the field is facing is to further develop its domain-specific language and body of knowledge, to foster a shared understanding of CSS and social phenomena, beyond description and prediction alone.

This volume brings together a group of researchers from various backgrounds and career stages. It opens with two discussions of the conceptual and methodological foundations for rigorous computational social science on cohesion and polarization and is followed by nine original chapters that showcase state-of-the-art applications. Together, they offer a lens into the practice of CSS and serve to inspire social cohesion and polarization researchers to follow in their footsteps.

This book emerged from two collaborative research incubators designed specifically to foster interdisciplinary collaboration. As detailed in Chap. 12, the incubators expand the concept of summer schools to not just educate, but to start collaborations.

We hope this book informs and inspires. Whether you are a researcher, student, policymaker, or simply curious, we invite you to explore the questions addressed in this book and hope it helps to fertilize new ideas and innovative research.

Toulouse, France — Marijn A. Keijzer
Bremen, Germany — Jan Lorenz
Warsaw, Poland/Barcelona, Spain — Michał Bojanowski
Summer 2025

Acknowledgements

All chapters in the book, as well as the book project itself, were initiated during two Summer Schools and Research Incubators on Computational Social Science enabled by a grant from the VolkswagenStiftung. The first research incubator was on social cohesion and was organized by Jan Lorenz, Andreas Flache, and Michael Mäs. It took place in Groningen, the Netherlands, in the summer of 2022. The second incubator was on Democratic Debate, organized by Jan Lorenz, Marijn A. Keijzer, and Bruce Edmonds. The event took place at the Bremen International Graduate Schools for Social Sciences at Constructor University Bremen, Germany, in 2023. The research incubators offered an opportunity for junior and senior researchers (or 'experts') to interact in small groups and work on a joint project. Additionally, each of the experts gave a lecture or tutorial during the summer school. In Chap. 12 of this book, Jan Lorenz outlines the concept of these research incubators, arguing that they are ideal tools to promote and disseminate interdisciplinary research practices.

We are greatly appreciative to all the reviewers who provided crucial support to the editors and provided valuable feedback to each chapter. Furthermore, we thank the VolkswagenStiftung not only for funding the research incubators but also for providing the funds to make this book open access.

About This Book

What holds societies together—and what drives them apart? As worry over political polarization and social cohesion intensifies across the globe, this volume explores timely and vital questions of social cohesion and polarization through the lens of Computational Social Science. It brings together leading and junior scholars who harness the power of computational methods to analyze, model, and understand discourse, social relationships, and beliefs. Drawing on tools such as agent-based modeling, social network analysis, and natural language processing, the book offers a range of innovative approaches to study how belief systems form, attitudes polarize, and communities fragment.

Aimed at researchers, students, and practitioners across disciplines, this volume is both an introduction to the field and a showcase of its most promising applications. It is an introduction into CSS of social cohesion and polarization, and an invitation to rethink how we study—and perhaps even how we can repair—the social fabric.

About This Book

Contents

Contributors

Regina Arant Bremen International Graduate School of Social Sciences, Constructor University, Bremen, Germany

Marlene C. L. Batzke Royal Holloway, University of London, London, UK

Klaus Boehnke Bremen International Graduate School of Social Sciences, Constructor University, Bremen, Germany

Michał Bojanowski Autonomous University of Barcelona, Bellaterra, Spain; Kozminski University, Warsaw, Poland

Susanne Böller University of Bonn, Bonn, Germany

Hilke Brockmann Constructor University, Bremen, Germany

Dino Carpentras Computational Social Science, ETH Zürich, Zurich, Switzerland

Yijing Chen Department of Network and Data Science, Central European University, Vienna, Austria

Christian S. Czymara Netherlands Interdisciplinary Demographic Institute, The Hague, The Netherlands

Bart de Bruin Department of Industrial Engineering and Innovation Sciences, Eindhoven University of Technology, Eindhoven, The Netherlands

Georgi Dragolov School of Business, Social and Decision Sciences, Constructor University, Bremen, Germany

Wiebke Drews University of the Bundeswehr Munich, Munich, Germany

Bruce Edmonds UiT The Arctic University of Norway, Tromsø, Norway;
The Centre for Policy Modelling, Manchester, UK;
Umeå University, Umeå, Sweden

Lukas Erhard Department for Computational Social Science, University of Stuttgart, Stuttgart, Germany

Pedro Fierro University Adolfo Ibanez, Santiago, Chile

Joris Frese European University Institute, Florence, Italy

Carina Hartz Bremen International Graduate School of Social Sciences, Constructor University, Bremen, Germany

Gert Jan Hofstede Vrije Universiteit Amsterdam, Amsterdam, Netherlands

Till Hovestadt Nuffield College, University of Oxford, Oxford, UK

František Kalvas University of West Bohemia, Pilsen, Czech Republic

Barbara Kamińska Faculty of Management, Wroclaw University of Science and Technology, Wroclaw, Poland

Marijn A. Keijzer Institute for Advanced Study in Toulouse, Toulouse School of Economics, University of Toulouse Capitole, Toulouse, France

Yara Khaluf Vrije Universiteit Amsterdam, Amsterdam, Netherlands

Zarine Kharazian Department of Human-Centered Design and Engineering, University of Washington, Washington, USA

Manika Lamba School of Library and Information Studies, University of Oklahoma, Norman, USA

Younghyun Lee University of Illinois, Urbana-Champaign, Illinois, USA

Jan Lorenz Bremen International School for Social Sciences, School of Business, Social and Decision Sciences, Constructor University, Bremen, Germany

Alla Loseva ICS, University of Groningen, Groningen, Netherlands

Miranda J. Lubbers Autonomous University of Barcelona, Barcelona, Spain

Adrian Lüders Institut für Kommunikationswissenschaft, University of Hohenheim, Stuttgart, Germany

André C. R. Martins Escola de Artes, Ciências e Humanidades, Universidade de São Paulo (EACH-USP), São Paulo, Brazil

Florencia Piñeyrúa National Council for Scientific and Technical Research, National University of San Martín, Buenos Aires, Argentina

Ivan Puga-Gonzalez Center for Modelling Social Systems, Norwegian Research Center (NORCE), Kristiansand, Norway

Paul Schuler University of Edinburgh, Edinburgh, Scotland

Anne Speer University of Bremen, Bremen, Germany

Peter Steiglechner Constructor University, Bremen, Germany;
Leibniz Centre for Tropical Marine Research (ZMT), Bremen, Germany;
Complexity Science Hub, Vienna, Austria

Daniel Triana National Autonomous University of Mexico, Mexico City, Mexico

Kai Unzicker Bertelsmann Stiftung, Gütersloh, Germany

Philip Warncke Department of Psychology, University of Limerick, Limerick, Ireland;
SCRIPTS Data and Methodology Center, Freie Universität Berlin, Berlin, Germany

Maximilian Weber University Mainz, Mainz, Germany

Valeria Widler Modeling and Simulation of Complex Processes, Zuse Institute Berlin, Berlin, Germany

Bernd Wurpts Independent Researcher, Lucerne, Switzerland

Weijun Yuan University of Chicago, Chicago, USA

Nikolas Zöller Max Planck Institute for Human Development, Berlin, Germany

Chapter 1
Computational Social Science of Social Cohesion and Polarization

Marijn A. Keijzer, Jan Lorenz, and Michał Bojanowski

Abstract The emergence of Computational Social Science (CSS) marks a transformative shift in the study of social phenomena, triggered by advancements in computational technology and large-scale collection of (digital) behavioral trace data. CSS promises to provide an accurate and deep understanding of social behavior through the analysis of social interactions, movement patterns, and communication networks at scale. However, the lack of a common theoretical language and clearly defined scientific agenda complicates CSS' ability to build a common understanding of social phenomena. In this chapter, we establish CSS as a scientific paradigm, emphasizing the integration of computational tools with rigorous theoretical modeling. Specifically, we position CSS within the trajectory of a maturing science and emphasize the synthesis of data-driven CSS with theoretically-informed modeling for understanding social phenomena like social cohesion and polarization. To illustrate how CSS can advance these fields specifically, we unpack a range of conceptualizations of political polarization and social cohesion, and demonstrate how they have evolved in Europe over recent decades. Finally, we discuss how the subsequent chapters in this book aim to bridge the gap between theoretical and empirical CSS for social cohesion and polarization.

Keywords Computational social science · Social cohesion · Polarization · Agent-based modeling · Network analysis · Belief alignment · Affective polarization

---

M. A. Keijzer (✉)
Institute for Advanced Study in Toulouse, Toulouse School of Economics, University of Toulouse Capitole, Toulouse, France
e-mail: marijn.keijzer@iast.fr

J. Lorenz
Bremen International School for Social Sciences, School of Business, Social and Decision Sciences, Constructor University, Bremen, Germany

M. Bojanowski
Autonomous University of Barcelona, Bellaterra, Spain

Kozminski University, Warsaw, Poland

M. A. Keijzer et al. (eds.), *Computational Social Science of Social Cohesion and Polarization*, Computational Social Sciences,
https://doi.org/10.1007/978-3-032-01373-6_1

1.1 A Computational Science for Social Phenomena

The new millennium has witnessed the Computational Social Science (CSS) revolution (Lazer et al. 2009; Conte et al. 2012; Lazer et al. 2020). Technological advancements have enabled the use of advanced computational techniques that require unprecedented computational power. Concurrently, digitization in many parts of society, including the emergence of the Internet as a public sphere for many social interactions, has created enormous amounts of behavioral data. This has not only aided traditional techniques for analyzing commonly used data sources, such as surveys and register data in our ability to execute more complex techniques on larger datasets (Edelmann et al. 2020), but also enabled the analysis of data that was previously unavailable or inaccessible (Salganik 2018). The CSS revolution enables us to analyze social interaction in digital communication technologies, movement patterns revealed through location tracking, or semantic structures in newly digitized archives, to name a few.

Much like any developing paradigm, establishing CSS has not gone without hiccups. Since CSS researchers draw from a variety of disciplines, there is a lack of common understanding about what has and ought to be done. Psychology, sociology, political science, economics, and related disciplines all benefit from histories rich in theoretical ideas, collective approaches and critical reflection. CSS researchers who come from a natural science or engineering background like physics, computer or information science will be accustomed to having a larger common body of knowledge about the world captured in laws and regularities. None of that exists in CSS, which has yet to develop its proprietary language, methods, and paradigms. As a consequence, a significant amount of work has been descriptive in nature, or has tested rudimentary ideas that are perhaps more developed in the longer theoretical literature of the disciplinary social sciences.

Here, we define Computational Social Science as a *scientific* approach to understanding *social* phenomena using *computational* tools. That definition explicitly departs from the data-driven, descriptive version of CSS that has become paramount in recent years. CSS has primarily focused on analyzing pre-existing, digital, behavioral trace data. In many domains, bridging the gap from self-report to observational data has advanced our understanding by forming *how-actually* descriptions of social systems–explanations that map closely to the social phenomenon, but lack parsimony (Ylikoski 2017). To move from description to explanation, however, we cannot rely on empirical observation alone, but have to understand the dynamics of a system that led to the particular observed outcome (Keuschnigg et al. 2017; Flache et al. 2022). The empirical verdict is only the final stage of a deductive research cycle (Popper 1959). To develop a proper scientific paradigm, CSS will need to incorporate rigorous theory formation through formal tools like generative micro-simulations (agent-based models), evolutionary modeling, game theory, or even through closer integration with simple verbal theorizing. Here, we argue for a broader understanding of CSS, and a tighter link between theoretical and empirical work. To argue why this is necessary and how that tight link should be established, let us delve a little deeper into CSS by unpacking each of its components.

1.1.1 Computational (Social Science)

With the emergence of CSS, the social sciences have undergone a natural evolution of modern sciences, complementing traditional *theoretical* and *empirical* components with a *computational* one (see Fig. 1.1) (Hummon and Fararo 1995). Traditional sciences link theorizing to empirical analysis through generalization (inductive) and hypothesis testing (deductive approach). With the addition of a computational component, two new scientific activities become part of CSS' practice.

First, complex data analysis has become feasible to the point that our predictive models frequently outperform theoretical ones (Salganik 2020). We have moved from *how-possibly* explanations–illustrative for the phase of theory-building in early social sciences–to evidence in insight into *how-actually* explanations (Ylikoski 2017). Data analysis practices have gained so much sophistication it has shortly led some to naively proclaim "the end of theory" (Anderson 2008). To the contrary, theory formation has benefited greatly from the computation-shift. While agent-based and other simulation models have been around for longer than the computer has, their potential has been boosted by computational advancements (Flache et al. 2022). A common misunderstanding around computational models is that they would share the same goal as deeply calibrated computational models for the analysis (and prediction) of relationships in complex systems like those on the arrow between 'Computational X' and 'Empirical X' in Fig. 1.1. However, the position of simulation in Fig. 1.1 is crucial, signifying its use as a computational theoretical tool. Simulation models have the advantage over empirical models in that they are better at making generalizations, cutting out what is less important, and focus on mechanisms in isolation. Even the most refined model using the largest and most precise dataset may be vulnerable to common problems with 'big' data like incompleteness, inaccessibility, non-representativity, drift, algorithmic confounds, and the like (Salganik 2018). Moreover, modeling complex empirical data almost always entails with a trade-off between accuracy and tractability. As a consequence, predictive models tend to be 'black boxes' that do not contribute to a deeper understanding of social phenomena at the level of the explanation (Molina and Garip 2019).

The methodological toolkit in CSS is extensive, and any attempt to provide a comprehensive inventory would inevitably fall short. Nevertheless, several methodologies stand out for their particular promise and relevance in linking theoretical insights with computational modeling. Theory-driven agent-based modeling emphasize the generative role of formal models in hypothesis development (Flache et al. 2022), allowing researchers to explore how micro-level assumptions–such as bounded confidence or social influence–can produce unexpected macro-level dynamics like polarization (e.g., see Chap. 10: Widler et al. 2025) or segregation (Chap. 11: Khaluf et aal. 2025). In contrast, data-driven agent-based modeling (Lorenz 2021) incorporates

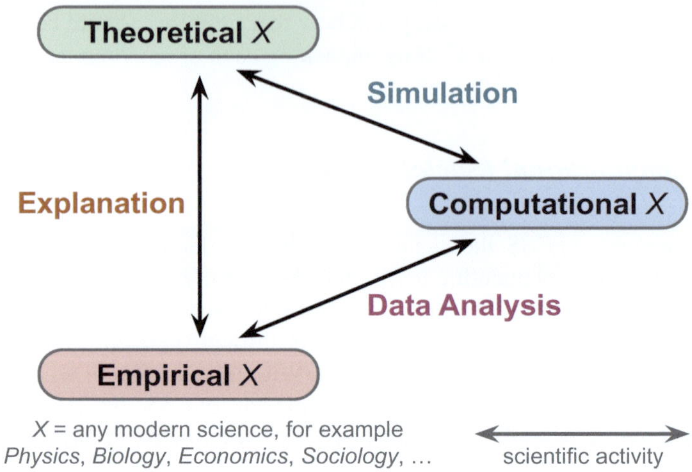

Fig. 1.1 **The three components of modern sciences** and the related scientific activities (adapted from Hummon and Fararo 1995)

empirical data to calibrate agent behavior (e.g., see Chap. 9: Edmonds et al. 2025) or validate simulation outcomes, thereby enhancing the realism and explanatory power of models. Natural language processing (NLP), which builds on traditional text analysis and increasingly leverages transformer-based models, enables the extraction of ideological positions, sentiment, and framing from large-scale textual data, offering a lens through which to study discourse and alignment (e.g., see Chaps. 6–8: Brockmann et al. 2025; Lee et al. 2025; Yuan 2025). Other machine learning techniques are also widely used to uncover complex patterns in behavioral or communicative data, support predictive modeling, and classify group identities or polarization trajectories (Molina and Garip 2019). Social network modeling is typically computationally expensive, and hence benefited greatly from the computational shift. In CSS, social network models can be applied to study interpersonal relationships (e.g., see Chap. 3: Bojanowski et al. 2025), of course, but have also been used to study other kinds of networks like belief networks (Chap. 5: Warncke et al. 2025) or informational networks (Chap. 4: Keijzer et al. 2025). Online experiments (Salganik 2018) facilitate controlled testing of social mechanisms in digital environments and are increasingly used in conjunction with simulations or observational data (Keijzer et al. 2024). Digital trace data–from social media posts to behavioral logs–provide an empirical foundation for tracking the evolution of social alignments at scale (Lazer et al. 2009). Finally, causal inference techniques for observational data, including matching and instrumental variables, are gaining traction in CSS as tools to estimate the effects of interventions or exposures in complex, real-world settings (Morgan and Winship 2014).

At the end of the day, what sets computational sciences apart from fields without an explicit computational component is that they use cutting-edge computational technologies to solve problems. This makes CSS almost exclusively a quantitative science. Ultimately, computers count things, and computational methods are thus, by definition, almost entirely quantitative. However, advancements in topic modeling and AI, and in particular the introduction of LLMs, also present an opportunity to use the computer as a central part in qualitative analysis.

1.1.2 (Computational) Social Science

Social sciences concern themselves with social phenomena. In his seminal book 'Dissecting the social,' Hedstrom (2005) defines social (or collective) phenomena as phenomena that belong to one of

1. Typical actions, beliefs, or desires among the members of society or a collectivity.
2. Distributions and aggregate patterns such as spatial distributions and inequalities.
3. Topologies of networks that describe relationships between members of a collectivity.
4. Informal rules or social norms that constrain the actions of the members of a collectivity.

As a scientific discipline, CSS is concerned with the production of generalizable knowledge about social phenomena. That is, it ought to go beyond detailed descriptions of social systems, and attempt to deduce generalizable rules from theory, supported by empirical data. It may be implicit, but data-driven CSS appears to have taken an inductive approach; learning from real-world observations alone. To generate knowledge, we should use data for a different purpose: to falsify what we hold as true (Popper 1959). Enough attempts at falsification then ultimately leave fewer and fewer hypotheses likely to explain a phenomenon. But there is one step before falsification: the formulation of falsifiable hypotheses. A mature CSS will need to emphasize the generation of falsifiable hypotheses–that is, the production of social theory.

One way CSS could develop into its own rigorous social science is by more clearly defining the scope of their explanations. Arvidsson et al. (2024), for example, argue that CSS should focus on middle-range theories (Merton 1968). On that account Arvidsson et al. note that "CSS researchers outside of the social sciences often frame their research as if they were in the business of establishing law-like relations in social data (e.g., scale-free networks, scaling laws). The accumulated knowledge of the social sciences suggests that this is not a route to be followed, however. The generality of the social is not found in universal laws, but in semi-general processes that operate according to similar principles in different social situations." (Arvidsson et al. 2024).

Various disciplines have integrated CSS into the production of theory and generalizable knowledge to different degrees. In quantitative sociology, CSS has had a major impact across the board, overtaking fields like social network analysis and group formation, collective behavior and political sociology, the sociology of knowledge, cultural sociology, social psychology, and emotions, the production of culture, economic sociology and organizations, and demography and population studies (Edelmann et al. 2020). Yet, recently, the call for stronger integration of strong empirical work with traditional and formal theory can be heard loud and clear (Flache et al. 2022; Arvidsson et al. 2024). In particular the link to analytical sociology–a branch of sociology that focuses on actor-based and mechanistic explanations of social phenomena–should be better established through a more solid theoretical basis for CSS (Keuschnigg et al. 2017; Arvidsson et al. 2024). Anthropology–a research field primarily built on ethographic, qualitative work–has leveraged computational opportunities mainly for analysis and calculation, but "there is an ongoing transition from the instrumentalisation of computers as tools for calculations, to the implementation of information science methodologies for analysis, deduction, knowledge representation, and reasoning, as part of the research process in social anthropology" (Peponakis et al. 2024). Similar interest is voiced in psychology and cognitive science–both fields where the analysis of 'big' data or digital trace data beloved by CSS researchers is traditionally less common–where scholars are promoting the use of formal theoretical tools (Cushman 2024) and social simulation (Schultheis 2021). Communication scientists explicitly place computational communication science as a subfield of CSS, and propose a traditional division of the field's tasks into experimental, observational and theoretical aspects of science (Hilbert 2019).

1.2 Social Cohesion and Polarization

Topically, this book focuses on the social phenomena of social cohesion and polarization. Social cohesion is the cornerstone of harmonious democratic societies. It ensures mutual understanding and care, promotes cooperation, increases health and well-being, and fosters economic growth. The promotion of social cohesion has long been on the political agenda of many governmental and supranational organizations. The United Nations Development Programme lists strengthening social cohesion as a core strategy for improving human development and cooperation (UNDP 2024). In Europe, social cohesion is a core policy goal, officially manifested in the Treaty of the European Union (Union 2012). Yet, social cohesion appears to have decayed in recent years. Loss of generalized trust, polarization in political debates, and loss of faith in democratic authorities have become a central concern in the debates of both policymakers and citizens alike. Social cohesion is under pressure (see Chap. 2: Boehnke et al. 2025), and this pressure is felt strongly in the political domain, manifesting as polarization. Political polarization has perhaps garnered even greater concern and interest in recent decades. Political polarization, and its consequences for the erosion of social cohesion, is named as one of the five greatest global risks of today by the World Economic Forum and the most severe societal challenge of tomorrow (World Economic Forum 2025).

Both social cohesion and polarization are examples of elusive concepts contested in the public debate, discussed across (social) sciences, and are therefore difficult to define. Social cohesion has been described as a *quasi-concept* (Bernard 1999), a construct that politicians like because it sounds like a scientifically solid societal goal, yet remains vague enough to be adapted for different interpretations in different situations. Political polarization is less ambiguous than social cohesion, but still, there is considerable variance in what is typically understood when discussed in news media, by politicians, and across social sciences.

In the following subsections, we provide an overview of conceptualizations and operationalizations of social cohesion and polarization. After this discussion, we provide some empirical evidence trends in social cohesion and polarization in Europe and North-America, building on those conceptualizations.

1.2.1 Social Cohesion

As signaled above, conceptual clarity is not social cohesion's strong suit. Many elements contribute to the cohesiveness of a society, making the concept broad and heterogeneous, to the point of being impractical. Before considering how researchers theorize about social cohesion, it is worth noting that there seems to be a relative consensus that a cohesive society is characterized by features such as rarity of social conflicts, cooperation, mutual trust among members, prevalent pro-social behavior, civic engagement, trust in institutions, equal access and lack of exclusion, shared social norms, and resilience. The list could go on, and, on a general level, none of the items would be individually challenged.

There is less consensus regarding the details and how researchers theorize the concept. As "it is better to be vaguely right than exactly wrong" (Read 2007) let it suffice to start with the fact that, historically, notions of social cohesion in sociology can be traced to Durkheimian notions of solidarity–a force that maintains social order (Durkheim 1893). According to Durkheim, the origins of solidarity come from shared activities and beliefs, such as group hunting and gathering, mythology, or religion. This "mechanical solidarity" characterized human sociality in the early stages of societal development. In later stages, characterized by "organic solidarity," the increasing specialization of labor creates mutual interdependencies between people. In other words, people have to rely on each other in order to meet their needs. Both forms of solidarity refer to elements of social cohesion–shared sentiments and cooperation (see also Doreian and Fararo 1998; Moody and White 2003; Friedkin 2004).

Many elements of social cohesion can also be found in the literature on social capital, albeit in different forms depending on the conceptualization of social capital itself (Erices-Ocampo et al. 2025). While the following notions of different conceptualizations might not be specific to any particular author, they are related to social cohesion. For example, Putnam (2000) highlights the importance of contributing to public goods and participation in voluntary organizations. In the concept of Portes and Sensenbrenner (1993), social capital (e.g., of migrants) comes from resources and social support available in cohesive social networks of people of the same origin.

Table 1.1 Dimensions of social cohesion as conceptualized by Schiefer and Noll (2017)

Relational	Ideational	Distributive
(1) *Social relations*—social networks, quality and closeness of social relations, mutual trust and reciprocity	(3) *Orientation towards common good*—pro-social behavior, willingness to contribute to public goods, internalization of group's goals	(5) *Quality of life*—security in long-term well being, low risk
(2) *Identification*—sense of belonging to a social group, geographical territory or culture, recognition as a member of a group, culture or territory	(4) *Shared values*—alignment of axiological positions, group consensus, deliberation	(6) *Inequality*—Equal opportunities, inclusion, lack of consequential social and economic divisions

Thus, some authors conceptualize social cohesion as a state, in which there is a lot of social capital that can be utilized by members of a group or society. Other authors define it as the structural features of networks of social relationships that provide beneficial conditions for social capital to be created, accumulated, and utilized (see also Lin 2002; Bourdieu 2011).

An exhaustive review of different conceptualizations of social cohesion is beyond the scope of this introduction (such reviews are to be found in Chan et al. 2006; Dragolov et al. 2016; Schiefer and Noll 2017, among others). It is, however, instructive to recall the work of Schiefer and Noll (2017) as an example of a conceptualization that led to an operationalization for survey measurement. They distinguish three general dimensions that can be broken down into six specific concepts, given in Table 1.1. Closely related to that conceptualization is the Social Cohesion Radar (Berger 1998; Dragolov et al. 2016)–a survey measurement tool consisting of blocks of questions leading to scales corresponding to the cohesion dimensions. The tool has been applied in an international cross-sectional survey, which allows for dynamic and cross-country comparisons of how different aspects of social cohesion change or remain stable in different countries. The scales and the results are further discussed by Boehnke et al. (2025 Chap. 2 in this book).

In contrast, a more macro-level perspective on cohesion is exemplified by the work of Green and Janmaat (2011). Their starting point is influenced by comparative welfare state theory (e.g., Esping-Andersen 1990), but they go beyond this framework by explicitly focusing on cultural and social integration, not just economic redistribution. They are also informed by the Durkheimian theory we mentioned earlier, which sees social cohesion as the glue holding societies together, as well as by political economy and globalization studies. They challenge the notion that globalization leads to convergence in social models and instead propose that different regimes of social cohesion persist and evolve in distinct ways. The definition of cohesion comprises four dimensions: social inclusion (e.g., income equality, access to services), social capital and trust, social mobility and opportunity, and shared values and identity. Similar to the conceptualizations above, these dimensions are both structural/distributive (e.g., distribution of resources) and cultural/ideational (e.g., values, trust, solidarity). Using both qualitative and quantitative methods, Green and Janmaat (2011) identify four main regimes of social cohesion in the developed world:

Nordic Regime (e.g., Sweden, Denmark, Finland) characterized by high levels of trust, low inequality, universalistic welfare states, strong civic engagement and with cultures rooted in egalitarianism, solidarity, and active citizenship.

Continental Regime (e.g., Germany, France, Austria, The Netherlands) characterized by social insurance-based welfare systems, moderate inequality, corporatist traditions, medium trust, and a culture rooted in duty-based citizenship, respect for hierarchy and order.

Anglo-Saxon Regime (e.g., UK, USA, Canada, Australia) characterized by a liberal welfare model, higher inequality, a more individualistic culture, and lower social trust. The culture is based on the emphasis on individual responsibility and a limited state role.

East Asian Regime (e.g., Japan, South Korea, Taiwan) characterized by strong social order, family-based welfare provision, low public welfare spending, high educational achievement, with cultures rooted in Confucian values, respect for authority, and group loyalty.

The concept of social cohesion is also closely related to the notion of social resilience. While it has long been considered in physics and complex systems literature (Fraccascia et al. 2018), it has also came under the attention of social scientists with respect to institutions (Easterly et al. 2006), socio-ecological systems (Adger 2000), or societies as a whole (Jenson 1998). These studies intend to capture and assess the capacity of a society to absorb or withstand shocks while maintaining its function–institutions operating, citizens able to secure their needs, and so on. It also includes societal features that facilitate collective action during crises (Aall and Chester 2019).

The discussion so far focused on social cohesion as a macro-level, and a rather static characteristic of societies–an aggregate state reflecting solidarity, shared norms, and cooperative relations. However, this macro-level condition emerges from a myriad of micro-level interactions and decisions. Understanding the interplay between individual actions and collective outcomes is, therefore, essential to grasping how cohesion is produced, maintained, or eroded over time. This calls for a focus on micro-macro linkages and the dynamic, emergent nature of social cohesion. Such a link can be established by connecting structural conditions, actor choices, and interaction dynamics, which together give rise to collective phenomena (Raub et al. 2011).

Examples of this approach include studies of social conventions, where coordination among individuals leads to stable patterns of behavior that are self-reinforcing (Ullmann-Margalit 1977; Young 1993; Lewis 2002). Once established, conventions help reduce uncertainty and facilitate predictable interaction, both of which are essential components of cohesion. This approach has been applied to other types of social norms (Bicchieri 2006). Going further, social cohesion can be understood as a stylized "second-order convention"–not just a specific behavioral rule, but a shared expectation that others will follow rules and coordinate or cooperate. These expectations are sustained by, among other things, network effects and reciprocal observation (e.g., reputational effects), making the social structure itself an important driver of cohesion (Bojanowski et al. 2011; Corten 2014; Raub and Weesie 1990).

Survey research and qualitative inquiry provide valuable insights into such aspects of social cohesion as perceptions, attitudes, or identities. Computational Social Science (CSS) provides a useful complement to traditional social science research methods, which often struggle to capture the emergent, interactional, and system-level properties of cohesion. CSS offers a uniquely powerful paradigm for understanding cohesion as a multi-level, dynamic, and networked phenomenon, integrating theory–including model-building–with simulation and large-scale behavioral data. A key advantage of CSS lies in its ability to model the micro-macro link explicitly. Through agent-based models, researchers can simulate how individual-level behaviors–such as norm-following or social influence–lead to emergent patterns of cohesion or fragmentation. CSS also enables the exploration of complex dynamics such as tipping points, path dependence, and feedback loops, which are central to understanding how cohesive societies develop, persist, or deteriorate.

Beyond modeling, CSS also enables the empirical measurement of cohesion at scale, using digital trace data. Online communication platforms, mobility traces, and interaction logs provide fine-grained, temporally rich data on how individuals form communities, express agreement or dissent, and respond to social or political events. When paired with NLP, sentiment analysis, or geospatial modeling, these data can serve as proxies for cohesion-related phenomena such as polarization, collective identity, or shared norms. This observational richness is especially valuable in settings where traditional survey instruments are too coarse or too slow to capture fast-changing social dynamics.

1.2.2 *Polarization: From Attitudes to Affect*

The study of political polarization has been a subject of interest to the scientific community for over a century. In recent decades, the perception that polarization is ever-increasing and has amounted to worrying proportions (Lees et al. 2021) has only amplified this interest. Whether this perception is actually true, however, depends greatly on how we think about and measure polarization. Early days of political polarization research focused on polarization of individual attitudes towards specific (policy) issues. Scholars were primarily interested in how individual attitudes aligned with party stances on political and economic issues (Stokes 1999). *Issue-based polarization* research focused on the growing divide between partisans, highlighting the role of issue salience as its natural cause (Converse 1964).

Measuring issue-based polarization is straightforward. Maximal polarization occurs when two equally sized groups have internal consensus at maximally discrepant opinions, and minimal polarization is when all individuals have consensus on a single opinion anywhere in the opinion space.[1] Between maximal and minimal polarization, it is less clear how polarization should be quantified; hence, several measures exist. Some focus on the existence of consensual groups with distinct opinions, others on fragmentation or coverage of all possible opinions (see Bramson et al. 2016, for an overview of issue-based polarization measures). The conceptual diversity for the simple case of single-issue based polarization on a bounded attitude scale is visualized in Fig. 1.2.

Contrary to folk belief, long-term trends of single-issue polarization reveal no clear trend of issue-based polarization, across the board (DiMaggio et al. 1996; Gestefeld et al. 2022). To some extent, this may be due to different ways of measurement in the middle ground between minimal and maximal polarization, but even so, it appears that actual issue-based polarization is not the main driver of increased perceived polarization.

By the 1990s, attention shifted to polarization as a consequence of underlying and deepening cultural conflict. The notion of 'culture wars' entered the debate, signifying that political conflict was driven by cultural, religious, and moral conflict, not by argumentative and substantive disagreement (Hunter 1992). The research on attitude consolidation within (DellaPosta 2020) and outside of the sphere of political topics (DellaPosta et al. 2015) can be seen as a natural extension of this line of work. Polarization in terms of *attitude consolidation* or *issue alignment* means that over time, attitudes become increasingly predictive of each other. When attitudes become correlated, divisions between groups with different attitudes may feel deeper, even in the absence of any change in single-issue polarization on the macro-level. Contrary to issue-based polarization, attitude consolidation does find considerable empirical support analyzing survey data from the United States of America using belief network

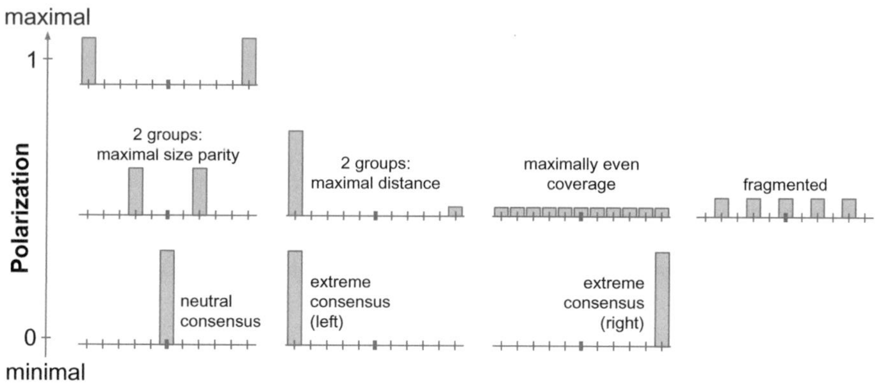

Fig. 1.2 Issue-based polarization and its different manifestations on a single attitude dimension

[1] Notable exception to this is psychology, where polarization can sometimes refer to the extremization of the opinion of a single individual.

analysis (DellaPosta 2020). In Europe, we see a similar upward trend, as we show in Sect. 1.3.

Most recently, polarization has been studied extensively in terms of *affective polarization*–measured as the difference between positive feelings towards the partisan ingroup and outgroups. This measure of polarization is by far the closest to the subjective experience of 'perceived polarization' too, completing the shift from a traditional, elite-polarization view to mass-polarization. The actual observed level of ideological polarization no longer plays a part (Dias and Yphtach 2022). The contemporary view of polarization research thus shifted the focus away from substantive disagreement to a story of identity-based conflict and processes of group distinction.

Long-term trends in affective polarization reveal a substantial increase in North America (Iyengar et al. 2019; Finkel 2020; Boxell et al. 2024). Globally, there is a lack of research on polarization in general, and affective polarization in particular (Falkenberg 2025). In Sect. 1.3, we show the significance of this by revealing considerable differences in affective polarization trends across Europe and North America.

Computational Social Science has contributed to the study of political polarization through large-scale multiple-world experiments (Macy et al. 2019), the analysis of attitude and taste consolidation using digital trace data, and the use of network-scientific methods in studying belief and attitude networks (DellaPosta 2020). The definitional nuances and challenges addressed above, however, also highlight that research on polarization is neither predominantly computational nor possible to address without a deeper understanding of its conceptualization.

1.3 Trends in Polarization and Social Cohesion Across Europe

To pave the way for the remaining chapters in this book, we take the opportunity here to show some general trends in polarization and social cohesion, focusing on the last few decades of large population studies in Europe and North America.

1.3.1 Polarizing Issue Alignment

Using belief network analysis, DellaPosta (2020) showed how polarization increased over the last half a century in the USA. Increasing issue alignment is also visible in Europe as we demonstrate here, using a classical method from statistics: Principal component analysis (PCA). Like belief network analysis, PCA is based on the correlation matrix of attitudes. PCA is the eigendecomposition of the correlation matrix. The eigenvectors of the correlation matrix are called principal components, and the sum of the corresponding eigenvalues represents the total variance of the standardized attitude variables. Thus, we can compute the percentage of the total variance of the data that is explained by the eigenvector by computing the variance share of its eigenvalue. That way, the eigenvalues create a natural hierarchy of the principal components, and the higher the percentage of total variance explained by the first principal component, the more issues are aligned along the direction it points to. However, issue alignment does not mean that attitudes become polarized! They align around a line in multidimensional attitude space but can be consensual, spread out, or even bipolarized along that line.

For the alignment trends, we use data from 212,387 individuals from 15 countries over nine years on five items from the European Social Survey (ESS 2024): political left-right self-identification, and attitudes towards European unification, homosexuality, immigration, and redistribution. In principle, there is no governing rule that all these attitudes should be related. Yet, a left-wing position is traditionally associated with a preference for reducing income differences, a positive stance towards immigration, homosexuality, European unification, and immigration.

Figure 1.3a shows the loadings on five principal components (PCs), and their explained variance (in percentages). PC1 has a negative loading for being politically right and a positive loading for all other attitude dimensions. However, the actual sign is not important; what matters is the relationship among the variables. If an individual indicates a strong right-wing position, the weights from PC1 will predict negative attitudes on all four other items. PC1 is also represented by the flipped vector with

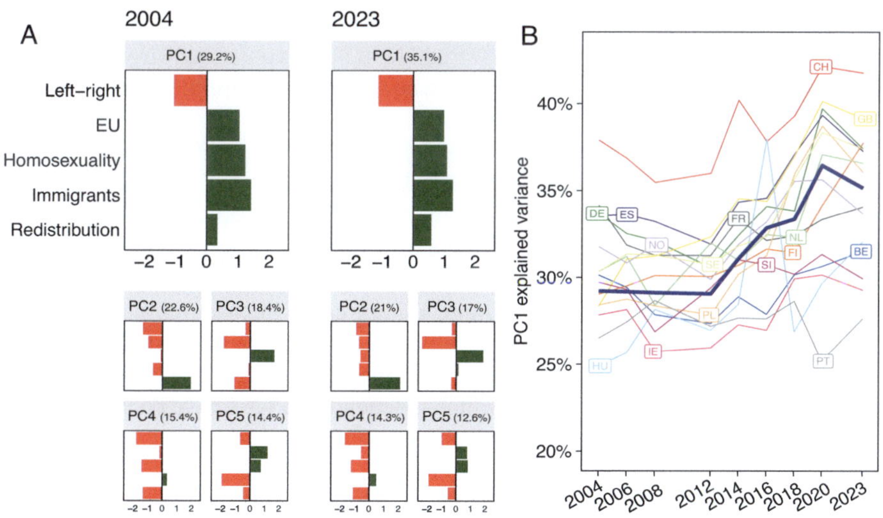

Fig. 1.3 Ideological alignment in Europe using a principal component analysis (PCA) of conceptually unrelated five attitude dimensions with data of representatively sampled individuals from the European Social Survey. Panel **A** shows the five principal components for PCA among all individuals in the years 2004 and 2023. Panel **B** shows the variance explained of the first principal component (PC1) for independent PCAs for all years and all country-year combinations

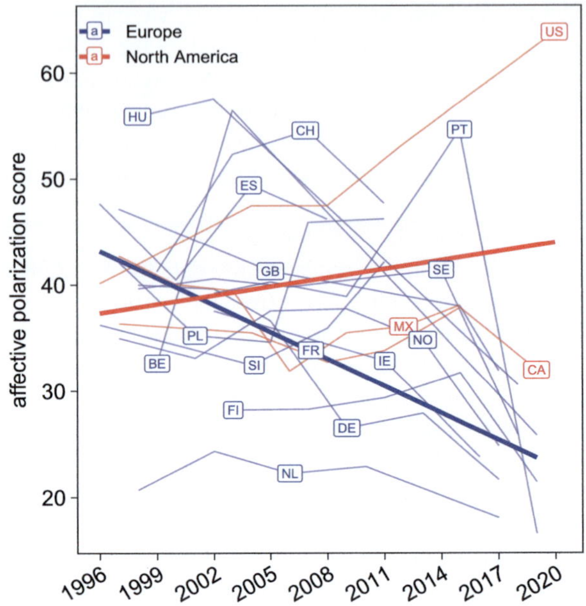

Fig. 1.4 Affective polarization in Europe and North-America. Data come from the CSES, waves 1 through 5 (CSES 2023)

all signs switched. PC2 represents a more traditional conception of being left with a strong loading pro redistribution and a slightly negative loading against the EU and the other attitudes. The similarity in PC loadings between the snapshots from 2004 and 2023 is striking, indicating that the structure of beliefs remained largely the same from 2004 to 2023. It is also very similar when PCAs are computed independently for each country-year combination.

The increasing relative importance of PC1 (from 29.2 to 35.1%, on average, between 2004 and 2023), as shown in Fig. 1.3b, indicates that attitude consolidation has increased in Europe, too. We argue that the explained variance of the first principal component is a measure of issue alignment because it shows how much of the total variance in attitude diversity can be explained along a single line in the multidimensional opinion space. The more a single component can explain the shape of the data, the more individuals use the same mental model to structure their beliefs. While there is considerable variance across European countries, the trend holds true for almost all of the 15 countries for which independent PCAs have been computed.

1.3.2 Affective Polarization

The study of affective polarization has been a hot topic in the social sciences in recent years. To a great extent, this is due to the stark increase in affective polarization observed in the USA. Internationally, there is a considerable gap in our knowledge, however. Part of this is because affective polarization is harder to measure in multiparty systems, as is the case in many European countries (Reiljan 2025; Wagner

2024). The cross-national research that does exist, however, shows that the upward trend in political intergroup affect is not at all as pronounced as in the USA (Boxell et al. 2024).

Here, we use data from all modules of the Comparative Study of Electoral Systems (CSES 2023), which collects information in as many countries as possible using a standard survey right after an election. We calculate affective polarization scores for multiparty systems by taking the difference between feelings towards voters for a respondent's own party and the average of feelings towards voters of other parties, weighted by the share of votes this party got in the most recent election.

Figure 1.4 reveals a high degree of variance in affective polarization scores over 25 years of measurement. What is more, grouping countries from North America and from Europe reveals a startling difference in trend. The stark increase in affective polarization that has alarmed the scientific literature recently does not appear to hold in Europe. There, affective polarization scores have, on average, decreased in the last 30 years.

1.3.3 Social Cohesion

A fair amount of research focuses on generalized and institutional trust as indicators of social cohesion. Generalized trust captures the degree to which people think others can be trusted, referring to the relational component of social cohesion in the

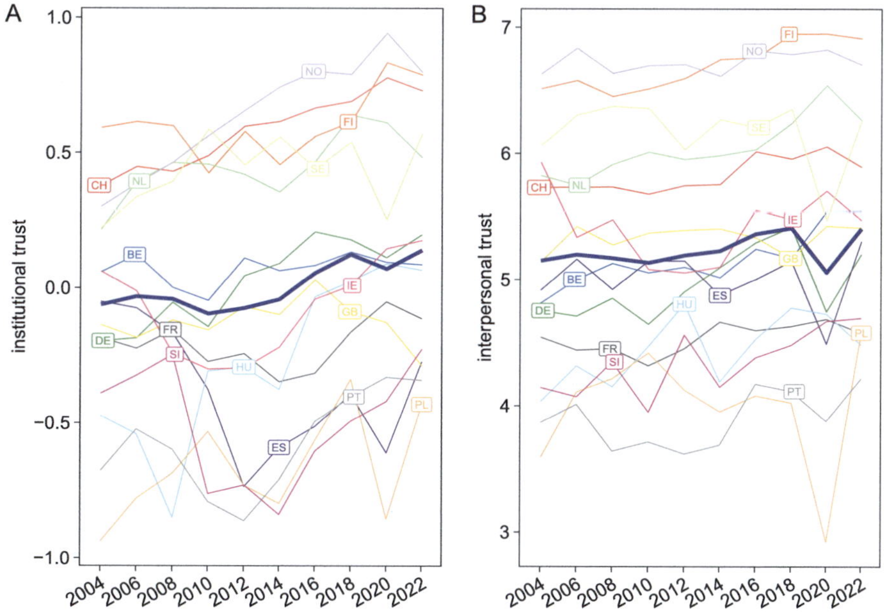

Fig. 1.5 **Social cohesion in Europe** measured as trust in institutions (Panel **A**) and as social trust (Panel **B**). Data come from the European Social Survey, waves 2 through 11

definition of Schiefer and Noll (2017). Institutional trust refers to the degree to which citizens trust social order, and hence relates to their orientation towards the common good in the definition of Schiefer and Noll (2017). Both concepts strongly relate to feelings of cooperation, unity, and identification, and are considered prerequisites of economic prosperity and growth (Schiefer and Noll 2017).

We use data from the European Social Survey (ESS 2024) to plot trends of social cohesion between and across 15 European nation-states over almost 20 years. Interpersonal trust is measured through the famous generalized trust question, where subjects indicate whether 'most people can be trusted' or 'you can't be too careful' on a scale from 0 to 10. Institutional trust is measured as the common reflective factor in trust in the legal system, the police, politicians, the country's parliament, and political parties, computed using confirmatory factor analysis. The five variables load well onto the common factor, with an average loading of .78 (ranging from .58 to .89) and an explained variance of 62%.

Both institutional and interpersonal trust show a similar, mostly stable or ever so slightly upward trend in cohesion across Europe, as shown in Fig. 1.5. Notable is a dip in interpersonal trust in 2020, potentially driven by the COVID-19 pandemic (as also discussed in Chap. 2: Boehnke et al. 2025). Next to the stability across time, we observe a large degree of variance across countries. At face value, that variance is partly explained by the social cohesion regimes by Green and Janmaat (2011), discussed in Sect. 1.2.1. The Nordic regimes plus Switzerland and The Netherlands score on the higher side of both scales, whereas the Continental regimes in central and southern Europe group together in the middle and lower end of the trust distributions.

1.4 Computational Approaches in Understanding Social Cohesion and Polarization

At this point, it should not come as a surprise that social cohesion and polarization share a fair amount of conceptual similarity, substantively and methodologically. We have discussed a wide array of conceptualizations of social cohesion, each touching on some kind of social 'glue,' holding society together. We have also discussed the transition in political polarization research from the study of opinions per se to the study of opinions as social bonds and, finally, opinions about others. It is there that we can see how social cohesion and polarization are two sides of the same coin, covering some degree of social or political distance between individuals. As a consequence, computational approaches to studying social cohesion and polarization can draw from the same pool of methods and ideas. The chapters in this book cover many of those approaches, presenting an array of starting points for that cross-fertilization.

In Chap. 2, Boehnke, Unzicker, Dragolov, Hartz, and Arant 2025 take a deeper look into the practical matters of measuring social cohesion using the multidimensional concept of the Social Cohesion Radar, developed by Schiefer and Van Der

Noll (2017); Dragolov et al. (2016). They report a substantial decline in social cohesion in Germany in the time of the COVID-19 pandemic, echoing the dip in social and institutional trust reported in the previous section. This showcases that social cohesion is fragile. A remarkable finding, because former results showed differences in profiles and level of social cohesion between countries, but rather small changes over time (Dragolov et al. 2016; Delhey et al. 2018).

The following nine application chapters are divided into three parts along the lines of the primary methodological tool used in the chapters. The three parts cover chapters that use tools from (social) network analysis, natural language processing, and agent-based modeling.

Chapter 3 by Bojanowski et al. (2025) addresses the challenge of studying social cohesion through a nationwide egocentric sample of core discussion ties among adults in Spain. The authors demonstrate how statistical network modeling, specifically Exponential-family Random Graph Models (ERGMs), can be used to analyze the underlying structural processes shaping observed network patterns. They then use the estimated model to simulate empirically calibrated network datasets, which provide insights into the global characteristics of society-wide core discussion networks. Notably, the results suggest that migrants and unemployed individuals are more likely to occupy peripheral positions in the network, indicating that country of origin and employment status may be important social cleavages that undermine social cohesion.

Using the SNA apparatus in a completely different context, in Chap. 4, Keijzer et al. (2025) study structural characteristics of informational ‘rabbit holes’ on the world’s second most visited website: YouTube. The access to information through what a platform will offer its users to view, read or watch next is telling of how similar perspectives are established and fed. CSS has enabled us to access and gauge belief segregation using ecologically valid data at an unprecedented scale. This chapter introduces and extensively explains a method for collecting and analyzing digital trace data such as recommendation graphs, and explores how ‘rabbit holes’ should and actually do look like.

Next to studying social relationships and informational structures, tools from network science are being applied the study of belief networks, too. Belief network analysis (BNA) focuses on the relationships between beliefs; that is, if the same person holds the same beliefs, a link exists between those beliefs. Much like the method for studying belief alignment described in Sect. 1.2.2, BNA can capture which beliefs are good predictors of other beliefs, and to what extent we can capture polarization as belief clustering across time, topics, and societies. In Chap. 5, Warncke et al. (2025) introduce a novel method for studying belief networks. Their method dichotomizes typical Likert-scale attitude items–relaxing otherwise restrictive assumptions of linearity and monotonicity–and constructs a network of items and co-endorsement dyads. Then, reducing dimensionality again by means of a physics simulation, they uncover relational patterns that other BNA methods have failed to capture.

Natural Language Processing (NLP) occupies an essential place in the Computational Social Science toolbox. Sentiment analysis, named entity recognition, and topic modeling are just a few examples of techniques that allow researchers to systematically analyze large volumes of textual data. These methods enable the extraction of patterns, trends, and structures in language use across diverse contexts such as traditional and social media, political discourse, or online communities. By leveraging NLP, researchers can gain insights into public opinion, collective identity, polarization, and the diffusion of ideas, often at scales and levels of granularity that would be impossible with manual analysis alone. In Chap. 6, Brockman et al. (2025) provide an analysis of Twitter/X discourse of top EU politicians related to the Russian-Ukrainian war. Using topic modeling, sentiment analysis, and related machine learning models, they demonstrate how the discourse reacted to the outbreak of the war and how the attention fluctuated in the months that followed. Moreover, their analysis provides insights into the polarized character of the discourse, manifested in the negative sentiment of the messages sent by actors on the political extremes.

Lee et al. (2025) examine how political polarization shapes the language used to discuss minority issues in parliamentary speeches in Germany and the UK over the past four decades, in Chap. 7. Using NLP techniques on an extensive corpus of parliamentary debates, the authors analyze linguistic polarization in discussions of immigration and sexual minorities. They show that both issues have become more salient over time, and that left- and right-leaning parties increasingly diverge in their rhetoric. Right-leaning parties tend to emphasize economic and security concerns, while left-leaning parties focus on rights and inclusion. The findings offer valuable insights into how political discourse reflects and reinforces ideological divisions regarding minority representation.

In Chap. 8, Yuan (2025) investigates the evolution of media framing of the LGBTQ rights movement in the United States over six decades, using semantic network analysis of nearly 6,000 newspaper headlines. The chapter documents how dominant master frames such as ‘rights’ and ‘same-sex marriage’ emerged and shifted over time in national media discourse. The analysis reveals that early news coverage favored dichotomous, morally charged framings, while later stages saw more inclusive and legitimizing frames aimed at broader audiences. Importantly, the rise of the ‘same-sex marriage ’ frame was driven not by the largest or most established organizations, but by groups perceived as morally resonant, such as those representing families and children. The chapter provides new methodological and theoretical insights into the dynamic construction of political frames in the public sphere.

The three chapters in the last application part use agent-based modeling to study the emergence of different aspects of polarization and social cohesion. Chapter 9 of Edmonds et al. (2025) provides an agent-based model of belief coherence and belief change through social influence. In this model, the authors build on empirical for the European Social Survey from the same five political dimensions as used in Sect. 1.2.2 for Germany. They derive coherence preferences as correlation matrices between beliefs for three groups of individuals using correlational class analysis. These groups differ in their beliefs, but more importantly, they differ in how they think beliefs should go together. Their simulation shows that agents striving for coherence tend to polarize on some beliefs but converge on others. Polarization happens sometimes within groups and sometimes between groups.

Widler et al. (2025) study the emergence of consensus in the choices of individuals, in Chap. 10. Conceptualizing political discourse as hierarchical coarse-graining, they study "upward causation" where individual outcomes influence group-level opinion and "downward causation" capturing how dominant collective views shape individual opinions. They use a model of continuous opinions and discrete actions (CODA) simulating Bayesian belief updates, social identityâŁ"driven information integration, and migration between identity groups to capture coarse-graining across micro-, meso-, and macroscopic scales, showcasing three distinct regimes of dynamics: independent local convergence, parallel rapid local and global convergence, and iterative slow global convergence.

Chapter 11 of Khaluf et al. (2025) looks at group cohesion through the lens of social exchange theory. In their model, agents engage in reciprocal interaction and decide to leave or join groups. It is shown that memory and learning from past interactions increase group cohesion with respect to the average time agents spend in groups and the duration of group existence.

1.5 Conclusion

Social cohesion and polarization both reflect varying degrees of social proximity and strength of social bonds. This chapter has argued that CSS offers a uniquely powerful lens for studying such phenomena–using a tight connection between theoretical expectations and empirical patterns. To achieve that, CSS must resist the temptation of mere description and commit to theoretical and analytical rigor. The tools are in place; the challenge now lies with us to deploy them with conceptual clarity and scientific ambition.

Data and materials The data presented in this chapter come from the Comparative Study of Electoral Systems (CSES 2023) and the European Social Survey (ESS 2024). All code to perform the described analyses and generate the presented figures is available publicly at Zenodo doi:10.5281/zenodo.15699651.

Acknowledgements Marijn Keijzer acknowledges funding from the Occitanie region, the European Regional Development Fund (ERDF), and the French government, through the France 2030 project managed by the National Research Agency (ANR) with the reference number "ANR-22-EXES-0015." Jan Lorenz acknowledges funding by Horizon Europe project "European City Squared: Computational Social Science Simulation for Democracy" (EuropeanCity2 grant agreement ID: 101178170, doi: 10.3030/101178170). Michał Bojanowski acknowledges funding support from European Research Council through grant 101020038 for the project "PATCHWORK: A network science approach to social cohesion in European societies" (PI Miranda J. Lubbers).

References

P. Aall, C.A. Crocker, Building Resilience and Social Cohesion in Conflict. Global Pol. **10**(S2), 68–75 (2019). https://doi.org/10.1111/1758-5899.12681

W.N. Adger, Social and Ecological Resilience: Are They Related? Prog. Hum. Geogr. **24**(3), 347–364 (2000). https://doi.org/10.1191/030913200701540465

C. Anderson, The end of theory: the data deluge makes the scientific method obsolete. Wired Mag. **16**(7), 16-07 (2008)

M. Arvidsson, P. Hedström, B. Jarvis, M. Keuschnigg, in *On the Intersection of Analytical Sociology and Computational Social Science* (2024). https://doi.org/10.31235/osf.io/4h5ys

Berger, (ed.), *The Limits of Social Cohesion: Conflict and Mediation in Pluralist Societies; A Report of the Bertelsmann Foundation to the Club of Rome* (Westview Press, Boulder, 1998)

P. Bernard, *Social Cohesion: A Critique*. CPRN Discussion Paper F90 (1999)

C. Bicchieri, *The Grammar of Society: The Nature and Dynamics of Social Norms* (Cambridge University Press, Cambridge, 2006)

K. Boehnke, K. Unzicker, G. Dragolov, C. Hartz, R. Arant, Social Cohesion and its development in Germany before, during, and after COVID-19: the Bertelsmann Social Cohesion Radar, in *Computational Social Science of Social Cohesion and Polarization*, ed. by L. Keijzer, Bojanowski (Springer, Berlin, 2025), Chap. 2

M. Bojanowski, V. Buskens, Coordination in dynamic social networks under heterogeneity. J. Math. Soc. **35**(4), 249–286 (2011). https://doi.org/10.1080/0022250X.2010.509523

M. Bojanowski, A. Loseva, P. Schuler, S. Boeller, M.J. Lubbers, Simulating an Empirically Informed Population Network of Core Discussion Ties. In: *Computational Social Science of Social Cohesion and Polarization*, ed. by L. Keijzer, Bojanowski (Springer, 2025), Chap. 3

P. Bourdieu, The Forms of capital. Cult. Theor. Anthol. **1**, 81–93 (2011)

L. Boxell, M. Gentzkow, J.M. Shapiro, Cross-country trends in affective polarization. Rev. Econ. Stat. **106**(2), 557–565 (2024)

A. Bramson, P. Grim, D.J. Singer, S. Fisher, W. Berger, G. Sack, C. Flocken, Disambiguation of social polarization concepts and measures. J. Math. Sociol. **40**(2), 80–111 (2016). https://doi.org/10.1080/0022250x.2016.1147443

H. Brockmann, W. Drews, P.F. Zamorra, J. Frese, D. Triana, Elites and polarisation: a text and sentiment analytical approach on the dynamics of polarized political discourses during times of crises, in *Computational Social Science of Social Cohesion and Polarization*, ed. by Keijzer, Lorenz, Bojanowski (Springer, 2025) Chap. 6

J. Chan, H.-P. To, E. Chan, Reconsidering social cohesion: developing a definition and analytical framework for empirical research. Soc. Indic. Res. **75**(2), 273–302 (2006). https://doi.org/10.1007/s11205-005-2118-1

R. Conte et al., Manifesto of computational social science. Eur. Phys. J. Spec. Top. **214**(1), 325–346 (2012). https://doi.org/10.1140/epjst/e2012-01697-8

P.E. Converse, The nature of belief systems in mass publics, in *Ideology and Its Discontents*, ed. by Apter (The Free Press of Glencoe, New York, 1964)

R. Corten, *Computational Approaches to Studying the Co-Evolution of Networks and Behavior in Social Dilemmas*. Wiley Series in Computational and Quantitative Social Science. (Wiley, Hoboken, 2014)

CSES, *Comparative Study of Electoral Systems Module 5 Full Release [dataset and documentation]* (2023). https://doi.org/10.7804/cses.module5.2023-07-25

F. Cushman, Computational social psychology. Ann. Rev. Psychol. **75**, 625–652 (2024). https://doi.org/10.1146/annurev-psych-021323-040420

J. Delhey, K. Boehnke, G. Dragolov, Z.S. Ignácz, M. Larsen, J. Lorenz, M. Koch, Social cohesion and its correlates: a comparison of western and asian societies. Comp. Sociol. **17**(3–4), 426–455 (2018). https://doi.org/10.1163/15691330-12341468

D. DellaPosta, Pluralistic collapse: the "oil spillâŁž model of mass opinion polarization. Am. Sociol. Rev. **85**(3), 507–536 (2020). https://doi.org/10.1177/0003122420922989

D. DellaPosta, Y. Shi, M. Macy, Why do liberals drink lattes? Am. J. Sociol. **120**(5), 1473–1511 (2015). https://doi.org/10.1086/681254

N. Dias, Y. Lelkes, The nature of affective polarization: disentangling policy disagreement from partisan identity. Am. J. Polit. Sci. **66**(3), 775–790 (2022). https://doi.org/10.1111/ajps.12628

P. DiMaggio, J. Evans, B. Bryson, Have American's social attitudes become more polarized? Am. J. Sociol. **102**(3), 690–755 (1996)

P. Doreian, T.J. Fararo, *The Problem of Solidarity: Theories and Models* (Gordon and Breach, Amsterdam, 1998)

G. Dragolov, Z.S. Ignácz, J. Lorenz, J. Delhey, K. Boehnke, K. Unzicker *Social Cohesion in the Western World -What Holds Societies Together, Insights from the Social Cohesion Radar* (Springer, 2016)

É. Durkheim, *The Division of Labor in Society* (1893)

W. Easterly, J. Ritzen, M. Woolcock, Social cohesion, institutions, and growth. Econ. Polit. **18**(2), 103–120 (2006). https://doi.org/10.1111/j.1468-0343.2006.00165.x

A. Edelmann, T. Wolff, D. Montagne, C.A. Bail, Computational social science and sociology. Ann. Rev. Sociol. **46**(1), 61–81 (2020). https://doi.org/10.1146/annurev-soc-121919-054621

B. Edmonds, P. Steiglechner, J. Lorenz, F. Kalvas, M.C.L. Batzke, Understanding mutual social influence when people prefer coherent beliefs, in *Computational Social Science of Social Cohesion and Polarization*, ed. by Keijzer, Lorenz, Bojanowski (Springer, 2025) Chap. 9

P. Erices-Ocampo, M.J. Lubbers, J. Adams, Toward a unified conceptualization of social capital. Ann. Rev. Sociol. (2025). https://doi.org/10.1146/annurev-soc-090924-032037

European Union, Consolidated version of the treaty on European Union. Off. J. Eur. Union **C326**, OJ 13 (2012)

G. Esping-Andersen, *The Three Worlds of Welfare Capitalism* (Polity Press, Cambridge, UK, 1990)

ESS, *ESS Rounds 2-11 Data, European Social Survey European Research Infrastructure (ESS ERIC)*. ESS—integrated file (2024)

M. Falkenberg et al, *Towards Global Equity in Political Polarization Research* (2025)

E.J. Finkel et al., Political sectarianism in America. Science **370**(6516), 533–536 (2020). https://doi.org/10.1126/science.abe1715

A. Flache, M. Mäs, M.A. Keijzer, Computational approaches in rigorous sociology: agent-based computational modeling and computational social science, *Handbook of Sociological Science*. ed. by Gërxhani, De Graaf, Raub. (Edward Elgar Publishing, 2022) , pp. 57–72. https://doi.org/10.4337/9781789909432.00011

L. Fraccascia, I. Giannoccaro, V. Albino, Resilience of complex systems: state of the art and directions for future research, in *Complexity*, ed. by De Domenico (2018), vol. 1, p. 3421529. https://doi.org/10.1155/2018/3421529

N.E. Friedkin, Social cohesion. Ann. Rev. Sociol. **30**(1), 409–25 (2004)

M. Gestefeld, J. Lorenz, N.T. Henschel, K. Boehnke, Decomposing attitude distributions to characterize attitude polarization in Europe. SN Soc. Sci. **2**(7), 110 (2022). https://doi.org/10.1007/s43545-022-00342-7

A. Green, J.G. Janmaat, *Regimes of Social Cohesion: Societies and the Crisis of Globalization* (Palgrave Macmillan, Basingstoke, 2011)

P. Hedstrom, *Dissecting the Social: On the Principles of Analytical Sociology* (Cambridge University Press, 2005)

M. Hilbert et al., Computational communication science: a methodological catalyzer for a maturing discipline. Int. J. Commun. **13**, 23 (2019)

N.P. Hummon, T.J. Fararo, The emergence of computational sociology. J. Math. Soc. **20**(2–3), 79–87 (1995). https://doi.org/10.1080/0022250X.1995.9990155

J.D. Hunter, *Culture Wars: The Struggle to Control the Family, Art, Education, Law, and Politics in America*. Avalon Publishing (1992)

S. Iyengar, Y. Lelkes, M. Levendusky, N. Malhotra, S.J. Westwood, The origins and consequences of affective polarization in the United States. Annu. Rev. Polit. Sci. **22**(1), 129–146 (2019). https://doi.org/10.1146/annurev-polisci-051117-073034

J. Jenson, *Mapp. Soc. Cohes. State Canad. Res.* (Family Network, CPRN, Ottawa, 1998)

M.A. Keijzer, L. Erhard, Z. Kharazian, M. Lamba, The anatomy of rabbit holes: studying information segregation in YouTube's recommendation graph, in *Computational Social Science of Social Cohesion and Polarization*, ed. by Keijzer, Lorenz, Bojanowski (Springer, 2025) Chap. 4

M.A. Keijzer, M. Mäs, A. Flache, Polarization on Social Media: micro-level evidence and macro-level implications. J. Artif. Soc. Soc. Simul. **27**(1), 7 (2024)

M. Keuschnigg, N. Lovsjö, P. Hedström, Analytical sociology and computational social science. J. Comput. Soc. Sci. **3–14**(2017). https://doi.org/10.1007/s42001-017-0006-5

Y. Khaluf, T. Hovestadt, N. Zöller, B. Wurpts, G.J. Hofstede, Modeling social cohesion: the influence of memory and learning, in *Computational Social Science of Social Cohesion and Polarization* ed. by Keijzer, Lorenz, Bojanowski (Springer, 2025) Chap. 11

D.M.J. Lazer, A. Pentland, L. Adamic et al., Computational social science. Science **323**(5915), 721–723 (2009). https://doi.org/10.1126/science.1167742

D.M.J. Lazer, A. Pentland, D.J. Watts et al., Computational social science: obstacles and opportunities. Science **369**(6507), 1060–1062 (2020). https://doi.org/10.1126/science.aaz8170

Y. Lee, F. Piñeyrúa, C.S. Czymara, M. Weber, Linguistic polarization in minority representation: analyzing parliamentary speeches in Germany and the UK (1980-2021), in *Computational Social Science of Social Cohesion and Polarization*, ed. by Keijzer, Lorenz, Bojanowski (Springer, 2025) Chap. 7

J. Lees, M. Cikara, Understanding and combating misperceived polarization. Philos. Trans. R. Soc. B **376**, 1822 (2021)

D.K. Lewis, *Convention: A Philosophical Study* (Blackwell, Oxford, 2002)

N. Lin, *Social Capital: A Theory of Social Structure and Action* (Cambridge University Press, 2002)

J. Lorenz, Data-driven agent-based modeling in computational social science, in *Handbook of Computational Social Science*, vol. 1, p. 18. (Routledge, 2021)

M. Macy, S. Deri, A. Ruch, N. Tong, Opinion cascades and the unpredictability of partisan polarization. Sci. Adv. **5**(8), eaax0754 (2019)

R.K. Merton, *Social Theory and Social Structure*. Google-Books-ID: dyqZOcux9o0C. Simon and Schuster (1968)

M. Molina, F. Garip, Machine learning for sociology. Ann. Rev. Sociol. **45**, 27–45 (2019). https://doi.org/10.1146/annurev-soc-073117-041106

J. Moody, D.R. White, Structural cohesion and embeddedness: a hierarchical concept of social groups. Am. Sociol. Rev. 103–127 (2003)

S.L. Morgan, C. Winship, *Counterfactuals and Causal Inference: Methods and Principles for Social Research*. Cambridge University Press (2014)

M. Peponakis, S. Kapidakis, M. Doerr, E. Tountasaki, From calculations to reasoning: history, trends and the potential of computational ethnography and computational social anthropology, in *Social Science Computer Review* (SAGE Publications Inc, 2024), vol. 42, no. 1, pp. 84–102. https://doi.org/10.1177/08944393231167692

K. Popper, *The Logic of Scientific Discovery* (Hutchinson, London, 1959)

A. Portes, J. Sensenbrenner, Embeddedness and immigration: notes on the social determinants of economic action. Am. J. Sociol. **98**(6), 1320–1350 (1993). https://doi.org/10.1086/230191

R.D. Putnam, *Bowling Alone: The Collapse and Revival of American Community* (Simon & Schuster, New York, 2000)

W. Raub, V. Buskens, M.A.L.M. Assen, Micro-macro links and microfoundations in sociology. J. Math. Soc. **35**(1–3), 1–25 (2011). https://doi.org/10.1080/0022250X.2010.532263

W. Raub, J. Weesie, Reputation and efficiency in social interactions: an example of network effects. Am. J. Sociol. **96**, 626–654 (1990)

C. Read, *Logic: Deductive and Inductive* (Dodo Press, 1898–2007), 392pp

A. Reiljan, Affective polarization in Europe, in *Handbook of Affective Polarization* (2025), Chap. 8, 176–201

M.J. Salganik, *Bit by Bit: Social Research in the Digital Age* (Princeton University Press, Princeton, NJ, 2018)

M.J. Salganik et al., Measuring the predictability of life outcomes with a scientific mass collaboration. Proc. Natl. Acad. Sci. **117**(15), 8398–8403 (2020). https://doi.org/10.1073/pnas.1915006117

D. Schiefer, J. Noll, The essentials of social cohesion: a literature review. Soc. Indic. Res. **132**(2), 579–603 (2017). https://doi.org/10.1007/s11205-016-1314-5

D. Schiefer, J. Noll, The essentials of social cohesion: a literature review. Soc. Indic. Res. **132**(2), 579–603 (2017). https://doi.org/10.1007/s11205-016-1314-5

H. Schultheis, Computational cognitive modeling in the social sciences, in *Handbook of Computational Social Science* (2021), vol. 1, p. 13

S.C. Stokes, Political parties and democracy. Annu. Rev. Polit. Sci. **2**, 243–267 (1999). https://doi.org/10.1146/annurev.polisci.2.1.243

E. Ullmann-Margalit, *The Emergence of Norms* (Oxford University Press, Oxford, UK, 1977), p.224

UNDP (ed.), Breaking the gridlock: reimagining cooperation in a polarized world, in *Human Development Report 2023/2024* (United Nations Development Programme (UNDP), New York, 2024)

M. Wagner, Affective polarization in Europe. Eur. Polit. Sci. Rev. **16**(3), 378–392 (2024)

P. Warncke, Y. Chen, A. Speer, B. de Bruijn, A. Lüders, D. Carpentras, ResIN: a new method to analyze socio-political attitude systems, in *Computational Social Science of Social Cohesion and Polarization*, ed. by Keijzer, Lorenz, Bojanowski (Springer, 2025) Chap. 5

V. Widler, B. Kamińska, A.C.R. Martins, I. Puga-Gonzalez, An investigation into the causal mechanism of political opinion dynamics: a model of hierarchical coarse-graining with community-bounded social influence, in *Computational Social Science of Social Cohesion and Polarization*, ed. by Keijzer, Lorenz, Bojanowski (Springer, 2025). Chap. 10

World Economic Forum, *The Global Risks Report 2025* (Switzerland, Geneva, 2025)

P. Ylikoski, Social mechanisms. In: *The Routledge Handbook of Mechanisms and Mechanical Philosophy*, 1st ed., ed. by Glennan, Illari (Routledge, New York, 2017), pp. 401–412. https://doi.org/10.4324/9781315731544-30

H.P. Young, The evolution of conventions. Econometrica **61**(1), 57 (1993). https://doi.org/10.2307/2951778

W. Yuan, Convergence in framing: a semantic network analysis of news coverage of the LGBTQ movement in the United States (1960s–2010s), in *Computational Social Science of Social Cohesion and Polarization*, ed. by Keijzer, Lorenz, Bojanowski (Springer, 2025) Chap. 8

Chapter 2
Social Cohesion and Its Development in Germany Before, During, and After COVID-19: The Bertelsmann Social Cohesion Radar

Klaus Boehnke, Kai Unzicker, Georgi Dragolov, Carina Hartz, and Regina Arant

Abstract The subsequent chapter introduces the conceptual and measurement approach of the Bertelsmann Social Cohesion Radar (SCR). It then continues by reporting the scores obtained by the SCR in country-wide representative studies in Germany in 2017, 2020, and 2023, i.e., before, during, and after the coronavirus pandemic. Results show that in Germany during these years, social cohesion, measured on a scoring scheme from 0 (zero), lowest possible cohesion, to 100 (highest possible cohesion), dropped from 61 to 52. Additional studies in the State of Baden-Württemberg, conducted more closely in time to the coronavirus pandemic's onset and apex, showed that the drop indeed occurred over COVID-19. The most pronounced drop in scores for the single dimensions of social cohesion between 2017 and 2023 was found for Dimension 3.1, Solidarity and Helpfulness. This suggests that COVID-19 indeed had detrimental consequences for the neighborhood quality of life: The percentage of Germans who responded, "(between) at least once every week and daily" to the question "How often do you volunteer in your free time to help other people?" dropped from 26 to 14% over COVID.

K. Boehnke (✉) · C. Hartz · R. Arant
Bremen International Graduate School of Social Sciences, Constructor University, Bremen, Germany
e-mail: kboehnke@constructor.university

K. Unzicker
Bertelsmann Stiftung, Gütersloh, Germany

G. Dragolov
School of Business, Social and Decision Sciences, Constructor University, Bremen, Germany

M. A. Keijzer et al. (eds.), *Computational Social Science of Social Cohesion and Polarization*, Computational Social Sciences,
https://doi.org/10.1007/978-3-032-01373-6_2

2.1 Introduction

Data on the strength and development of social cohesion in the Western world has been available since the late 1980s. With its Social Cohesion Radar (SCR), Bertelsmann Stiftung initially presented several secondary data analytical studies assessing social cohesion in OECD and Asian countries (Dragolov et al. 2016; Stiftung 2018). Subsequently, population-representative surveys have been conducted three times since 2017 to record the level of social cohesion in Germany. This chapter first introduces the SCR concept of social cohesion. It then turns to findings for Germany for 2017 (Arant et al. 2017), 2020 (Follmer et al. 2020), and 2023 (Boehnke et al. 2022), i.e., before, during, and after the coronavirus pandemic.

2.1.1 Defining Social Cohesion

Following the theoretical assumptions of the SCR (Schiefer and van der Noll 2017), the present study assumes that cohesion is (a) a feature of a territorially defined community and not a characteristic of individuals; (b) a gradual phenomenon, i.e., communities can be more cohesive or less cohesive, and (c) a multidimensional concept. Despite being a characteristic of geopolitical entities, i.e., a collective quality, the degree of cohesion is reflected in the attitudes, behaviors, and experiences of individual members and groups within the respective community. A cohesive society is characterized by (1) resilient social relationships between the people who belong to it, (2) a positive emotional connection between its members and the community, and (3) a pronounced orientation towards the common good. These three aspects represent the core domains of cohesion, each subdivided into three dimensions (see Fig. 2.1). In addition to the integrity of social networks (Dimension 1.1), the domain "Social relationships" addresses general trust in people (Dimension 1.2) and acceptance of diversity (Dimension 1.3). The domain "Connectedness" measures the extent of identification with the respective community (Dimension 2.1), trust in its institutions (Dimension 2.2), and the subjective experience of fairness (Dimension 2.3). Whether people show solidarity and helpfulness towards others (Dimension 3.1), respect basic social rules (Dimension 3.2), and are socially and politically engaged (Dimension 3.3) is assessed in the domain of "Orientation towards the common good."

According to the SCR approach, social cohesion has nine constitutive building blocks or dimensions. The guiding principles listed in Fig. 2.1 concisely characterize each dimension.

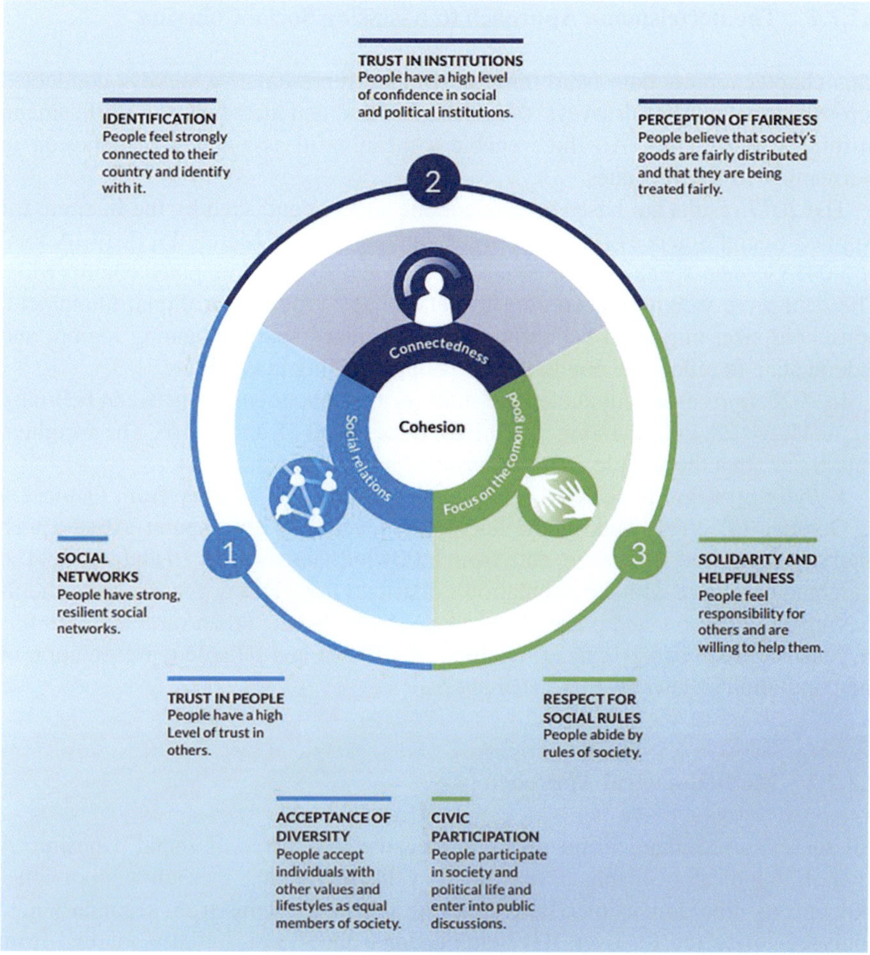

Fig. 2.1 Domains and dimensions of social cohesion

2.1.2 How is Cohesion Measured?

Following the aforementioned concept, the level of social cohesion within a social entity is assessed by asking its members about their attitudes, behaviors, and experiences. This approach intentionally avoids posing direct questions about the subjective experience of social cohesion. However, before turning to the report on the current level of social cohesion in the German federal states, we briefly reiterate the pathway from the initially secondary analytic approach of assessing social cohesion to the contemporary measurement strategy.

2.1.2.1 The Bertelsmann Approach to Assessing Social Cohesion

This chapter reports data from three population-representative surveys conducted across Germany. These surveys were designed and conducted for the Bertelsmann Stiftung's SCR series. All three enable a meaningful assessment of cohesion in Germany's 16 federal states.

The 2017 results are based on a telephone survey conducted by the Institute for Applied Social Sciences (*infas*) between January 10 and March 25, 2017. A total of 5,041 German-speaking individuals aged 16 and above participated countrywide. The data were weighted according to gender, age group, educational attainment, household size, migration background, homogenized spatial planning region, and federal state to reflect the population of people residing in Germany.

In 2020, *infas* again conducted the study as a telephone survey between February 5 and March 28, 2020, among 3,010 individuals aged 16 and above. The weighted data ensure that the sample reflects Germany's resident population.

Pollytix Strategic Research GmbH conducted the 2023 survey from October 4 to October 17, 2023. This online survey, conducted as a computer-assisted web interview, gathered analyzable data from 5,004 individuals aged 16 and above. The weighted data align with the population's distribution regarding gender, age, school-leaving qualification, and place of residence (federal state, urban/rural area). In this respect, our 2023 survey can be regarded as a robust and reliable representation of the population's views on these characteristics.

2.1.2.2 Methodological Approach

All surveys used identical questions to measure the degree of social cohesion. A total of 36 indicators enable an empirically valid and reliable measurement of cohesion and its nine dimensions. Item selection originally stems from secondary data analyses conducted for over 100 items deemed face-valid, initially sourced from open-access databases, including the World Values Survey and Eurobarometer. The selection process is described in detail in *Social Cohesion in the Western World. What Holds Societies Together: Insights from the Social Cohesion Radar* by Dragolov et al. (2016). It should be emphasized here that the assessment of the overall social cohesion of a given social entity follows the logic of a formative index or, in other terminology, the basket-of-goods logic. Scores obtained for the nine dimensions of the Bertelsmann Social Cohesion Radar are aggregated due to their agreed-upon construct validity rather than because they form a second-order factor, as would be required by a psychometric, reflective-indicator approach.

To calculate the nine dimension-specific index scores, negatively formulated indicators (see below) were first recoded so that higher numerical codes always reflected a positive statement on the surveyed dimension. All indicators were rescaled further so that agreement with a statement is assessed on a scale from 0 (weakest agreement) to 100 (strongest agreement) to make them interpretable as percentage scores. This means that, for example, items that had to be answered by survey respondents in the original study as 'no'/'yes' (0/1) were rescaled to scores of 0 and 100. For items that required responses on a Likert scale ranging from 0 to 3 in the studies from which they were taken, the responses were recoded to 0, 33.33, 66.67, and 100. The described procedure implies that all items of a specific dimension received an equal weight, as is known from classic psychometric scale formation. This approach differed from the initial approach used in the secondary data analyses documented by Dragolov et al. (2016). There, factor scores were averaged, which gives the items of a specific dimension a weight based on how strongly they load on the factor constituted by the items.

The nine dimension scores at the federal-state level in Germany were calculated by arithmetically averaging the respective indicators across individuals surveyed in a given state. The overall social cohesion index was then calculated by averaging the nine dimension scores arithmetically within a state. Using the same set of indicators and methodological approaches for measuring social cohesion enables comparisons across the three survey years: 2017, 2020, and 2023. Data were weighted for all three subsequently reported studies to guarantee population representativeness following the GESIS guidelines (Sand and Kunz 2020).

2.2 Social Cohesion in Germany from 2017 to the Present Day

What is the current state of social cohesion in Germany? How has cohesion changed compared to 2017 and 2020? As the developments in 2017 and 2020 have already been discussed in detail elsewhere (Follmer et al. 2020; Brand et al. 2021), this study focuses on comparing the years 2020 and 2023. Nevertheless, we summarize the most critical findings from both previous studies below to provide the best possible account of the current situation.

2.2.1 Looking Back: Cohesion in 2017 and 2020

As mentioned, Bertelsmann Stiftung already surveyed social cohesion in Germany in 2017 and 2020 (Arant et al. 2017; Follmer et al. 2020). The results of those studies supported the basic assumption that social cohesion is a highly stable phenomenon that only changes over the long term (Dragolov et al. 2016; Delhey et al. 2018). The overall index was 61 points on a scale of 0 to 100 at both measurement points in Germany and was stable.

The differences between the federal states were also minor in both years. In 2017, the difference between the strongest and weakest federal states was 6 points, compared to 8 points in 2020. With an average score of 61 points, Germany's states of Hesse, Bavaria, Baden-Württemberg, Rhineland-Palatinate, and Saarland achieved the highest scores on the overall index in 2017, with 63 points. In contrast, the lowest score of 57 points was achieved in Saxony. In 2020, Bavaria, Rhineland-Palatinate, Saarland, and Schleswig–Holstein scored the highest 63 points, whereas Bremen scored the lowest 55.

However, the range between the federal states was considerably more remarkable in the single dimensions. As for "Identification with the community" (Dimension 2.1), for example, the difference between the highest score in Mecklenburg-Western Pomerania (86 points) and the lowest score in Berlin (67 points) was 19 points in 2020. The differences between the federal states were also high in the dimensions "Respect for social rules" (Dimension 3.2), "Social networks" (Dimension 1.1), "Acceptance of diversity" (Dimension 1.3), and "Trust in institutions" (Dimension 2.2). In addition, a clear East–West divide was evident in both years, with the West German states consistently exhibiting higher cohesion than the East German states. Bremen and Mecklenburg-Western Pomerania were an exception in 2020.

Further, there were only negligible fluctuations in the nine dimensions between 2017 and 2020. This underscores that social cohesion is a stable characteristic that only changes slowly. However, the dimensions "Acceptance of diversity" (1.3) and "Perception of fairness" (2.3) each saw a notable increase of 3 points from 2017 to 2020. This indicates that openness to diversity and perceptions of justice have improved, on average, during this period. Between 2017 and 2020, "Trust in institutions" (Dimension 2.2) and "Respect for social rules" (Dimension 3.2) declined slightly by about 3 points each.

Looking not only at the changes but also at the respective level of the single dimensions, "Acceptance of diversity" (Dimension 1.3) had by far the highest average score (82 points) in 2020. Similarly, high scores were achieved in the following dimensions: "Identification with the community" (76 points, Dimension 2.1), "Respect for social rules" (74 points, Dimension 3.2), and "Social networks" (71 points, Dimension 1.1). On the other hand, "Perception of fairness" (Dimension 2.3) was characterized by the lowest scores overall, with 41 points. At around 50 points, the dimensions "Solidarity and helpfulness" (3.1), "Civic participation" (3.3), and "Trust in institutions" (2.2) were at the lower end. At 56 points, "Trust in people" (Dimension 1.2) recorded only slightly higher scores.

It is important to note that the Germany-wide survey in 2020 took place at the beginning of the year (February and March) and thus coincided with the initial phase of the coronavirus pandemic. A two-time follow-up survey of a small sample of these respondents in 2020 (Brand et al. 2021; Hartz 2021) reveals a development: Whereas the cohesion scores at the beginning of 2020 (i.e., before the full outbreak of the pandemic) were similarly high as in 2017 and even improved in Summer 2020, a noticeable drop was observed in December 2020. In any case, it should be noted that the SCR did not find the social disintegration frequently lamented in the wake of the coronavirus pandemic for these years.

However, a series of additional studies on cohesion in Baden-Württemberg empirically corroborated a 10-point decline in the degree of cohesion as a result of the coronavirus pandemic based on a comparison of spring 2019 (Dragolov et al. 2020) and the turn of the year 2021/2022 (Boehnke et al. 2022). In addition, the 2020

Germany-wide study revealed an increasing social divide: Poorer and less educated respondents were already experiencing significantly less social cohesion at that time than they had in 2017.

2.2.2 *Social Cohesion in 2023*

A central concern of the current study is to examine the extent to which social cohesion in Germany has changed. Table 2.1 documents the scores for the overall index across all federal states for the years 2017, 2020, and 2023. The "Difference" column indicates the extent of the change in the specified period.

The latest data indicate that cohesion in Germany has declined visibly for the first time since it was first recorded at the end of the 1980s. The scores decreased in every federal state between 2020 and 2023. On average, across Germany, cohesion currently stands at 52 points on a scale of 0 to 100. It is close to the implicit mean score of the measurement scale (50); however, the trend points in the same direction for the overall index and all individual dimensions. The dimension scores have decreased by

Table 2.1 Overall cohesion index compared over time by federal state

Federal state	2017	Difference 2020–2017	2020	Difference 2023–2020	2023	Difference 2023–2017
Hamburg	62	– 2	60	– 5	55	– 7
Hesse	63	– 1	62	– 8	54	– 9
Bavaria	63	0	63	– 10	53	– 10
Lower Saxony	62	– 1	61	– 8	53	– 9
Baden-Württemberg	63	– 2	61	– 8	53	– 10
Schleswig–Holstein	62	1	63	– 10	53	– 9
Rhineland-Palatinate	63	0	63	– 11	52	– 11
Mecklenburg-Western Pomerania	59	2	61	– 9	52	– 7
Saarland[a]	63	0	63	– 11	52	– 11
North Rhine-Westphalia	61	0	61	– 9	52	– 9
Germany	**61**	**0**	**61**	**– 9**	**52**	**– 9**
Berlin	59	0	59	– 8	51	– 8
Brandenburg	58	– 1	57	– 6	51	– 7
Thuringia	59	– 1	58	– 8	50	– 9
Saxony	57	0	57	– 8	49	– 8
Bremen[a]	62	– 7	55	– 6	49	– 13
Saxony-Anhalt	59	1	60	– 13	47	– 12

Note The table displays the average scores of the federal states for the overall index of social cohesion in the years 2017, 2020, and 2023, as well as the differences in scores across these years
[a] Sample size N < 40

between 3 points ("Civic participation") and 14 points ("Solidarity and helpfulness"), as shown in Table 2.2.

In the spring of 2020, optimism prevailed, and it seemed that society could overcome the challenges and restrictions associated with the coronavirus pandemic (Brand et al. 2021). In the meantime, however, it must be assumed that life with ever-new, constantly worsening crises has not left people unscathed but has, after all, impacted their sense of cohesion (see also More in Common 2023). Nevertheless, these figures should not be overinterpreted: The social challenges of recent years are identifiable and can be seen as a burden on cohesion. Furthermore, although the decline in cohesion scores is striking in a long-term comparison, it is not a sign of severe erosion. The score for the overall index is still in the upper half of the measurement range. Despite the decline, the foundations of cohesion in Germany are still solid. Nevertheless, the negative trend should not be ignored politically and socially. It remains to be seen whether this is merely a temporary "corona dip" with no recovery phase in the wake of further crises or whether a sustained downward trend is emerging that could also lead to a societal divide. A study conducted in 2024, although using an abbreviated instrument (Hartz 2021), supports the latter. It reports a score of only 45.1 for Germany as a whole.

Table 2.2 Overall cohesion index and its dimensions compared over time in Germany as a whole

Social cohesion	2017	Difference 2020–2017	2020	Difference 2023–2020	2023	Difference 2023–2017
Total index	61	0	61	– 9	52	– 9
Dimensions						
1.1 Social networks	71	0	71	– 10	61	– 10
1.2 Trust in people	56	0	56	– 9	47	– 9
1.3 Acceptance of diversity	79	3	82	– 13	69	– 10
2.1 Identification	77	– 1	76	– 11	65	– 12
2.2 Trust in Institutions	55	– 4	51	– 5	46	– 9
2.3 Perception of justice	38	3	41	– 6	35	– 3
3.1 Solidarity and helpfulness	48	0	48	– 14	34	– 14
3.2 Respect for social rules	77	– 3	74	– 7	67	– 10
3.3 Civic Participation	51	– 1	50	– 3	47	– 4

2.2.3 A Closer Look: The Nine Dimensions of Cohesion

This section examines each of the nine cohesion dimensions in more detail, illustrating changes over time at the federal level using single indicators. This helps to understand the issues that have been affecting people in recent years. A comparison of the last two survey periods also shows where there have been particularly large shifts.

2.2.3.1 Social Relations

Social relations play an essential role in the strength of cohesion. They represent the horizontal network that characterizes the interaction between individuals and groups within a community, such as a federal state or a region. Each of the three dimensions within this domain—"Social networks," "Trust in people," and "Acceptance of diversity"—has lost around 10 points compared to 2020. However, social relationships in Germany can still be described as intact compared to the other dimensions (see Table 2.3). According to the study by Hartz (2021), social cohesion is still higher in Germany than in the four so-called Visegrad countries (Poland, 44.8; Slovakia, 40.9; Hungary, 38.9; Czech Republic, 43.1).

Dimension 1.1—Social Networks

It is crucial for solid cohesion that people are integrated into an intact social network in the sense of "bridging social capital," according to Putnam (2000), which goes

Table 2.3 Indicators of Dimension 1.1 "social networks" compared over time

Guiding principle: people have strong and resilient social networks			
Indicator	2017	2020	2023
How large is your circle of friends and acquaintances?			
Rather large/very large	35	32	22
How often do you privately meet with friends, acquaintances, or work colleagues?			
Very often/rather often	49	49	35
If you had difficulties: do you have friends you can always count on for help?			
Yes	90	91	86
Do you have friends or acquaintances outside your family who would lend you 1000 euros in an urgent emergency?			
Yes	70	77	64

Note The table presents the average scores of the federal states on the overall index of social cohesion and its nine dimensions for the years 2017, 2020, and 2023, as well as the changes in scores across these years.

beyond the narrower family circle, i.e., "bonding social capital." The strength of such a network is measured by the frequency and quality of interactions, for example, with friends, acquaintances, neighbors, or work colleagues (Schiefer and van der Noll 2017). A comprehensive study by Teichler et al. (2023) recently highlighted the centrality of social networks to social cohesion.

As in the previous studies, the "Social networks" dimension was measured using four indicators. For example, we asked people about the size of their circle of friends, the intensity with which they maintain it, and whether they have friends they can count on in times of need. The results of our analyses are precise: In 2023, people not only have a much smaller circle of friends but also meet less often in private. Whereas just under 35% of respondents reported having a large circle of friends in 2020, this figure had decreased to just under 22% by 2023. In contrast, almost half of all respondents (43%) have a very small or small circle of friends, which is 16 percentage points more than in 2020. People are also meeting up less often. Whereas almost half of the respondents frequently met up with their friends in 2020, this figure has fallen to just over a third in 2023. Therefore, people's social lives have become less intense over the past three years.

Dimension 1.2—Trust in People

Trust in others is a crucial prerequisite for positive social interaction and a fundamental aspect of social cohesion. Those who trust their fellow human beings, on the whole, do not have to weigh all the risks and exercise caution in every contact and situation. It is also reasonable to assume that the less trust you have in other people, the less interest you show in them and the less willing you are to interact with them. Another indicator of trust is the belief that most people have good intentions and behave as can be expected, and—which is often an unquestioned and rarely checked assumption—largely "tick" in a similar way.

The current study distinguishes between generalized trust in others and trust in specific individuals (see Table 2.4). Compared to 2020, not only did generalized trust decrease (from an average of 6 to 5 points on a scale of 0 to 10), but also trust in people met for the first time. While almost a fifth (19%) had a great deal or very great deal of trust in 2020, this figure had fallen to just 10% by 2023.

Almost twice as many citizens also doubt that most people have good intentions (23% compared to 12% in 2020). The change in the agreement, with the statement that you can no longer rely on anyone, is particularly striking. Whereas only a minority of just under 15% shared this view in 2020, it is now almost a third of respondents, at just over 29%.

One reason for a breakdown in interpersonal trust could be that differences in opinion and attitude increase among people in their immediate surroundings, such as in families and at work. This development gained prominence in public discourse during the coronavirus pandemic but appears to persist in the context of military conflicts, such as those in Ukraine and Gaza. Opinions diverge more frequently, assumptions about others suddenly prove to be incorrect, and trust in others is sometimes shaken. The increasingly disrespectful culture of discussion, especially on social media, is probably also contributing to this (El-Menouar and Unzicker 2021).

Table 2.4 Indicators of Dimension 1.2 "trust in people" compared over time

Guiding principle: People have great trust in their fellow human beings			
Indicator	2017	2020	2023
Most people can be trusted			
Mean score (0 to 10)	5	6	5
How much do you trust people you meet for the first time?			
Trust reasonably/trust completely	15	19	10
I am convinced that most people have good intentions			
Fairly true/completely true	40	50	29
You can't rely on anyone these days			
Not true at all/not very true	47	46	29

Teney et al. (2024) argue against a general polarization trend, citing that polarization is observed in only approximately 20% of the attitudinal items in large open-access datasets. In light of the *de*polarization trend identified by Munzert and Bauer (2013) for the period between 1980 and 2010, based on data from the German General Social Survey (ALBUS), the current development may also be a mere 'swing back to normal' effect.

Dimension 1.3—Acceptance of Diversity

Modern societies are characterized by growing diversity in lifestyles, worldviews, religious beliefs, and cultural practices. The main topic of public debate is the influence of immigration on growing social diversity, such as the admission of refugees in recent years. In these debates, diversity is often given a negative connotation. It is considered a potential cause of weak social cohesion, and in some cases, this is also supported by the academic literature. The underlying argument is that increasing diversity diminishes the common cultural value base (Green and Janmaat 2011). It is also argued that increasing diversity can reduce the quality of communication between members of a society, thereby reducing cohesion (Dahrendorf 2004).

In their overview article, Schiefer and van der Noll (2017) conclude that diversity is not a fixed entity, but rather, its acceptance in society influences the strength of cohesion. Thus, this dimension is defined here as measuring the extent to which respondents accept people with different values and lifestyles, i.e., the degree to which individuals who might be considered "different" are accepted in the neighborhood for various reasons.

Despite a decline, "Acceptance of diversity" is the dimension with the highest average score in Germany at 69 points. A majority of the German population, therefore, still has no problem with having people with a completely different lifestyle, a different religion, foreigners, or homosexuals as neighbors. The single indicators support this, although approval has declined over the past three years (see Table 2.5).

Rejection has always been the lowest for homosexual neighbors. Just under 10% of respondents (an increase of 3 percentage points compared to 2020) stated that

Table 2.5 Indicators of Dimension 1.3 "acceptance of diversity" compared over time

Guiding principle: people accept people with different values and lifestyles as an equal part of society			
Indicator	2017	2020	2023
Would you like to have people with a completely different lifestyle as neighbors?			
No reservation to have as neighbors	72	75	67
Do you dislike having people of other religions as neighbors?			
No reservation to have as neighbors	84	87	77
Do you dislike having foreigners/migrants as neighbors?			
No reservation to have as neighbors	74	78	54
Would you like to have homosexuals as neighbors?			
No reservation to have as neighbors	86	90	87
Would you say that life in Germany, in general, is threatened or enriched by increasing diversity?			
Mean score (0 to 10)	6.1	6.6	4.7

they would not like to have homosexuals in their neighborhood. At just under 28%, the share of respondents who would not like to have people with a different lifestyle as neighbors is considerably higher. However, the rejection here has always been comparatively strong (2017: 23%, 2020: just under 21%). There has, therefore, been little change overall for both groups.

The situation is different for people of other religions and foreigners. In the current study, the share of those who would not prefer people of other religions in their neighborhood almost doubled by eight percentage points to 18%. Attitudes towards foreigners have changed even more: Whereas 17% said they disliked having foreigners as neighbors in 2020, their share more than doubled to almost 40% in 2023. Fewer people also believe that life in Germany is enriched by increasing diversity: The score on a scale of 0 to 10 was 6.6 points in 2020 but has since dropped to 4.7 points, already placing it in the negative range of the answering scale. This means that the majority tend to see diversity as a threat.

Overall, acceptance of diversity has declined in recent years. Given that our society is increasingly characterized by cultural and ideological diversity, it is essential to acknowledge this trend regarding regional differences: Acceptance of diversity is significantly lower in the East than in the West.

2.2.3.2 Connectedness

Connectedness is people's positive attachment to the community and its institutions. Dimensions of this core domain of cohesion are "Identification with the community," "Trust in institutions," and "Perception of fairness".

Table 2.6 Indicators of Dimension 2.1 "identification" compared over time

Guiding principle: people feel strongly connected to their community and identify as part of it			
Indicator	2017	2020	2023
How strongly do you feel connected to your federal state?			
Fairly connected/very connected	74	72	60
How strongly do you feel connected to your region?			
Fairly connected/very connected	77	76	62
How strongly do you feel connected to your place of residence?			
Fairly connected/very connected	78	79	60
How strongly do you feel connected to your neighborhood?			
Fairly connected/very connected	62	59	43

Dimension 2.1—Identification

How strongly do citizens in Germany feel connected to their neighborhood, place of residence, region, or federal state? The answers to these questions are essential because strong cohesion can develop when people see themselves as part of their community (Arant and Boehnke 2016). Conversely, people who feel disconnected from their neighborhood or residence are likely to have little interest in community involvement.

As in the previous studies, the "Identification" dimension comprises four single indicators (see Table 2.6). Our analyses indicate that people feel significantly less connected to all community levels in 2023 compared to 2020. Whereas 72% of people across Germany still felt fairly or very connected to their federal state, this share has declined to just 60% in 2023. Regional solidarity has also fallen by 14 percentage points to 62%.

The change is even more pronounced in people's local areas. Identification with one's place of residence decreased by around 19 percentage points to 60%, and identification with one's neighborhood decreased by 16 percentage points to 43%. The fact that mainly the small-scale identification has fallen so sharply is food for thought and may be due to the coronavirus pandemic. The sudden limitation of social contact and often drastic changes in daily routines due to working from home, a lack of childcare (particularly in West Germany), and the general retreat into one's own home have likely contributed to a decline in the importance of the living environment beyond one's family. Now, it seems that these cutbacks have left lasting traces. This conclusion also aligns with the study on cohesion in Baden-Württemberg from the turn of 2021/2022 (Boehnke et al. 2022).

Although the connection to the community is rarely consciously reflected upon in "normal" times and is predominantly taken for granted as part of one's identity (Billig 1995), it changes when one's affiliation is called into question. For example, this is often the case for people with a migration background (Berry 2001) or when, as in the case of the pandemic, one suddenly depends on the support and attention

Table 2.7 Indicators of Dimension 2.2 "trust in institutions" compared over time

Guiding principle: people have great trust in social and political institutions			
Indicator	2017	2020	2023
How much trust do you place in the political parties?			
Great confidence/very great confidence	9	8	7
How much trust do you place in the courts?			
Great confidence/very great confidence	48	48	45
How much trust do you place in the police?			
Great confidence/very great confidence	70	67	57
How much trust do you place in the federal government?			
Great confidence/very great confidence	30	23	19
How much trust do you place in the Bundestag?			
Great confidence/very great confidence	28	22	19

of one's environment. The double disappointment stemming from a lack of support and unreliable guidelines can thus lead to a distancing from the community.

Dimension 2.2—Trust in Institutions

Those who feel fairly treated by politicians and well-represented by the political system tend to have greater trust in social and political institutions such as the police, political parties, and the government. This is closely tied to a lower fear of corruption or arbitrariness on the part of the state. We, therefore, see trust in institutions as a "vertical" component of social cohesion.

What is the state of institutional trust in Germany? As Table 2.2 shows, the 5-point drop is comparatively tiny. However, at just 46 points, trust in institutions is weak overall. The single indicators reveal relevant differences (see Table 2.7).

The proportion of people placing great or very great trust in the Bundestag (the legislative branch) and the federal government (the executive branch) has remained essentially unchanged since 2020. The situation differs for those with little or no trust in these institutions. Their share has risen considerably—by 12 and 17 percentage points, respectively. Currently, just under 46% of respondents report having little to no trust in the Bundestag, whereas the figure for the federal government is almost 49%. The political parties fared even worse: The proportion of those with great trust in them has remained roughly the same, although it is very low at 7%. The majority now do not trust the parties or only a little; their share rose by almost 14 percentage points to 55%.

Typically, regulatory institutions, such as the police and courts, enjoy the greatest support among the population (Baier and Ellrich 2014; ROLAND Rechtsschutz 2023). However, whereas the share of people who trust the police has also fallen by around ten percentage points to just under 57%, trust in the courts has remained relatively constant: Around 45% of respondents (− 3 percentage points) say they have very high or high trust, and 18% (+ 3 percentage points) say they have only low or no trust at all.

Overall, the results awaken concerns. Frustration and disappointment with political decisions, as well as skepticism towards politics, have either increased or are being expressed more resolutely than they were three years ago. The growing group of people who feel politicians are not paying enough attention to their needs plays a key role here.

Dimension 2.3—Perceived Fairness

Justice plays a central role in social cohesion. Subjective perceptions are crucial here: Only when objective inequalities are perceived as unjust does resistance arise in the population (Sachweh and Sthamer 2016). This is why objective inequality indicators, such as differences in income or wealth, are not included in the measurement of this dimension. Instead, we use survey indicators that provide information on whether people perceive the distribution of material goods in society fairly and whether they feel fairly treated.

A look at the four items for this dimension reveals a widespread feeling of a lack of justice (see Table 2.8). Only 11% of respondents feel that social differences in society are fair. Around two of three respondents—just under 64%—do not share this opinion; in 2020, the figure was only 46%.

The situation is similar regarding the distribution of economic gains: more than two-thirds (72%) feel that this is unfair (up from 56% in 2020), while only 8% are satisfied with the current distribution. Just under half of the respondents (48%) believe that people in Germany are not remunerated according to their performance. Differences in rank between people are also only accepted by around a fifth of respondents (21%). In 2020, their share was about four percentage points higher.

Table 2.8 Indicators of Dimension 2.3 "perceived fairness" compared over time

Guiding principle: People see the distribution of goods in society as fair and feel they are treated fairly			
Indicator	2017	2020	2023
I think the social differences in our country are fair on the whole			
Completely true/fairly true	16	18	11
The differences in rank between people are acceptable because they essentially express what you did with the opportunities you had			
Completely true/fairly true	21	25	21
By and large, economic gains are distributed fairly in Germany today			
Completely true/fairly true	8	9	8
In Germany, you are paid according to your performance			
Completely true/fairly true	20	22	18

Table 2.9 Indicators of Dimension 3.1 "solidarity and helpfulness" compared over time

Guiding principle: people feel responsible for and help their fellow human beings			
Indicator	2017	2020	2023
Some people make monetary donations to social or charitable causes from time to time. Have you made such donations in the last 12 months?			
Yes	61	64	46
How often do you volunteer in your free time to help other people?			
at least once every week and daily	22	26	14
Most people don't care what happens to their fellow human beings			
true a little/not true at all	21	21	11

The index scores for the perception of fairness in Germany were already relatively low in our previous studies. Other studies also confirm the perceived lack of justice (Baarck et al. 2022; More in Common 2023). In 2023, the Germany-wide average for this dimension was 35 points (see Table 2.2). Therefore, the current perception of fairness is 6 points lower than the 2020 score and 3 points lower than the 2017 score. The change in this dimension is relatively small compared to most other dimensions, presumably due to a floor effect, i.e., the already low past scores limit the downward scope.

2.2.3.3 Orientation Towards the Common Good

Orientation towards the common good describes community members' actions and attitudes expressing responsibility for others and the community. This includes solidarity and helpfulness, the recognition of social rules, and the strength of civic participation.

Dimension 3.1—Solidarity and Helpfulness

Supporting society's weaker members is essential for solid cohesion. We use the "Solidarity and helpfulness" dimension to measure whether and to what extent people feel responsible for their fellow human beings. The focus here is on people becoming active instead of relying on state institutions or facilities.

This dimension is measured using three single indicators. Compared to 2020, Germans' willingness to donate and take on voluntary work has declined (− 18 percentage points). Currently, half of respondents state that they never volunteer in their free time—compared to 32% in 2020. The share of those who think that most people do not care about what happens to their fellow human beings has also increased: In 2020, just over a third (36%) agreed with this statement; today, it is more than half at 58%. As many as 79% believe that everyone only looks after themselves.

Four years ago, this share was 63%. A study by More in Common (2023) on social cohesion in the current time of crisis reached a similar conclusion: Since 2019, there has been growing dissatisfaction with a society perceived as increasingly selfish.

A certain degree of solidarity fatigue was already evident in 2022 (Boehnke et al. 2022; Unzicker 2022). However, it is worth noting that solidarity was repeatedly activated on a large scale in exceptional situations, such as the flood disaster in the Ahr Valley and the reception of refugees from Ukraine.

Dimension 3.2—Respect for Social Rules

The extent to which people adhere to the basic social rules in their community determines the strength of local social cohesion. This is not primarily about avoiding crime in the legal sense but rather about behavior that complies with the applicable, in some cases, "unspoken" norms and conventions (Bliesener and Bergmann 2016).

The Bertelsmann studies measure this cohesion dimension using three single indicators (see Table 2.10), for example, by asking whether people feel safe in their neighborhoods. This was the case for 88% of respondents in 2017, 85% in 2020, and 81% in 2023. The change is more pronounced regarding areas near respondents' homes where they would not want to go alone at night: 31% said yes in 2017, 38% in 2020, and 47% in 2023. Another question addressed whether there are problems in the neighborhood, including dog excrement, garbage on the streets, graffiti, or cars parked in violation. It is not a question of how much litter there is in a park, for example, but whether the careless throwing away of litter is perceived as a breach of the rules and, therefore, a nuisance. Only 25% of the 2023 respondents reported having no problems in their neighborhood. Around one in three people (34%) report one to two problems, and 41% report three or more. In spring 2020, 28% experienced three or more problems in their neighborhood.

Table 2.10 Indicators of Dimension 3.2 "respect for social rules" compared over time

Guiding principle: people adhere to basic social rules			
Indicator	2017	2020	2023
Generally speaking, how safe do you feel in your neighborhood?			
Very safe/rather safe	88	85	81
Is there any area around here—I mean within a radius of one kilometre—that you wouldn't want to go to alone at night?			
No	68	61	53
Are there problems in your neighborhood with ...?[a]			
No problems	24	26	25

[a] This variable is the sum of the yes-answers to the following issues: (1) dog excrement on the street, (2) cars parked in violation or an obstructive manner, (3) damaged playgrounds, (4) graffiti, (5) garbage in the streets or green spaces, (6) disturbance of the peace, (7) loitering drunks, (8) harassment or verbal abuse

Overall, compliance with basic social rules is viewed somewhat more critically in Germany in 2023 than in 2020. Above all, respondents report a more significant burden of problems in their surroundings. However, only a minority perceive their neighborhood as unsafe.

Dimension 3.3—Civic Participation

Civic participation is the ninth dimension of social cohesion. It focuses on actively shaping society and local communities through participation in social and political life, as well as public debates. It is captured using four indicators.

For example, a representative survey by the Institut für Demoskopie Allensbach (2023a) shows a connection between volunteering and democracy. This clearly shows that volunteering is essential for trust in democracy: "Trust in the system, approval of democracy and the feeling of self-efficacy is much more pronounced among those who get involved and, in turn, among those who do so in roles of responsibility—be it in a voluntary position, in responsibility for a specific task area, be it in a sports club, in work with refugees, in the fire department or culture." (Institut für Demoskopie Allensbach 2023b, p. 1).

The indicators assigned to this dimension show two contrasting developments (see Table 2.11). In 2020 and 2023, just over a quarter (30 and 26%, respectively) of respondents reported being highly politically engaged in the past twelve months. The proportion of people who are more politically engaged than average has, therefore, only fallen slightly over the last three years. On the other hand, the share of those who are inactive has increased by 12 percentage points. Today, 43% of respondents state that they are not politically active. The situation is similar regarding membership in non-profit associations or organizations: Whereas a good third (36%) said yes in 2020, only a quarter (25%) did so in 2023. The coronavirus pandemic and its consequences have presented numerous non-profit organizations, ranging from sports clubs to refugee aid organizations, with significant challenges, including the loss of members. It may take years for this sector to recover.

However, civic participation is expressed through active engagement and an interest in the political processes of society. In contrast to almost all indicators in the other dimensions, we do not observe a decline here, but rather an increase: the share of those not interested has remained relatively unchanged. However, those interested in politics have grown from 43 to 48%. The situation is similar when it comes to voting intentions. In 2020, approximately 85% of respondents believed it was likely that they would vote in the next election; by 2023, this share had increased to 89%.

These results indicate that our country is currently experiencing a highly politicized period. Political decisions are perceived as having a significant impact on people's everyday lives—both positively and negatively. The Fridays for Future movement has mobilized many people, especially the young, to stand up for the climate through demonstrations and protests. At the beginning of 2024, thousands of farmers and truck drivers protested across the country, seeing the climate policy measures of the European Commission and the German government as a threat to their economic existence. A thousand others are taking to the streets to send a clear signal against right-wing radicalism and xenophobia. At least now, there is little sign

Table 2.11 Indicators of Dimension 3.3 "civic participation" compared over time

Guiding principle: people participate in social and political life and public debates			
Indicator	2017	2020	2023
Political engagement in the last twelve months			
Many activities (three or more)	17	30	26
How interested are you in politics?			
Rather strong/very strong	42	43	48
When the next elections for which you are eligible to vote are due, how likely is it that you will actually vote for the go to the polls?			
very likely/rather likely	85	85	89
Are you a member of a non-profit association or organization?[a]			
Yes	35	36	25

[a] This variable is the sum of the yes-answers to the following items: There are different ways to campaign for something. In the last 12 months, have you (1) signed petitions, (2) worn badges or stickers, (3) held a political office, (4) taken part in a demonstration or (5) citizens' initiative, (6) attended a citizens' meeting, (7) contacted a politician/official, (8) taken a political stance on the Internet?

of the much-discussed disenchantment with politics and lethargy among the people. On the contrary, people are once again interested in political events and want to exert influence. The recent federal elections in February 2025 saw the highest voter turnout since German unification (82.5%).

2.3 The Regional Level—Structural Differences in the Experience of Social Cohesion

Social cohesion is primarily lived locally, so it is also necessary to examine it at a small regional or even local level (Arant et al. 2017; Boehnke et al. 2022). We do this at the level of the spatial planning regions,[1] which are formed based on Germany's districts and independent cities. For our studies, we have reduced the original 96 spatial planning regions to 79 homogenized spatial planning regions by collapsing some original regions from the same federal state and those that are adjacent to one another. They share several socio-economic characteristics. Interested readers can find out more about the methodology used in our 2017 study.

The 79 regions examined here primarily serve to measure empirically and better illustrate key factors influencing social cohesion. In other words, we aim to determine the extent to which a region's structural characteristics contribute to strengthening or

[1] In German: Raumordnungsregionen.

weakening cohesion. The insights gained can inform policymakers with evidence-based recommendations on the essential factors for social cohesion. Examining structural factors, we do not provide the cohesion scores for the regions.

Our SCR studies repeatedly show that social cohesion is, by and large, more pronounced in West German regions than in the East. What can these differences be attributed to? What are the specific mentalities, demographics, and economic characteristics of the regions? The almost proverbial US "Rust Belt" also exists in Germany, i.e., regions characterized by a dying manufacturing industry. In their study, Decker et al. (2022) observed that certain attitudes often occur in regions characterized by specific structural features. Although such regions are more likely to be in East Germany, there are also West German regions with the same structural profile.

To find out whether specific structural patterns characterize regions with solid or weak cohesion, we examined characteristics from the following six thematic areas: (1) prosperity and economic situation, (2) inequality and the welfare state, (3) modernization and restructuring, (4) demography, (5) education, and (6) migration. The characteristics were selected based on current social developments, theoretical considerations, and empirical findings from previous studies on cohesion in Germany (Dragolov et al. 2016; Arant et al. 2017). The measures for the analyzed characteristics are based on official statistics, primarily from the Federal Statistical Office's data pool, the Statistical Offices of the Federal States, and independent scientific institutes. The data included relate to the period from 2021 to 2023, with most of the data being available for 2021 and 2022.

We examine the relationship between the structural characteristics of the regions and the overall strength of social cohesion using bivariate and partial correlations. Bivariate correlations provide information on the strength and direction of the relationship between two variables. The correlation coefficient r can assume values between 0 and $\pm$ 1, whereby the sign (plus or minus) indicates the direction of the relationship (positive or negative). If the correlation coefficient is 0, there is no correlation between the variables. The closer the coefficient approaches 1, the stronger the relationship between the two variables.

In addition to bivariate (simple) correlations, we also report partial correlations. These provide information on the relationship between two variables controlled for a third variable and, like correlation coefficients, assume values between 0 and $\pm$ 1. For our purposes, the regional gross domestic product (GDP) per capita—the central measure of prosperity—is partially outside the bivariate relationship between the respective structural characteristics and social cohesion. The resulting partial correlation has been adjusted to account for the possible influence of GDP. In this way, it can be shown that social cohesion is not simply the result of a high standard of living or high economic prosperity. In a second step, the respective correlation is further partialled for the region's belonging to East or West Germany.[2] This allows

[2] Due to the fact that residence of respondents in former West or East Berlin in not recorded, the East/West variable is contrast-coded as '− 1' (East), '0' (Berlin), and + 1 (West).

the correlation to be additionally controlled for the possible influence of Germany's former division.

It is essential to note that cause-and-effect relationships cannot be inferred from correlations. However, the time lag in the data increases the plausibility of such an interpretation: The structural characteristics of the regions were recorded several years prior to the collection of the survey data. In addition, previous SCR studies have empirically shown that the characteristics analyzed here can be regarded as influencing factors of cohesion rather than its outcomes (Dragolov et al. 2016; Delhey et al. 2023).

The findings from the correlation analyses presented here are limited to results that are statistically highly significant ($p < 0.001$) at least once, either as simple correlations or partialled for GDP or for both GDP and East/West.

Level of Prosperity and Economic Situation

In comparative macro-sociological research, GDP per capita is a key indicator of economic performance and living standards. It has a moderately positive correlation with social cohesion ($r = 0.43$): The more prosperous a region is, the stronger the sense of togetherness there. This effect remains after partialling for the differences between East and West, though then somewhat weaker ($r = 0.27$). The situation is very similar with disposable income: Regional cohesion has a moderately positive correlation with income per inhabitant ($r = 0.48$). If the correlation is adjusted for the influence of GDP and East–West differences, it remains but weakens considerably ($r = 0.21$).

Notably, there is a correlation between the price index for housing costs in a region and local cohesion, which remains moderately strong and positive even after partialling ($r = 0.41$). The higher the housing costs in a region, the greater the cohesion within it. As housing costs are exceptionally high in metropolitan areas and economically attractive residential locations, the finding provides initial indications of the character of regions with strong cohesion. It is not the case that high housing costs drive down cohesion; rather, the positive correlation between housing costs and cohesion means that more people who experience high cohesion levels tend to live in areas with high housing costs.

Another interesting indicator is the female employment rate. We measure it relative to that of men, whereby the latter is set to 100. A score of 50 on this indicator means that the number of employed women in this location is 50% of the number of employed men. Simply put, out of 150 workers, 50 would be women, and 100 would be men. The simple correlation with social cohesion is weak and negative ($r = -0.19$). In other words, cohesion is lower (predominantly in eastern Germany) where the share of women in employment approaches that of men (also predominantly in the eastern German regions). If this correlation is first partialled for regional prosperity, the effect disappears. However, if the differences between East and West are then balanced out by partialling, the result is a moderately positive correlation ($r = 0.40$). In other words, a more intensive activation of women in the labor market is by no means detrimental to cohesion; on the contrary, it is beneficial. However, its positive influence is distorted by the still unclosed gap between the East and West of the country.

Surprisingly, our analyses show no correlation between cohesion and unemployment. Neither the unemployment rate overall or in certain age groups nor the share of long-term unemployed has any influence here. Overall, the average social cohesion in the regions depends on both the level of prosperity and the economic situation. The cost of housing, in particular, makes it clear that prosperous regions have solid cohesion (Table 2.12).

Inequality and the Welfare State

We examine the extent to which cohesion is associated with inequality and poverty and welfare state measures to reduce these externalities using two characteristics: first, the at-risk-of-poverty rate, i.e., the share of people with less than 60% of the federal median income in a region; second, the share of employable women who are entitled to welfare benefits and are dependent on basic income support (SGB II rate) at the time of data collection.

Social cohesion is weaker in regions where a higher proportion of people have an income below 60% of the federal median income. This correlation remains even when the influence of GDP and East–West differences are controlled for ($r = -0.23$). The same applies if the welfare system has to intervene more frequently to support women: Where more employable women receive SGB II benefits, cohesion is lower. This correlation is negative and weak but remains even after partialling for GDP and the East–West location ($r = -0.19$). As in previous studies (Arant et al. 2017), we again find that poverty is a crucial risk factor for social cohesion.

Demography

The results in the domain of demographics also support the assumption that cohesion is stronger in flourishing urban regions than in less attractive regions. Two key findings should be emphasized here: the higher the number of deaths per 10,000 inhabitants in a region, the lower the level of cohesion within that region. The correlation is strong and negative in the bivariate case ($r = -0.60$) and remains even after controlling for GDP and East–West differences, albeit only moderately so ($r = -0.31$). It is consistent with the other finding that population development has a moderate and positive correlation with social cohesion ($r = 0.28$). This means that cohesion is more robust in regions where the population is growing than in regions characterized by aging, regardless of whether they are in the West or East of the country.

Education

What is the relationship between the level of education in a region's population and its social cohesion? We consider an indirect, so-called proxy indicator, namely the childcare rates, as these are considerably higher for more highly educated parents than for less educated parents. The results are interesting: If we first look at the simple correlation for children under 3, we find a moderately negative effect ($r = -0.32$). Where particularly large numbers of children are cared for in daycare centers,

Table 2.12 Bivariate and partial correlations between the overall index of social cohesion and selected characteristics of the homogenized spatial planning regions ($N = 79$)

	Correlation					
	Simple		*Adjusted for*			
			GDP		*East/West*	
	r	*p*	*r*	*p*	*r*	*p*
Level of prosperity and economic situation						
(ln) Gross domestic product per capita	0.43	***			0.27	**
Disposable income per inhabitant	0.48	***	0.27	**	0.21	*
Price index for housing costs	0.56	***	0.40	***	0.41	***
Employment rate women vs. men	– 0.19	*	– 0.09	n.s	0.40	***
Inequality and the welfare state						
At-risk-of-poverty rate (federal median)	– 0.28	***	– 0.16		– 0.23	**
Deaths per 10,000 inhabitants	– 0.60	***	– 0.47	***	– 0.31	***
Population development per 10,000 inhabitants	0.39	***	0.37	***	0.28	**
Education						
Childcare rate for children aged 0–2	– 0.32	***	– 0.25	**	0.31	***
Migration and asylum						
Share of tolerated foreigners of all foreigners	– 0.53	***	– 0.40	***	– 0.19	*
Share of rejected asylum seekers of all asylum seekers	– 0.39	***	– 0.36	***	– 0.21	*
Share of unemployed foreigners	– 0.40	***	– 0.34	***	– 0.19	*

Note The correlation coefficient r between the overall cohesion index and the respective characteristic is shown for the simple (bivariate) correlation, the partial correlation for GDP, and the partial correlation for GDP and East–West location. Only highly significant correlations in at least one column are reported ($p < 0.01$). The significance of the correlations in two-sided tests is as follows: * $p \leq 0.10$, ** $p \leq 0.05$, *** $p \leq 0.01$

cohesion is worse at first glance. However, this finding is very strongly influenced by regional prosperity and differences between East and West. If both correlations are adjusted for GDP and East–West differences, the correlations become moderately positive ($r = 0.31$). A high rate of early childhood care is associated with greater social cohesion.

Migration and Asylum

The ongoing high level of immigration from abroad has sparked concerns in certain sections of the German population. Such concerns are partly responsible for the rapid rise of the AfD. We, therefore, took a closer look at how immigration is linked to cohesion.

The simple correlation between the share of non-Germans in the resident population of the regions and the level of cohesion there is initially clearly *positive* ($r = 0.44$). However, this correlation weakens after partialling out for GDP. It reduces further when differences between East and West are also taken into account. This can mean that immigrants prefer to settle in prosperous regions of Germany due to the generally better life opportunities rather than in economically worse-off regions. The effect is also due to a peculiar distribution between the old and new federal states: Far fewer foreigners live in the new federal states. If this is considered in the partial correlation, the original finding becomes considerably less significant.

Higher shares of tolerated foreigners among all foreigners or rejected asylum seekers among all asylum seekers in a region are negatively correlated with cohesion ($r = -0.53$ and $r = -0.39$, respectively). A weak negative correlation remains after partialling out the influence of GDP and the East–West differences ($r = -0.19$ and $r = -0.21$, respectively). It is important to note that higher shares of non-EU foreigners, tolerated and rejected asylum seekers, and unemployed foreigners occur primarily in regions that have a significantly lower share of both foreigners and asylum seekers in the total population. This could indicate that these correlations are due less to the characteristics of the foreigners themselves and more to the specific immigration history of the regions.

Summary

We examined the relationship between several relevant structural characteristics of German regions and social cohesion. The reason for this was the recurring finding over several decades that cohesion was weaker in East Germany than in the West. We attempted to determine whether the reasons lie in the unique characteristics of the old and new federal states or whether structural characteristics generally found everywhere play a—perhaps even more central—role.

Our analyses show that the economic situation and level of prosperity are the primary factors that make a difference: Cohesion is exceptionally high in prosperous regions, whereas it is weaker in regions with a higher risk of poverty. A high rate of early childhood care also goes hand in hand with greater cohesion. The shift towards a modern service society also appears to play a role: where it is more advanced and has a less industrial character, cohesion is stronger. However, this also applies to rural regions. After all, cohesion is stronger in regions where the population is growing than in those characterized by aging populations.

2.4 Conclusion

Summarizing the findings of this study is not an easy task. The trend in social cohesion is clear: we are witnessing declines in all dimensions. Nevertheless, the scores fall within a range that allows us to speak of relatively solid social cohesion; however, it should not be overlooked that a state of permanent crisis can strain cohesion over time. Given the challenges of our time, it would have been even more surprising if these had not been reflected in our results. Our study reinforces our findings on Baden-Württemberg (Boehnke et al. 2022). However, the long-term perspective has shown that cohesion, as measured by our model, is a relatively sluggish phenomenon. In the past, it has hardly been subject to short-term fluctuations and has proven stable even in challenging times.

Cohesion Has Proven Its Worth Despite Crises.

What is remarkable about the past three years? People probably tend to perceive their era as the most unique of all times. However, the current period brings together developments that make it unique to previous decades: the coronavirus pandemic was a once-in-a-century event, and, although some may already have forgotten, it radically changed everyone's daily lives within a matter of days. During this period, conspiracy narratives permeated public and private discourse on a massive scale, reinforced by radical political forces that exploited widespread uncertainty to further their agendas.

A short time later, the Russian attack on Ukraine called into question fundamental certainties that had applied at least since the end of the Soviet Union. All this is happening at a time when far-reaching transformation processes are progressing inexorably and coming to the fore: droughts and heavy rainfall are making climate change palpable, the shortage of skilled workers is a factor in societal aging, and the rapid development of technology, including ChatGPT, is also a contributing factor. At the same time, the constellation of figures and power in the political domain is shifting due to the rise of a party that, to a certain extent, is anti-constitutional. This is accompanied by an increasingly shrill public debate, the pace and quality of which is increasingly determined by social media logic. Under these conditions, transformation efforts and crises of all kinds are accompanied by significant agitation.

Leaving aside the detrimental consequences of COVID-19, none of the above phenomena would have individually put a noticeable strain on cohesion. However, the combination and persistence of crises and transformations scratch its foundations. Above all, when there is no time to catch your breath and rest, stress builds up continuously. Our data show the result.

The findings demonstrate a weakening of cohesion in all its sub-dimensions. Nevertheless, the results do not show a dramatic collapse or deep societal divide. So far, we have interpreted them as an exhaustion effect of this phase characterized by crises and worries about the future. On the contrary, one could argue that cohesion has generally proven effective in the current crisis phase. However, it must be actively maintained and strengthened.

Good Living Conditions Help People to Live Together

Our study yields an essential finding: regional living conditions, particularly socioeconomic factors, play a significant role. Although cohesion is not a foregone conclusion even in prosperous and demographically growing regions, a stable economy, attractive living conditions, and favorable prospects make successful social cohesion much more likely. There has been much discussion in Germany about equal living conditions and the completion of German unity. Our analyses confirm that these objectives still belong on the political agenda.

References

R. Arant, K. Boehnke, Identifikation mit dem Gemeinwesen—Welches Wir-Gefühl ist ein gutes Wir-Gefühl?, in *Der Kitt der Gesellschaft [The sealant of society].* ed. by B. Stiftung (Bertelsmann Stiftung, 2016), pp.145–173

R. Arant, G. Dragolov, K. Boehnke, *Sozialer Zusammenhalt in Deutschland 2017 [Social Cohesion in Germany 2017]* (Bertelsmann Stiftung, 2017)

J. Baarck, M. Dolls, K. Unzicker, L. Windsteiger, *Gerechtigkeitsempfinden in Deutschland [Sense of justice in Germany]* (Bertelsmann Stiftung, 2022)

D. Baier, K. Ellrich, Vertrauen in die Polizei im Spiegel verschiedener Befragungs-studien [Trust in the police as mirrored in various survey studies], in *Polizeibeamte als Opfer von Gewalt. Ergebnisse einer Mixed-Method-Studie*, ed. by K. Ellrich, D. Baier. Verlag für Polizeiwissenschaft (2014), pp. 43–90

J.W. Berry, A psychology of immigration. J. Soc. Issues **57**(3), 615–631 (2001)

M. Billig, *Banal nationalism* (Sage, 1995)

T. Bliesener, M.C. Bergmann, Anerkennung sozialer Regeln—Die Entwicklung normenabweichender Einstellungen und Verhaltensweisen junger Menschen in Deutschland, in *Der Kitt der Gesellschaft.* ed. by B. Stiftung (Bertelsmann Stiftung, 2016), pp.287–311

K. Boehnke, G. Dragolov, R. Arant, *Gesellschaftlicher Zusammenhalt in Baden-Württemberg 2022 [Social cohesion in Baden-Württemberg]* (Bertelsmann Stiftung, 2022)

T. Brand, R. Follmer, J. Hölscher, K. Unzicker, *Gesellschaftlicher Zusammenhalt in Zeiten der Pandemie. Ergebnisse einer Längsschnittstudie in Deutschland 2020 mit drei Messzeitpunkten [Social Cohesion in times of the pandemic. Results of a three-wave panel study in Germany 2020]* (Bertelsmann Stiftung, 2021)

R. Dahrendorf, *Der Wiederbeginn der Geschichte: Vom Fall der Mauer zum Krieg im Irak* (C.H. Beck, 2004)

O. Decker, J. Kiess, A. Heller, E. Brähler, *Autoritäre Dynamiken in unsicheren Zeiten. Neue Herausforderungen - alte Reaktionen? Leipziger Autoritarismus Studie 2022 [Authoritarian dynamics in insecure times. New challenges—Old reactions? The Leipzig Authoritarianism Study 2022]* (Psychosozial-Verlag, 2022)

J. Delhey, K. Boehnke, G. Dragolov, Z.S. Ignácz, M. Larsen, J. Lorenz, M. Koch, Social cohesion and its correlates: a comparison of Western and Asian societies. Comp. Sociol. **17**(3–4), 426–455 (2018)

J. Delhey, G. Dragolov, K. Boehnke, Social cohesion in international comparison: a review of key measures and findings. Kölner Zeitschrift Für Soziologie und Sozialpsychologie **75**, 95–120 (2023)

G. Dragolov, R. Arant, K. Boehnke, K. Unzicker, *Gesellschaftlicher Zusammenhalt in Baden-Württemberg [Social cohesion in Baden-Württemberg]* (Bertelsmann Stiftung, 2020).

G. Dragolov, Z.S. Ignácz, J. Lorenz, J. Delhey, K. Boehnke, K. Unzicker, *Social cohesion in the Western world. What holds societies together: insights from the Social Cohesion Radar* (Springer International, 2016)

Y. El-Menouar, K. Unzicker, *Klimawandel, Vielfalt, Gerechtigkeit. Wie Werthaltungen unsere Einstellungen zu gesellschaftlichen Zukunftsfragen bestimmen [Climate change, diversity, justice. How value orientations determine our attitudes toward questions on the societal future]* (Bertelsmann Stiftung, 2021)

R. Follmer, T. Brand, K. Unzicker, *Gesellschaftlicher Zusammenhalt in Deutschland 2020. Eine Herausforderung für uns alle. Ergebnisse einer repräsentativen Bevölkerungsstudie [Social cohesion in Germany 2020. A challenge for us all. Results from a representative population study]* (Bertelsmann Stiftung, 2020)

A. Green, J.G. Janmaat, *Regimes of social cohesion: Societies and the crisis of globalization.* (Palgrave, MacMillan, 2011)

C. Hartz, *Reducing Citizens' Worries Through Resilience: A Two-Wave Panel Study During the Corona Pandemic.* Master thesis. Jacobs University Bremen (2021)

Institut für Demoskopie Allensbach, *Demokratische Integration. Zweite Vorstudie. Repräsentative Bevölkerungsbefragung 2022/2023 [Democratic integration. Second pretest. Representative population survey 2022/2023]* (2023a). https://www.deutsche-stiftung-engagement-und-ehrenamt.de/wp-content/uploads/2023/06/Langbericht_Bevoelkerungsbefr_Dem_Integration_Mai_2023.pdf. Accessed 7 Apr 2024

Institut für Demoskopie Allensbach, *Demokratische Integration in Deutschland [Democratic integration in Germany. Short report]* (Kurzbericht, 2023b). https://www.deutsche-stiftung-engagement-und-ehrenamt.de/wp-content/uploads/2023/05/Kurzbericht_Bevoelkerungsbefragung_Demokratische_Integration_Mai_2023.pdf

More in Common, *Zukunft, Demokratie, Miteinander: Was die deutsche Gesellschaft nach einem Jahr Preiskrise umtreibt [Future, democracy, cooperation: What plagues the German society after a year of price crisis].* More in Common e.V. (2023)

S. Munzert, P.C. Bauer, Political depolarization in German public opinion, 1980–2010. Polit. Sci. Res. Methods **1**, 67–89 (2013). https://doi.org/10.1017/psrm.2013.7

R.D. Putnam, *Bowling Alone: The Collapse and Revival of American Community* (Simon & Schuster, 2000).

ROLAND Rechtsschutz, *ROLAND Rechtsschutz 2023 [ROLAND law report 2023].*

P. Sachweh, E. Sthamer, Befunde zum Gerechtigkeitsempfinden der Deutschen und potenzielle soziale Folgen empfundener Ungerechtigkeit [Findings on the perception of justice among Germans and potential consequences of experiencing injustice], in *Der Kitt der Gesellschaft [The sealant of society].* ed. by B. Stiftung (Bertelsmann Stiftung, 2016), pp.207–251

M. Sand, T. Kunz, *Gewichtung in der Praxis [[Weighting in practice]]* Gesis—Leibniz-Institut für Sozialwissenschaften. GESIS Survey Guidelines (2020)

D. Schiefer, J. van der Noll, The essentials of social cohesion: a literature review. Soc. Indic. Res. **132**(2), 579–603 (2017)

B. Stiftung (ed.) *What holds Asian Societies Together? Insights from the Social Cohesion Radar* (Verlag Bertelsmann Stiftung, 2018)

N. Teichler, J-Y. Gerlitz, C. Cornesse, C. Dilger, O. Groh-Samberg, H. Lengfeld, E. Nissen, J. Reinecke, S. Skolarski, R. Traunmüller, L. Verneuer-Emre, *Entkoppelte Lebenswelten? Soziale Beziehungen und gesellschaftlicher Zusammenhalt in Deutschland. Erster Zusammenhaltsbericht des FGZ. SOCIUM, Forschungsinstitut Gesellschaftlicher Zusammenhalt [Decoupled life worlds? Social relations and societal cohesion in Germany. First cohesion report of the FGZ]* (2023). https://doi.org/10.26092/elib/2517

C. Teney, G. Pietrantuono, T. Wolfram, What polarizes citizens? An explorative analysis of 817 attitudinal items from a non-random online panel in Germany. PLoS ONE **19**(5), e0302446 (2024). https://doi.org/10.1371/journal.pone.0302446

K. Unzicker, *Umfrage Februar 2022. Erschöpfte Gesellschaft. Auswirkungen von 24 Monaten Pandemie auf den gesellschaftlichen Zusammenhalt [Survey February 2022. Exhausted society. Consequences of 24 months of the pandemic on social cohesion]* (Bertelsmann Stiftung, 2022)
C.R. Williamson, R.L. Mathers, Economic freedom, culture, and growth. Public Choice **148**(3/4), 313–335 (2011)

Part I
Networks

Chapter 3
Simulating an Empirically Informed Population Network of Core Discussion Ties

Michał Bojanowski, Alla Loseva, Paul Schuler, Susanne Böller, and Miranda J. Lubbers

Abstract Social cohesion and polarization can be studied with society-wide networks, however such data are not easy to collect. The alternatives—stylized networks often used in agent-based models (ABM) and small-scale empirical networks—might misrepresent societal structure at the macro-level, in terms of both topological properties and differences in network positions of social groups. We demonstrate how more realistic society-level networks can be generated from ego-network data that can be reasonably collected even for large populations. The empirical data we use come from a large-scale survey on a representative national sample about individuals' core discussion ties, collected by the Spanish Institute for National Statistics (INE). In this paper, we describe our methods and the properties of the resulting networks. We find that large-scale core discussion networks do not have small-world properties, resembling population-level familial networks rather than friendship networks. At the same time are characterized by assortativity on dimensions such as age, gender, working status and political views. We also demonstrate how model-based simulations of complete networks can be further analyzed to make inferences that go beyond personal network analysis, such as centrality and connectivity. Together with this paper, we release the simulated full networks for secondary use by ABM modelers and wider research community interested in studying cohesion in realistic networks.

M. Bojanowski (✉) · M. J. Lubbers
Autonomous University of Barcelona, Barcelona, Spain
e-mail: mbojanowski@kozminski.edu.pl

M. Bojanowski
Kozminski University, Warsaw, Poland

A. Loseva
ICS, University of Groningen, Groningen, Netherlands

P. Schuler
University of Edinburgh, Edinburgh, Scotland

S. Böller
University of Bonn, Bonn, Germany

M. A. Keijzer et al. (eds.), *Computational Social Science of Social Cohesion and Polarization*, Computational Social Sciences,
https://doi.org/10.1007/978-3-032-01373-6_3

3.1 Introduction

Social cohesion is a pivotal concept in the social sciences, reflecting the degree to which a society is characterized by absence of social conflict and polarization and presence of strong social bonds (e.g., Durkheim 1893). Social relations between groups and individuals, and social networks as their component, are the most prominent aspect of social cohesion (Schiefer and van der Noll 2017). Of particular significance are core discussion networks—3–5 typically strong ties with whom individuals discuss important matters (Marsden 1987). Structural patterns found in these networks could scale up to societal-level segregation, as well as lay out the pathways of information diffusion and polarization. The role of social networks in these macro-level phenomena is frequently studied with agent-based modeling (ABM).

To make empirically sound conclusions about cohesion, one needs to work with population networks of realistic structure. In much of the ABM literature, agents' interaction spaces are initialised using stylised networks like complete graphs, random graphs, scale-free graphs, or small-world networks (Amblard et al. 2015; Hedström & Manzo 2015). While different levels of model realism may be desirable depending on the research question, network topology can significantly affect the model results (e.g., Guilbeault et al. 2018; Rolfe 2014). Research has shown that empirical networks, drawn from real-world data, can more accurately capture complex social dynamics than stylised networks, particularly for processes like knowledge diffusion (Cointet and Roth 2007).

However, researchers have limited understanding of what network structures arise empirically at the population level, as population-level networks are scarce and notoriously hard to collect. Available large-scale networks mostly come from online networks and national registries (e.g., Chetty et al. 2022; Corten 2012; Kazmina et al. 2024; Bokányi et al. 2023). Although examining their structure is insightful, they do not necessarily represent core discussion ties.

While using stylized networks results in limited insight into empirical context and obtaining real large-scale networks is challenging, a practical alternative is to use realistic but artificially generated large-scale networks. Among the various methods available (Heß et al. 2021), inferring a sociocentric network from ego network data stands out as the most efficient one as it does not require complete data about all interdependencies in the population or even in its subset. This approach involves collecting data from individuals about their connections, such as friends or confidants, and then using a graph-generating model based, for instance, on Exponential-family Random Graph Modeling (ERGM) to infer a global network structure (Smith 2012).

So far, however, this method has only been used on small samples, which limits its potential to represent relationship patterns accurately, especially for smaller subpopulations. Here, we present a version of this strategy applied to unique, large-scale survey data from Spain, to generate empirically-informed population networks based on a wealth of relationship data. We compare the structure of our empirically calibrated networks to stylised networks sampled from classic network models. Together with this paper, we release a dataset that includes these realistic full networks.

Our simulations are valuable for two main reasons. Firstly, despite the extensive collection of personal network data, there is still a gap in understanding what these data reveal about the structure of strong sociability ties within the larger society. By simulating the networks, we can gain insights into how these data collected at the individual level reflect broader network features at the larger society level. Secondly, using the data about core discussion networks to create empirically-informed networks can enhance the realism and applicability of ABMs in the domain of opinion diffusion and polarisation (e.g., Boero and Squazzoni 2005; Bruch and Atwell 2015; Chattoe-Brown and Gabbriellini 2021; Lorenz 2021). Although we do not aim to create 'hyperrealistic' networks,[1] our study is informative in that we pinpoint where the simulated networks differ from stylized structures. We also demonstrate how analysis of distribution of such empirically-calibrated networks provides insights into relative differences between certain groups in centrality and connectivity—features which are not directly observed in egocentric data, but can be subject of inference given the partial network information available in the personal networks.

The structure of the chapter is as follows. The next section discusses the network structures used in cohesion research and argues for our approach. Then, we present the range of methods that have been used so far to insert empirical realism into ABM network environments and justify our choice of method. Then, we detail how the method works and our modeling decisions. Afterwards, we present the empirical data and the outcomes, which we discuss further in the conclusion.

3.2 Background

3.2.1 Network Structures in Cohesion Research

To approach the macro-phenomenon of cohesion, one can start by examining micro-level interpersonal networks. Core discussion partners—small egocentric networks of 3–5 people with whom individuals discuss "important matters" (e.g., Marsden 1987)—provide useful data. These core network members are typically contacted weekly and discuss personal and significant societal topics, such as politics (Klofstad et al. 2009). Therefore, core networks are particularly valuable for studying communicative processes related to social cohesion, including opinion diffusion and the emergence of shared norms.

Empirically, core discussion networks are often "small, kin-centered, relatively dense, and homogeneous" (Marsden 1987, p. 122). They typically show segregation by ethnicity and socio-economic status (SES; McPherson et al. 2001). For example, among Turkish and Moroccan minorities in the Netherlands, three-quarters of confidants are from the same ethnic group, which overlaps with categorical boundaries of

[1] We thank an anonymous reviewer for this notion.

SES (van Tubergen 2015). Ethnic closure is even more pronounced among women, those living in immigrant concentration areas, and individuals with strong ethnic or religious identities. A longitudinal study using US General Social Survey data reveals that core discussion networks remain segregated by race and age despite increased societal diversity over time. Moreover, young people become more isolated from older generations outside the family, and there is weak evidence of rising educational and religious homophily (Smith et al. 2014).

To study cohesion at the macro scale, one would need to work with a society-wide core discussion network. However, such networks might not exhibit the same structures as small-scale core networks. Theoretically, Blau (1974) suggested that if social networks consisted solely of core discussion network ties, they would primarily comprise small, isolated "islands" lacking overall cohesion.

Empirical large-scale discussion networks are hard to collect. The two mostly used types of representations of empirical population-level networks are online friendship networks (Chetty et al. 2022; Corten 2012) and networks based on administrative register data (Bokányi et al. 2023; Cremers et al. 2024; Kazmina et al. 2024; Menyhért et al. 2024). Studies show that these empirical networks deviate from synthetic ones (such as scale-free networks) in various ways, for example in local transitivity. One caveat is that it is unclear whether ties in these networks (e.g., between family members, next-door neighbors, colleagues, classmates) correspond to core discussion ties, as neither registers-based networks nor online friendship networks show any indication of tie strength or communication intensity.

When accessing large-scale networks is not an option, researchers can use artificially generated network structures. Most agent-based modeling studies of social influence and information diffusion use artificial networks: Only 3% of the studies published in the field between 1998 and 2015 used empirical data to inform the generated networks (Amblard et al. 2015). Researchers using artificial data typically draw on complete, random, scale-free, lattice, or small-world graphs (Albert and Barabási 2002). These networks are either grown during simulations based on agents' behavioral rules (e.g., Zachara and Piskor-Ignatowicz 2016) or formed by assuming ties between agents who are adjacent in some appropriately defined social space (e.g., Hamill and Gilbert 2009).

The choice of network topology significantly influences the outcomes of various models (Guilbeault et al. 2018; Rolfe 2014). For example, the diffusion of retirement norms differs between grid-based and random networks (Axtell 2001), and continuous opinion dynamics yield varied opinion landscapes based on network structure (Amblard and Deffuant 2004; Deffuant 2006). Rolfe (2014) shows that simple contagion models produce vastly different outcomes depending on the network used, while Guilbeault et al. (2018) find similar variations for complex contagion models. Even different types of small-world networks do not produce consistent results in models of epidemics, opinion, and cultural dynamics (Thiriot 2020).

The impact of network topology is particularly striking when comparing stylised networks to empirical ones. For example, Bearman et al. (2004) highlight differences between empirically observed sexual partner networks and those used in epidemiological models, noting variations in infection rates and discussing policy implications. Therefore, Cointet and Roth (2007) recommend using a real-world network of similar size from an adjacent domain to accurately represent real-world processes.

Empirically-based synthetic networks have been suggested as a viable compromise between data accessibility and realism of the resulting structure. Heß et al. (2021) demonstrate that such synthetic networks more closely resemble empirical ones than random networks, in their case affecting the discussed migration models. These insights highlight the importance of using realistic network topologies to improve the accuracy of social dynamics models.

3.2.2 Methods of Generating Realistic Networks

Multiple approaches have been proposed for generating realistic networks. For the sake of brevity we skip studies relying on theoretical and "feature-driven" (Lim et al. 2016) models such as ones generating scale-free (Barabási and Albert 1999) or small-world graphs (Watts and Strogatz 1998) with "plausible" generating parameters, and concentrate on models and approaches more directly focused on empirical data. We group them into the following rough categories:

1. **Methods not requiring direct social network measurement**. These approaches usually rely on multiple data sources on distributions of characteristics of the whole society: census data on demographics and household structure. Such statistics are often combined with data on population activities such as mobility and daily routine sequences. Network ties are then introduced via mechanisms such as spatial proximity, co-affiliation in schools and workplaces, or other theoretically informed procedures and their parameters are usually set by assumption or trial-and-error. Examples include Barrett et al. (2009), Burger et al. (2017), Eubank et al. (2004), Jiang et al. (2022), and Thiriot and Kant (2008). Such methods are often used in epidemiology or transportation policy planning. While based on population statistics, the network-generating part of these approaches heavily relies on theoretical assumptions.

The other two approaches involve simulating networks using a more explicit model of a target system.

2. **Methods relying on direct measurement of a complete social network**. When the full network is available, the data can be used to estimate/train a generative network model, and at a later stage, use the model to generate/sample data for the actual ABM simulations. This approach includes both generic methods utilising genetic programming or symbolic regression (Menezes and Roth 2014, 2019; Heß et al. 2021) and models specifically developed for social networks such as Exponential-family Random Graph Model (ERGM; Frank and Strauss 1986; Wasserman and Pattison 1996; Lusher et al. 2013; Snijders et al. 2006) or, if

dynamic network data is available, the Link Probability Model (McCulloh et al. 2010) or Stochastic Actor-Oriented Modeling (SAOM) (Snijders et al. 2010). The available network of the population of interest can of course be used in the simulations directly. Still, it is useful to work with a model fitted to that network and use it to produce a population of networks to consider possible variation in network structure while keeping the crucial structural features consistent with the empirical data.

3. **Methods relying on partial social network measurement**. Several methods have been proposed for scenarios when complete network data is unavailable. A variant of an ERGM can be used to infer and simulate complete networks from ego network samples (Smith 2012, 2015). Studies have shown that networks generated with this method closely resemble known complete networks in terms of diffusion dynamics and network-level cohesion (Smith and Burow 2020; Smith and Gauthier 2020). This approach works well if the network under study has a relatively low degree such that frequencies of types of simulated personal networks can be monitored and compared to the observed frequencies. As an alternative, more recent developments in the ERGM methodology allow directly fitting a subclass of these models to egocentrically-sampled data. The sub-class consists of models containing terms for which the sufficient statistics are recoverable from an egocentric sample. The list includes exogenous terms related to attribute-based degree heterogeneity, assortativity, and endogenous terms such as degree effects and triadic effects related to the distribution of edgewise shared partners (Krivitsky et al. 2011, 2019, 2022; Krivitsky and Morris 2017). We will use this method in the remainder of this article.

Adopting the Exponential-family Random Graph Model (ERGM) as the statistical framework for this study offers several compelling advantages over the other approaches. First, ERGMs are grounded in a rigorous and principled statistical foundation. These models are members of the exponential family of distributions, with properties that have been extensively studied. Their estimation relies on established statistical methods, such as Maximum Likelihood Estimation, rather than relying on less formal or ad hoc generative algorithms. This approach enables robust evaluation of model convergence and goodness of fit within a well-defined framework (Hunter et al. 2008).

Second, the coefficients of ERGMs have meaningful interpretations related to social processes of tie formation. These include concepts such as attribute-related degree heterogeneity, assortativity, mutuality, and triadic closure, making the model particularly relevant for sociological research.

Third, even when ERGMs are fitted to egocentrically sampled data, they retain the capacity to generate complete network datasets. These generated datasets exhibit properties consistent with those observed in the egocentric sample, enhancing the model's utility for analyzing and extrapolating network characteristics.

The analysis presented below applies ERGM framework to a large, representative sample from the national population of Spain, thus contributing to the growing body of literature of egocentric ERGM applications. Our model specifications not only include dyad-independent terms (e.g. in Krivitsky and Morris 2017) but also degree and triadic effects (as in Krivitsky et al. 2019).

3.3 Methods

An ERGM specifies a probability distribution over a set of all networks of specified size (number of nodes):

$$P(Y = y) = \frac{exp(\theta^T g(y))h(y)}{k(\theta)}$$

where the probability of observing a particular network y is a function of a vector of network statistics g(y), θ is a vector of model coefficients to be estimated, h(y) is the reference measure defining the baseline behavior of the model when $\theta = 0$, and k(θ) is a normalizing constant ensuring that the sum of the probabilities over all y's is equal to 1. Specifying an ERGM for the given dataset primarily consists of proposing a set of network statistics, g(y), that the researcher hypothesised to correspond to important mechanisms responsible for the network structure. Once the model is fit, the estimated values of model coefficients, θ, indicate, roughly speaking, how the probability of a tie changes given that it is to form a particular structural feature encapsulated in the network statistic, ceteris paribus other effects present in the model.

As discussed in the preceding section, our approach builds on the methodologies outlined by Krivitsky and Morris (2017) and further developed by Krivitsky et al. (2019, 2022). In a nutshell, it is an approach to estimate an ERGM but, instead of computing its sufficient statistics directly from a "complete", sociocentrically-collected network data, they are estimated based on an egocentric sample. In applying this framework to our study, we have tailored the model specifications to align with the characteristics of our dataset (see the section "Data"). We estimate two specifications. The first contains the following effects:

- Degree heterogeneity effects related to the following attributes: age, education, gender, country of birth, occupational status, political views, and religion.
- Endogeneous effects: number of nodes with degree 0 (isolates), 1, 2, 3, and 4 (5 parameters in total), number of edges with the number of shared partners equal to 0, 1, and 2 (three parameters).

The second specification extends the first with the following assortativity effects:

- Modeled with absolute difference, related to age, education, and political views.
- Modeled with categorical uniform assortativity effects related to gender, country of birth, occupational status, and religion.

Together, these specifications provide a rather detailed representation of the interplay between individual attributes and the network structure, keeping in mind that the data comes from a nationally representative survey. We estimate the models via the Maximum Pseudo-Likelihood (MPLE)[2] method using Statnet and the package 'ergm.ego' (Krivitsky 2025).

The estimated models will be used in three ways:

1. Model coefficients have substantive interpretations regarding social mechanisms related to node and tie characteristics, e.g. assortativity, reciprocity. It is then of interest to investigate which important structural effects are responsible for the presence or absence of core discussion ties.

   To further understand the probability distribution over networks, we will draw a sample of 100 networks, each of a size equal to the sample size (5094 respondents). The distribution of various properties of these networks will be utilised in the remaining two investigations:
2. We compare the ERGM-generated distribution to Erdős–Rényi graphs in features such as transitivity and average path length. Apart from each being of interest in their own right, together they constitute a fingerprint of the Small World phenomenon, i.e. the combination of high transitivity (clustering) and low average path length is a symptom of that phenomenon. In this way, we verify whether the empirically estimated network distribution has the Small World property.
3. We analyze social cohesion in the ERGM-generated network. The concept of social cohesion is often related to the general extent of the "integration" in a society. As such, a lack of social cohesion can be related to the overall prevalence of individuals who are relatively less well connected with others. We use three indicators of social cohesion: closeness centrality, betweenness centrality, and the fraction of nodes outside of the largest connected component.

Analyses were performed using the R package 'igraph' (Csardi and Nepusz 2005).

3.4 Data

3.4.1 Sample

We used data from the Spanish General Social Survey, collected by the Spanish Center for Sociological Research (CIS) between the 11th and 30th of April, 2013. The data are openly accessible via the CIS website.[3] A large, multistage, representative sample of the national adult population was drawn and interviewed face-to-face about their

---

[2] While MPLE has known limitations—primarily leads to underestimated standard errors of the coefficients—we used it because the network size and model size made the preferred MCMCMLE method computationally and technically intractable, even on High Performance Computing hardware.

[3] Encuesta Social General Española (study number 2975), see www.cis.es.

core discussion networks (realised sample size $N = 5094$; 54% response rate; see CIS 2013).

The following name generator was used to collect the data about core discussion networks:

> From time to time, most people discuss important issues with others. Thinking back over the last six months, with which people have you talked with about issues that are important to you? Please tell me the first name, initials, or nickname of these people (or family relationship).

While respondents could mention more than five people, interviewers recorded the (nick)names or initials of the first five people they nominated as well as the total number of persons a respondent answered. Follow-up information on these ties was collected on 15,580 ties, of which we excluded 157 because they were ties to children.

After the names were elicited, respondents ("egos") were asked follow-up questions about each of the (first) five nominated persons ("alters"), such as their gender, age, country of birth, years of education, occupation, religion, and political orientation, and about the relationships among each pair of those alters, which allows us to measure transitivity. Furthermore, respondents were asked to report their own sociodemographic attributes, which allowed us to measure the similarity between respondents and their network members as well as attribute-related degree heterogeneity.

3.4.2 *Measures*

The interviewers assessed respondents' *sex* as man, woman, or don't know. Respondents were asked to report the sex of each nominated alter. Using this information, we define egos' and alters' sex as binary variables.

Ego's *age* is a continuous variable, calculated as the survey year minus their birth year, while each alter's age was reported by ego in years.

Respondents were also asked about their own *country of birth* and that of their nominated alters. Based on their responses, we defined egos' and alters' countries of origin as binary variables, differentiating between people born in Spain and abroad.

To define egos' and alters' *level of education*, we rely on responses to an open question about egos' highest level of completed education and a closed question on each alter's highest level of completed education. CIS used other response categories for ego than for alter. We unified the responses by transforming them into years of education, which is the typical number of years needed to complete each level of education.

Information on egos' *occupation* is based on an open question about egos' employment status (e.g., working, retired, unemployed, student) and, if they work, their jobs. For alters, respondents were first asked about alters' employment status, and if they worked or had worked before, open questions enquired about alters' jobs. CIS coded the answers to the occupation questions according to the National Classification of Occupations (CNO-11). Combining employment status and occupation, we differentiate between five categories: Unemployed, employed in a high-level job (CNO-11 levels 1–3), employed in a middle- and low-level job (CNO-11 levels 4–9), student, and inactive or other.

Respondents were further asked about their *religion* (Catholic, believer of another religion, non-believer, agnostic, or atheist) and that of their nominated alters (Catholic, believer of another religion, not religious/atheist/agnostic, don't know). Based on this information, we define egos' and alters' religion in three categories: Catholic, other religion, and no religion.

Finally, we define ego's *political orientation* based on respondents' self-placement on an 11-point left–right scale ("When talking about politics, the terms "left" and "right" are commonly used. On this card there is a series of boxes from left to right. In which box would you place yourself?"). They reported their perceptions of alters' political orientation on the same scale.

For *network structure*, respondents were asked to indicate, for each pair of alters, "Do [name person 1] and [name person 2] know each other, or do they not know each other at all, that is, they wouldn't recognise each other if they met on the street?". For those pairs of alters for which respondents reported a tie, they were additionally asked, "And do they have an especially close relationship among them, or is their relationship not especially close?". We coded alter-alter ties 1 if they were especially close and 0 if they did not know each other or did not have a close relationship, to ensure that the relationship between alters was similar in strength as ego-alter ties.

The sample consists of slightly more women than men (51% vs. 49%), reflecting their population prevalences in Spain. Respondents were between the ages of 18 and 97 (average age: 50 years) of whom the large majority was Catholic (77%) and born in Spain (91%). The average number of years of education is just over nine years, and most respondents were employed in high- (22%) or low-level employment (27%) or are inactive (26%).

Table 3.1 gives the descriptive statistics of all ego-alter pairs in the empirical data. The average number of ties respondents reported is 5.4, and most respondents have fewer than ten alters, but a few respondents nominated many more contacts. Follow-up questions were asked on a maximum of 5 alters, which had a mean number of 3.03. The set of egos is on average quite similar to the set of alters in these characteristics (see Table 3.1), except for education, employment, and religion, showing that respondents tended to nominate people who received on average three more years of education than they had received, were more often employed, and were more often Catholic. The higher educational and employment status of alters could possibly be explained by the nature of the relationships under study: People might prefer more resourceful individuals as their confidants. Since these are close ties, we see recall bias as a less likely, but potentially also valid, explanation.

For network modeling presented in the "Results" section, we imputed the missing values once using multivariate imputation by chained equations (van Buuren 2018).

Table 3.1 Summary table of descriptive statistics of the original data, at the tie level

Variables		Attributes of egos	Attributes of alters	*N* ego-alter pairs for which is available	
				Ego attribute	Alter attribute
Sex	*N* (%) man	2460 (48.3%)	7153 (47.0%)	15,657	15,222
	N (%) woman	2629 (51.7%)	8069 (53.0%)		
Age: Mean (*SD*)		48.7 (17.9)	46.3 (15.8)	15,665	15,063
Birth country:	*N* (%) abroad	447 (8.79%)	1113 (7.4%)	15,649	15,126
	N (%) Spain	4640 (91.2%)	14,013 (92.6%)		
Education: Mean (*SD*)		8.59 (4.21)	12.5 (4.7)	3169	14,554
Occupation:	*N* (%) employed high level	991 (19.6%)	4056 (27.1%)	15,539	14,942
	N (%) employed low level	1333 (26.4%)	4398 (29.4%)		
	N (%) student	258 (5.11%)	792 (5.3%)		
	N (%) unemployed	942 (18.6%)	1998 (13.4%)		
	N (%) inactive and other (non-student)	1528 (30.2%)	3698 (24.7%)		
Religion	*N* (%) Catholic	3859 (76.8%)	11,663 (79.4%)	15,439	14,682
	N (%) not religious	969 (19.3%)	2560 (17.4%)		
	N (%) other	197 (3.92%)	459 (3.1%)		
Political orientation: Mean (*SD*)		4.47 (2.09)	4.7 (2.1)	12,058	11,053
Number of ties (no upper limit): Mean (*SD*)		4.04 (4.37)	–	15,637	–

3.4.3 Group Differences and Assortativity

Two important features of real-life social networks are the variation in network structural features such as degree or closure by sociodemographic group (e.g., age, gender, or country of birth), and the tendency to associate with people who are similar to oneself in sociodemographic characteristics (assortativity). This is also the case in these data. People born in Spain, women, and highly educated individuals tend to have larger personal networks than people born abroad, men, and lower-educated individuals. The proportion of individuals with fully transitive networks is highest for inactive individuals and employed individuals with low occupational prestige (see Fig. 3.1), and lowest for individuals with high occupational prestige.

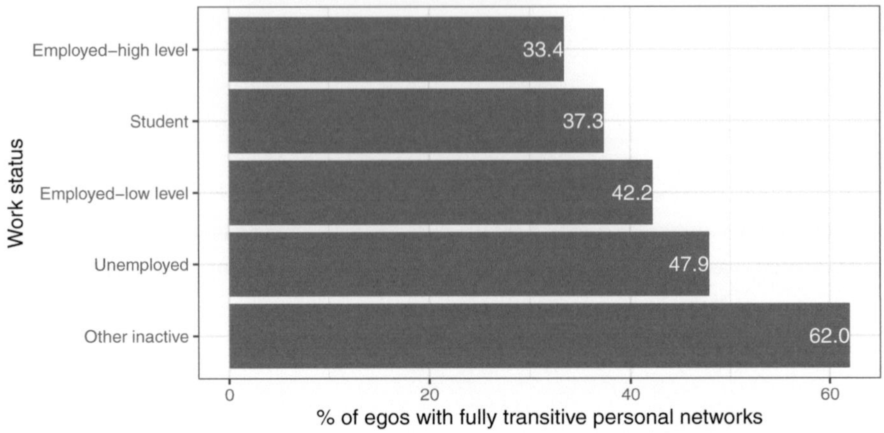

Fig. 3.1 Proportion of nodes with maximally transitive personal networks broken down by ego occupation

Regarding assortativity, individuals from different groups mix fairly well. Still, especially for higher status occupation and higher education of actors, we can see that for most categories of egos the largest fraction of alters belong to the same category, which suggests assortativity (see Fig. 3.2). Only a tiny proportion of high-level employed egos have core discussion alters who are unemployed or inactive. Similarly, the majority of alters of egos with primary education also have primary education. Assortativity is even stronger for egos with higher education who have very few alters with primary education. The ERGM we discuss in the next section will provide a more stringent test for this pattern.

3.5 Results

We first present the ERGM model estimated based on the survey data and its goodness of fit. The model was fit in two versions: on ego-alter data only, and on data including alter-alter ties. The results of the latter model are presented and discussed, unless specified otherwise. The ERGM model was then used to simulate a sociocentric network with the same size as the survey sample ($N = 5094$). The next sections compare the simulated networks with raw empirical data and pure random graphs. Finally, we describe the simulated networks in terms of social cohesion.

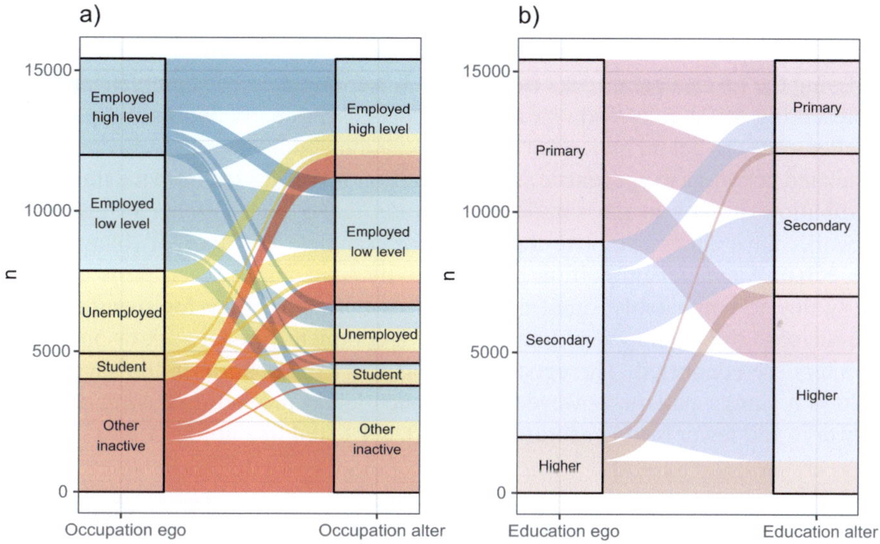

Fig. 3.2 Alluvial diagrams of ego-alter pairs by characteristics of ego (left hand side) and characteristics of alter (right hand side) for **a** work status and **b** educational level

3.5.1 ERGM

The ERGM, fitted to the Spanish data, largely confirms the descriptive patterns (see Figs. 3.1, 3.2 and Table 3.1). Older people tend to have more discussion ties, and confidants tend to be close in age to each other. Highly educated people tend to have more ties than lower-educated individuals, but these confidants do not necessarily come from the same educational backgrounds (positive distance coefficient indicating heterophily). When assortativity tendencies are accounted for, including gender assortativity, women appear to have less discussion ties. People born in Spain discuss important matters with more people, especially with Spaniards, while people born abroad tend to be surrounded by other foreign-born discussion partners. Students do not have significantly more (or fewer) confidants compared to people employed at more prestigious positions. Every other employment category has more confidants compared to people employed at more prestigious positions. At the same time, there is assortativity by occupational status. The number of confidants is not significantly related to ego's political views, however there is assortativity on this dimension. Finally, both Catholics and people of other religions have more discussion ties than nonreligious people, and alters tend to belong to the same religion category as egos.

The model fits the data reasonably well (see Fig. 3.9 in the Appendix). It slightly overestimates the number of isolates and egos who name four and more confidants, and it tends to overestimate smaller values of edgewise shared partners distribution. Substantively, this means that the model underestimates the tendency of egos to discuss important matters with only two or three people, and the tendency of alters to discuss important matters between each other (triadic closure).

Using the ERGM parameters from Fig. 3.3, we simulated 100 complete networks representing the society-wide structure of core-discussion networks in Spain on a smaller scale. To get an indication of the simulation goodness of fit, we compare the simulated networks to egocentric survey data (Fig. 3.10). We see from the transitivity distribution of egos in the simulated networks that a high number of egocentric networks have either complete transitivity or complete lack thereof (blue lines in Fig. 3.10). A smaller proportion has transitivity scores in between. This might be partly due to comparably small network sizes that only allow for specific values and increase the likelihood of having either a complete ego-network or one where no alters are connected. The egocentric transitivity distribution in the survey data follows a similar pattern, however with a much larger proportion having complete networks and fewer having scores between 0 and 1 (red line in Fig. 3.10).

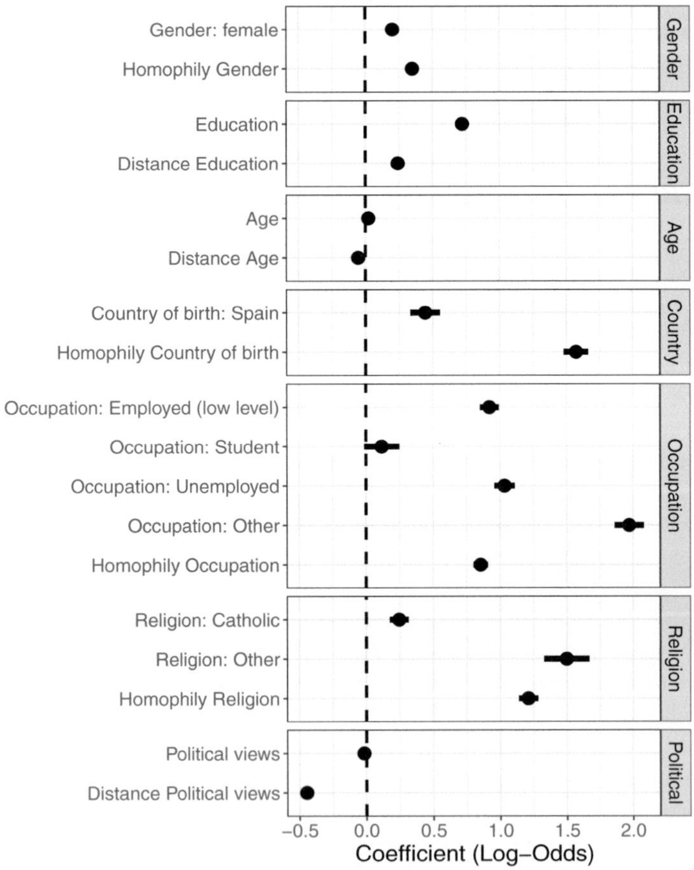

Fig. 3.3 Coefficients of node-related model terms

3.5.2 *Topological Properties*

Next, we compare the 100 simulated networks to 100 random networks with a similar size and density, as a 'neutral' null model, to evaluate structural differences, including group segregation. We see that in the empirically based simulation, more realistic network structures occur. Other than the classic 'hairball' of a random network, we observe more cohesive structures of many smaller clusters that are connected by few ties to form a larger component (Fig. 3.4). Zooming into network neighbourhoods (Fig. 3.5), the different smaller communities and the bridges in between become more apparent.

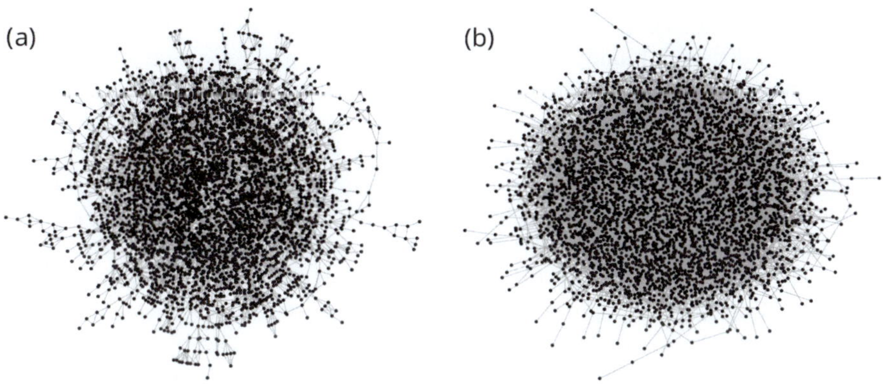

Fig. 3.4 Examples of the giant components of **a** an empirically-calibrated simulated network and **b** an Erdős–Rényi random network of the same size and density. Both figures use the stress majorization layout (Gansner et al. 2005)

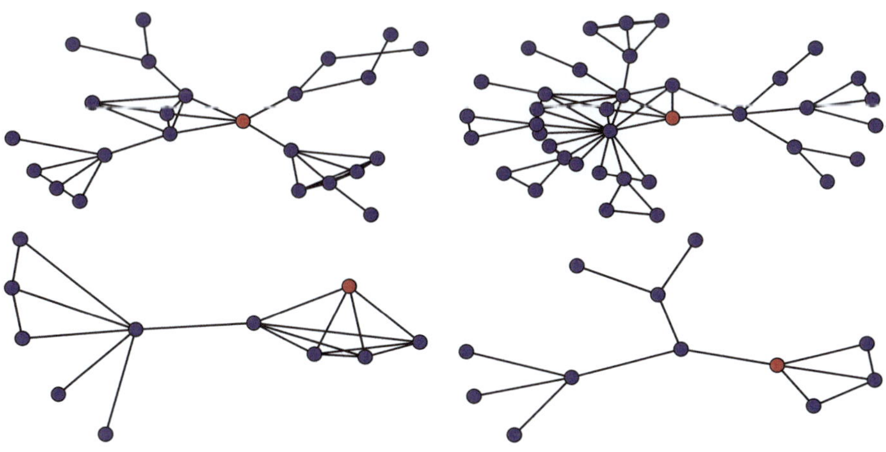

Fig. 3.5 Four examples of three-step neighborhoods in the empirically calibrated network simulation. *Note* In red, the focal node whose ego-network the neighborhood is formed around

We then compare the 'small-world' properties, i.e. the average clustering and shortest paths, to Erdős–Rényi models of similar size and density, as well as empirical large-scale networks. When alter-alter ties are not included in the model and only nodal and dyadic effects are used to calibrate the network simulation, the created networks show higher average transitivity and shorter average paths than random networks of similar size and density. In this scenario, the social network of the Spanish General Social Survey, representing the Spanish population, resembles a small-world more than expected by chance. However, when alter-alter ties are added and triadic closure effects are a part of the model, the shortest paths become much longer on average. This may be due to the lower number of isolates.

We next compare this result to complete society-level networks, namely the Dutch (Bokányi et al. 2023) and Danish register-based multilayer population network (Cremers et al. 2024). We see that the observed shortest path lengths correspond closely to the distances found among extended family members (around 10 on average in the Netherlands and 12 in Denmark). Empirical networks of neighbors, classmates, and colleagues have substantially shorter distances (around 5–6 on average in both countries). Similar short distances occur in online friendship networks, where the effective diameter (the smallest number of steps in the network at which at least 90% of all connected pairs of nodes can be reached) is around 7 (e.g., Corten 2012).

Therefore, the society-wide core-discussion network of people in Spain has higher transitivity but also longer shortest paths than random networks (in contrast to what Watts and Strogatz 1998, suggested), thus cannot be considered to have the small-world property. Comparison with register-based networks of family ties shows that our network shows analogous properties, therefore can be considered to capture relatively strong ties. This also serves as further evidence that networks of strong ties in general show less small-world properties.

Departing from the macro-comparison of ERGM-based simulated networks and random networks, we analyse potential differences in the position and embeddedness of different groups. After randomly adding node attributes with the same baseline distribution as the empirical data to the random networks, we can compare segregation patterns in empirically informed and artificial data. For gender (panel (a) in Fig. 3.6), we find higher segregation in the empirically informed network than in a random network, while for education, we find lower levels of segregation than in random networks (panel (b) in Fig. 3.6).

3.5.3 Social Cohesion by Centrality and Isolation

Finally, we interpret the simulated networks in terms of social cohesion. We compare the location of selected social groups in two ways. In the first approach, we compare the harmonic centrality and betweenness centrality scores in each group. Average closeness and betweenness centrality scores might indicate whether actors in some groups occupy more prominent positions in society. Moreover, the two indicators serve as an example of positional characteristics that are computed using a whole

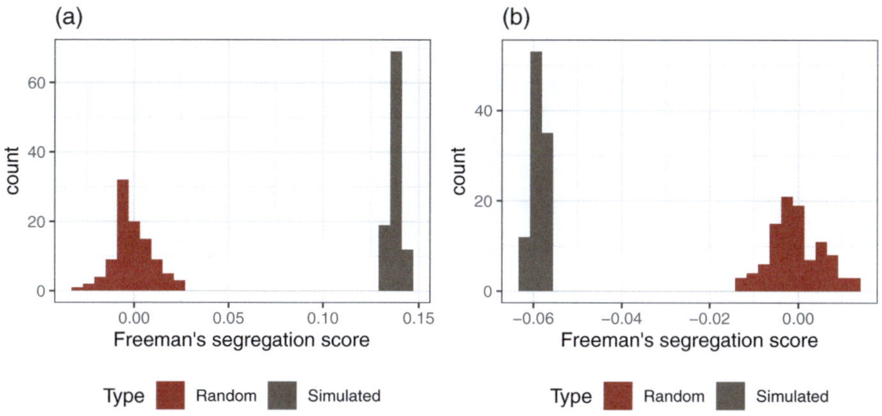

Fig. 3.6 Freeman's segregation scores for **a** gender and **b** educational levels in random networks (red) compared to empirically calibrated network simulations (gray)

network rather than personal networks only, which is impossible with the raw egocentric data we work with. In the second approach, we compare the fractions of a given social group outside of the largest connected component. We interpret this as an indicator of the extent to which members of different groups are "excluded" from the society, which points at a relative lack of social cohesion.

The differences in harmonic centrality[4] and betweenness centrality between native-born and foreign-born individuals are minimal (see Fig. 3.7). In both cases distributions have largely similar shapes suggesting that the positions of people from these two groups are by and large similar in terms of their centralities. Still, network-wide median values are slightly higher for people born in Spain. The variation in medians between the 100 simulated network is smaller than the difference between the two groups implying that the difference might not be substantively convincing, but is nevertheless statistically significant.

There are different relational structures on the periphery of the graph, outside of the largest connected component. The majority of nodes there still reside in components of sizes up to 15 (Fig. 3.13), which in some cases reflects a well-connected group of people. Nevertheless, isolates are the most frequent component pattern while dyads are also present, which means that there are people who have only one confidant, if any.

In the following, we test if any of the social categories are overrepresented in the smaller components on the periphery of the network. Figure 3.8 shows what share of the corresponding category ends up outside the largest connected component (LCC), and how these values are distributed across 100 simulated networks. If members of all categories were equally likely to appear on the network peripheries, there would

[4] We opted for using harmonic centrality (sum of inverse distances) rather than classical closeness centrality (inverse of the sum of distances) because the former is better at handling isolates while describing the same phenomenon—reachability of other nodes from the focal node.

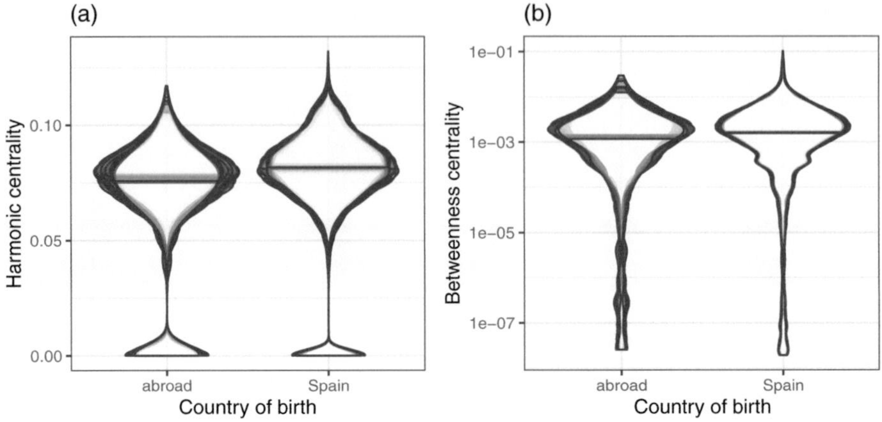

Fig. 3.7 Violin plots of **a** harmonic centrality and **b** betweenness centrality people born in Spain and abroad. Overplotted violins and horizontal lines show distributions and their medians from simulations from the fitted model

be no difference in the distribution shapes. In Fig. 3.8 we see that this is not the case. Simulations suggest that approximately 8% of people born in Spain occupy network positions outside of the largest connected component while for people born abroad this percentage is roughly twice as large. We also see that the unemployed and other people inactive on the labour market are more often in the network peripheries than the employed and the students.

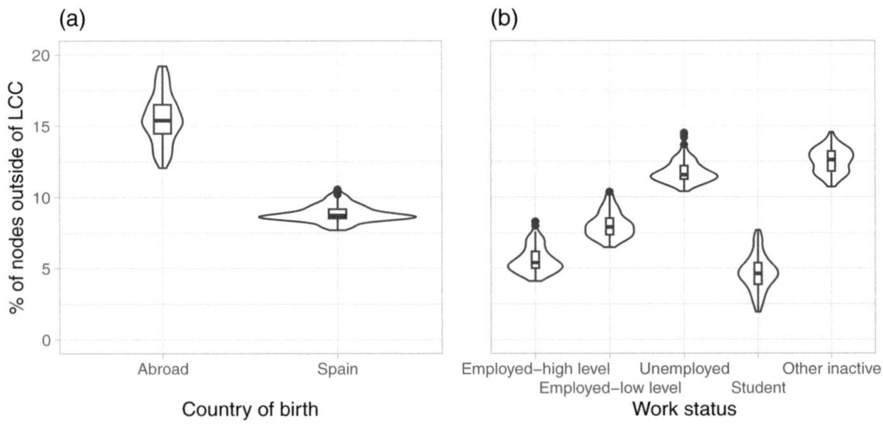

Fig. 3.8 Percentage of nodes outside of the largest connected component by **a** country of birth and by **b** work status, across 100 simulations. The Y axis is common for both panels

3.6 Discussion

The simulations presented in this study mark a significant step toward more realistic approximations of society-wide core discussion networks, especially in the context of further analysis such as with agent-based models. We contribute to the body of existing applications of Exponential Random Graph Models (ERGMs) to model egocentrically-sampled network data, by simulating society-wide networks using information on nodal, dyadic and triadic network features. We construct and analyze the properties of large-scale core discussion networks of people in Spain based on a unique ego-network dataset. We also release our empirically-calibrated simulated networks, which can hopefully serve as a baseline with included variation for agent-based models that concern core discussion networks and related phenomena.[5]

The simulated society-wide core discussion networks have notable topological properties. Comparison to random networks showed that our networks have higher transitivity but also substantially longer average shortest paths, which means that they do not exhibit small-world properties (where distances between nodes are shorter). Comparison with society-wide register-based networks showed that topologically, our networks look most similar to networks of family ties, where distances are as long. Therefore, even though previous research has shown that approximately half of the people with whom people discuss important matters are not their closest relationships (Small 2013), we find that large-scale networks of discussion ties are more similar to networks of strong family ties than of colleagues or online friends. An alternative explanation for the longer distances in our networks could be that we did not capture important discussion relationships with the collected data, or the method did not allow us to generate important macro-level structures. Should this be the case, it could be related to the fact that our simulations remain constrained by their focus on local effects. When modeling networks spanning larger populations it seems worthwhile to also empirically measure more complex network structures beyond triadic level. We believe that it remains an important challenge for future research. Importantly, longer distances appeared in the simulations made with the model version that included information about alter-alter ties and thus transitive closure. Without this data, distances in simulated networks were shorter. This has crucial implications for data collection strategies with the aim of generating large-scale networks from ego-network data. When simply using single-item questions on ego-centric network sizes, the resulting networks might misrepresent key aspects of cohesion. Should such networks be further used in models of diffusion (Valente and Vega Yon 2020) or complex contagion (Centola and Macy 2007), overestimated degree of small-worldness might bias model results. Researchers must carefully consider how to balance data collection efforts and model accuracy.

Through the ERGMs' assortativity estimates, we obtained a measure of net network segregation. This measure partially accounts for endogenous network mechanisms (Goodreau et al. 2009) and by-product effects (Smith et al. 2014). However, it

[5] The simulated network datasets are available at https://osf.io/v52wt/.

is crucial to recognise that these estimates may still be influenced by various mechanisms, including individuals' preferences for similarity (McPherson et al. 2001), the higher likelihood of interaction among similar others due to proximity (Kruse et al. 2016), or other network amplification effects not captured by the model (Wimmer and Lewis 2010). The inclusion of kinship relations and geographic information would be particularly valuable in future analysis and simulations.

The analysis of the distribution of complete networks simulated from the model with tools capturing aspects of social cohesion demonstrates two elements. Firstly, how the information in the egocentrically collected data can be used to make inferences about macro network features—such as betweenness and closeness scores or component sizes. Secondly, how one can make inferences about relative positions of different groups, such as natives and migrants, in a society-wide network using such seemingly limited data. Our analysis suggests that people residing in Spain but born abroad occupy positions of lower centrality and are relatively more often in the peripheries of the society-wide network compared to people who were born in Spain.

One of the primary features and limitations of the presented method is that attempts at utilizing the network information available in an egocentric sample of personal networks. It is a lot of information: about attribute mixing and assortativity and about degree distribution and certain types of social closure. This however is by no means exhaustive. Egocentric data, and thus the models for such data, are not able to represent any higher-order network features such as community structure unrelated to observed attributes or over- or under-prevalence of higher-order cycles. It is also important to measure, both ego- and alter-levels, as many nodal attributes relevant for tie formation as possible to avoid omitted variable problems.

Presented methods rely on, among other things, assumptions regarding the collected personal networks. In particular, that (1) ego-alter and alter-alter ties pretend to be the same type of social relationship, (2) all the ties are undirected and reported as such by both actors, and finally (3) that these reports are all 100% reliable. In other words, all the reports on ego-alter and alter-alter ties are taken at face value. One can argue that this is not realistic especially with respect to the alter-alter ties—for example ego's reports on ties of a socially distant alter might be less reliable than her reports on ties of a socially close alter. We believe that this asks for future research on improving the methods of data collection and incorporating reliability assessment into statistical models based on personal network data.

Another avenue of future research on the presented methods should look into applying it to other relationships than core discussion ties, like most intimate ties, acquaintanceships, or friendships. Previous research has shown that approximately half of the people with whom people discuss important matters are not their closest relationships (Small 2013), and that such relationships can change rapidly (Small et al. 2015). A comparative analysis with the simulated core discussion network could extend knowledge of society-wide relationship patterns, including social cohesion.

Acknowledgements We thank Aswathi Padmavilochanan for her contributions to the project during the BIGSSS summer school. Michał Bojanowski and Miranda Lubbers are grateful for the funding of the European Research Council (ERC) under the European Union's Horizon 2020 research and innovation programme (Grant Agreement No. 101020038; "A network science approach to social cohesion in European societies"; PATCHWORK). Furthermore, Miranda Lubbers is grateful for the support of the ICREA Acadèmia program (2021-2025). Paul Schuler is grateful for the funding through the Scottish Graduate School of Social and Political Science International Award scholarship (ESRC Grant Ref: ES/P000681/1). Susanne Böller is grateful for funding of the Deutsche Forschungsgemeinschaft (DFG, German Research Foundation, 458745130). Alla Loseva is grateful for funding of the Dutch Research Council (NWO, 406.18.SW.038).

Appendix

See Figs. 3.9, 3.10, 3.11, 3.12, 3.13 and Table 3.2.

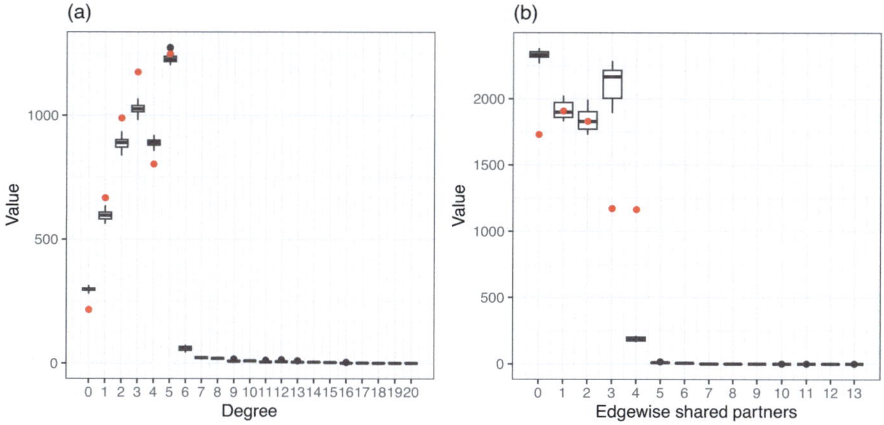

Fig. 3.9 ERGM fit for **a** degrees and **b** edgewise shared partners. Red dots indicate empirical values, boxplots show distributions over 100 simulated networks

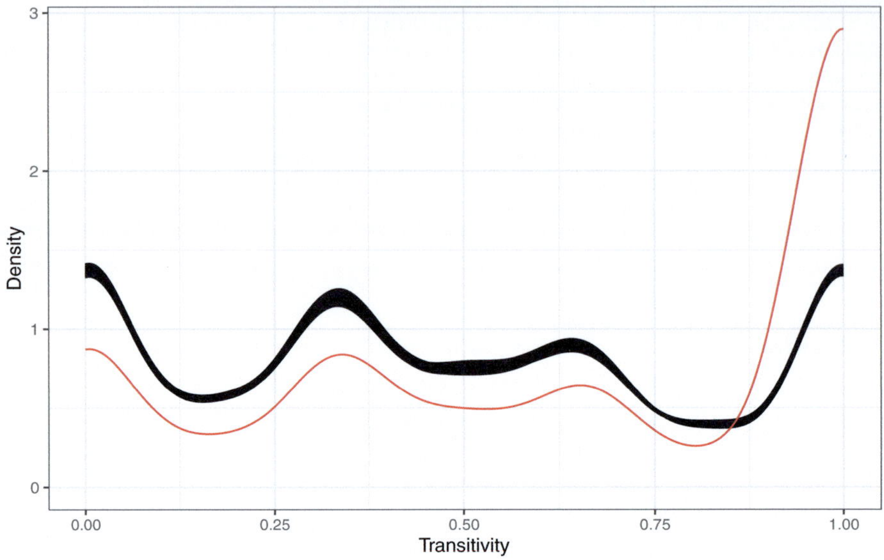

Fig. 3.10 Density plot of ego transitivity scores across 100 empirically-calibrated networks (blue lines) and the transitivity scores of the egocentric transitivity scores in the original survey data

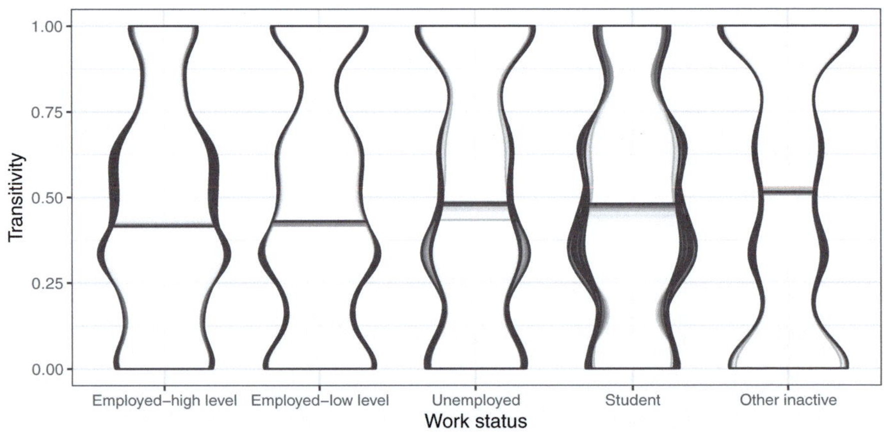

Fig. 3.11 Violin plots for transitivity by ego's employment

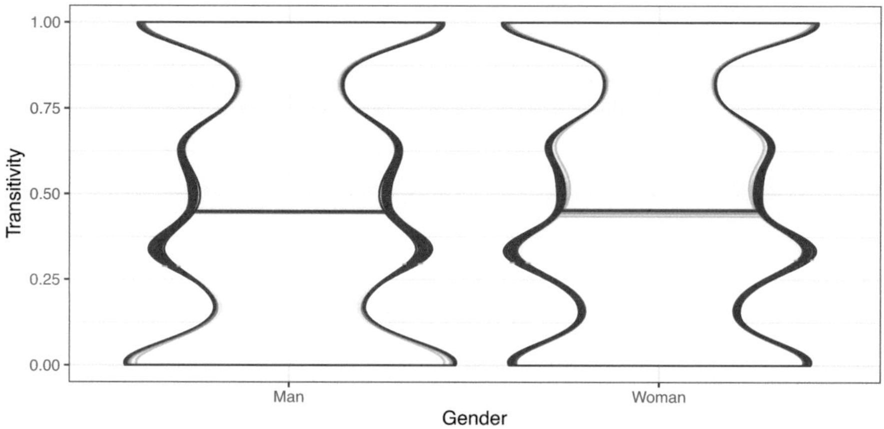

Fig. 3.12 Violin plots for transitivity by ego's gender

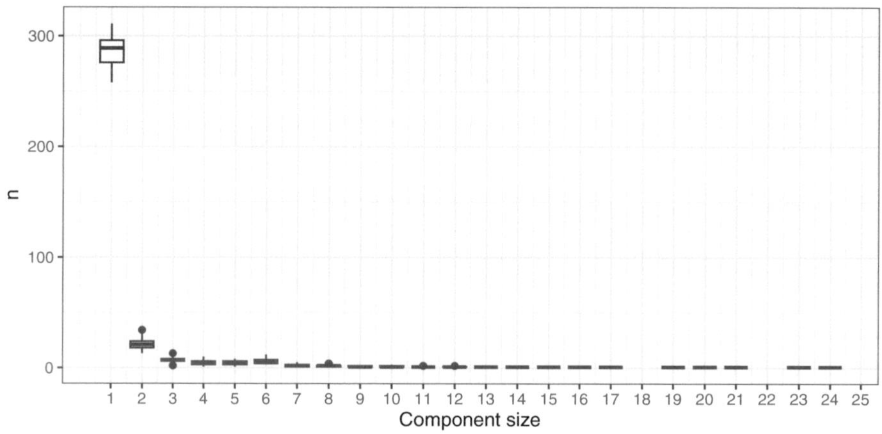

Fig. 3.13 Distribution of frequencies of smaller component sizes across 100 simulated networks

Table 3.2 ERGM results

Term	Model 1. Base			Model 2. Base + assortativity		
	β	SE	*t*	β	SE	*t*
Offset	− 8.54***	0.00	-Inf	− 8.54***	0.00	-Inf
Edges	− 81.94***	8.91	− 9.20	− 31.03***	1.53	− 20.32
Isolates	− 100.04***	10.68	− 9.37	− 40.09***	1.69	− 23.67
Degree: 1	− 72.40***	7.78	− 9.31	− 29.82***	1.26	− 23.60
Degree: 2	− 48.03***	5.11	− 9.40	− 20.28***	0.86	− 23.60
Degree: 3	− 27.39***	2.96	− 9.26	− 12.14***	0.51	− 23.66
Degree: 4	− 12.91***	1.34	− 9.66	− 6.03***	0.24	− 25.44
Edgewise shared partners: 0	− 4.76***	0.50	− 9.43	− 3.26***	0.11	− 29.17
Edgewise shared partners: 1	− 4.78***	0.38	− 12.64	− 3.64***	0.09	− 42.05
Edgewise shared partners: 2	− 2.69***	0.22	− 12.18	− 1.79***	0.05	− 35.83
Node characteristics						
Age in years	0.05***	0.01	8.70	0.02***	0.00	10.68
Education in years	1.90***	0.20	9.49	0.72***	0.03	20.66
Gender—woman (ref.: Man)	− 0.13	0.09	− 1.42	0.20***	0.04	4.64
Country of birth—Spain (ref.: Abroad)	3.13***	0.36	8.61	0.44***	0.11	4.02
Occupation—low level (ref.: High level)	2.49***	0.28	8.98	0.92***	0.07	13.32
Occupation—student	− 0.91**	0.29	− 3.08	0.12	0.13	0.90
Occupation—unemployed	3.06***	0.34	8.91	1.03***	0.08	13.69
Occupation—inactive	5.23***	0.57	9.18	1.97***	0.11	17.73
Political views (0–10)	− 0.01	0.03	− 0.39	− 0.02	0.01	− 1.60
Religion—Catholic (ref.: None)	1.93***	0.25	7.83	0.25***	0.07	3.51
Religion—other	3.67***	0.52	7.04	1.50***	0.17	8.81
Assortativity						
Distance: age in years				− 0.05***	0.00	− 24.52
Distance: education in years				0.24***	0.01	18.79
Assortativity: gender				0.35***	0.04	9.32
Assortativity: country of birth				1.57***	0.09	16.97
Assortativity: occupation				0.86***	0.05	15.56

(continued)

Table 3.2 (continued)

Term	Model 1. Base			Model 2. Base + assortativity		
	β	SE	*t*	β	SE	*t*
Distance: political views				– 0.45***	0.02	– 21.52
Assortativity: religion				1.21***	0.07	16.80

Note $N = 5094$. Asterisks denote statistical significance: $p < 0.05$ (*); $p < 0.01$ (**); $p < 0.001$ (***)

References

R. Albert, A.-L. Barabási, Statistical mechanics of complex networks. Rev. Mod. Phys. **74**(1), 47–97 (2002). https://doi.org/10.1103/RevModPhys.74.47

F. Amblard, A. Bouadjio-Boulic, C. Sureda Gutiérrez, B. Gaudou, Which models are used in social simulation to generate social networks? A review of 17 years of publications in JASSS. Winter Simulat. Conf. (WSC) **2015**, 4021–4032 (2015). https://doi.org/10.1109/WSC.2015.7408556

F. Amblard, G. Deffuant, The role of network topology on extremism propagation with the relative agreement opinion dynamics. Physica A **343**, 725–738 (2004). https://doi.org/10.1016/j.physa.2004.06.102

R. Axtell, Effects of interaction topology and activation regime in several multi-agent systems, in *Multi-Agent-Based Simulation*, ed. S. Moss, P. Davidsson (Springer, 2001), pp. 33–48. https://doi.org/10.1007/3-540-44561-7_3

A.-L. Barabási, R. Albert, Emergence of scaling in random networks. Science **286**(5439), 509–512 (1999). https://doi.org/10.1126/science.286.5439.509

C.L. Barrett, R.J. Beckman, M. Khan, V.S.A. Kumar, M.V. Marathe, P.E. Stretz, T. Dutta, B. Lewis, Generation and analysis of large synthetic social contact networks, in *Proceedings of the 2009 Winter Simulation Conference (WSC)*(2009), pp. 1003–1014. https://doi.org/10.1109/WSC.2009.5429425

P.S. Bearman, J. Moody, K. Stovel, Chains of affection: the structure of adolescent romantic and sexual networks. Am. J. Sociol. **110**(1), 44–91 (2004). https://doi.org/10.1086/386272

P.M. Blau, Presidential address: parameters of social structure. Am. Sociol. Rev. **39**(5), 615–635 (1974). https://doi.org/10.2307/2094309

R. Boero, F. Squazzoni, Does empirical embeddedness matter? Methodological issues on agent-based models for analytical social science. J. Artif. Soc. Soc. Simulat. **8**(4), 6 (2005). https://jasss.soc.surrey.ac.uk/8/4/6.html

E. Bokányi, E.M. Heemskerk, F.W. Takes, The anatomy of a population-scale social network. Sci. Rep. **13**(1), 9209 (2023). https://doi.org/10.1038/s41598-023-36324-9

E. Bruch, J. Atwell, Agent-based models in empirical social research. Sociol. Methods Res. **44**(2), 186–221 (2015). https://doi.org/10.1177/0049124113506405

A. Burger, T. Oz, A. Crooks, W.G. Kennedy, Generation of realistic mega-city populations and social networks for agent-based modelling, in *Proceedings of the 2017 International Conference of The Computational Social Science Society of the Americas* (2017), pp. 1–7. https://doi.org/10.1145/3145574.3145593

D. Centola, M. Macy, Complex contagions and the weakness of long ties. Am. J. Sociol. **113**(3), 702–734 (2007). https://doi.org/10.1086/521848

E. Chattoe-Brown, S. Gabbriellini, *How to Improve Network Science: The Potential of (Empirically Calibrated and Validated) Agent-Based Modelling* (OSF, 2021). https://doi.org/10.31235/osf.io/bym74

R. Chetty, M.O. Jackson, T. Kuchler, J. Stroebel, N. Hendren, R.B. Fluegge, S. Gong, F. Gonzalez, A. Grondin, M. Jacob, D. Johnston, M. Koenen, E. Laguna-Muggenburg, F. Mudekereza, T. Rutter, N. Thor, W. Townsend, R. Zhang, M. Bailey, N. Wernerfelt et al., Social capital I: measurement and associations with economic mobility. Nature **608**(7921), 108–121 (2022). https://doi.org/10.1038/s41586-022-04996-4

CIS—Centro de Investigaciones Sociológicas, *Estudio 2975, Encuesta Social General Española, Abril –julio 2013: Informe metodológico* (2013)

J.-P. Cointet, C. Roth, How realistic should knowledge diffusion models be? J. Artif. Soc. Soc. Simulat. **10**(3), 5 (2007). https://www.jasss.org/10/3/5.html

R. Corten, Composition and structure of a large online social network in the Netherlands. PLoS ONE **7**(4), e34760 (2012). https://doi.org/10.1371/journal.pone.0034760

J. Cremers, B. Kohler, B.F. Maier, S.N. Eriksen, J. Einsiedler, F.K. Christensen, S. Lehmann, D.D. Lassen, L.H. Mortensen, A. Bjerre-Nielsen, *Unveiling the Social Fabric: A Temporal, Nation-Scale Social Network and its Characteristics* (2024) (No. arXiv:2409.11099). arXiv. https://doi.org/10.48550/arXiv.2409.11099

G. Csardi, T. Nepusz, The Igraph software package for complex network research. Int. J. Complex Syst. **1695**, 1–9 (2005). https://igraph.org

G. Deffuant, Comparing extremism propagation patterns in continuous opinion models. J. Artif. Soc. Soc. Simulat. **9**(3), 8 (2006). https://www.jasss.org/9/3/8.html

E. Durkheim, *The Division of Labor in Society* (MacMillan, New York, 1893)

S. Eubank, H. Guclu, V.S. Anil Kumar, M.V. Marathe, A. Srinivasan, Z. Toroczkai, N. Wang, Modelling disease outbreaks in realistic urban social networks. Nature **429**(6988), 180–184 (2004). https://doi.org/10.1038/nature02541

O. Frank, D. Strauss, Markov graphs. J. Am. Stat. Assoc. **81**(395), 832–842 (1986). https://doi.org/10.1080/01621459.1986.10478342

E.R. Gansner, Y. Koren, S. North, Graph drawing by stress majorization, in *Graph Drawing*, ed. by J. Pach. Springer (2005), pp. 239–250. https://doi.org/10.1007/978-3-540-31843-9_25

S.M. Goodreau, J.A. Kitts, M. Morris, Birds of a feather, or friend of a friend? Using exponential random graph models to investigate adolescent social networks. Demography **46**(1), 103–125 (2009)

D. Guilbeault, J. Becker, D. Centola, Complex contagions: a decade in review, in *Complex Spreading Phenomena in Social Systems: Influence and Contagion in Real-World Social Networks*, ed. by S. Lehmann and Y.-Y. Ahn (Springer International Publishing, 2018), pp. 3–25. https://doi.org/10.1007/978-3-319-77332-2_1

L. Hamill, N. Gilbert, Social circles: a simple structure for agent-based social network models. J. Artif. Soc. Soc. Simul. **12**(2), 3 (2009). https://www.jasss.org/12/2/3.html

M.S. Handcock, D.R. Hunter, C.T. Butts, S.M. Goodreau, P.N. Krivitsky, M. Morris, L. Wang, K. Li, S. Bender-deMoll, C. Klumb, M. Bojanowski, B. Bolker, C. Schmid, J. Cheng, A. Karami, *ergm: Fit, Simulate and Diagnose Exponential-Family Models for Networks* (Version 4.6.0) (Computer Software, 2023). https://cran.r-project.org/web/packages/ergm/index.html

P. Hedström, G. Manzo, Recent trends in agent-based computational research: a brief introduction. Sociol. Methods Res. **44**(2), 179–185 (2015). https://doi.org/10.1177/0049124115581211

K. Heß, J. Himmelspach, O. Reinhardt, A.M. Uhrmacher, A generalized network generation approach for agent-based models. Winter Simulat. Conf. (WSC) **2021**, 1–12 (2021). https://doi.org/10.1109/WSC52266.2021.9715377

D.R. Hunter, S.M. Goodreau, M.S. Handcock, Goodness of fit for social network models. J. Am. Stat. Assoc. **103**(481), 248–258 (2008). https://doi.org/10.1198/016214507000000446

N. Jiang, A.T. Crooks, H. Kavak, A. Burger, W.G. Kennedy, A method to create a synthetic population with social networks for geographically-explicit agent-based models. Comput. Urb. Sci. **2**(1), 7 (2022). https://doi.org/10.1007/s43762-022-00034-1

Y. Kazmina, E.M. Heemskerk, E. Bokányi, F.W. Takes, Socio-economic segregation in a population-scale social network. Soc. Netw. **78**, 279–291 (2024). https://doi.org/10.1016/j.socnet.2024.02.005

C.A. Klofstad, S.D. McClurg, M. Rolfe, Measurement of political discussion networks: a comparison of two "name generator" procedures. Public Opin. q. **73**(3), 462–483 (2009). https://doi.org/10.1093/poq/nfp032

P.N. Krivitsky, *ergm.ego: Fit, Simulate and Diagnose Exponential-Family Random Graph Models to Egocentrically Sampled Network Data* (The Statnet Project, 2025). https://statnet.org. R package version 1.1.2, https://CRAN.R-project.org/package=ergm.ego

P.N. Krivitsky, M. Bojanowski, M. Morris, *Inference for Exponential-Family Random Graph Models from Egocentrically-Sampled Data with Alter–Alter Relations* (Working Paper Nos. 08–19) (National Institute for Applied Statistics Research Australia, University of Wollongong, 2019). https://niasra.uow.edu.au/workingpapers/UOW255140.html

P.N. Krivitsky, M.S. Handcock, M. Morris, Adjusting for network size and composition effects in exponential-family random graph models. Statist. Methodol. **8**(4), 319–339 (2011). https://doi.org/10.1016/j.stamet.2011.01.005

P.N. Krivitsky, M. Morris, Inference for social network models from egocentrically-sampled data, with application to understanding persistent racial disparities in HIV prevalence in the US. Ann. Appl. Stat. **11**(1), 427–455 (2017). https://doi.org/10.1214/16-AOAS1010

P.N. Krivitsky, M. Morris, M. Bojanowski, Impact of survey design on estimation of exponential-family random graph models from egocentrically-sampled data. Soc. Netw. **69** (2022). https://doi.org/10.1016/j.socnet.2020.10.001

H. Kruse, S. Smith, F. Van Tubergen, I. Maas, From neighbors to school friends? How adolescents' place of residence relates to same-ethnic school friendships. Soc. Netw. **44**, 130–142 (2016). https://doi.org/10.1016/j.socnet.2015.07.004

S.-H. Lim, S. Lee, S.S. Powers, M. Shankar, N. Imam, *Survey of Approaches to Generate Realistic Synthetic Graphs* (No. ORNL/TM-2016/3) (Oak Ridge National Lab. (ORNL), Oak Ridge, TN, USA, 2016). https://doi.org/10.2172/1339361

J. Lorenz, Data-driven agent-based modeling in computational social science, in *Handbook of Computational Social Science* (Routledge, 2021), vol. 1, pp. 150–167

D. Lusher, J. Koskinen, G. Robins, *Exponential Random Graph Models for Social Networks: Theory, Methods, and Applications* (Cambridge University Press, 2013)

P.V. Marsden, Core discussion networks of Americans. Am. Sociol. Rev. **52**(1), 122–131 (1987). https://doi.org/10.2307/2095397

I. McCulloh, J. Lospinoso, K.M. Carley, in *The Link Probability Model: A Network Simulation Alternative to the Exponential Random Graph Model* (SSRN Scholarly Paper 2729285) (2010). https://doi.org/10.2139/ssrn.2729285

M. McPherson, L. Smith-Lovin, J.M. Cook, Birds of a feather: homophily in social networks. Ann. Rev. Sociol. **27**, 415–444 (2001). https://doi.org/10.1146/annurev.soc.27.1.415

T. Menezes, C. Roth, Symbolic regression of generative network models. Sci. Rep. **4**(1), 6284 (2014). https://doi.org/10.1038/srep06284

T. Menezes, C. Roth, Automatic discovery of families of network generative processes, in F. Ghanbarnejad, R. Saha Roy, F. Karimi, J.-C. Delvenne, B. Mitra (eds.), *Dynamics On and Of Complex Networks III* (Springer International Publishing, 2019), pp. 83–111. https://doi.org/10.1007/978-3-030-14683-2_4

M. Menyhért, E. Bokányi, R. Corten, E.M. Heemskerk, Y. Kazmina, F.W. Takes, *Connectivity and Community Structure of Online and Register-based Social Networks*(2024). arXiv. https://doi.org/10.48550/arXiv.2406.17752

M. Rolfe, Social networks and agent-based modelling, in *Analytical Sociology*, ed. G. Manzo (Wiley, 2014), pp. 233–260. https://doi.org/10.1002/9781118762707.ch09

D. Schiefer, J. van der Noll, The essentials of social cohesion: a lliterature review. Soc. Indic. Res. **132**(2), 579–603 (2017). https://doi.org/10.1007/s11205-016-1314-5

J.A. Smith, Macrostructure from microstructure: generating whole systems from ego networks. Sociol. Methodol. **42**(1), 155–205 (2012). https://doi.org/10.1177/0081175012455628

M.L. Small, Weak ties and the core discussion network: why people regularly discuss important matters with unimportant alters. Soc. Netw. **35**(3), 470–483 (2013). https://doi.org/10.1016/j.socnet.2013.05.004

J.A. Smith, Global network inference from ego network samples: testing a simulation approach. J. Math. Sociol. **39**(2), 125–162 (2015). https://doi.org/10.1080/0022250X.2014.994621

J.A. Smith, J. Burow, Using ego network data to inform agent-based models of diffusion. Sociol. Methods Res. **49**(4), 1018–1063 (2020). https://doi.org/10.1177/0049124118769100
J.A. Smith, G.R. Gauthier, Estimating contextual effects from ego network data. Sociol. Methodol. **50**(1), 215–275 (2020). https://doi.org/10.1177/0081175020922879
M.L. Small, V. Deeds Pamphile, P. McMahan, How stable is the core discussion network? Soc. Netw. **40**, 90–102 (2015). https://doi.org/10.1016/j.socnet.2014.09.001
J.A. Smith, M. McPherson, L. Smith-Lovin, Social distance in the united states: sex, race, religion, age, and education homophily among confidants, 1985 to 2004. Am. Sociol. Rev. **79**(3), 432–456 (2014). https://doi.org/10.1177/0003122414531776
T.A.B. Snijders, P.E. Pattison, G.L. Robins, M.S. Handcock, New specifications for exponential random graph models. Sociol. Methodol. **36**(1), 99–153 (2006). https://doi.org/10.1111/j.1467-9531.2006.00176.x
T.A.B. Snijders, G.G. van de Bunt, C.E.G. Steglich, Introduction to stochastic actor-based models for network dynamics. Soc. Netw. **32**(1), 44–60 (2010). https://doi.org/10.1016/j.socnet.2009.02.004
S. Thiriot, *Small World is not enough: Criteria for Network Choice and Conclusiveness of Simulations*(2020). https://doi.org/10.48550/arXiv.2002.03717
S. Thiriot, J.-D. Kant, *Generate Country-Scale Networks of Interaction from Scattered Statistics* (2008) https://doi.org/10.48550/arXiv.2004.01031
T.W. Valente, G.G. Vega Yon, Diffusion/contagion processes on social networks. Health Educ. Behav. **47**(2), 235–248 (2020). https://doi.org/10.1177/1090198120901497
S. van Buuren, *Flexible Imputation of Missing Data*, 2nd ed. (Chapman and Hall/CRC, 2018)
F. van Tubergen, Ethnic boundaries in core discussion networks: a multilevel social network study of Turks and Moroccans in the Netherlands. J. Ethn. Migr. Stud. **41**(1), 101–116 (2015). https://doi.org/10.1080/1369183X.2014.886955
S. Wasserman, P. Pattison, Logit models and logistic regressions for social networks: I. An introduction to Markov graphs and p^*. Psychometrika **61**(3), 401–425 (1996). https://doi.org/10.1007/BF02294547
D.J. Watts, S.H. Strogatz, Collective dynamics of 'small-world' networks. Nature **393**(6684), 440 (1998)
A. Wimmer, K. Lewis, Beyond and below racial homophily: documented on facebook. Am. J. Sociol. **116**(2), 583–642 (2010). https://doi.org/10.1086/653658
M. Zachara, C. Piskor-Ignatowicz, Agent-based creation and simulation of artificial social networks and the analysis of their properties. Comput. Sci. Eng. **18**(4), 34–41 (2016). https://doi.org/10.1109/MCSE.2016.46

Chapter 4
The Anatomy of Rabbit Holes: Studying Information Segregation in YouTube's Recommendation Graph

Marijn A. Keijzer, Lukas Erhard, Zarine Kharazian, and Manika Lamba

Abstract The impact of YouTube's recommendation algorithm has been subject to much debate. Case studies and anecdotal evidence have suggested that algorithmic recommendations may lure the platform's users into informational 'rabbit holes' where they are exposed to biased content and misinformation. However, empirical research on the phenomenon has been challenging to conduct because the effects of the algorithm are inherently confounded by user and creator behavior. In this chapter, we study the net effect of algorithmic recommendations through a comparative network approach. That is, we collect the recommendation links between videos for various political and non-political issues. The resulting networks are then compared on various structural network characteristics. If the algorithm creates rabbit holes, one would expect the recommendation networks of videos on conspiratorial content to be more modular, less centralized and intra-topically dense. We analyzed 15,455 videos and 154,311 recommendation links on 40 different topics, each belonging to one of four main categories: news, science, conspiracy, and non-controversial. On the macro level, we find that conspiratorial video networks are small, sparse and centralized, with their density partly explained by lower view counts and network size. The sentiment of their videos is negative on average–like news networks, but unlike science and non-controversial networks. However, sentiment does not but view count does predict how often videos are recommended.

Supplementary Information The online version contains supplementary material available at https://doi.org/10.1007/978-3-032-01373-6_4.

M. A. Keijzer (✉)
Institute for Advanced Study in Toulouse, Toulouse School of Economics, University of Toulouse Capitole, Toulouse, France
e-mail: marijn.keijzer@iast.fr

L. Erhard
Department for Computational Social Science, University of Stuttgart, Stuttgart, Germany

Z. Kharazian
Department of Human-Centered Design and Engineering, University of Washington, Washington, USA

M. Lamba
School of Library and Information Studies, University of Oklahoma, Norman, USA

M. A. Keijzer et al. (eds.), *Computational Social Science of Social Cohesion and Polarization*, Computational Social Sciences,
https://doi.org/10.1007/978-3-032-01373-6_4

Keywords YouTube · Social network analysis · Echo chambers · Information segregation · Rabbit holes

4.1 Introduction

With over a third of US adults receiving news regularly from YouTube (Pew Research Center 2024), worry over the role of this and other social media platforms in hardening opinion polarization in western democracies has grown. Information consumption has become scattered, individual and of questionable quality, and hence may have contributed to disruptive events of political conflict such as the Yellow Vest movement, Brexit, rising populism, and the Capitol riots. In particular, scholars and experts argue that recommender algorithms installed on these platforms may bias users' information diets, exposing them to information that does not challenge their opinions and may even reinforce their views (Keijzer and Mäs 2022; Pariser 2011; Ribeiro et al. 2020). YouTube, like many other social media platforms, uses a recommendation algorithm primarily informed by overlap in viewing history of the focal and similar users. It will pair videos on similar topics, with similar perspectives or otherwise related content, because both videos have been watched by the same users. Watch one, and the recommendation algorithm will suggest the other. Assuming that people with similar attitudes have similar viewing preferences, and that attitudes across topics are coherent, this creates the potential for a problematic chain reaction. Users following the algorithm's recommendations may be dragged into a *rabbit hole*–an informational pathway of algorithmically driven suggestions for content that is increasingly narrow in scope as the users progress along the path (Pariser 2011; Sunstein 2018).

YouTube is the world's second most visited website (Similarweb 2025). Yet, there is very little empirical research on the platforms information ecosystem. Most research focused on whether or not YouTube's recommendation algorithm contributes to a vicious circle of biased media content and opinion polarization (Hosseinmardi et al. 2024; Ledwich et al. 2022; Munger and Phillips 2020). While important, this focus on political radicalization and algorithmic influence has left a broader question underexplored: what does the overall structure of information on YouTube actually look like? In particular, we still lack a clear understanding of how segregated or connected the platform's recommendation network is–and whether patterns of segregation vary across topics, from highly controversial to seemingly trivial. This chapter addresses that gap by introducing a comparative methodological approach for mapping and analyzing YouTube's recommendation graph. Using data generated directly from the platform's recommender system, we apply tools from social network analysis to investigate the presence and structure of 'rabbit holes,' and evaluate the extent of information segregation across networks of non-controversial, science, news, and conspiracy videos.

The debate about the undesired effects of algorithms on user content diets and the resulting societal consequences is complex and characterized by ambiguous terminology (Bruns 2019). Concepts like 'filter bubbles', 'echo chambers', and 'rabbit holes' are strong metaphors that communicate warnings about complex dynamics caused and influenced by algorithms. But, empirically, these concepts are hard to quantify in a valid and reliable way. A key challenge is that rabbit holes are macroscopic phenomena. That is, they do not describe single pieces of content or individual recommendations generated by the algorithms. Rather, a rabbit hole is a characteristic of a large set of recommendations. On YouTube, for example, a user who has consumed a video on a COVID-19 conspiracy theory might receive only recommendations to videos that also support this theory.

We define the rabbit holes using concepts from network analysis. We treat YouTube videos as nodes in a network and recommendations as directed edges connecting those nodes. When YouTube's algorithm recommends a set of videos after consumption of a given video, each of these recommendations constitutes a directed connection between the watched and the recommended video. Next, we apply tools from network science to describe the networks in their degree of 'rabbit-holeness.' In particular, we argue that a recommendation network can be characterized as a rabbit hole when the network is strongly modular and low in density–such that multiple hubs with many connections within and few between the hubs will expose only a section of the whole graph to a given user–and low centralization–such that walking the recommendation graph from different starting points does not always converge to the same information consumption patterns.

We compared the degree of network modularity, centralization and intra-topical density in different parts of the YouTube recommendation network, comparing networks for different types of content. This allowed us to test the hypothesis that networks of videos on uncontroversial issues should be characterized by weaker network modularity than networks of videos on polarized issues. To this end, we identified 40 controversial and uncontroversial issues and measured the recommendation networks for each issue. In total, the networks contained information on 15,455 videos and 154,311 recommendation links. We find that recommendation networks on conspiratorial content are generally less dense, indicating that consumers of that content are less likely to encounter much more of it. They contain more negative sentiment in their captions and direct more often to politically left-leaning channels. However, controlling for views, the differences in the incoming recommendations largely disappear between the different network categories.

This chapter makes two main contributions. First, we outline a novel methodological approach that allows valid micro- and macro-level comparisons between networks of videos on conspiratorial, news, scientific, and non-controversial topics. This approach can be further developed and applied to YouTube recommendation networks on other types of topics to better understand the content available to different kinds of users interested in different topics. Second, applying this method to 40 topical networks, we find that this method exposes significant and considerable differences in structural characteristics of recommendation graphs on controversial and non-controversial topics. This might explain why regular YouTube users experience the filter bubble effect (when watching non-controversial content), but asserts that this algorithmic filtering will not push consumers of potentially harmful content into rabbit holes.

The remainder of this chapter is organized as follows. In the following section, we provide an overview of previous research on YouTube rabbit holes. Next, we describe our empirical and analytical approach (we refer readers of this book who are primarily interested in the analysis of recommendation graphs to Sect. 4.4.1). Finally, we present our results and discuss the implications of our findings for the debate about rabbit holes, sketching other applications of this method for future research in the concluding section.

4.2 Rabbit Holes and Radicalization on YouTube

The literature on YouTube and its algorithm is relatively young and small, but has already made great progress in advancing our understanding of information consumption in sociotechnological systems. The first wave of studies on information consumption on YouTube focused on actual user consumption, auditing observed behavior and information consumption pathways. Ribeiro et al., for example, were able to track users who commented on multiple videos and found some indications for right-wing radicalization (2020). They found that, over time, some of their commenters did migrate to more extreme right-wing content. What is more, this study was one of the first to study the recommendation graph and found an interesting mismatch between the connectedness of radical channels. The most radical videos appeared to be easily reachable through the suggestions of the channels themselves but not through the video recommendations of the platform (Ribeiro et al. 2020). Overall, their results paint the picture that users indeed radicalize, but that the responsibility for their viewing decisions cannot be attributed to the recommendation algorithm alone.

The importance of individual choice is echoed by Munger and Phillips (2020). Taking a supply and demand perspective, this study looked at the quantity, popularity, and provocativeness of conservative, alt-lite and alt-right content on YouTube. They find that the increase in amount of videos and views does not keep up with the demand for radical content. In an analysis of the ratio of comments to views–indicative of demand by viewers who are intensely engaged–they show that the demand for radical content has consistently increased between 2013 and 2019 and that demand is diverging between content of different degrees of extremity (Munger and Phillips 2020).

In their compelling study from 2021, Hosseinmardi et al. investigated the browsing behavior of over 300,000 Americans and found that radical content–albeit growing in popularity over the last years–is only in the media diets of a very small percentage of users. What is more, users seek out this consumption themselves as opposed to this consumption being triggered by YouTube's recommendation algorithm. Zooming in on consumers of political content, they do not find evidence for radicalization pathways that steer users from mild to more radical, extreme (right-wing) content (Hosseinmardi et al. 2021).

While valuable to understand the magnitude of the problem on the information consumption side, neither of the audit studies can capture the actual causal effect of YouTube's personalization algorithm. A method that can was pioneered by Ledwich et al. (2022) who used bots to build up a user history, and examined the political leaning of their personalized recommendations. The user histories were based on 'personas' of particular political leaning. This method allows to focus on the recommendations that users with a history of viewing, for example, conspiratorial, religiously conservative, or (anti-)woke content would receive. While the algorithm does appear to create informational bubbles for these users, they refute the idea that YouTube is steering its users heavily towards radical and right-wing pipelines. Using a similar method, Hosseinmardi et al. (2024) design personas based on observational data, combining empirically plausible viewer historics with a causal test of recommendations. They conclude that "on average, relying solely on the recommender results in a more moderate experience on YouTube relative to the real user" (Hosseinmardi et al. 2024).

Zooming out and studying the relationships between channels more generally, Ledwich and Zaitsev labeled over 800 YouTube channels that focus on political content and collected data on the recommendation links between videos of those channels. They refute the idea that the YouTube algorithm is actively steering users towards radical rightist content. To the contrary, most links seem to point to mainstream and leftist media sources (Ledwich and Zaitsev 2020).

Another approach is to use the YouTube API directly to obtain search results for a particular topic, and study the recommendation links between the videos obtained in that search. Keijzer et al., for example, study a large recommendation graph for videos about COVID-19, in the first year after the pandemic (2022). They find that the structure in this news-dominated graph is mostly driven by what countries the videos are about. A few problematic clusters emerge from that analysis, but they are considerably less dense and central than the other clusters.

A review of 23 studies that investigated recommendations for problematic content concluded that "the YouTube recommender system can facilitate pathways to problematic content," with some caveats. Overall, 14 of the 23 studies implicated the recommender system in facilitating problematic content pathways, with the remaining studies indicating mixed results or no impact (Yesilada and Lewandowsky 2022). The reviewed studies had some common limitations, however. Many did not consider users' personal search history or interactions, and instead relied on random walk algorithms from seed videos.

The evidence that challenges the popular belief that YouTube's recommendation algorithm drives users toward radical right-wing content (Hosseinmardi et al. 2024; Ledwich and Zaitsev 2020; Hosseinmardi et al. 2021; Munger and Phillips 2020; Ribeiro et al. 2020) should not be mistaken for evidence that the structure of YouTube's recommendation system is unimportant. On the contrary, most decisions about what to watch on YouTube are shaped by a combination of algorithmic suggestions, user preferences, and content creator strategies (Bakshy et al. 2015; Keijzer et al. 2022). Studies that isolate the causal effects of the recommendation algorithm are valuable–but by focusing narrowly on algorithmic influence and extreme content, they leave open a broader and arguably more foundational question: what does the information ecosystem on YouTube actually look like? Crucially, we still know little about the degree of information segregation that exists on YouTube-how content clusters, how fragmented the ecosystem is, and how these patterns vary across different topics, from the controversial to the mundane. This study addresses that gap by proposing a method to empirically map the structure of YouTube's recommendation graph. Using data generated by the recommender system itself and applying tools from social network analysis, we offer a new lens to assess whether and where 'rabbit holes' emerge within the platform's information landscape.

4.3 Hypotheses

4.3.1 Macro

Despite the lack of empirical support for 'radicalization pipelines' in audit and causal studies, we can still expect to see between-category differences in network structure. That is, while the general tendency of the YouTube algorithm appears to be that it directs its users towards moderate (or even leftist) and popular content, that tendency might differ across networks for different topics. Based on worry over informational rabbit holes in conspiratorial and controversial content, we hypothesize that the degree to which networks exhibit structural characteristics of informational rabbit holes varies across whether the topic is conspiratorial, news, science or non-controversial.

H1 Networks in the conspiracy category exhibit more characteristics of rabbit holes than all other categories.

H2 Networks in the news category exhibit more characteristics of rabbit holes than those in the non-controversial category.

H3 Networks in the science category exhibit more characteristics of rabbit holes than those in the non-controversial category.

4.3.2 Micro

There is substantial evidence that negative emotions drive engagement on social media platforms, as people tend to react more strongly to negative content than to neutral or positive content (Tsugawa and Ohsaki 2015; Watson et al. 2024). This phenomenon, known as negativity bias, suggests that negative sentiment in YouTube video titles may increase their attractiveness, leading to more recommendations. Given that conspiracy theories often rely on emotionally charged narratives and fear appeals, we assume that videos with more negative sentiment receive more recommendations, particularly in conspiracy networks. However, while negativity might generally increase engagement, the YouTube algorithm optimizes for watch time and user retention rather than sentiment alone. Thus, the extent to which sentiment influences recommendations may depend on the category of the video. Assuming that conspiracy theories thrive on emotionally provocative content, we expect a stronger relationship between negative sentiment and recommendation likelihood in these networks that in others. Additionally, since conspiratorial narratives often revolve around fear, distrust, or outrage, we anticipate that videos in the conspiracy category will, on average, contain more negative sentiment than those in other categories.

H4a Sentiment is negatively related to the number of incoming recommendations in all networks.

H4b The sentiment-recommendation relationship is stronger for videos in the conspiracy category.

H5 There are proportionally more videos with negative sentiment in the conspiracy category compared to all other categories.

4.4 Method

4.4.1 Studying Behavioral Traces on YouTube

In this chapter, we focus on a method for studying digital trace data. Unlike the data sources social scientists typically use (like surveys or experiments), digital trace data have the advantage of being 'always-on' and highly ecologically valid. They are continuously collected data of primary (social) behavior collected at extraordinary scale. What is more, they are by definition high in ecological validity, since, in the case of YouTube, the platform is the context we want to generalize to, and the behavioral data can be collected without (a researcher's) observational bias. Those benefits do come at the cost of losing control over confounders. Particularly, algorithmically confounding–the complex and powerful ways in which the system itself impacts user behavior and makes it hard to disentangle algorithmic from behavioral traces in observed outcomes (Salganik 2019)–presents a significant challenge. Another major issue is that many of the data we are truly interested in are proprietary to commercial enterprises (Lazer 2020; Yesilada and Lewandowsky 2022). While collaboration between industry and university may sometimes be possible, maintaining academic independence in such collaborations is challenging.

On YouTube, there are many digital traces to analyze, but we focus here on the graph of between-video recommendations. The recommendation graph is a huge network comprising of all videos present on YouTube, connected by links that indicate that one video appears as a suggestion to be watched next for another video. Conceptually, this makes the network very interesting because it contains traces of user, creator and platform behavior (Keijzer et al. 2022). The recommendation graph is ever-changing, so the data studied here refer to a snapshot of that graph for a small subset of YouTube videos selected by us. Rather than exploring a single network from a (randomly) chosen subset of the YouTube recommendation graph, we first select topics within categories of interest, retrieve some of the videos' characteristics and collect all the links between this and the other videos in the topic. Those networks then enable within-network as well as cross-network and cross-category comparisons.

Our aim was to identify different subgraphs: ones that focus on controversial and ones that focus on uncontroversial issues. That way, we can better answer the question as to whether recommendation networks on controversial topics are structured differently than expected. The comparison of these networks' structures is the central contribution of our work. Most naturally, we compare videos on conspiracy content to non-controversial topics like hobbies or instructional videos. Furthermore, we wanted to select video categories that fall somewhere in between fully non-controversial and conspiratorial. To that end, we selected videos on scientific topics and on news events.

4.4.2 Collecting Topical Subgraphs of YouTube's Recommendation Graph

Using the overview of most popular search terms on YouTube as listed on Google Trends, we selected 40 topics that each apply to one of four broad categories of interest: non-controversial, science, news, or conspiracy.[1] The topics were chosen to represent unambiguous issues with a sufficient number of videos and views–as best as possible. Next, for each of the 40 issues, we collected the recommendation network using the public YouTube API, gathering information about a total of 21,774 videos and (up to) 20 recommendation links per video. These links are directed, with a source and target video, and hence the obtained network is treated as a directed network whenever possible. While the cap on 20 recommendation per video is arbitrary,[2] the retrieved network structure in terms of modularity and clustering configurations tends to stabilize after retrieving about the 14 most relevant videos (Keijzer et al. 2022). For most issues, we were able to obtain about 550 videos and their recommendation

[1] We focused our search on Google Trends data on most popular search terms in the United States on YouTube for all 23 main video categories in the period July 9 2021–July 8 2022. Whenever there were no suitable search queries available, the research team made a decision on a topic to include, and retrieved the best possible search query using behavioral data from Google Trends for the same period and geographical area.

[2] The YouTube API defaults at 20, but allows to retrieve up to 50 recommendations.

links to any other video on the platform. Using this 'catch-all' method, we assume that the initial search includes all potentially relevant videos, plus a surplus of videos that the YouTube algorithm haphazardly included in the raw dataset. To select the videos that are relevant for the recommendation network we wanted to study, we thus had to select the subset of videos most related to the search term. To this end, we selected the largest connected component (LCC) in each graph, filtering out those videos that did not link to or are linked by any of the videos in the LCC. The search queries, total number of videos in the raw dataset, number of videos in the LCC and the total number of views for all videos combined are reported in Table 4.1. While we discuss the implications of this at greater length in Sect. 4.6 ("Discussion"), it should be noted here that the videos included recommended videos are not personalized, not ranked in relevancy to a user, and mono-topical. In short, here are the five steps of data collection:

Step 1. Find a currently popular topic on Google Trends.
Step 2. Retrieve the first 550 videos on this topic using the public YouTube API.
Step 3. Get 20 recommendation links for each video using the public YouTube API.
Step 4. Construct a directed network of videos recommending other videos among the original 550 videos.
Step 5. Select the largest connected component, removing all videos that do not link to (or are not linked-to by) any other video in the original 550.

4.4.3 What Does a Rabbit Hole Look Like?

The metaphor of a 'rabbit hole' evokes a strong image of an individual tumbling ever deeper into a tunnel of one-sided information. A tunnel that brings us farther away from reality and further into the bizarre world of Caroll's Alice in Wonderland. In the context of online information consumption and extremism, it has come to define not just thematic filtering, but a narrowing trajectory towards homogeneous and extreme content. Translating this into network indicators or macro-level metrics for our topical subgraphs is challenging. Several structural measures offer partial but not exhaustive proxies for aspects of a narrowing and extremist information diet–a diet that lies farther away from the average casual YouTube viewer.

First, we can consider *density* of the graph (or average degree of its nodes) as indicator for the likelihood of intra-topic reinforcement. Because the number of recommendation links for every video is constant, the proportion of links pointing to videos on the same topic directly translates to density on the macro-level. Graphs that are sparse, have many links pointing 'outward,' and away from the sampled topic.

Second, *centralization* reflects whether a graph has a dominant hub or whether no videos or hubs in the networks are at the end of a particularly high number of paths.

Third, *modularity* captures the degree to which the graph could be further divided into groups of videos that recommend each other more than they recommend themselves. High modularity suggests that there are 'islands' of videos within the network

Table 4.1 Complete list of networks collected for the study

	Search query	Videos	Videos in BCC (% of total)	Modularity	Views
Non-controversial	ab workout	504	455 (90%)	0.538	2,664,570,462
	How to draw	515	376 (73%)	0.368	1,893,777,121
	Minecraft	412	299 (73%)	0.533	2,108,329,539
	Pokemon go	554	510 (92%)	0.372	1,013,820,353
	Power tools	573	292 (51%)	0.503	71,574,366
	Urban gardening	583	392 (67%)	0.478	179,673,393
	Van life us	575	433 (75%)	0.442	415,832,870
	Vintage jewelry	576	481 (84%)	0.458	8,032,313
	Warrior cats	576	553 (96%)	0.464	221,730,300
	Wordle	489	453 (93%)	0.354	69,928,513
	Subtotal	*5,357*	*4,244 (79%)*	*0.448*	*8,647,269,230*
Science	Autism	576	473 (82%)	0.361	472,792,683
	Blockchain	501	428 (85%)	0.409	146,903,002
	Climate change	546	471 (86%)	0.312	318,486,715
	Filter bubbles	575	136 (24%)	0.422	6,342,847
	Game theory	544	461 (85%)	0.442	2,312,904,339
	Machine learning	521	476 (91%)	0.375	275,318,766
	Monkeypox virus	561	433 (77%)	0.283	25,113,752
	Nanotechnology	570	450 (79%)	0.288	92,332,837
	nft	534	387 (72%)	0.579	197,310,079
	Tourette syndrome	497	412 (83%)	0.329	280,807,107
	Subtotal	*5,425*	*4,127 (76%)*	*0.392*	*4,128,312,127*
News	Antifa	547	334 (61%)	0.399	108,648,757
	Baby formula	574	475 (83%)	0.287	40,625,938
	Critical race theory	550	433 (79%)	0.306	66,231,303
	Derek chauvin	585	473 (81%)	0.333	109,284,065
	Dominion voting system	520	342 (66%)	0.315	25,742,495
	Gas prices	544	487 (90%)	0.430	68,059,221
	Johnny depp amber heard trial	363	325 (90%)	0.375	661,045,532
	Roe v wade	537	464 (86%)	0.300	103,259,849
	Transgender	546	302 (55%)	0.554	395,431,204
	Vaccine mandate	548	424 (77%)	0.441	56,038,564
	Subtotal	*5,314*	*4,059 (76%)*	*0.369*	*1,634,366,928*
Conspiracy	5g covid	549	99 (18%)	0.645	18,542,753
	9 11 Building 7	587	252 (43%)	0.357	208,600,921
	Adrenochrome	562	314 (56%)	0.449	20,063,547
	Chemtrails	582	333 (57%)	0.373	92,035,165
	Death elvis presley	572	467 (82%)	0.302	600,961,114
	Great replacement theory	556	355 (64%)	0.299	76,581,541
	Is earth flat	569	456 (80%)	0.247	557,082,623
	Pizzagate	552	229 (41%)	0.420	250,993,689
	Plandemic	570	138 (24%)	0.453	26,216,144
	Qanon	579	372 (64%)	0.382	115,634,250
	Subtotal	*5,678*	*3,015 (53%)*	*0.389*	*1,966,711,747*
	Total	**21,774**	**15,445 (71%)**	**0.400**	**16,376,660,032**

that prevent the user from freely accessing other information on the same topic at the same rate as in its low-modularity counterfactual.

Taken together, these three indicators offer a structural perspective on the extent to which a topical network exhibits rabbit-hole characteristics. In developing a measurable and rigorous approach, we move away from the common association of rabbit holes with ideological extremity–an aspect that cannot be captured solely with network-level features. Instead, we conceptualize rabbit holes as content-agnostic and in terms of informational segregation: the extent to which algorithmic recommendations limit exposure to diverse or opposing viewpoints. More concretely, we understand highly segregated recommendation graphs as those where access to information varies significantly depending on the user's point of entry.

With this understanding of rabbit holes as a form of information segregation, we can now clarify how each of our three structural metrics relates to this concept. First, modularity offers a direct approximation: highly modular networks are more likely to trap users within cohesive content clusters, making it structurally difficult to reach content in other parts of the graph. In this sense, modularity may provide the clearest structural signal of information segregation. However, it does not capture whether users are likely to be exposed to some central content, nor does it reflect the presence of recommendation links that lead outside the observed network. Second, network density can be interpreted in more than one way. Lower density may reflect a structure in which videos link outward-to content with different perspectives or unrelated topics. But these links could either broaden users' exposure (e.g., by connecting to counter-narratives or mainstream information) or redirect them into other fringe or conspiratorial content. To distinguish between these possibilities, density should be interpreted alongside modularity: a network that is both high in modularity and low in density is more likely to represent a fragmented and ideologically insulated information environment. Finally, high centralization speaks to whether the network steers users toward a common core of content. This could counteract segregation by creating shared reference points, or, conversely, reinforce it by channeling users into a dominant, potentially biased narrative. At minimum, centralization informs us about the consistency of user experiences: whether most users engaging with a topic are exposed to similar content or not.

4.4.4 Data

With the data collected as described in Sects. 4.4.1 and 4.4.2, we focus our analysis on a handful of indicators on one of three levels of analysis: the network, the channel, and the video-level.

On the network-level, we capture 'rabbit-holeness' by operationalizing the indicators from Sect. 4.4.3. *Density* is measures as the average number of (outgoing) ties of each video–which we refer to as average degree. The maximum number of outgoing ties a video can have is 20, by design–because if a recommendation from a video included in our network goes to a video outside of the network, that tie is removed from the analysis–so a network with an average degree of 20 is maximally dense.

Centralization captures inequality in the distribution of incoming ties such that a network where all videos recommend the same or a few of the same videos is considered centralized. We operationalize centralization by taking the Gini coefficient, a continuous measure ranging from 0 (perfect equality) to 1 (perfect inequality).

To calculate *modularity* of the graph, we first need to assign cluster membership to all videos in the graph. The goal is to find a configuration of clusters optimizing for modularity, such that many ties connect videos that belong to the same cluster while few ties connect videos that belong to different communities. It has the range $[-0.5, 1]$ where -0.5 indicates full non-modal clustering and 1 indicates maximal density within each cluster in the configuration. We find a solution for each model using the Louvain algorithm. Community detection has shown to be an effective way of unraveling structure between videos on YouTube, like, for example, topical similarity (Woma et al. 2019).

In our main analyses, and in the analyses in the supplementary information, we use information from the channel-level. To enrich our data with information of the channels, we build on the efforts of Ledwich and Zaitsev (2020), who manually labeled the political slant and category of 816 American YouTube channels. These channels were selected based on size (at least 10,000 subscribers) and content (at least 30% of content is political). *Slant* refers to the political leaning of the channel (left, center or right). *Channel category* refers to the kind of political content included on the channel. In total, Ledwich and Zaitsev (2020) use 21 different categories, like socialist, state funded, QAnon or mainstream news (a full description of each category can be found in Ledwich and Zaitsev 2020). We matched our datasets to the dataset of Ledwich and Zaitsev (2020) and were able to obtain information for 3596 videos (23.28%), responsible for 1,316,425,677 views (8.03% of total).

On the video-level, we collect and use five variables: sentiment, view count, comments, likes and duration. *Sentiment* of a video is captured through computing a sentiment score on the video title. Scores were computed using the 2022 version of the Twitter-roBERTa-base model for Sentiment Analysis (Loureiro et al. 2022), which is also integrated into the TweetNLP package for python (Camacho-Collados et al. 2022). Although specifically trained on Twitter data, we assume linguistic similarities across social media platforms are sufficient for sophisticated models like RoBERTa to detect meaningful signals. To minimize potential confounding factors, URLs and the original search queries were removed from the text before sentiment analysis. The sentiment model is a multiclass classifier, categorizing each input as negative, neutral, or positive, and returning a composite score as well. The latter is used as the main indicator of video (title) sentiment. We calculated sentiment scores exclusively based on video titles, since these are the primary textual information users see when deciding whether to click on a recommended video or not. *View counts* refer to the number of views of a given video at time of collection, and were logged because of their heavily right-tailed distribution. The variables *comments* and *likes* capture the number of comments and likes for a video.

4.4.5 *Analytical Strategy*

To compare the structure of networks across video categories, we compare several macro-level characteristics, controlling for number of videos and total (logged) view count in each of our 40 networks. We present both the raw category differences using t-tests, and the differences as controlled for view counts and network size in OLS regression models.

The analyses at the micro-level focus on directed dyads of one video (the source) recommending another video (the target), and uncover the relationship between characteristics of the source, the target and their similarity on the probability that such a link exists. We turn to our variables on the video-level and on the channel-level. We test whether a channel's political slant (of the target and in similarity), channel ideological category (target and similarity) and sentiment in the video title (of the target) affects the number of incoming recommendations a video receives, controlling for the (logged) number of views a video had at the time of collection, the duration of the video, the number of comments and the number of likes. We turn to a permuation test, specifically the Multiple Regression Quadratic Assignment Procedure (MRQAP) (Krackhardt 1988; Dekker et al. 2007) through the 'netlm' function of the 'sna' package in R (Butts 2024). We run two MRQAP models per network; one for political slant and sentiment in the video title, and one for channel category. Sentiment scores, logged view counts, normalized comment counts, normalized like counts and video durations were all standardized on a per network basis.

4.5 Results

4.5.1 *Macro*

The LCCs of the 40 collected networks are visualized in Fig. 4.1. Visually, it is hard to form a picture of the differences across network categories, but some general network shapes stand out. Most networks appear very centralized with only a few videos clearly in the periphery, if at all (e.g., 'ab workout', 'monkeypox virus', 'dominion voting system' or 'adrenochrome'). The lack of clear clustering patterns, at least visually, could be indicative of well-balanced supply of information available on the platform. Some networks maintain this degree of centralization, but show clearer branches of clusters (e.g., 'how to draw', 'nft', 'derek chauvin' and 'plandemic'). Finally, few networks show a lack of connectivity and are formed around mutliple network cores (e.g., 'filter bubbles', '5g covid', 'chemtrails'). Those networks may be the least informative to an actor who wants to learn about a topic from many angles. For such an actor, it would take a long time to receive recommendations for all videos in the network, starting from any given node in the network.

We can study the degree to which our networks resemble 'rabbit holes' in a more rigorous way. Table 4.2 presents the results from three OLS regression models on

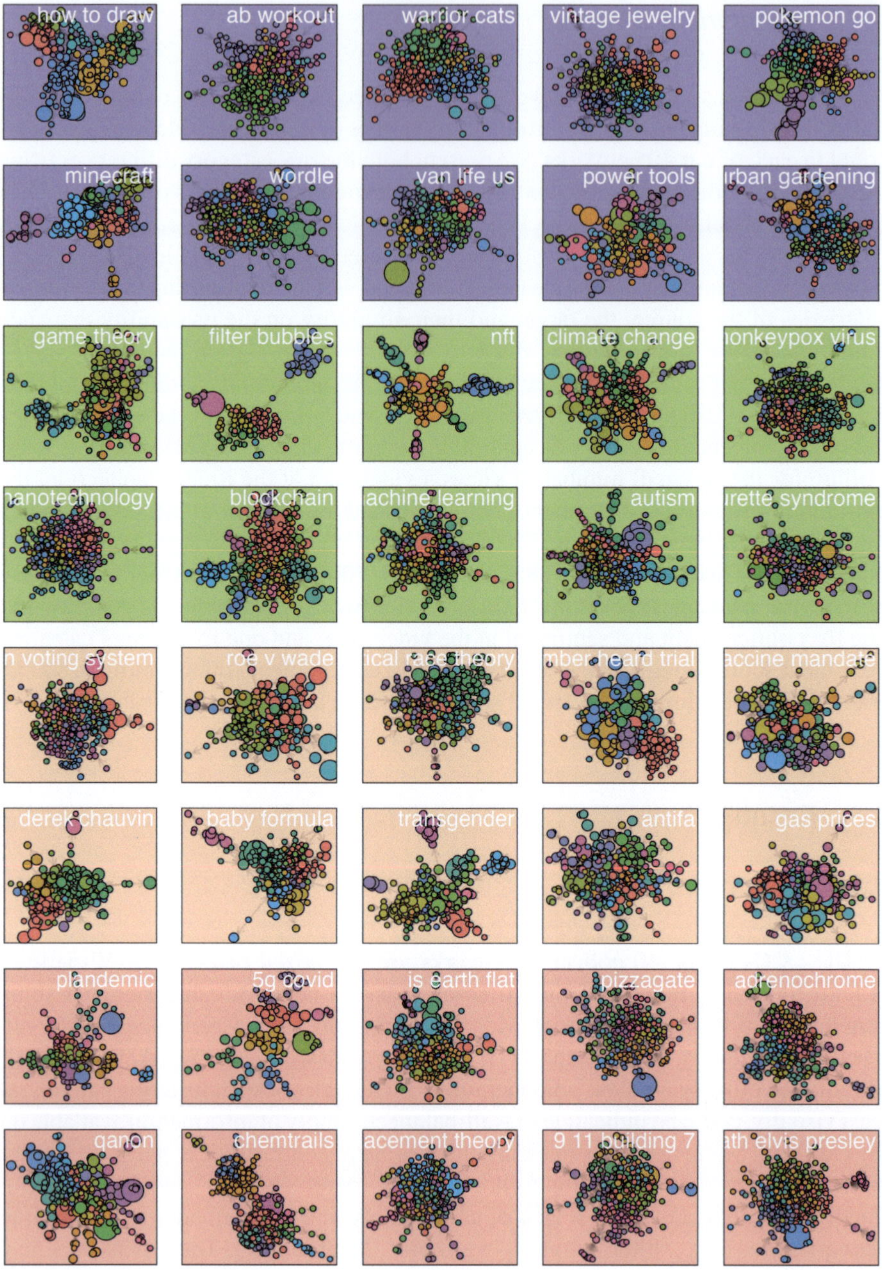

Fig. 4.1 All largest connected components of the 40 networks analyzed in this chapter. Panel background indicates whether networks belong to the non-controversial (blue), science (green), news (orange) or conspiracy (red) category. Nodes are colored by assigned cluster and sized by view count. Networks are laid out using the Fruchterman-Reingold algorithm

Table 4.2 OLS regression models on indicators of clustering in the graphs

	(1) Modularity	(2) Density	(3) Centralization
Category[a]			
Science	−0.063*	0.932	0.011
	(0.034)	(1.229)	(0.020)
News	−0.082**	0.665	0.035
	(0.035)	(1.262)	(0.021)
Conspiracy	−0.106***	−0.458	0.064***
	(0.038)	(1.352)	(0.022)
Views (log)	0.008	0.614*	−0.016***
	(0.009)	(0.321)	(0.005)
Size ($\times 10^{-2}$)	−0.049***	2.190***	0.008
	(0.014)	(0.487)	(0.008)
Constant	0.630***	−1.549	0.797***
	(0.061)	(2.206)	(0.037)
Observations	40	40	40
R^2	0.364	0.578	0.419
F Statistic (df = 5; 34)	3.893***	9.315***	4.914***

Note [a]reference is *Non-controversial*; *p<0.1; **p<0.05; ***p<0.01

different indicators of clustering at the network level. Some of those characteristics are also shown, raw, in Fig. 4.2.

Informational rabbit holes should have a high average degree, strong modularity and a relatively flat degree distribution (low centralization). Panels A and B of Fig. 4.2 clearly present the networks on conspiracy content as outliers. Some of these differences occur because the conspiracy networks are considerably smaller than networks from the other three categories. While the original sample of videos is similar in across all categories, many videos in the conspiracy category drop out of the network once we select the LCC. The lack of cross-recommendations indicates that many recommended videos will point to content that takes the user out of this particular topic–a finding that may well reflect YouTube's policies to de-popularize conspiratorial or low-credibility content. To interpret the density difference in terms of whether it indicates the presence of rabbit holes, we expect low density to occur alongside high modularity (as argued in Sect. 4.4.3). Panel D positions each of the networks by modularity and average degree. The networks in the conspiracy category do show a negative relationship between modularity and density ($r(8) = -0.88$, $p < .001$) while no such relationship exists for any of the other categories). Controlling for network size and number of views, the difference in average degree disappears, as shown in Table 4.2 (model 2).

The expected lack of centralization and high degree of modularity expected of informational rabbit holes is less clearly visible for the networks in our study. Contrary to expectation, the degree of centralization rises slightly with sensitivity of the

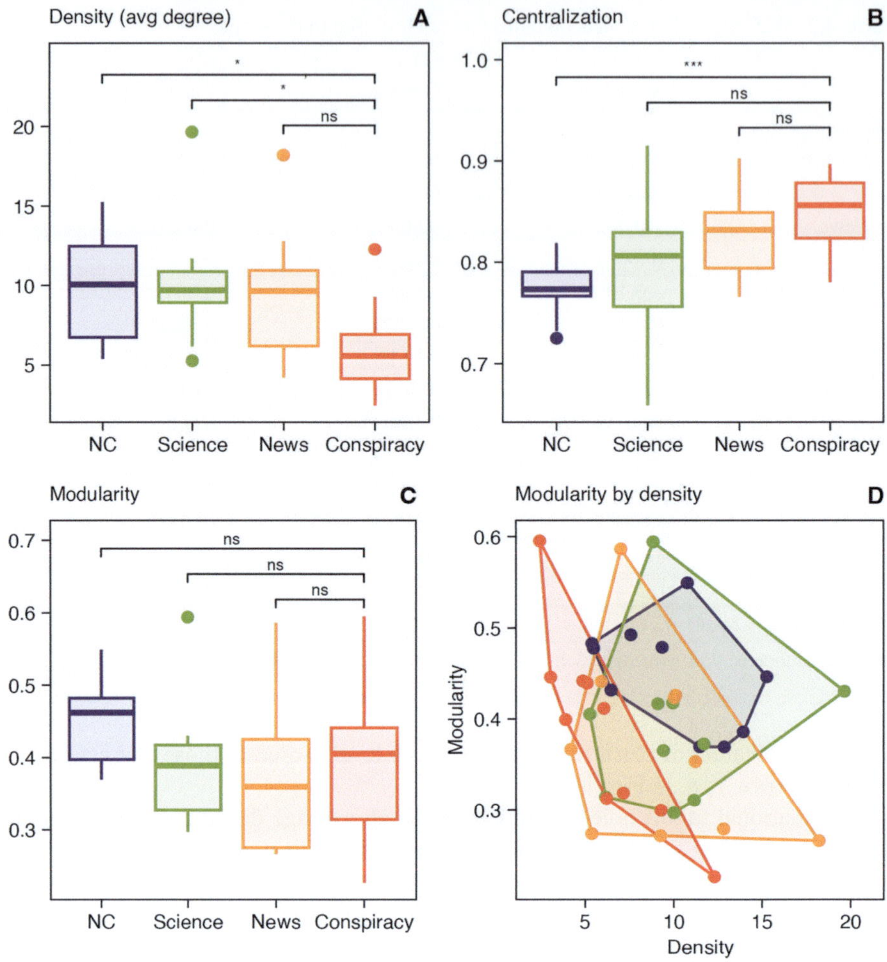

Fig. 4.2 Network-structural indicators of rabbit holes in informational subgraphs. In panels A, B and C, boxplots refer to the per-network average of density, centralization and modularity, respectively. Brackets show the significance level of p-values for simple between-category differences (t-tests), where * $p<.05$; ** $p<.01$; *** $p<.001$; and ns = non-significant. Panel D presents graph modularity by degree and visualizes the hull of each category

topic, from non-conspiratorial through science to news and conspiracy (Panel B in Fig. 4.2). What is more, while it appears that non-controversial topics have a higher degree of modularity, the networks all vary around quite similar values, and also have quite similar numbers of clusters for their modularity fit. The ordinary least squares regression models that control for network size and number of views do pick up on significant differences in modularity: conspiracy networks are less modular and more centralized.

All in all, there is not enough evidence that conspiracy networks exhibit more characteristics of rabbit holes on the macro-level and we refute hypotheses 1, 2 and 3.

4.5.2 Micro

Figure 4.3 shows the average sentiment scores of videos in the four different categories. The differences are crystal clear. The networks on non-controversial videos contain content that is more positive, on average. The science networks are mildly negative or neutral and both news and conspiracy networks have clearly more negative sentiment on average. We can partially accept hypothesis 5 as indeed the conspiracy networks tend to have more negative sentiment, but only as compared to non-controversial and science topics.

The within-network effects of sentiment are less pronounced. Surprisingly, sentiment does not seem to affect the number of recommendations a video receives, neither positively nor negatively. Controlling for network structure, the panels in Fig. 4.4 present the effects in the MRQAP of (cross-)video characteristics (panel A) and (cross-)channel characteristics (panel B) on a video's propensity to receive recommendations. On the video-level, recommendations are driven primarily, if not exclusively, by view count. Surprisingly, the number of comments, likes (both proportional to the number of views), or duration of the video do not affect incoming recommendations. The only exceptions to this regularity seem to exist in the news

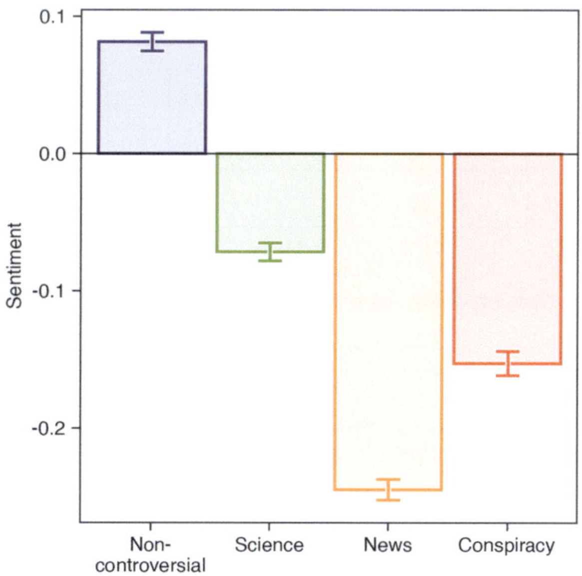

Fig. 4.3 Sentiment value in captions of videos included in the networks, averaged for each network and grouped by category. Whiskers refer to standard errors

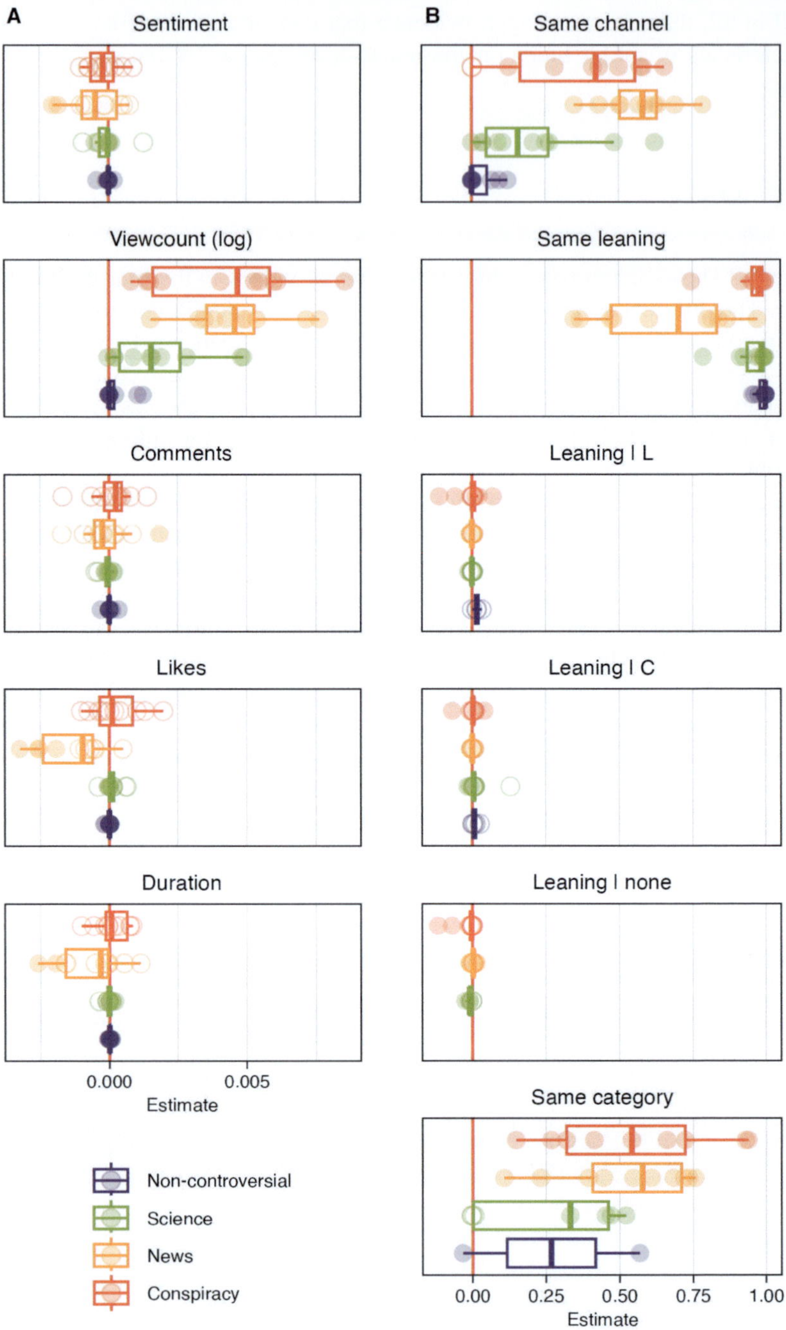

Fig. 4.4 Effects in 40 independent multiple regression quadratic assignment procedure (MRQAP) models. Panel A shows video-level effects. Panel B shows channel-level effects. All effects are estimated jointly. Solid circles indicate that the effect was significant (p<.05) while open circles indicate non-significant effects

category, where, contrary to expectations about the logic of recommendations, both proportion of likes and video duration seem to negatively affect the likelihood to receive a recommendation. The effects of sentiment are significant only in a few networks, and overall do not show any particular direction. We refute hypotheses 4a and 4b and conclude that sentiment does not play a role in receiving recommendations from the YouTube algorithm within the 40 networks studied here.

4.6 Discussion

This chapter studied the graph structure of 154,311 recommended videos next to 15,455 YouTube videos as a directed network, on 40 different topics across four topic categories. Specifically, we looked at how the structure of recommendation graphs for conspiratorial content differed from non controversial, science or news content. We find that, overall, networks of conspiratorial videos are sparse, small and more centralized. Their density, however, can be partially explained by their smaller overall network size and a lack of views. The sentiment of videos in conspiracy networks is remarkably negative–which is also true for news networks, but not for science (neutral) and non-controversial (positive sentiment) networks. In none of the networks is sentiment a good predictor for indegree; most recommendations on a video-level are driven by view count.

The null effect of sentiment overall is somewhat puzzling, but resonates with recent insights into the complex relationship between creator sentiment and content attractiveness (Cui et al. 2024). Cui et al. find that while strong sentiments (both positive and negative) in thumbnails boost the number of views, video captions with strong sentiments have a negative effect on a video's popularity and for titles the effect should in fact be linear and positive (2024).

Studying the YouTube API comes with some considerable limitations. First, all of the results discussed here are on non-personalized recommendations. For a logged-in user, the experience is much less mono-topical and its recommendations are much more complex (as demonstrated in Ledwich et al. 2022). Whether those personalized recommendations will be and stay more diverse over time is hard to tell. On the one hand, they will surely offer a more diverse set of topics to the user in the short-run (more between-topic recommendations for any viewing session). On the other, a user with a much clearer profile for YouTube will possibly be less likely to have a diverse viewing experience long term. Future work using bots could merit our comparative YouTube research approach by having bots explore video networks of different topics. Second, we analyze the networks as independent subgraphs, but in reality, they are, of course, part of the larger recommendation graph. For all links that point away from the network, to a video outside of the current graph, we do not know whether that link will point to a harmless other topic or perhaps to other subgraphs on other harmful topics. However, while possible, given the evidence presented in this chapter, warnings that such pathways may exist are not grounded.

While our approach captures structural properties of topical recommendation graphs, it does not yet account for how users enter these networks in the first place. The metaphor of a rabbit hole suggests a dynamic process–users do not start at the bottom, but "fall" into increasingly narrow informational spaces. In our analysis, we simulate this process by starting from specific queries, such as "plandemic" or "5G covid." However, real-world users may encounter rabbit-hole content through less intentional pathways: prior research has shown that users can be nudged toward conspiratorial or extreme content even when starting from neutral or mainstream queries (Ribeiro et al. 2020; Ledwich and Zaitsev 2020). Others have emphasized the role of "bridge" or "gateway" videos that serve as ideological intermediaries, connecting mainstream content to fringe narratives (Papadamou et al. 2022). This raises the question of where the entrance to a rabbit hole lies and how accessible these structures are from the broader YouTube ecosystem. Future work should therefore go beyond topical subgraphs to map recommendation trajectories from general-interest content and examine the frequency and visibility of transitional nodes. Doing so would clarify not just the internal structure of rabbit-hole networks, but also their integration into–or insulation from–the broader platform architecture.

In this chapter we have proposed a method for studying information segregation on YouTube. This comparative approach benefits from repeated monitoring and case studies. We hope it triggers and inspires computational social scientists to build a body of work understanding information consumption on social media, to gain a better understanding of belief formation in a Western political reality where a shared common ground is softly eroding.

Data and materials Data were collected using the YouTube API. All materials and data used in this project are publicly available via github.com/luerhard/yt_rabbit_hole

Acknowledgements We would like to thank Michael Mäs and Annika Deubel for their contributions to the project during the BIGSSS-CSS summer school 2022. Marijn Keijzer acknowledges funding from the Occitanie region, the European Regional Development Fund (ERDF), and the French government, through the France 2030 project managed by the National Research Agency (ANR) with the reference number "ANR-22-EXES-0015." Lukas Erhard acknowledges the support of the Deutsche Forschungsgemeinschaft (DFG, German Research Foundation, under the reference number UP 31/1) for the Stuttgart Research Focus Interchange Forum for Reflecting on Intelligent Systems (IRIS).

References

E. Bakshy, S. Messing, L.A. Adamic, Exposure to ideologically diverse news and opinion on Facebook. Science **348.6239**, 1130–1132 (2015)

A. Bruns, *Are Filter Bubbles real?* (John Wiley and Sons, 2019)

C.T. Butts, sna: tools for social network analysis. R package version **2**, 8 (2024)

J. Camacho-Collados, K. Rezaee, T. Riahi, A. Ushio, D. Loureiro, D. Antypas, J. Boisson, L. Espinosa-Anke, F. Liu, E. Martínez-Cámara, et al., TweetNLP: cutting-edge natural language processing for social media'. in *Proceedings of the 2022 Conference on Empirical Methods in Natural Language Processing: System Demonstrations*. Abu Dhabi, U.A.E.: Association for Computational Linguistics (2022)

G. Cui, S. Yu-Ho Chung, L. Peng, Q. Wang, Clicks for money: predicting video views through a sentiment analysis of titles and thumbnails. J. Business Res. **183**, 114849 (2024)

D. Dekker, D. Krackhardt, T.A.B. Snijders, Sensitivity of MRQAP tests to collinearity and autocorrelation conditions. Psychometrika **72**, 563–581 (2007)

H. Hosseinmardi, A. Ghasemian, A. Clauset, M. Mobius, D.M. Rothschild, Examining the consumption of radical content on YouTube. in *Proceedings of the National Academy of Sciences* vol. 118.32 (2021), pp. 1–8

H. Hosseinmardi, A. Ghasemian, M. Rivera-Lanas, M.H. Ribeiro, R. West, D.J. Watts, Causally estimating the effect of YouTube's recommender system using counterfactual bots. in *Proceedings of the National Academy of Sciences* vol. 121.8 (2024), pp. e2313377121

M.A. Keijzer, E. Golan, A. Coiciu, B. Burgerhof, A. Llulla, Y. Faber, CovidTube: mapping information segregation on YouTube (2022). SocArXiv

M.A. Keijzer, M. Mäs, The complex link between filter bubbles and opinion polarization. Data Sci. **5.2**, 139–166 (2022)

D. Krackhardt, Predicting with networks: nonparametric multiple regression analysis of dyadic data. Social Netw. **10.4** 359–381 (1988)

D.M.J. Lazer et al., Computational social science: obstacles and opportunities. Science **369.6507** 1060–1062 (2020)

M. Ledwich, A. Zaitsev, Algorithmic extremism: examining YouTube's rabbit hole of radicalization. First Monday **25.3** (2020). eprint: 1912.11211

M. Ledwich, A. Zaitsev, A. Laukemper, Radical bubbles on YouTube? Revisiting algorithmic extremism with personalised recommendations. First Monday (2022)

D. Loureiro, F. Barbieri, L Neves, L.E. Anke, J. Camacho-Collados, *TimeLMs: Diachronic Language Models from Twitter* (2022). arXiv: 2202.03829 [cs.CL]

K. Munger, J. Phillips, Right-wing YouTube: a supply and demand perspective. Int. J. Press/Polit. (2020)

K. Papadamou, S. Zannettou, J. Blackburn, E. De Cristofaro, G. Stringhini, M. Sirivianos, "It is just a flu: assessing the effect of watch history on YouTube's pseudoscientific video recommendations. in *Proceedings of the International AAAI Conference on Web and Social Media*. vol. 16 (2022), pp. 723–734

E. Pariser, *The Filter Bubble: What the Internet is Hiding From You* (Penguin, London, 2011), p.304

Pew Research Center, *Social Media and News Fact Sheet* (2024). en-US

M.H. Ribeiro, R. Ottoni, R. West, V.A.F. Almeida, W. Meira, Auditing radicalization pathways on YouTube (2020), pp. 131–141. arXiv:1908.08313

M.J. Salganik, *Bit by Bit: Social Research in the Digital Age* (Princeton University Press, 2019)

Similarweb, *Top Websites Ranking—Most Visited Websites in December 2024* (2025). en

C. Sunstein, *# Republic: Divided Democracy in the Age of Social Media* (Princeton University Press, 2018)

S. Tsugawa, H. Ohsaki, Negative messages spread rapidly and widely on social media. In: *Proceedings of the 2015 ACM on Conference on Online Social Networks* (2015), pp. 151–160

J. Watson, S. van der Linden, M. Watson, D. Stillwell, Negative online news articles are shared more to social media. Scient. Reports **14.1** 21592 (2024)

J. Woma, K. Ngo, Comparisons of community detection algorithms in the YouTube network (2019)

M. Yesilada, S. Lewandowsky, Systematic review: YouTube recommendations and problematic content. Internet Policy Rev. **11.1** 1–22 (2022)

Chapter 5
ResIN: A New Method to Analyze Socio-political Attitude Systems

Philip Warncke, Yijing Chen, Anne Speer, Bart de Bruin, Adrian Lüders, and Dino Carpentras

Abstract Investigating attitude systems is of key interest to many social scientists. However, "classic" approaches to studying such systems like linear scaling or dimensionality reduction risk hiding useful information and may artificially narrow the scope of explanatory theories. As an alternative, scholars have recently turned to Belief Network Analysis (BNA), which formalizes mass attitudes as sets of statistically interconnected nodes. However, BNA inherits many of the assumptions typical of latent variable methods which can preclude explorations of more complex phenomena, such as inter-group asymmetries and non-linearities. This chapter discusses Response Item Networks (ResIN)—an extension of BNA which is detached from several assumptions inherent in latent variable models. In particular, we demonstrate how ResIN can detect attitudinal asymmetries without "forcing" specific (linear or monotonic) dependencies onto source data. In ResIN, structural patterns instead emerge organically from co-endorsement patterns. We use simulations and investigate real-world survey data to highlight how ResIN provides parsimonious, yet realistic reproductions of diverse attitude structures in cases that are difficult to handle both for latent variable models and "classic" BNA. We further discuss

P. Warncke
Department of Psychology, University of Limerick, Limerick, Ireland

SCRIPTS Data and Methodology Center, Freie Universität Berlin, Berlin, Germany

Y. Chen
Department of Network and Data Science, Central European University, Vienna, Austria

A. Speer
University of Bremen, Bremen, Germany

B. de Bruin
Department of Industrial Engineering and Innovation Sciences, Eindhoven University of Technology, Eindhoven, The Netherlands

A. Lüders
Institut für Kommunikationswissenschaft, University of Hohenheim, Stuttgart, Germany

D. Carpentras (✉)
Computational Social Science, ETH Zürich, Zurich, Switzerland
e-mail: dcarpentras@ethz.ch

M. A. Keijzer et al. (eds.), *Computational Social Science of Social Cohesion and Polarization*, Computational Social Sciences,
https://doi.org/10.1007/978-3-032-01373-6_5

unitary, bi-nary, and trinary attitude structures based on survey responses across three European countries as well as non-linearities within the US liberal-conservative spectrum.

Keywords Attitude systems · Latent variables · Non-linearities · Asymmetries · Belief network analysis (BNA) · Response item networks (ResIN) · European social surveys (ESS) · American national election studies (ANES)

5.1 Latent Variable and Belief Network Models

5.1.1 Limitations of Latent Variable Models

A common approach to the study of social and political attitude systems involves "summarizing" a given set of attitudes (e.g., answers to multiple survey items) through statistical techniques that involve some form of dimensionality reduction. For instance, when interested in learning about overall trends across individuals' political preferences, researchers often rely on principal components analysis (Ellis and Stimson 2012), factor models (Ansolabehere et al. 2008; Feldman and Johnston 2014), or item-response theory (Treier and Hillygus 2009) to generate estimates of citizens' positions along various issues at once. Dimensionality reduction methods, in other words, allow scholars to reduce the multi-dimensional nature of issue preference data on topics as diverse as gun control, immigration, and vaccine mandates by parsimoniously mapping each respondent's summary positions onto a lower-dimensional space, such as the well-known left-right ideological spectrum. Such lower dimensional representations are often referred to as "latent variables" since the thus obtained quantities (e.g. people's summaries positions) cannot be directly measured but require processing of manifest (or "proxy") variables.

While latent variable models have become a standard practice across the social sciences, they continue to evoke criticism due to several assumptions they impose on data-generating processes (Uher 2021; Scheel 2022). For instance, most latent variable models assume that survey responses ultimately emanate from an individual's "true score" on some latent construct plus some amount of measurement error. In the context of the above example, this implies that a person's attitude on a 5-point Likert scale on vaccination mandates linearly maps onto the left-right spectrum (i.e., the more right-wing a person is, the more they reject such mandates) plus some amount of zero-centered noise. However, truly consistent measurement is impossible to achieve unless the data in question has, in fact, been generated by a (single) underlying latent variable—a proposition which is impossible to falsify in practice (Carpentras and Warncke 2024).

Moreover, latent variable models generally suffer from a lack of falsifiability (Scheel 2022). At first glance, this may seem surprising because many established latent variable models allow for statistical tests of model-fit (da Rocha et al. 2013;

Gaskin and Happell 2014). However, these tests merely verify whether the data are generally compatible with the chosen methodological framework to begin with. They do not demonstrate that the extracted variable is indeed the "correct" one—namely, that researchers have successfully identified the precise latent construct they intended to measure in the first place (Uher 2021).

Furthermore, classic latent variable models fail to account for non-linear and non-monotonic expressions. Once again, consider how the issue of vaccine mandates maps onto the left-right ideological spectrum. Factor and item-response theory (IRT) models assume that an increasing intensity of agreement with a given proposition (in this case, vaccine mandates) corresponds to monotonic changes in the underlying latent variable (i.e., political ideology). However, it might be the case that people on the far left are just as likely as people on the far right of the ideological spectrum to reject the proposition while individuals at the center possess the highest level of agreement. In this case, latent variable models would fail to reproduce any dependency between ideology and issue agreement because they are limited to reproducing monotonic dependencies.[1]

What is more, recent studies have demonstrated that different operationalizations of the same latent variable can yield incompatible and even contradictory findings (Schweinsberg et al. 2021; Breznau et al. 2022; Carpentras and Warncke 2024). For example, Schweinsberg et al. (2021), enlisted numerous analysts to test whether participants with higher status were more verbose than their lower-status counterparts in interactive chats. All analysts had access to the same dataset and complete freedom to define each construct. As a result, some measured verbosity by counting the number of words per comment, others by total characters typed, and still others by the number of conversations participants engaged in. Similar variations occurred in the operationalization of "status," as well as in the choice of statistical models and potential covariates. Although these decisions might appear to be minor technicalities, they led to irreconcilable results. This issue also extends to agent-based models, where differing operationalizations have produced entirely different model dynamics (Carpentras and Quayle 2022).

A recently proposed solution involves cross-checking multiple operationalizations to see if they yield consistent outcomes (Carpentras 2024). However, "some constructs may just be too complex to be reduced to a single measurement" (p. 3). Consequently, although it may be mathematically feasible to reduce dimensionality, critical information inevitably gets lost in the process. Even among multiple valid modes of dimensionality reduction, certain aspects of the data will be overemphasized while others are overlooked.

---

[1] Although extensions to classic IRT models exist that can accommodate non-linear response functions (e.g., Roberts et al. 2000), such solutions are computationally quite expensive as they require full Bayesian parameter estimation and are currently limited to modeling only a single latent variable/dimension at a time (Duck-Meyr and Montgomery 2019).

5.1.2 *Belief Network Analysis and Response Item Networks (ResIN)*

Belief network analysis (BNA) promises to address many of the shortcomings of traditional latent variable models in the study of mass attitude systems. BNA refers to a broad family of methods that model attitude systems as dedicated statistical networks (Boutyline and Vaisey 2017). Among others, BNA has been applied to describe architectures of individual belief systems (Brandt and Sleegers 2021), intergroup differences (Lüders et al. 2024), and macro-level dynamics (DellaPosta 2021).

Practically, BNA models attitude items such as responses to survey questions as nodes and their correlations as link weights. By permitting researchers to simultaneously explore individual relationships between attitudes, as well as the holistic "Gestalt" of all such relationships, BNA can advance the understanding of a range of processes linked to belief systems, such as social influence, group dynamics, identity management, and attitude change (e.g., Daenekindt et al. 2017; Brandt et al. 2019; Fishman and Davis 2022). Furthermore, while latent variable methods attempt to "reduce information" by imposing a lower-dimensional representation of the original data, BNA generally preserves the complexity of interconnections between individual attitudes.

While BNA is a powerful tool for exploring belief systems, it also harbors important limitations stemming from the fact that it provides mere graphical representations of inter-item correlation matrices. Like linear factor models, classic BNA thus also cannot adequately represent or reproduce asymmetrical or non-linear attitude structures.

Response-Item Networks (ResINs) were designed to address many of the previous limitations in BNA (Carpentras et al. 2024).[2] The main difference between ResIN and "classic" BNA approaches consists of modeling attitude systems not at the item, but at the item-response level. This means that ResIN considers not just the content but also the valence of attitudes. In other words, whereas BNA represents every item, such as abortion and gun control, as singular nodes, ResIN assigns a dedicated node to every possible *item response*, e.g. strongly supporting gun control, mildly supporting gun control, strongly rejecting gun control, etc.

Furthermore, ResIN produces so-called spatial networks—that is, networks with spatially interpretable node locations. Thus, proximity and distance between attitude nodes are not random values generated by network plotting algorithms but carry

[2] Note that this chapter does not claim that ResIN solves all problems associated with more established methods such as latent variable models and belief network analysis. Also, we do not claim that ResIN is superior to any other method or approach. What we claim here is that latent variable approaches have important limitations which provide grounds for exploring alternative models. Among these alternatives, ResIN stands out as being able to detect features of data-generating processes that often remain hidden in other methodological frameworks. Thinking of methodologies as tools, factor analysis, belief network analysis, and ResIN could be thought as a screwdriver, a hammer, and a wrench, respectively; each one excels for some tasks but is highly unsuitable for others.

deeper meaning (Carpentras et al. 2024). In the remainder of the chapter, we shall discuss each of these advantages in turn using practical examples.

5.1.3 *The Impact of ResIN*

Figure 5.1 reproduces the ResIN network depicted in Carpentras et al. (2022). The source dataset for this figure consists of a cross-national survey on trust in vaccines, doctors, and institutions, with responses ranging from complete trust to complete distrust. Interestingly, attitude nodes which correspond to strong trust in all these institutions (represented in green) appear completely separated from the remainder of the network. To test whether the spatial location of each node in the network provided reliable information, the authors opted to study network distance between the neutral and the strong trust attitudes (hereafter called "isolation"). Using agent-based simulations, Carpentras et al. (2022) showed that countries in which the isolation parameter was greater were also more likely to show greater distrust in vaccination. These results were corroborated by significant empirical correlations between (1) isolation and vaccination coverage and (2) isolation and trust in vaccination. Indeed, the isolation parameter allowed the authors to predict which countries would experience an increase in vaccination coverage at an accuracy of 72%.

In sum, Carpentras et al.'s (2022) vaccination study demonstrated that ResIN networks contain information critical to understanding future trajectories in mass attitude and behavior. Moreover, the results suggested that network distance was equivalent to the spatial distance in the visualization.

Carpentras et al. (2024) further explored this connection in a follow-up study, comparing spatial distance of attitude node position in ResIN with estimates derived from IRT. As a latent variable model, IRT associates each item response (e.g., strongly opposing abortion restrictions) with a dedicated probability of endorsement curve.

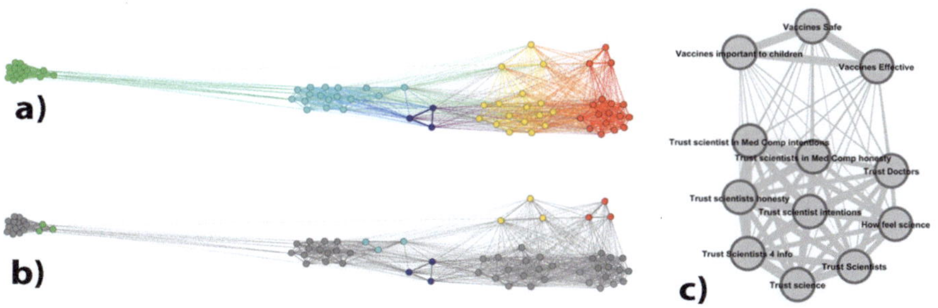

Fig. 5.1 **a** ResIN network from Carpentras et al. (2022), **b** the same network with only the vaccine response colored and **c** the BNA network obtained from the same data. In the ResIN network each color represents a different level of trust. In both BNA and ResIN, it is possible to see that the three vaccination items are slightly separated from the others. However, ResIN also shows the isolation of the attitudes expressing strong trust—something that is not visible in BNA

This study showed that, when data are generated by a latent variable, ResIN produces spatial estimates for each node which are strongly correlated with the mean of the corresponding IRT curves. Furthermore, ResIN outperformed a series of off-the shelves dimensionality reduction methods, including multi-dimensional scaling (MDS). For example, in one test in which unidimensional data was generated by an IRT model, ResIN correctly identified a unidimensional structure while MDS suggested the existence of an artificial second dimension[3] (Carpentras et al. 2024).

If ResIN can produce equivalent estimates to more established approaches such as IRT, wherein lies the added benefit of using this method? Should one not just simply rely on latent variable models? One distinct advantage of ResIN lies in its powerful visualization potential that can deliver high-level information more efficiently than latent variable models. For instance, noticing the isolation of the strong trust attitudes through IRT would require researchers to evaluate 17 different plots (one for each item), while ResIN effectively visualizes this anomaly within a single plot (Fig. 5.1).

Secondly, not all attitude systems possess a uni-dimensional, bipolar structure. Indeed, in many cases, such as in multi-dimensional ideological systems or in trifurcated user spaces (such as PC operating systems consisting of Windows, Linux, and MacOS users) it is common for data to possess three or more equally opposed extremes. Thus, while IRT and ResIN tap into complementary information in strictly bipolar structures, for ternary or more complex systems, IRT rapidly becomes overly complex and cumbersome to use. ResIN, in contrast, continues to produce readily interpretable results.

In what follows, we more specifically discuss how ResIN can produce insights on non-bipolar attitude structures. As mentioned above, data are often analyzed and simulated by evoking latent variables. Instead, we opted for a simulation procedure which solely requires the presence of attitude-based groups (i.e., groups forming through attitude sharing, Quayle 2025), allowing us to explore ResIN networks under more complex scenarios. Section 5.2 offers a more formal introduction to ResIN and explains how researchers can simulate different attitude-based groups with this framework. In Sects. 5.3 and 5.4 we analyze the results of our simulations and draw parallels with ResIN networks that we obtained from real-world, public opinion data. Section 5.5 summarizes our main findings and explores possible avenues for future research and methodological developments.

[3] This discrepancy between IRT and MDS may be surprising to some as both methods belong to the latent variable class of models. However, it is important to note that only IRT models include a dedicated theory on how responses and latent variables are related. On the contrary, MDS is a dimensionality reduction method which makes no assumptions about the data generation process.

5.2 Methodology

5.2.1 *Simulations*

In this section, we use simulations to investigate how different macro-structures of attitude-based groups are reflected in ResIN networks. While previous simulation studies on ResIN relied on latent variable models to generate synthetic data (Carpentras et al. 2024), we opted to directly simulate correlated response patterns here. This approach has the advantage in that it avoids embedding the inherent limitations of latent-variable models such as symmetry, linearity, and monotonicity into the data-generating process.

We introduce n groups, labelled P_i, where $i\epsilon[1:n]$ is the index identifying each group. Each group, P_i, is also associated with a set of attitudes $A_i = \{a_j\}$, where A_i is the set and a_j are the attitudes. These sets are mutually exclusive, so that each attitude a_j belongs to one and only one of them. Notice that while the terms "group" and "set" can be used synonymously, we will use the first to refer to people and the second to refer to attitudes. Unless stated otherwise, the total number of people N equals 1000, distributed approximately equally among the groups (for example, two groups of 500 respondents each).

A positive association between group membership and attitude sets mathematically mimics in-group members sharing similar attitudes. To implement this, we initially pose that each person selects their attitudes only from their respective in-group set, such that all members in P_i only pick attitudes from A_i. Then, a fraction $r\epsilon(0, 1)$ of these attitudes is replaced with another attitude.

The "mode" parameter of our simulations governs how new attitudes will be selected. We rely on three such modes: "random", "ordinal" and "circular", which we explain in the following. If the simulation mode is set to "random", a new attitude will be randomly selected among all possible sets except the original one. If the simulation is in "ordinal" mode, a new attitude will be selected from a neighboring set, specifically such that the new attitude for a person in group P_i will be either in A_{i-1} or A_{i+1} with equal probability. If A_{i-1} or A_{i+1} do not exist, only the other neighboring set is selected. Finally, the "circular" mode is identical to the ordinal case, except for the fact that the first and the last sets are considered neighbors.

Notice that same values of the r parameter may produce qualitatively different results for different numbers of groups. For instance, for two groups, moving r beyond 0.5 would imply that respondents select out-group attitudes on average more frequently than in-group attitudes. However, in the case of three groups, setting $r = 0.5$ implies that respondents pick from their in-group set at least twice as often as any out-group set. We therefore do not show plots for all possible combinations of r and number of groups. Instead, we rely on the average intra-group correlation, defined as

$$\underline{\rho}_i = \frac{1}{|A_i|} \sum_{j,k \in A_i} \rho_{j,k} \tag{5.1}$$

where $|A_i|$ is the number of attitudes in A_i.

As we seek to also capture the spatial aspects of ResIN in our simulation, we define both set-specific quantities capturing spatial size and spatial distance. In general, we define the distance between any two sets i and l as:

$$d_{i,l} = \sqrt{E\left[\left(p_k - p_j\right)^2\right]} \textit{ for all pairs } j \in A_i \textit{ and } k \in A_l \tag{5.2}$$

where p_l is the spatial position of attitude l. With this formula, we can define the spatial size of a set:

$$s_i = d_{i,i} \tag{5.3}$$

where p_l is the spatial position of attitude l. With this formula, we can define the spatial size of a set:

This definition of "size" stems from the fact that attitude sets tend to form circular clusters in the visualization. Furthermore, leveraging the fact the average distance between two random points within a circle is $\frac{128}{45\pi}R \sim 0.9R$, where R is the radius of the circle (Alagar 1976), we can approximately equate the spatial size to the radius of the set.

Further, we define the normalized distance between sets as:

$$\hat{d}_{i,l} = d_{i,l} - \frac{s_i + s_l}{2} \tag{5.4}$$

The subtracted term ensures that if two sets completely overlap, $\hat{d}$ equals 0. This is because, $d_{i,l}$ approximately equals $\frac{s_i + s_l}{2}$ and not zero in this case.

5.2.2 *Producing ResIN Networks*

Many people possess an intuitive sense of how certain social attitudes tend to align. For example, US citizens, on average, recognize linkages among issues like gun control, gay rights, and welfare provision (e.g., Freeder et al. 2019; Groenendyk et al. 2023). This awareness likely stems from mental representations of belief systems associated with different political groups, making these groups identifiable through just a few core attitudes (Lüders et al. 2024). A similar logic underpins ResIN: if a dataset shows that individuals who support "Attitude A" also frequently support "Attitude B," a connection between these attitudes will emerge in a ResIN network.

For this chapter, we treat each isolated survey response as an attitude (e.g., "vaccines are useful: strongly agree," "vaccines are useful: neutral," etc.). At the data level, these attitudes (i.e., nodes in a ResIN network) are obtained by dummy-coding raw Likert-type items from social surveys. In other words, the first step in applying ResIN is to convert each response option into a separate binary variable, where a value of 1 indicates that a respondent endorsed that option, and 0 indicates that they did not.

Next, we assign link weights by calculating the pairwise correlation between responses.[4] It is important to note that ResIN sets correlation values between responses belonging to the same item to zero as these represent mutually exclusive options (e.g., one cannot select both "strongly agree" and "strongly disagree" to abortion restrictions).

The spatial coordinates are retrieved using a force-directed algorithm (Fruchterman and Reingold 1991). This algorithm—which has been validated in the initial formulation of ResIN (Carpentras et al. 2024) models each node as if it was an electrically charged particle, creating constant, linearly decaying repulsion between all nodes. Conversely, the links, which correspond to the strength of the pairwise correlation, act like springs pulling connected nodes back together. The greater the link weight gets, the stronger the pulling force becomes. Consequently, strongly correlated nodes will cluster more closely together, while less strongly correlated node clusters appear further apart.

Since force-directed algorithms strictly require only positive edge weights, negative correlations need to be removed from the network. One naturally arising concern from this operation is that the simple removal of such edges might result in the loss of important information. However, Carpentras et al. (2024) has shown that when a network is fully connected by only positive edges, setting negative correlation pairs to zero results in no noticeable loss in precision. Nevertheless, as many of the examples we will analyze present isolated groups (i.e. groups which are connected to each other through negative edges), we need to offset all correlations by subtracting the minimum correlation value, to be able to obtain interpretable solutions from the force-directed algorithm. Notice that both procedures (i.e. removing negative correlations and offsetting edges) are used only for the force-directed algorithm and do not impact the remainder of the analysis.

To illustrate how ResIN works, consider the simple scenario in Fig. 5.2, which depicts three groups, each holding a specific set of attitudes (10 per set). When we set the simulation mode to "ordinal," group members are very likely to hold only the attitudes corresponding to their own group. However, they still tend to adopt a few attitudes from the adjacent group. In other words, while members of Group 1 never accept views from Group 3 (and vice versa), both groups partially adopt attitudes from Group 2. This setup simulates two "extreme" groups with a third acting as a mediator. In real-world terms, this situation might mirror political landscapes in which two polarized camps (e.g., Democrats and Republicans) share little overlap but are linked by a moderate group of independents. To illustrate this visually, we color-code the attitudes of each group.

As illustrated in Fig. 5.2, ResIN naturally sorts clusters of co-endorsed attitudes together. In this example, the three groups form three distinct clusters in the network. The ordinal structure is evident as well: members who select attitudes from the middle

---

[4] For binary response, Pearson, Spearman, and Phi correlation coefficients yield identical results; we opted for Pearson correlations in the analysis of this chapter (Ekström 2011).

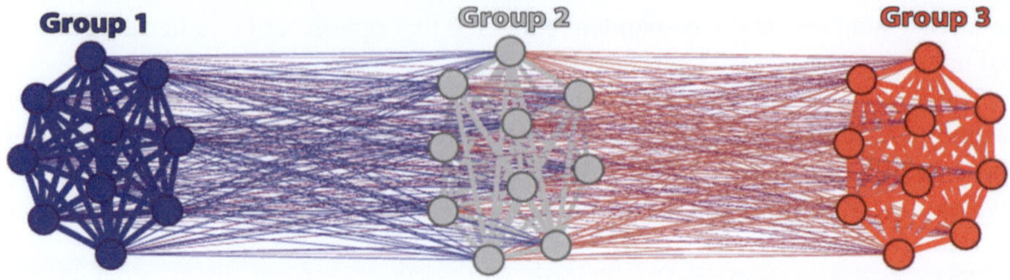

Fig. 5.2 Attitude network of a simulated population presenting 3 attitude clusters. Visualization has been made using Gephi's ForceAtlas 2

group also co-endorse attitudes from the other two, making Set 2 a spatial bridge. Meanwhile, because Sets 1 and 3 are mutually exclusive, they appear farther apart in the ResIN layout.

Notably, many latent variable models could reproduce this kind of result by assuming an ordinal data generation process, naturally leading to a similar, linear, unidimensional arrangement. In contrast, ResIN achieves such an arrangement without any assumptions about the data's underlying source or the form of latent associations. Instead, the network's ordinal structure emerges directly from the ordinal nature of the simulated data.

Although ResIN does not rely on any unconventional measurement strategy (e.g., Kullback-Leibler distance; Kertzer et al. 2019), some readers may be unsure how to interpret correlations between item responses. Conceptually, this correlation measures co-endorsement patterns—i.e., whether individuals who choose response X also tend to choose response Y. A correlation of 1 indicates that everyone who selected X also selected Y; a correlation of -1 means that anyone who selected X did not select Y; and a correlation of 0 shows no association whatsoever between choosing X and choosing Y.

Interestingly, we can also reframe item-response correlations in terms of conditional probability (i.e. the probability that a person selected X given the fact that they have selected Y). To arrive at this formulation, we can leverage the formula for the ϕ correlation for two arbitrary columns x and y (Ekström 2011):

$$\phi_{x,y} = \frac{Nn_{11} - n_{1\blacksquare}n_{\blacksquare 1}}{\sqrt{n_{1\blacksquare}n_{\blacksquare 1}(n - n_{1\blacksquare})(n - n_{\blacksquare 1})}} \tag{5.5}$$

where n_{ab} is the number of entries where the column x equals a and column y equals b (x and y refer to $\phi_{x,y}$ while a and b refer to n_{ab}). Thus n_{10} is the number of people who selected the response coded in column x but did not select the response of column y. The $\blacksquare$ symbol makes the selection independent of the respective column. Thus, $n_{1\blacksquare}$ equals the number of people who selected the response of column x, independent of their response in column y. Finally, N denotes the total number of people in a given sample.

For positive correlations, we can write, $\phi > 0$, substitute ϕ with its value from Eq. (5.5) and eliminate the denominator because it is always positive, thus obtaining:

$$Nn_{11} > n_{1\blacksquare}n_{\blacksquare 1}. \tag{5.6}$$

From here, we can rearrange the terms in order to rewrite the inequality in terms of probabilities as:

$$\frac{n_{11}}{n_{\blacksquare 1}} > \frac{n_{1\blacksquare}}{N} \Rightarrow \frac{P(X \cap Y)}{P(Y)} > P(X) \Rightarrow P(Y) > P(X). \tag{5.7}$$

Following similar steps, we find $P(X) > P(\underline{Y})$ under the same assumptions as before. Here, $\underline{Y}$ represents not selecting the response of column Y. Thus, we can overall state that

$$\phi_{x,y} > 0 \Rightarrow P(Y) > P(X) > P(\underline{Y}). \tag{5.8}$$

Thus, we can overall state that Eq. (5.8) tells us that if we know that X and Y are positively correlated and that a certain person selected attitude Y, it is more likely that this person also selected attitude X. Similarly, if we know that the person did not select attitude Y, it is less probable that they co-selected attitude X. This means that when we observe a cluster of attitudes, we can infer that if a person holds one of the attitudes within the same cluster, they are more likely to also select the other attitudes from that cluster. This is exactly what we would expect from attitude-based groups; if a Democrat holds a *Democratic* attitude, they are also likely to hold other *Democratic* attitudes.[5]

5.3 Simulation Results

5.3.1 Case of Two Groups

In this section, we use simulated data to investigate how different attitude-group structures give rise to particular network properties. This is crucial for understanding how features of attitude-based groups can be inferred from ResIN networks. More specifically, simulations allow us to explore groups with varying properties—such as

[5] Some readers may note that, it one could simply substitute the correlation for conditional probability in ResIN. Indeed, this would obviate the issue of negative edge-weights being unsuitable for force-directed algorithms. However, the problem of using conditional probability is that it is not a symmetric function, that is, PY$\neq$PX unless specific conditions are met. A directed network estimation and plotting strategy could address this problem but it would also increase the complexity of the solution. While such an extension to ResIN could be conceivable, for the scope of this chapter, we will focus on the use of correlation.

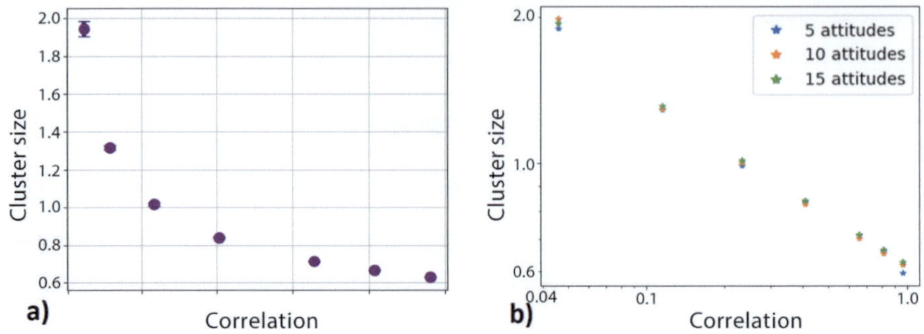

Fig. 5.3 **a** Case of 10 attitudes per set. As the average correlation increases, the cluster size decreases. **b** Same plot in logarithmic scale while also changing the number of attitudes per group. We can notice that the overall size is almost independent on the number of attitudes

different attitudinal coherence—and then observe how those differences are reflected in network characteristics (e.g., in the size or relative density of communities).

The first aspect we examine is how the size of ResIN-generated network clusters relates to the average inter-item correlation $\underline{\rho}_i$. A key challenge in investigating this relationship is that most force-directed algorithms rescale spatial layouts, making it impossible to compare the absolute sizes of networks across simulations. To address this limitation, we implemented a custom, size-preserving force-directed algorithm. Like other force-directed methods, it applies the usual attractive and repulsive forces, but without rescaling the space.[6]

To examine how cluster size relates to $\underline{\rho}_i$, we simulated two groups of 500 respondents, each with 10 attitudes. As shown in Fig. 5.3a, increasing $\underline{\rho}_i$ leads to smaller clusters within the ResIN network. Consequently, if a ResIN network contains a compact cluster, one can reasonably infer that the attitudes within it are strongly correlated.

Figure 5.3a also indicates that this relationship is non-linear: cluster size decreases sharply when the correlation ranges from 0 to 0.4, then levels off for correlations above 0.4. While non-linearity is often considered undesirable, correlations in the social sciences rarely approach 1. In fact, the steep decline between 0 and 0.4 makes it easier to distinguish among various levels of correlation in that range.

Figure 5.3b shows a repeated analysis that varies the number of attitudes per set. Somewhat surprisingly, cluster size remains almost unchanged despite the different numbers of attitudes, suggesting that cluster size primarily depends on average correlation.

To explore how the spatial properties of ResIN are affected by group-level properties, we also explore the normalized distance $\hat{d}_{i,l}$ between attitudes. Figure 5.4a–c present three network visualizations for average correlation values of $\underline{\rho}_i = 1, 0.5$, and 0.025, respectively. As $\underline{\rho}_i$ increases, groups become more compact (as seen before)

[6] We use this custom algorithm solely for the current test; for all other results in this chapter, we rely on off-the-shelf solutions.

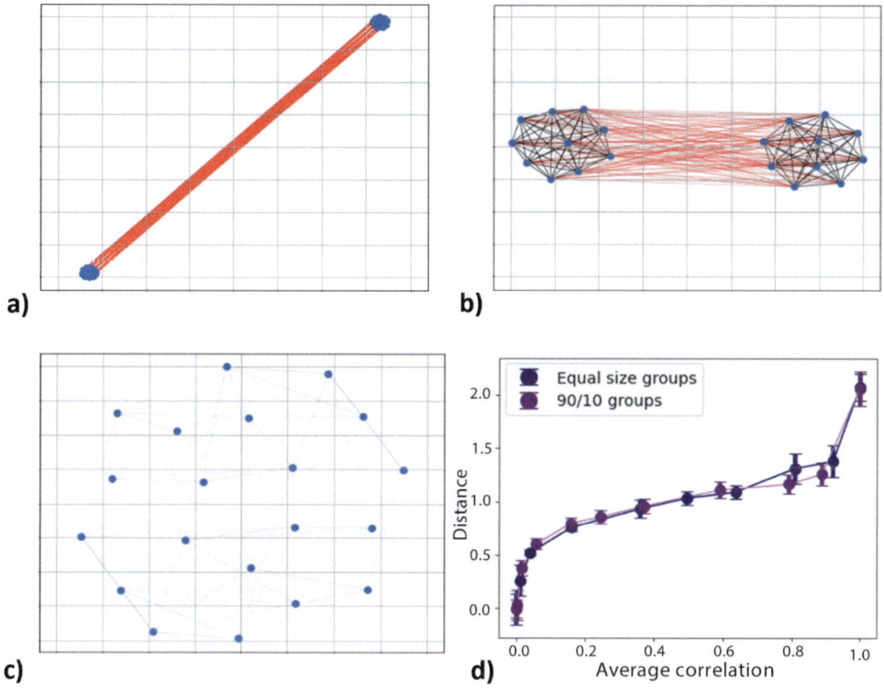

Fig. 5.4 **a–c** Network for average correlation of 1, 0.5, and 0.025, respectively. **d** Distance versus average correlation for equal and unequal group size. Red edges were negative before the offset

and more distant to each other. Figure 5.4d showcases this more effectively where we plotted the normalized distance $\hat{d}_{i,l}$ as a function of the average correlation coefficient. This figure represents the case of two groups of equal size in blue, and the case of one group representing 90% of the population and the other representing only 10%, in violet. Interestingly, the results do not change for uneven groups sizes.

5.3.2 Multiple Groups

Thus far, we have focused on relatively simple cases involving two mutually exclusive groups and corresponding attitude sets. However, some of the more intriguing findings that ResIN can produce arise when multiple groups and multi-level response items are involved. For example, in their vaccination study, Carpentras et al. (2022) used items with four to five response levels, allowing them to distinguish among strongly positive, mildly positive, neutral, mildly negative, and strongly negative attitudes. Similarly, ResIN has revealed notable asymmetries in survey items with more than two response levels, as reported by Lüders et al. (2024). By examining US citizens' belief systems on several hot-button political issues, these authors found that neutral responses were more closely associated with the Republican cluster.

Moreover, the presence of more than two groups allows for the exploration of qualitatively different structures, including ordinality, circularity, and n-ary configurations. A classic example of ordinality is when two political sides (e.g., Democrats and Republicans) are joined by a middle option (e.g., Independents). As illustrated in Fig. 5.2, the middle group would appear between the other two. Naturally, this chain-like layout need not be limited to three groups; for instance, Fig. 5.1 shows five sets ranging from strong trust to strong distrust.

An interesting extension of ordinality is a "circular" structure. Such a layout may emerge if groups at the extreme ends of a political spectrum share enough attitudinal overlap to bring them closer together. As we will see in Sect. 4.2, some empirical cases reveal semi-circular arrangements that can easily be visualized with ResIN.

Finally, by n-ary structures we refer to any arrangement featuring n groups that do not follow a strict ordinal or linear progression. For example, consider the question of which computer operating system is best—Windows, MacOS, or Linux. Because none of these positions serves as an intermediate "middle ground," the resulting network would likely exhibit an n-ary layout.

To simulate the three main structures—ordinal, circular, and n-ary—we rely on the different simulation modes outlined in Sect. 5.2. Besides ResIN, we also analyze each simulated dataset using hierarchical clustering (a common, state-of-the-art clustering method) using the Scipy package for Python (Virtanen et al. 2020). Comparing ResIN with hierarchical clustering will help us highlight which features of the data are uniquely recoverable/visible with ResIN.

In Fig. 5.5a, we present the results of a simulation involving 3 groups with an ordinal attitude structure while Fig. 5.5b summarizes a ternary system. Although these structures can easily be distinguished from one another visually with ResIN, the same is not true for their respective dendrograms (Fig. 5.5e, f) which were obtained using hierarchical clustering.

We carried out a similar analysis for simulations involving five groups. Here, we primarily focus on the differences between a 5-ary system (Fig. 5.5c) and a circular one (Fig. 5.5d). Since these simulations result in isolated groups (i.e. groups which are connected to each other through only negative correlations), we offset the correlations, following the procedure described above and coloring in red edges which were negative before the offset. Furthermore, we opted to plot only such correlational weights that reach a threshold of -0.2, allowing us to more clearly distinguish the 5-ary from the circular structures. Again, the dendrograms do not allow to observe the difference in these structures.

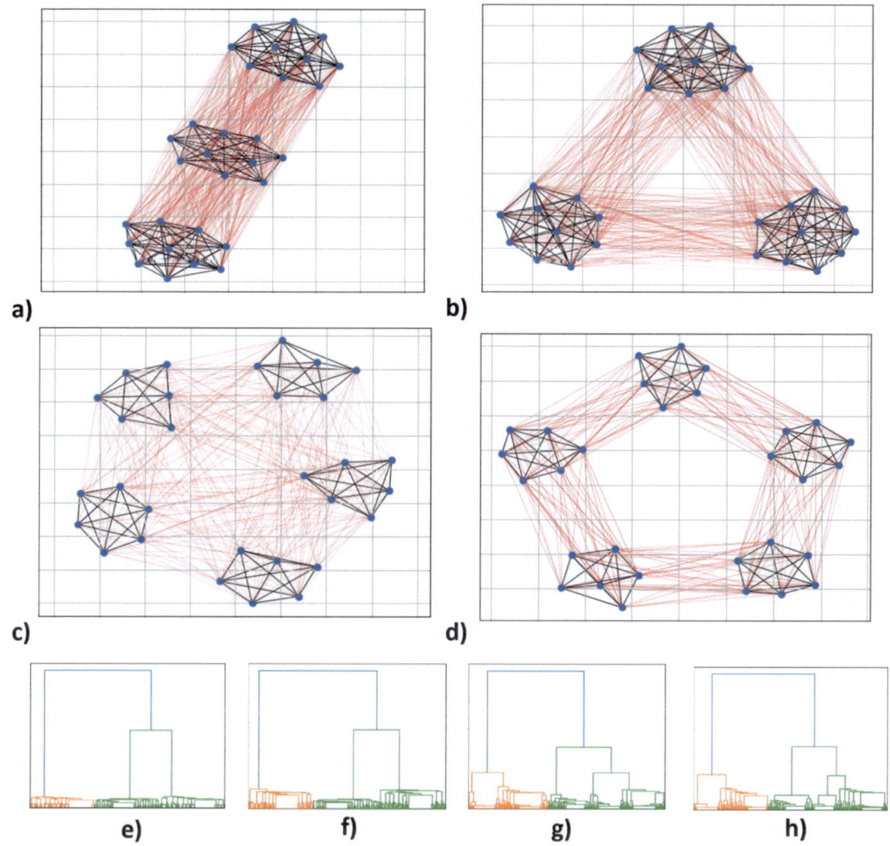

Fig. 5.5 **a** Ordinal system with three groups. **b** Ternary system. **c** 5-ary system. **d** Circular system with 5 groups. **e–h** Dendrograms of the datasets used to generate figures a–d

5.4 Applications to Survey Data

5.4.1 European Social Surveys 2018

In this section, we move from simulations to real-world applications by examining how ResIN can be used to study attitude-based groups using data from the European Social Survey 2018 (ESS 9). Specifically, we explore how several of the attitude structures discussed in the previous simulations can manifest in empirical public opinion data.[7]

[7] We do not suggest that these examples prove ResIN's superiority over more established methods; rather, we aim to showcase its potential for detecting asymmetric and non-linear dynamics within attitude groups—particularly where approaches like factor analysis or BNA might struggle to reveal comparable insights.

Belief systems can vary markedly across different political contexts (e.g., Warncke 2025). In the U.S., two major parties (i.e., Republicans and Democrats) form the primary poles along a conservative–liberal axis, making it reasonable to expect mass belief systems to cluster around these two camps. However, in many European countries, party landscapes are typically more diverse, and political cleavages do not always align neatly with a single ideological dimension (e.g., De Vries and Marks 2012). Under such conditions, mass belief systems likely exhibit more intricate structures.

As a belief-network model, ResIN offers a straightforward method to analyze the structural diversity of attitude systems across countries. Crucially, it does so without assuming any underlying ideological dimensions, allowing it to inductively detect core belief patterns without imposing an a priori ideological framework.

For our analysis, we selected five salient political issues that appear in all 27 countries participating in Wave 9 of the ESS (2018): attitudes toward (1) *immigration* (four response levels), (2) *redistribution* (five response levels), (3) *gay rights* (five response levels), (4) *European unification* (eleven response options, collapsed to five categories), and (5) *environmental protection* (six response levels).

We generated ResIN networks for each ESS-participating country but focus here on three illustrative cases—Slovakia, Spain, and Germany—presented in Fig. 5.6. To identify clusters within each network, we employed a simple Louvain community detection algorithm and color-coded the nodes according to the best-fitting solution (Javed et al. 2018). This method also provided us with thresholded modularity scores, which quantify how distinctly a network is partitioned into separate clusters.[8]

The country examples in Fig. 5.6 illustrate typical network solutions featuring one, two, and three clusters, as indicated by the nodes' visual separation and color coding. We discuss each case by first interpreting the overall network shape and clustering structure, after which we relate these interpretations to their respective socio-political context in order to gauge their plausibility.

The ResIN network generated from the Slovakian data shows only a single cluster. The ResIN network suggest that no single, collectively aligned belief system structures mass attitudes. Although there is some clustering—for instance, the most left-leaning positions on immigration and gay rights cluster together—these same attitudes lie near the most right-leaning positions on redistribution and European unification. Less extreme attitudes are even more mixed, showing no clear pattern. Rather than displaying multiple, internally coherent belief groups, the Slovakian public forms cross-cutting layers across various issues.

This outcome is typical of mass attitudes in post-communist Europe and reflects key features of Slovakia's wider political and societal landscape (Tomczuk 2016). Comparative public opinion studies suggest that under the totalitarian control of media, public assembly, and politics, many people in East-Central Europe disassociated from pluralistic competition for political ideas—a competition that might have

[8] Because the Louvain algorithm always produces at least two clusters, we established a decision criterion to cover scenarios in which a single cluster better represents the underlying community structure. Specifically, we set a modularity threshold of 0.4.

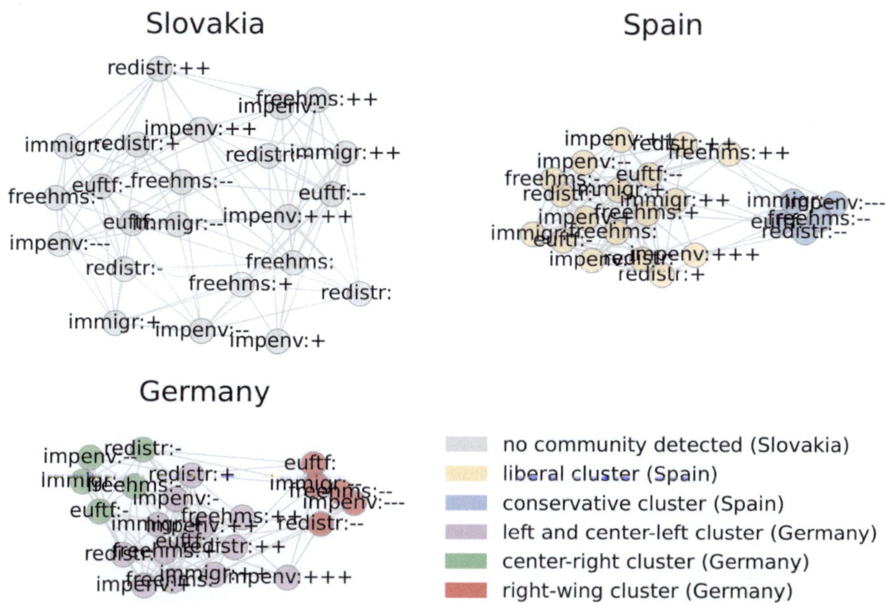

Fig. 5.6 ResIN snapshots for Slovakia, Spain, and Germany using data from Wave 9 of the European Social Surveys (2018). Node color indicates the community this node belongs to. Node communities were detected via Louvain community detection. The resolution parameter was set to 0.6, and the modularity threshold was set to 0.4

existed before Soviet-style communism (Pop-Eleches and Tucker 2017). Furthermore, after only about three decades of partly free political competition following the Iron Curtain's fall, voters may not have had enough time to form strong emotional attachments to parties, a prerequisite for structuring political positions (Converse 1969; Dalton 2018). Another explanation, rooted in historical path dependency, relates to the timing of democratic transitions. Whereas older European democracies often emerged through pressures to represent urban workers and, in some cases, religious or regional minorities—pushing party leaders toward more programmatically distinct electoral platforms—radical social and economic changes under Soviet-style communism in East-Central Europe severed many of these pre-existing ties. As a result, newly formed parties leaned toward personalist, loyalty-based election campaigns, often centered on strongman-type figures, rather than offering predictable, policy-driven alternatives (Howard 2003; Mainwaring and Zoco 2007; Pop-Eleches 2010).

Our second case focuses on Spain, where attitudes are split into two clusters with substantial spatial separation in Fig. 5.6's ResIN solution. The most conservative attitudes across all included issues cluster tightly together, while liberal and conservative positions remain distinctly apart. Notably, the two clusters also differ in size, suggesting an asymmetrical pattern of belief system consistency across the ideological divide. For instance, the second-most conservative attitudes on each issue already belong to the more liberal cluster—similar to patterns observed in Carpentras et al. (2022) and Lüders et al. (2024).

This network structure reflects Spain's historical legacy of left-right conflict, marked by frequent and, at times, violent confrontation. After the liberal revolution of 1820, Spain's early democratic experience led to a highly co-opted, largely non-ideological two-party system. However, rapid industrialization, severe land inequality, and the loss of its remaining colonial possessions at the end of the 19th century fostered the rise of strong, radical left-wing movements. Meanwhile, military, business, and clerical elites on the right organized staunchly against both redistribution and democracy. The Spanish Civil War—sparked partly by the electoral victory of a left-wing coalition—deeply polarized the citizenry, and the subsequent Franco dictatorship further entrenched these divisions. Even after the democratic transition in the early 1980s, remnants of the early 20th-century left-right clash persist in Spanish belief systems (Torcal and Montero 1997), aligning with the patterns observed in Fig. 5.6. Moreover, the asymmetric clustering in the ResIN network mirrors another enduring feature of Spanish electoral politics: while the ideological left tends to have broader popularity, it is also more diverse—made up of socialists, regional autonomists, and pro-environment/alternative lifestyle groups (Shabad and Gunther 1982; Diaz 1998). By contrast, the right remains cohesive and ideologically disciplined, allowing it to capitalize on divisions within left-leaning factions.

The German case, depicted in the third panel of Fig. 5.6, displays three distinct clusters: one comprised exclusively of the most right-wing attitudes, a second encompassing conservative-moderate attitudes, and a third consisting of left-wing and moderate attitudes. The mixed cluster is notably larger than either of the two right-wing communities. The presence of three well-defined clusters suggests that a sizable number of Germans co-endorse three distinct combinations of attitudes, pointing to three underlying attitude groups. Interestingly, the spatial distance between the moderately and the strongly right-wing clusters appears to be about the same as between the center-left and the far-right counterparts. This indicates that the clusters are not simply arranged along a single left-right spectrum, underscoring the need for caution when generalizing left-right divisions across political contexts.

In terms of values and social structure, German society appears more fragmented than polarized, at least in the classic bipolar sense (Groh-Samberg et al. 2023). These various groups may form coalitions around specific political issues, resulting in the three-cluster pattern observed in the ResIN network. This configuration may be partly traced to Germany's reunification, which blended an early democratizer in the West—where intense left-right competition was later tempered by the traumatic legacy of Nazism—with a post-communist, relatively diffuse attitude space in the East, where nostalgia for the old regime and populist strongman politics persisted (similar to Slovakia). As a result, Germany today exhibits both a left-right divide and a more diffuse, populist belief structure. Moreover, the ResIN network reflects another defining aspect of German politics: the far-right populist party AfD remains widely isolated, with even the conservative Christian Democrats (CDU/CSU) refusing formal coalitions. This aligns with Fig. 5.6, where the most conservative cluster is also the most isolated.

5.4.2 American National Election Survey 2020

In this final section, we briefly examine an empirical case from the United States that produces a semi-circular belief system structure. Our data stem from the 2020 wave of the American National Election Studies (ANES; American National Election Studies 2021); we selected 64 political items covering a broad range of both longstanding and pressing issues in American politics such as unemployment benefits, government healthcare provision, international free trade agreements, and the legality of business shutdowns and mask mandates during the COVID-19 pandemic. As shown in Fig. 5.7, positions favoring government intervention on issues like healthcare and unemployment cluster toward the left side of the attitude space, while right-leaning stances converge toward the right hand side of the network.

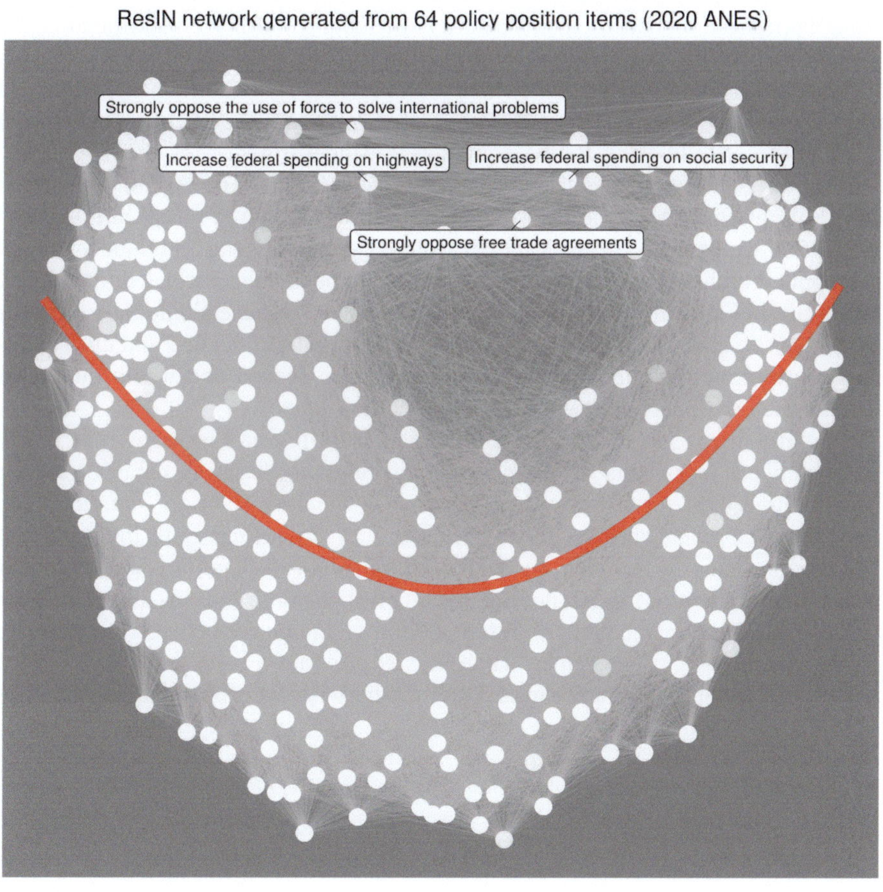

Fig. 5.7 Visualization of political attitudes from the 2020 American National Election Studies (ANES). A LOESS trend-line *(red curve)* highlights the curvature of the network

Interestingly, however, the network does not form a straightforward, unidimensional axis but rather takes on a stretched U-shape. To highlight this feature, we superimposed a LOESS (Locally Estimated Scatterplot Smoothing) trend line on the plot, revealing that attitudes at either ideological end curve the attitude space upward. In fact, many respondents who endorse the most conservative option on some questions also endorse a strongly liberal stance on others, and vice versa. While this does not constitute a fully circular pattern (as discussed in Sect. 5.3), it is similar in that both extremes are more interlinked than one might expect in a highly polarized political environment.

At this point, we would like to stress that ResIN can seamlessly highlight which of these item responses possess the greatest influence on this non-linear distortion of the familiar left-right attitude spectrum; items concerning international politics, such as foreign interventions and free trade deals are predominantly opposed by both respondents on the far left and the far right of the political spectrum. Likewise, we note strong opposition on cuts to social security spending towards the inner bend of the U-shaped trend-line. Surprisingly, both ideological extremes also strongly support the US government to spend more money on building and repairing highways and bridges—perhaps a testament to the poor state of road infrastructure prior to the passing of the 'Build-Back-Better' act under President Biden.

What would an equivalent analysis conducted with more conventional, linear latent variable methods such as principal axis factoring (PAF) reveal in this case? In Fig. 5.8, we present loading patterns from a two-dimensional, obliquely rotated PAF applied to these same items.[9] Both factors are positively correlated ($r = 0.68$), indicating they broadly capture similar aspects underlying the single, left-right (or liberal-conservative) division in American politics. Items in the first and third quadrants reinforce this alignment, whereas those in the second and fourth quadrants increase the dissimilarity between the two ideological axes.

Crucially, the response items that connect the far-left and far-right ends of the ResIN network (e.g., calls to "increase federal funds for highway repairs") appear to undermine the overall left-right coherence in the PAF solution—treating such items as if they were mostly "noise" because they do not neatly fit the dominant liberal-conservative dimension. By contrast, the ResIN visualization suggests a more nuanced interpretation: these items (specifically, response options like "increase spending on highway repairs") represent a point of agreement between respondents at opposing ideological extremes. Thus, ResIN provides a concise explanation for patterns that a traditional factor model might otherwise dismiss as anomalies.

[9] Recall that while ResIN works at the item-response-level, (i.e., "increase federal funds for highway repairs") traditional factor models operate at the item level (i.e., "highway repairs"). This is why Fig. 5.8 features far fewer item locations (dots) than Fig. 5.7.

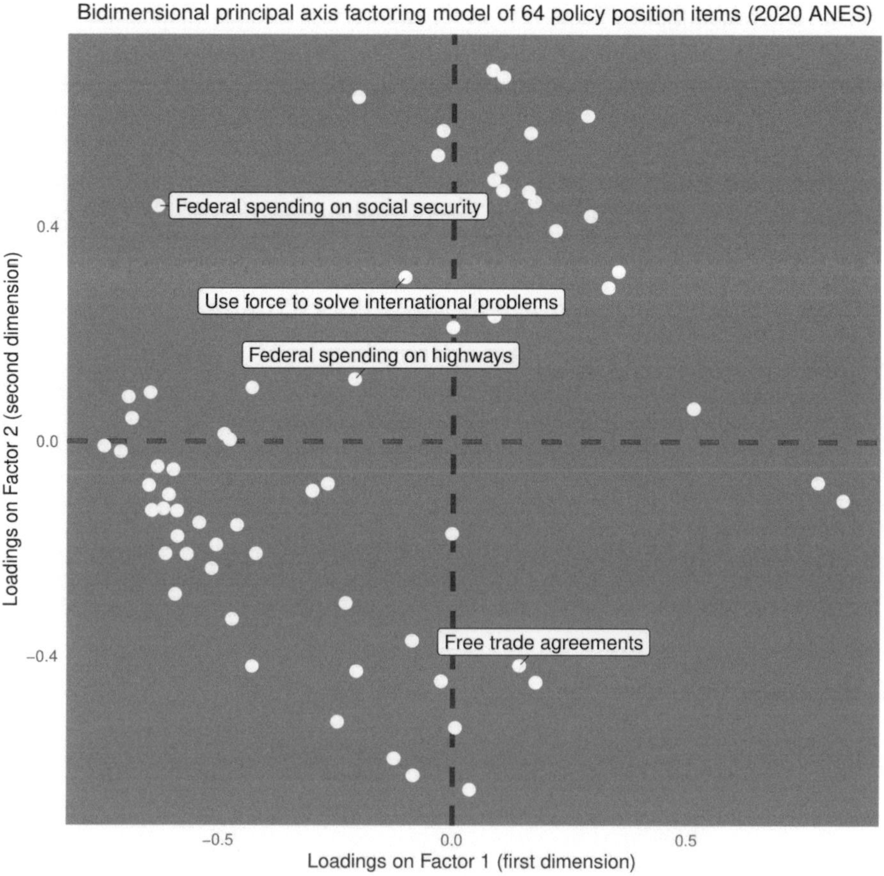

Fig. 5.8 Item factor loadings in two-dimensional, oblique rotation principal axis factoring solution using the same survey items as in Fig. 5.7. The first dimension *(x-axis)* uniquely explains about 21 percent while the second accounts for an additional 15 percent of the total item variance. Both dimensions are correlated at 0.68

5.5 Conclusion

In this chapter, we showcased ResIN—a novel, network-based approach for analyzing belief systems at the item-response level. By organically mapping structural features such as non-linearities and asymmetries, ResIN can visualize, explain, and help address limitations of traditional latent variable methods and Belief Network Analysis (BNA).

Moreover, through simulations and real-world applications, we have demonstrated ResIN's capacity to uncover distinct clusters and spatial relationships within attitude networks. We highlighted how ResIN can reveal the complexity of political belief systems across European countries, and how, in the United States, certain issues draw together ideological extremes, producing a curved, rather than strictly linear, network. These case studies illustrate ResIN's ability to capture the multifaceted nature of belief systems in diverse socio-political contexts.

To date, ResIN has primarily been applied to "classic" survey data, often using Likert-type scales for ease of comparison with other established methodologies. However, the method's flexibility extends to nominal data, non-exclusive response formats, and even unstructured data. Indeed, initial tests suggest ResIN could be applied to Twitter data (SobigData 2021), indicating broad potential beyond standard survey approaches. We hope this methodology will encourage researchers to leverage available and novel attitude data in innovative ways.

Acknowledgements DC is grateful for support from the project "CoCi: Co-Evolving City Life", which was funded by the European Research Council (ERC) under the European Union's Horizon 2020 research and innovation program under grant agreement No. 833168.

This work was funded in part by the European Union. Views and opinions expressed are however those of the author(s) only and do not necessarily reflect those of the European Union or the European Research Council Executive Agency. Neither the European Union nor the granting authority can be held responsible for them.

This work is supported by ERC grant (ID-COMPRESSION, grant number: 101124175)

References

V.S. Alagar, The distribution of the distance between random points. J. Appl. Probab. **13**(3), 558–566 (1976). https://doi.org/10.2307/3212475

American National Election Studies (ANES), *ANES 2020 Time Series Study Full Release (July 19, 2021 version)* (ANES, 2021). https://www.electionstudies.org

S. Ansolabehere, J. Rodden, J.M. Snyder, The strength of issues: Using multiple measures to gauge preference stability, ideological constraint, and issue voting. Am. Polit. Sci. Rev. **102**(2), 215–232 (2008). https://doi.org/10.1017/s0003055408080210

A. Boutyline, S. Vaisey, Belief network analysis: a relational approach to understanding the structure of attitudes. Am. J. Sociol. **122**(5), 1371–1447 (2017). https://doi.org/10.1086/691274

M.J. Brandt, W.W. Sleegers, Evaluating belief system networks as a theory of political belief system dynamics. Pers. Soc. Psychol. Rev. **25**(2), 159–185 (2021). https://doi.org/10.1177/1088868321993751

M.J. Brandt, C.G. Sibley, D. Osborne, What is central to political belief system networks? Pers. Soc. Psychol. Bull. **45**(9), 1352–1364 (2019). https://doi.org/10.1177/0146167218824354

N. Breznau, E.M. Rinke, A. Wuttke, H.H. Nguyen, M. Adem, J. Adriaans, J. Van Assche et al., Observing many researchers using the same data and hypothesis reveals a hidden universe of uncertainty. Proc. Natl. Acad. Sci. **119**(44), Article e2203150119 (2022). https://doi.org/10.1073/pnas.2203150119

D. Carpentras, A. Lüders, M. Quayle, Mapping the global attitude space to explain anti-vaccine attraction. Sci. Rep. **12**(1), 6188 (2022). https://doi.org/10.1038/s41598-022-10069-3

D. Carpentras, M. Quayle, Propagation of measurement error in attitude dynamics models: the case of the Deffuant model. Physica A **606**, 127993 (2022). https://doi.org/10.1016/j.physa.2022.127993

D. Carpentras, We urgently need a culture of multi-operationalization in psychological research. Commun. Psychol. **2**(1), 32 (2024). https://doi.org/10.1038/s44271-024-00084-7

D. Carpentras, A. Lüders, M. Quayle, Response Item Network (ResIN): a network-based approach to explore attitude systems. Human. Soc. Sci. Commun. **11**(1), 1–14 (2024). https://doi.org/10.1057/s41599-024-03037-x
D. Carpentras, P. Warncke, The hidden problem in Big Data: even infinite information does not guarantee consistent measurement. Soc. Regist. **8**(4), 7–30 (2024). https://doi.org/10.3929/ethz-b-000720100
P.E. Converse, Of time and partisan stability. Comp. Polit. Stud. **2**(2), 139–171 (1969)
N.S. da Rocha, E. Chachamovich, M.P. de Almeida Fleck, A. Tennant, An introduction to Rasch analysis for psychiatric practice and research. J. Psychiatr. Res. **47**(2), 141–148 (2013). https://doi.org/10.1016/j.jpsychires.2012.09.014
S. Daenekindt, W. De Koster, J. Van der Waal, How people organise cultural attitudes: Cultural belief systems and the populist radical right. West Eur. Polit. **40**(4), 791–811 (2017). https://doi.org/10.1080/01402382.2016.1271970
J.B. Duck-Mayr, J. Montgomery, Ends against the middle: scaling votes when ideological opposites behave the same for antithetical reasons (2019). http://jbduckmayr.com/papers/ggum.pdf
C.E. De Vries, G. Marks, The struggle over dimensionality: a note on theory and empirics. Eur. Union Polit. **13**(2), 185–193 (2012). https://doi.org/10.1177/1465116511435712
D. DellaPosta, Pluralistic collapse: The "oil spill" model of mass attitude polarization. Am. Sociol. Rev. **85**(3), 507–536 (2021). https://doi.org/10.1177/0003122420922989
E. Díaz, Ideologies in the making of the Spanish transition. West Eur. Polit. **21**(4), 26–39 (1998). https://doi.org/10.1080/01402389808425269
R.J. Dalton, *Citizen politics: public opinion and political parties in advanced industrial democracies* (Cq Press, 2018)
C. Ellis, J.A. Stimson, *Ideology in America* (Cambridge University Press, 2012)
Ekström, J., *The phi-coefficient, the tetrachoric correlation coefficient, and the Pearson-Yule debate [Working paper]* (UCLA Department of Statistics, 2011). https://escholarship.org/uc/item/7qp4604r
N. Fishman, N.T. Davis, Change we can believe in: Structural and content dynamics within belief networks. Am. J. Polit. Sci. **66**(3), 648–663 (2022). https://doi.org/10.1111/ajps.12626
S. Freeder, G.S. Lenz, S. Turney, The importance of knowing "what goes with what": Reinterpreting the evidence on policy attitude stability. J. Polit. **81**(1), 274–290 (2019). https://doi.org/10.1111/ajps.12626
S. Feldman, C. Johnston, Understanding the determinants of political ideology: implications of structural complexity. Polit. Psychol. **35**(3), 337–358 (2014)
T.M. Fruchterman, E.M. Reingold, Graph drawing by force-directed placement. Softw.: Pract. Exp. **21**(11), 1129–1164 (1991)
C.J. Gaskin, B. Happell, On exploratory factor analysis: a review of recent evidence, an assessment of current practice, and recommendations for future use. Int. J. Nurs. Stud. **51**(3), 511–521 (2014). https://doi.org/10.1016/j.ijnurstu.2013.10.005
E. Groenendyk, E.O. Kimbrough, M. Pickup, How norms shape the nature of belief systems in mass publics. Am. J. Polit. Sci. **67**(3), 623–638 (2023). https://doi.org/10.1111/ajps
O. Groh-Samberg, T. Schröder, A. Speer, Social milieus and social integration. From theoretical considerations to an empirical model. KZfSS Kölner Zeitschrift für Soziologie und Sozialpsychologie **75**(Suppl 1), 305–329 (2023)
M.M. Howard, *The Weakness of Civil Society in Post-Communist Europe* (Cambridge University Press, 2003)
M.A. Javed, M.S. Younis, S. Latif, J. Qadir, A. Baig, Community detection in networks: a multidisciplinary review. J. Netw. Comput. Appl. **108**, 87–111 (2018). https://doi.org/10.1016/j.jnca.2018.02.011
J.D. Kertzer, K.E. Powers, A. Mintz, L. Terris, Foreign policy attitudes as networks, in *The Oxford Handbook of Behavioral Political Science* (2019). https://doi.org/10.1093/oxfordhb/9780190634131.013.27

A. Lüders, D. Carpentras, M. Quayle, Attitude networks as intergroup realities: using network-modelling to research attitude-identity relationships in polarized political contexts. Br. J. Soc. Psychol. **63**(1), 37–51 (2024). https://doi.org/10.1111/bjso.12665

S. Mainwaring, E. Zoco, Political sequences and the stabilization of interparty competition: electoral volatility in old and new democracies. Party Politics **13**(2), 155–178 (2007). https://doi.org/10.1177/1354068807073852

G. Pop-Eleches, J.A. Tucker, *Communism's Shadow: Historical Legacies and Contemporary Political Attitudes* (Princeton University Press, 2017), vol. 3. https://doi.org/10.23943/princeton/9780691175591.001.0001

G. Pop-Eleches, Throwing out the bums: protest voting and unorthodox parties after communism. World Politics **62**(2), 221–260 (2010). https://doi.org/10.1017/s0043887110000043

M. Quayle, Social identity networks: people holding attitudes are a collective social identity information system and bipartite networks are a useful way to represent them. Eur. Rev. Soc. Psychol. 1–66 (2025)

J.S. Roberts, J.R. Donoghue, J.E. Laughlin, A general item response theory model for unfolding unidimensional polytomous responses. Appl. Psychol. Meas. **24**(1), 3–32 (2000). https://doi.org/10.1177/01466216000241001

A.M. Scheel, Why most psychological research findings are not even wrong. Infant Child Dev. **31**(1), Article e2295 (2022). https://doi.org/10.1002/icd.2295

M. Schweinsberg, M. Feldman, N. Staub, O.R. van den Akker, R.C.M. van Aert, M.A.L.M. van Assen, Y. Liu, T. Althoff, J. Heer, A. Kale, Z. Mohamed, H. Amireh, V. Venkatesh Prasad, A. Bernstein, E. Robinson, K. Snellman, S. Amy Sommer, S.M.G. Otner, D. Robinson, E. Luis Uhlmann, et al., Same data, different conclusions: radical dispersion in empirical results when independent analysts operationalize and test the same hypothesis. Organ. Behav. Hum. Decis. Process. **165**, 228–249 (2021). https://doi.org/10.1016/j.obhdp.2021.02.003

G. Shabad, R. Gunther, Language, nationalism, and political conflict in Spain. Comp. Polit. **14**(4), 443–477 (1982). https://doi.org/10.2307/421632

SobigData, *Bridging Networks with Linear Spaces to Study Attitudes and Political Polarization* (2021). http://www.sobigdata.eu/blog/bridging-networks-linear-spaces-study-attitudes-and-political-polarization

S. Treier, D.S. Hillygus, The nature of political ideology in the contemporary electorate. Public Attitude Quarterly **73**(4), 679–703 (2009). https://doi.org/10.1093/poq/nfp067

S.J. Tomczuk, Contention, consensus, and memories of communism: comparing Czech and Slovak memory politics in public spaces, 1993–2012. Int. J. Comp. Sociol. **57**(3), 105–126 (2016). https://doi.org/10.1177/0020715216658187

M. Torcal, J.R. Montero, *Party Change and Cleavage Formation: The Effects of Value Change on the Spanish Party System [Working Paper No. 132]* (Institut de Ciències Polítiques i Socials, 1997). https://ddd.uab.cat/record/44731

J. Uher, Psychometrics is not measurement: unraveling a fundamental misconception in quantitative psychology and the complex network of its underlying fallacies. J. Theor. Philos. Psychol. **41**(1), 58–84 (2021). https://doi.org/10.1037/teo0000176

P. Virtanen, R. Gommers, T.E. Oliphant, M. Haberland, T. Reddy, D. Cournapeau, P. Van Mulbregt, et al., SciPy 1.0: fundamental algorithms for scientific computing in Python. Nat. Methods **17**(3), 261–272 (2020). https://doi.org/10.1038/s41592-019-0686-2

P. Warncke, What explains country-level differences in political belief system coherence? Polit. Behav. (2025). https://doi.org/10.1007/s11109-025-10015-9

Part II
Text-Based Methods

Chapter 6
Political Elites and Polarization: Understanding Political Discourse in the European Parliament During Turbulent Times

Hilke Brockmann, Wiebke Drews, Pedro Fierro, Joris Frese, and Daniel Triana

Abstract In liberal democracies, both experts and laypeople are observing an increase in polarized public discussions. The rise of social networks and various crises are linked to this political fragmentation. What role do political elites play in this? Our study examines European elite politicians at the start of the Russia-Ukraine war. Using a dataset from Twitter/X and an unsupervised, pre-trained, transformer-based topic model, we analyze the discourse of all members of the European Parliament (MEP) and the European Commission. Our findings show that the attention of political elites to the conflict is immediate and brief. Sentiment analysis confirms the polarized nature of discussions related to the crisis. Notably, male politicians and those on the ideological extremes tend to express more negative sentiments than females and politicians of the political center. Additionally, a crisis event like the outbreak of the Russian-Ukrainian war tends to deepen this emotional divide. Our research adds to existing literature on polarized narratives by focusing on polarization dynamics driven by diverse political elites.

Hilke Brockmann, Wiebke Drews, Pedro Fierro, Joris Frese and Daniel Triana authors contributed equally and are listed in alphabetical order.

H. Brockmann (✉)
Constructor University, Bremen, Germany
e-mail: hbrockmann@constructor.university

W. Drews
University of the Bundeswehr Munich, Munich, Germany

P. Fierro
University Adolfo Ibanez, Santiago, Chile

J. Frese
European University Institute, Florence, Italy

D. Triana
National Autonomous University of Mexico, Mexico City, Mexico

M. A. Keijzer et al. (eds.), *Computational Social Science of Social Cohesion and Polarization*, Computational Social Sciences,
https://doi.org/10.1007/978-3-032-01373-6_6

Keywords MEPs · Russia-Ukraine war · Twitter · X · BERTopic · VADER · Machine learning

6.1 Introduction

Democratic institutions are coming under attack worldwide. The Economist reports a decrease of 5% in the Democracy Index in Europe and 12% in North America since 2006 (Economist Intelligence Unit 2023). Growing polarization is one of the reasons why democratic compromise is at risk, some experts say (Haggard and Kaufman 2021; Kingzette et al. 2021). However, polarization is not a new phenomenon. The Oxford English Dictionary dates the political connotation of the term back to 1862 (OED 2023; Schedler 2023). Different definitions circulate in the literature. Most recent papers refer to clusters of growing ideological and affective distance between social groups or parties, but do not specify clear boundaries (Schedler 2023). Thus, some empirical studies show a recent rise in polarization (Finkel et al. 2020), while others do not (Kreiss and McGregor 2023; Mau et al. 2023).

At the same time, the large supply and demand for polarization research is often linked to the rise of populism (Guriev and Papaioannou 2022), and to the simultaneous spread of social media (Brady et al. 2021; Harris et al. 2023). Digital platforms provide a perfect breeding ground for new and divergent political deliberations (Lorenz-Spreen et al. 2022). They allow responses in real-time, at no cost, and without geographical or social boundaries. Moreover, recommender algorithms tend to automatically connect like-minded individuals (Cinelli et al. 2021). These features make social media valuable communication tools even for established politicians. Since politicians are now more active on social media than ever, and since social media seems prone to polarized debates (Allcott et al. 2020), we are interested in whether political elites contribute to polarized political discussions.

Specifically, we aim to analyze how politicians respond to external shocks and whether these shocks can lead elite-level political communication to become more negative and polarized.

On social media, we follow an entire political elite during the outbreak of the Russia-Ukraine war. In times of acute crisis, we expect certain politicians to engage in new and polarized discourses to mobilize support for their political positions. We anticipate polarization to manifest as increasingly negative sentiments and widening sentiment gaps between opposing political camps.

Our findings shed light on the dynamics of polarization. They also may help us better assess whether, during times of polycrisis (Tooze 2022)—when people lack orientation because there is no single cause and simple fix—political polarization is a more likely response from elite politicians than political restraint.

The organization of the paper is as follows: First, we review the literature on polarization, social media, and political elites. Then, we explain our methodological approach. Our analysis is based on more than half a million tweets from all members of the European Parliament and the European Commission during the four months before and after the outbreak of the Russia-Ukraine war on February 24, 2022. We use machine learning methods—namely Transformer models and sentiment analysis—to identify topics and sentiments during the peak of the crisis. We present our results and conclude.

6.2 Literature Review

Political polarization, the growing ideological and emotional distancing between social groups (Phillips et al. 2023), is neither a new phenomenon nor a steady state. The concept encompasses both processes and outcomes (Arora et al. 2022). Its demand in scientific and public discussions is significant and growing however, a clear definition and consistent measurement are lacking (Kubin and Von Sikorski 2021). Still, there is a common understanding that political polarization refers to inter-group dynamics like social segregation and sorting, creates in-group identity and solidarity, and out-group differentiation or even demonization, and takes place in uncompromising, hardened political deliberations, which poses a threat to democracy (Haggard and Kaufman 2021; Wilson et al. 2020). Often unforeseen events trigger polarization processes (Macy et al. 2021; Mainych et al. 2023; Svozil et al. 2025; Weber et al. 2024; Westwood and Peterson 2022).

6.2.1 External Shocks and Crises

Politics is frequently driven by external shocks and crises. These extraordinary events offer elite politicians an opportunity to raise their profile. For example, during the COVID-19 pandemic polarization among U.S. Congress members grew stronger along the ideological lines of the two main political parties. Each party adopted different communication strategies that reflected and reinforced existing ideological divisions (Green et al. 2020). Similarly, economic recessions, which can be seen as a type of external shock, may lead to increased polarization as they frequently spark debates over government responsibility in their prevention, creation, and mitigation, as well as related market regulation and social welfare policies. These debates can deepen pre-existing ideological divisions (Funke et al. 2016; Macy et al. 2021).

However, shocks and crises not only exacerbate divisions among social groups, but they also serve as unifying forces that (temporarily) narrow social gaps by fostering a sense of group identity (Levendusky 2018). When a society or specific community faces wars, natural disasters, terrorist attacks, or global pandemics, the initial response can often trigger a mobilization effect, briefly reducing polarization as individuals and groups rally against a common threat. Events like the Russian invasion of Ukraine have been studied for their influence on cohesion or division among political elites. For instance, Chueri and Törnberg (2024) examined its influence on the European Parliament's unity through Twitter network analysis. While the crisis initially seemed to enhance communication and unity among members, this effect was temporary and did not lead to lasting cohesion. Despite increased focus on the war and a surge in European solidarity, pre-existing political and geographical divisions within the European Parliament persisted, and Eurosceptic groups remained isolated. The study concludes that the invasion did not produce enduring unification among European political elites, leaving existing fractures intact (Chueri and Törnberg 2024).

In our study, we examine the Russian invasion of Ukraine on February 24, 2022, as an pivotal turning point in European politics, focusing on how various politicians discuss the war and related issues before and after the large-scale invasion. First, we expect that European politicians will immediately shift their focus to the Russia-Ukraine war (H1: Attention Hypothesis).

6.2.2 Political Polarization and Social Media

Whether social media is a decisive factor in the rise of polarization is controversial (Graham and Svolik 2020; Lorenz-Spreen et al. 2022; Sunstein 2018; Zhuravskaya et al. 2020), as the interplay between social media and polarization turns out to be complex. Extensive research (Bail et al. 2018; Bakshy et al. 2015) investigated if and how exposure to ideologically diverse content on platforms like X/Twitter and Facebook affects the political views of users. Most findings prove that exposure to social media will reinforce existing beliefs rather than promote understanding. This narrowing within one camp is further supported by the algorithms that govern content distribution on these platforms and amplify partisan content (Banks et al. 2021). The role of platform design and user interaction is also critical to drive groups apart. Research shows that social feedback mechanisms reinforce expressions of moral outrage and polarization (Brady et al. 2021; Harris et al. 2023).

Beyond ideological dividing lines, emotions shape the polarization of political discourse and opinions (Webster and Albertson 2022). Affective polarization is connected to partisanship and elicits positive feelings towards the in-party but, more importantly, negative emotions towards the out-party. Particularly in situations of political threat, negative emotions prevail (Druckman et al. 2020; Iyengar et al. 2019).

Anger, resentment, and dissatisfaction ignite political movements for social change, regardless of the politician's gender (Traister 2018). Mechkova and Wilson (2021) demonstrate that women who make use of an angry rhetoric on social media are more likely to win a vote than more reserved female candidates. But women who challenge gender stereotypes also attract more hate comments. Overall, women show more emotions than men, with female politicians expressing more positive emotions while male politicians show more negative affect (Brescoll and Uhlmann 2008; Renner and Masch 2019).

Content that expresses animosity towards out-groups has been found to drive engagement on social media platforms (Rathje et al. 2021), indicating that the nature of the content itself, as well as the interactions it fosters, can contribute to polarization. This points to a potentially concerning aspect of social media: their tendency to reward content that fuels division and conflict, which can have real-world consequences for subjective well-being, social cohesion, democratic discourse, and political voting behavior (Allcott et al. 2020; Guriev and Papaioannou 2022).

In line with this research on polarization, we hypothesize that any political communication about the conflict will exhibit significantly more negative feelings than communication about other issues (H2a: Feeling Hypothesis). Men's conflict-related communication should be significantly more negative than that of women, as research has shown that women face harsher backlash when expressing negative emotions (H2b: Gendered Sentiment Hypothesis). In addition, ideologically extreme politicians are likely to express more negative emotions than moderate politicians because social media algorithms tend to amplify more engaging communication, and a marginalized political position requires fewer compromises in that regard (H2c: Ideological Sentiment Hypothesis). Lastly, we assume that politicians geographically close to Ukraine express more negative emotions than those representing countries further away, as negative emotions better emphasize the greater threat of the situation (H2d: Geographical Sentiment Hypothesis).

6.2.3 Political Elites

Elite polarization, particularly as it manifests within social media, has become a major topic of academic interest and social concern (Levin et al. 2021). Political divisions are wider, and extremist views are more common among elites than among ordinary voters (Macy et al. 2021). Theoretical perspectives often draw on the concept of echo chambers and filter bubbles (Pariser 2011; Sunstein 2001), where algorithmic curation strengthens existing beliefs and reduces exposure to opposing perspectives (Cinelli et al. 2021). This self-reinforcing cycle is thought to exacerbate ideological divides, as elites engage in performative polarization to galvanize their base, often at the expense of cross-ideological dialogue (Tucker et al. 2018). Furthermore, the architecture of social media platforms, which prioritizes engagement metrics such as likes, shares, and comments, may incentivize elites to adopt more radical positions to attract viewers (Bakshy et al. 2015). Therefore, we expect the emotional distance between ideological groups to grow after the Russian invasion of Ukraine (H3: Polarization Hypothesis).

6.3 Data and Methods

Through the Academic Twitter API,[1] we scraped every tweet posted by members of the European Parliament (MEPs) and the European Commission from October 13, 2021 to July 8, 2022. This period covers nineteen weeks before and after the start of the Russian invasion of Ukraine. In total, our dataset includes 520,871 tweets from over 600 parliamentarians and all commissioners at that time. Both original tweets and retweets are included. In addition to the data from the API, we enrich our dataset with a comprehensive set of demographic and political variables related to these EU politicians, such as their gender, age, country of origin, EU party group affiliation, national party affiliation, and the political position of their party (and their EU party family) on various policy issues (European Parliament 2022; Jolly et al. 2022; Kinkartz et al. 2019).

Since the tweets were originally posted in various languages, we first translated them into English, using the Python package deep-translator 1.1. (Baccouri 2020). The deep-translator 1.1 Python package is a versatile tool for machine translation, designed to facilitate translating texts from various languages into English. It connects to multiple translation services like Google Translate, Microsoft Translator, and others, providing broad language support. This package functions by sending the input text to the selected translation service's API, which then returns the translated version. When manually validating a random sample of translated tweets, the quality of the translations achieves face validity.

For the subsequent thematic and sentiment analyses, it was essential to preprocess the tweets: firstly, tweets were decoded from HTML and stripped of specific tags and URLs. The preprocessing also included normalizing quotation marks, unicode characters, and handling non-ASCII characters and whitespace. Additionally, Twitter handles, emails, and accents were removed, while dashes and special characters were replaced. The text was further converted to lowercase, with the removal of numbers and special characters, focusing solely on alphabetic characters. This meticulous cleaning ensured that the tweets were in a consistent and analyzable format.

In our thematic analysis, BERTopic is employed to extract latent topics from texts (Grootendorst 2022, p. 1). It starts by creating document embeddings, which are numerical representations that capture the semantic meaning of texts, using the all-mpnet-base-v2 sentence-transformers model.[2] This model tends to capture a wider range of semantic information and is often chosen for tasks that require a deep understanding of sentence context and structure. It is well-suited for processing short texts like tweets, because it is trained on over 1.17 billion sentences from various sources, including Reddit, WikiAnswers, and the S2ORC. After generating embeddings, BERTopic employs HDBSCAN, a clustering algorithm, to group similar embeddings and identify related topics. It then applies a class-based TF-IDF method to

[1] Data collection took place in mid-2022, i.e., before Elon Musk's takeover and the subsequent disablement of Twitter's Academic API.

[2] The sentence transformers model can be found here: ttps://huggingface.co/sentence-transformers/all-mpnet-base-v2.

select and emphasize key words for each topic cluster, helping to clarify the thematic content of each cluster. This structured approach allows for accurate extraction and interpretation of topics from our dataset, especially useful for short and informal texts such as tweets.

In our thematic analysis using BERTopic, we set the min_cluster_size parameter to 500 in the HDBSCAN clustering algorithm. This choice is crucial because it determines the minimum number of tweets required for a cluster to be considered a distinct topic. Choosing 500 as the minimum cluster size strikes a strategic balance. On the one hand, it ensures that each identified topic is supported by enough data, providing statistical significance and reliability. On the other hand, it prevents topics from fragmenting into too many small, potentially overlapping subtopics, which could complicate interpretation and dilute the thematic focus. This threshold is especially suitable for large datasets like ours, consisting of tweets, where it is important to identify substantial and coherent thematic clusters without missing meaningful patterns due to overly strict clustering criteria. A list of the top 20 topics classified by BERTopic is provided in Table 6.1.

To identify demarcated and polarized tweets, we classify emotional intensities in conversations. For this, we use the VADER (Valence Aware Dictionary for Sentiment Reasoning) lexicon (Hutto and Gilbert 2014). NLTK's VADER is a tool commonly

Table 6.1 Topics MEPs and the EU Commission tweeted about in 2021/22

Topics	Label	N (tweets)
1	Russia-Ukraine	55,991
2	Covid-19	35,847
3	France	30,125
4	Economy and finance	25,586
5	EP	19,639
6	Agriculture	18,662
7	Women's rights	17,610
8	Elections	16,304
9	Energy and resources	11,066
10	Immigration	10,940
11	Adjectives	9225
12	Gratitude	9142
13	Climate change	9079
14	Spain	8993
15	Digitization	8390
16	Italy	7484
17	Energy prices	7427
18	Poland	5963
19	MEP delegations	5505
20	Rule of law and executives	5147

used in NLP, designed to analyze sentiments in text. It is particularly effective at handling social media text, where sentiments are often expressed informally. VADER uses a combination of a sentiment lexicon and rules to assess the emotional tone of a text segment. It provides a compound score calculated by summing the valence scores of each word in the lexicon, adjusting them based on rules, and normalizing the results between -1 (most extreme negative) and $+1$ (most extreme positive). One advantage of VADER over other sentiment analyzers like Lexicoder is its ability to incorporate nuances like sarcasm and context into the sentiment output.

6.4 Results

In the following subsections, we first show the distribution of topics over time and the prevalence of the Russia-Ukraine topic across different groups, including gender, party affiliation, and ideology (measured by the GALTAN scale). Then, we highlight divergences and polarization in expressed sentiments before and after the Russian invasion of Ukraine, and again across various groups, including gender, party affiliation, and political ideology.

6.5 BERTopic Model

The BERTopic analysis of the dataset yielded a total of 65 distinct topics. Within these, we identified and merged five closely related topics into one comprehensive theme centered around Russia-Ukraine. This combined topic covers a wide range of issues: general Russia-Ukraine communication, discussions about Russian energy supplies during the conflict, insights into Ukraine's EU and NATO accession status, attention to Ukrainian refugees, and specific discourse on the German-Ukraine relationship.

This amalgamation resulted in a significant topic cluster, accounting for a total of 55,991 tweets related to the Russia-Ukraine topic over the entire observation period. Consequently, the Russia-Ukraine topic is the second most frequently discussed topic in the dataset, surpassed only by a more general topic that expresses gratitude or announces events (for example, the most frequent terms in this topic are 'thank', 'today', and 'right'). Figure 6.1 visualizes the frequency of tweets addressing the ten most common topics over time, including the Russia-Ukraine topic. In the legend (termed 'global topic representation'), the most frequent words for each topic are displayed. The figure reveals notable patterns in the data. There was an abrupt surge in the volume of Russia-Ukraine-related tweets following the Russian invasion on February 24, 2022, which aligns with our attention hypothesis. In fact, attention toward this topic was already increasing in the weeks before the invasion, likely due to build-up and anticipation effects. However, the intensity of this communication rapidly declined in March. This pattern suggests that while an exogenous shock,

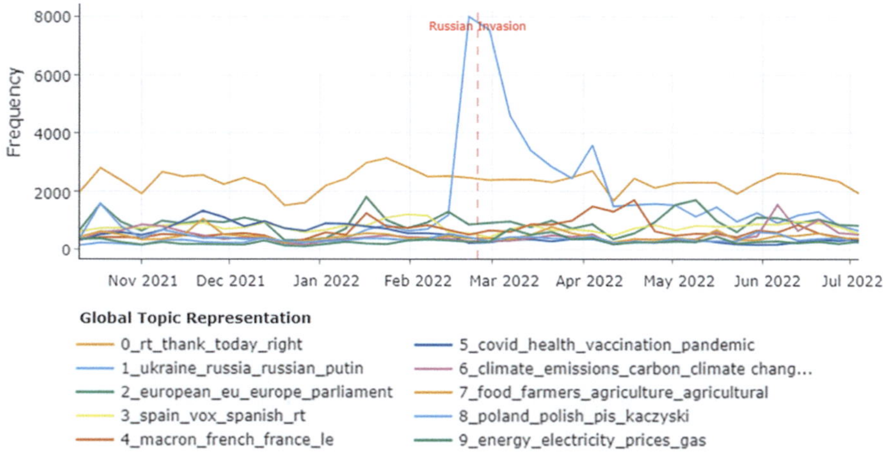

Fig. 6.1 Ten most frequent topics over time

such as the invasion, can trigger bursts of communication, interest among MEPs and Commissioners in the topic appears to wane shortly afterward. This observation might reflect the dynamic nature of political communication on social media, where initial reactions to major events are often intense but can quickly give way to other emerging issues.

To identify which EU politicians are most actively contributing to discussions about the war in Ukraine, we first visualize the percentage of Russia-Ukraine tweets out of all tweets from politicians in each EU country. As shown in the right panel of Fig. 6.2, where dark colors represent low percentages and light colors indicate high percentages, politicians from Eastern European countries discuss the Ukraine war in a much larger share of their tweets than those from Western Europe. For example, Polish politicians discuss the war in over 20% of their tweets, while Estonians do so in over 40%. In contrast, Spanish or French politicians mention it in less than 15% of their tweets. Since the total number of tweets varies significantly between countries, we also visualize the share of all war-related tweets for each country relative to the total across all countries, to better illustrate who dominates the discourse. In the left panel of Fig. 6.2, we see that Polish politicians contribute the largest share of war-related tweets compared to all other EU countries, with German politicians posting the second highest number. These findings suggest that geographical proximity greatly increases interest in the conflict.

After the invasion on February 24, the proportion of Russia-Ukraine related tweets increased across various groups, including gender, party affiliation, and ideology of EU politicans, as shown in Figs. 6.3, 6.4, and 6.5. However, some differences are noticeable: men discuss the topic significantly more than women (although it is debatable whether this difference is also substantially meaningful: roughly 18% of post-war male tweets are Russia-Ukraine related compared to about 16% of post-war female tweets). Furthermore, after the invasion, moderate politicians talk about the

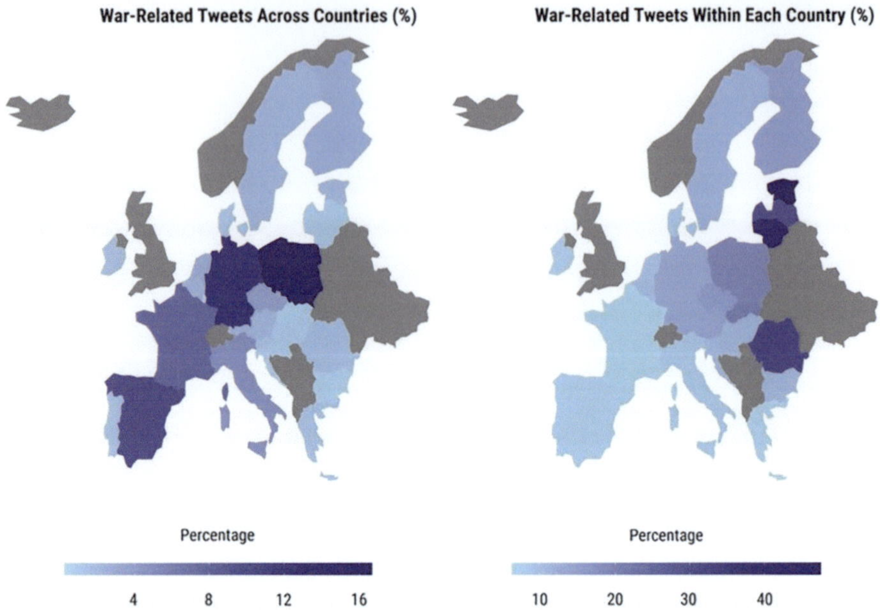

Fig. 6.2 Percentage of Russia-Ukraine related tweets across (left) and within (right) countries

topic significantly more than those at the extreme ends of the political spectrum (i.e., far-left or far-right parties and those with very high or very low GALTAN scores). For instance, members of the far-left GUE-NGL (The Left in the European Parliament) and the far-right ID (Identity and Democracy) mention Ukraine in roughly 9% and 10% of their tweets, respectively, while members of the liberal RE (Renew Europe) and the social democratic SD (Progressive Alliance of Socialists and Democrats) discuss Ukraine in over 20% and 15% of their post-invasion tweets, respectively.

6.6 Vader Sentiment Analysis

To assess the average sentiment in each of the 520,871 tweets, we use the VADER sentiment analyzer, as described above. In Fig. 6.6, we visualize the average daily sentiment of all tweets related to Ukraine and all tweets unrelated to Ukraine (as determined by the BERTopic model). Two observations are apparent: (1) the average sentiment in Ukraine-related tweets is consistently more negative than that in unrelated tweets. While Ukraine-related tweets are generally neutral or negative, unrelated tweets tend to be positive. This aligns with the sentiment hypothesis. (2) The divergence in sentiments between the two topics increases considerably after the Russian invasion of Ukraine. While the 95% confidence intervals for daily sentiments overlap

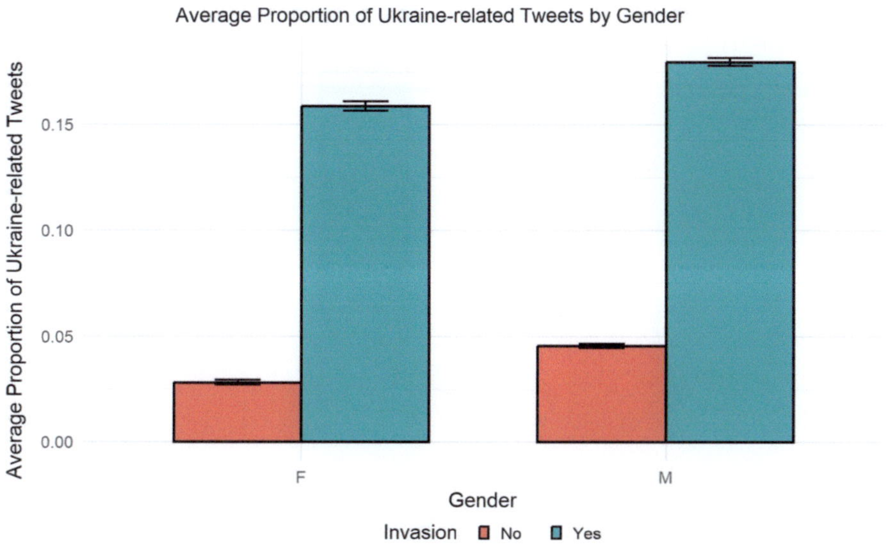

Fig. 6.3 Average proportion of Russia-Ukraine tweets before and after the invasion, split by gender. *Note* that the error bars represent 95% confidence intervals

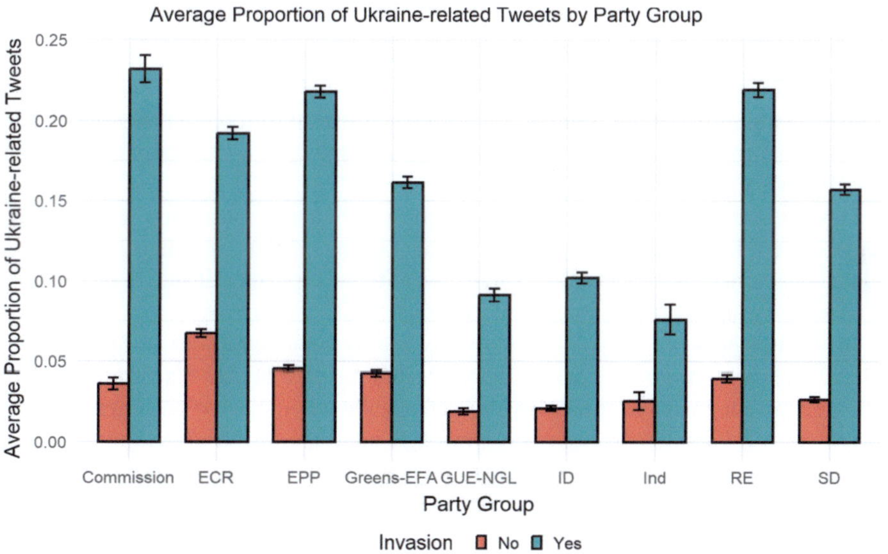

Fig. 6.4 Average proportion of Russia-Ukraine tweets before and after the invasion, split by party group. *Note* that the error bars represent 95% confidence intervals

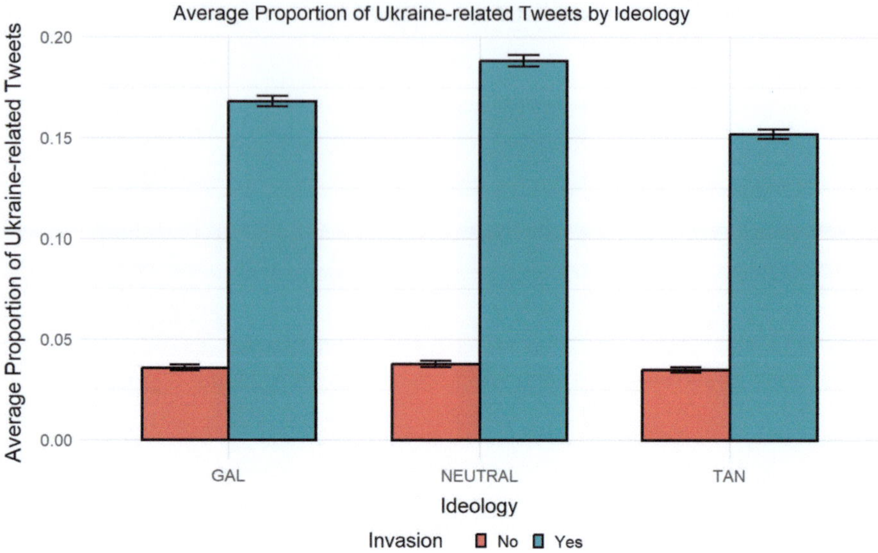

Fig. 6.5 Average proportion of Russia-Ukraine tweets before and after the invasion, split by GALTAN ideology. *Note* that the error bars represent 95% confidence intervals

to a large extent before the invasion, this is not the case for several months afterwards. Although the difference in sentiments between the two topics mainly was not statistically significant beforehand, it became significant following the invasion and remained so for a long period before gradually converging again roughly 100 days after February 24.

Having established that the Ukraine topic is discussed with significantly more negative sentiment than other topics, we next compare the sentiment of Ukraine-related tweets across the same strata analyzed with the topic model above: nationality, gender, party affiliation, and political ideology of EU politicians.

In the left panel of Fig. 6.7, we display the average sentiment of all Ukraine-related tweets within each country. Light colors indicate negative sentiments, dark colors represent positive sentiments. Apart from a few outliers, the sentiment in these tweets is overwhelmingly negative. However, contrary to the geographical sentiment hypothesis, it is not consistently more negative in countries closer to Ukraine. While some Eastern European countries are very negative (e.g., Estonia, Lithuania, or Poland), others are more positive (e.g., Latvia and Romania). Some Western European countries (e.g., the Netherlands and Germany) and some Southern European countries (e.g., Spain and Italy) are also very negative. The right panel of Fig. 6.7 shows the change in sentiment following the Russian invasion: for most countries, the political communication of their politicians shows a further increase in negative sentiments, with Scandinavian and Baltic countries experiencing particularly drastic

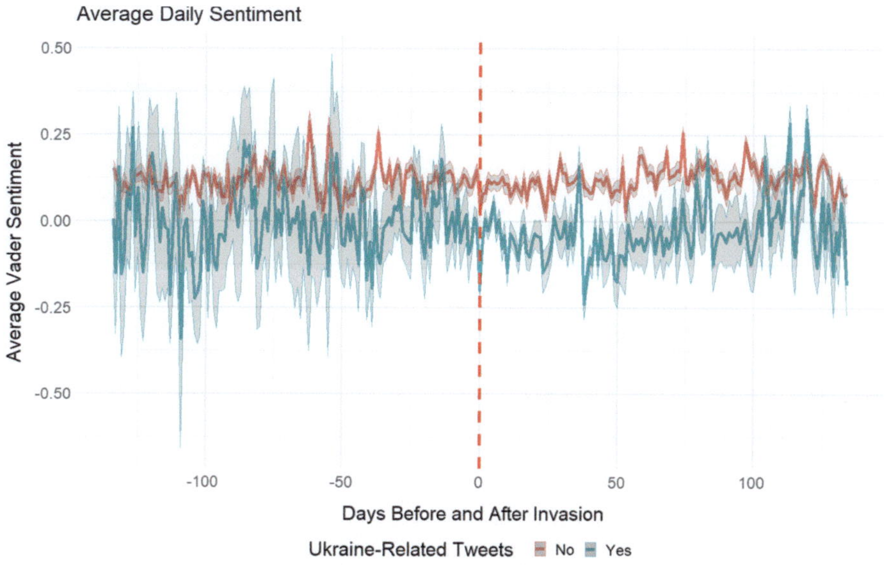

Fig. 6.6 Daily sentiment in Russia-Ukraine and non-related tweets. *Note* that the grey shades represent 95% confidence intervals

shifts in sentiment in the negative direction. Romanian politicians, who had previously held the most positive sentiments, also became significantly more negative after February 2022.

Further disaggregating the data, heterogeneity between sociopolitical groups becomes evident. In Fig. 6.8, we depict the average sentiment in Russia-Ukraine related tweets before and after the invasion, divided by gender. Male politicians are already somewhat more negative in their political communication than the female politicians prior to the invasion. After the invasion, the sentiment becomes significantly more negative for both genders, and it is significantly more negative for men than women. These findings confirm both the gendered sentiment hypothesis and the gendered polarization hypothesis.

Examining party affiliation in Fig. 6.9, the far-left GUE-NGL and the far-right ID are the most negative in their communication about Russia-Ukraine topics, while the more moderate RE and SD are more neutral, thus supporting the ideological sentiment hypothesis. Tweets from members of the EU Commission are significantly more positive than those from any parliamentary group. Across all parties and institutions, sentiment becomes more negative following the invasion, but, contrary to the ideological polarization hypothesis, this increase in negativity is not systematically stronger for ideologically extreme parties.

Finally, analyzing the political ideology of tweeting politicians (measured here by the GALTAN scale) in Fig. 6.10, the patterns of heterogeneity indicated by party affiliation remain salient. Politicians at both extremes of the political spectrum (i.e.,

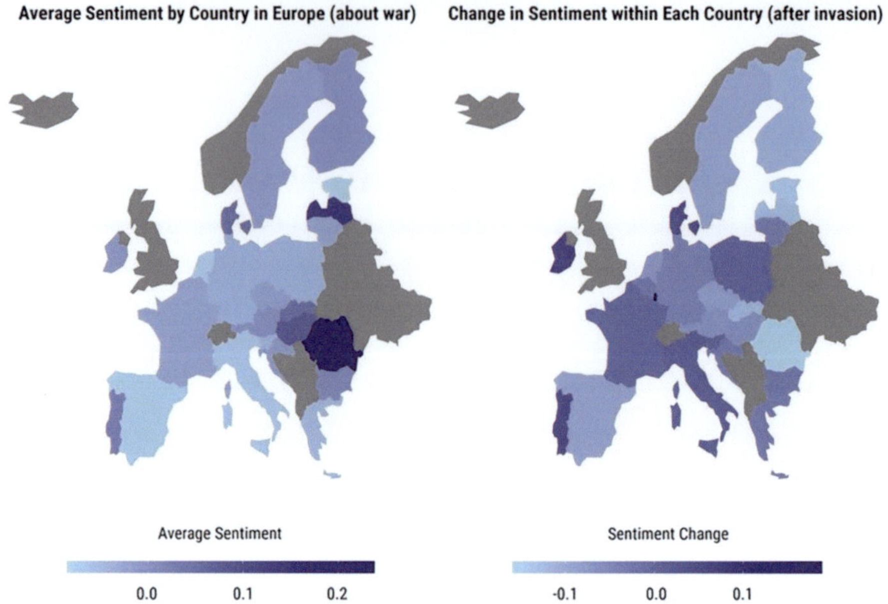

Fig. 6.7 Sentiment of all Russia-Ukraine related tweets (left) and sentiment-change after the invasion (right)

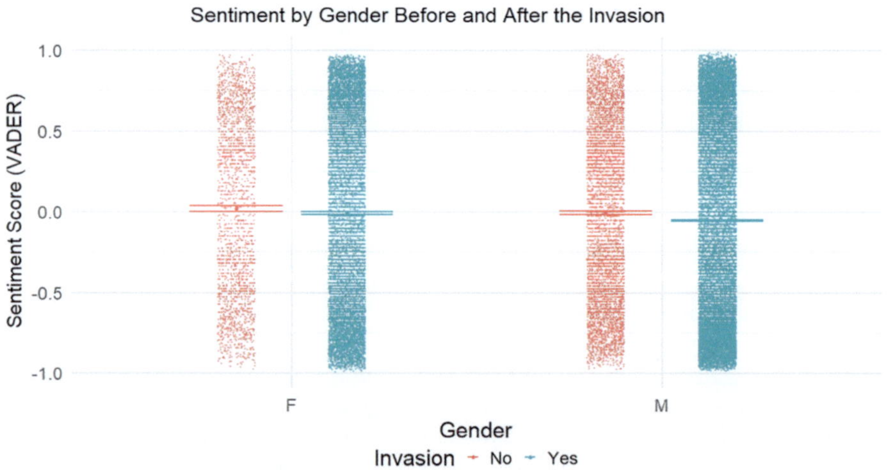

Fig. 6.8 Average sentiment in Russia-Ukraine tweets before and after the invasion, split by gender. *Note* that the error bars represent 95% confidence intervals

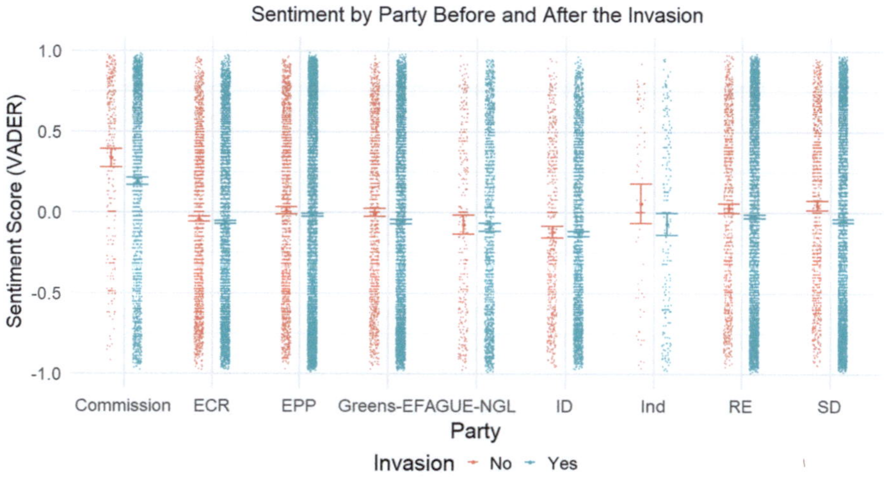

Fig. 6.9 Average sentiment in Russia-Ukraine tweets before and after the invasion, split by party affiliation. *Note* that the error bars represent 95% confidence intervals

those who are extremely green/alternative/liberal and those who are extremely traditional/authoritarian/nationalist) are more negative than moderate politicians, again supporting the ideological sentiment hypothesis.

Furthermore, unlike with party families, the gap in sentiment between ideologically extreme and moderate politicians on the GALTAN scale widens further after the invasion, supporting to the ideological polarization hypothesis.

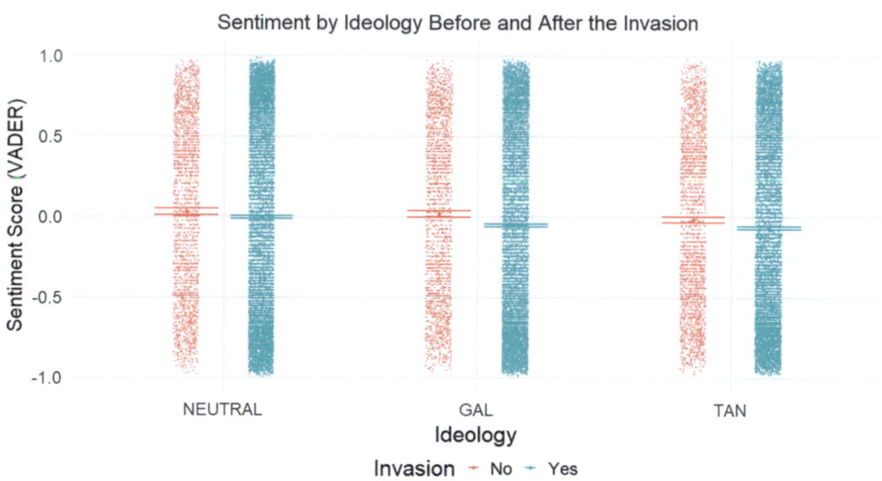

Fig. 6.10 Average sentiment in Russia-Ukraine tweets before and after the invasion, split by GALTAN ideology. *Note* that the error bars represent 95% confidence intervals

We also summarize our findings in Table 6.2, where we present the results from regression analyses (with standard errors clustered at the politician level). We show that (in line with H1) tweets after the invasion were 13 percentage points more likely to discuss the Russia-Ukraine topic ($p < 0.001$***), that (in line with H2a) tweets on the Russia-Ukraine topic are significantly more negative than others ($p < 0.001$***), that (in line with H2b) men tweeting about the war are significantly more negative than women ($p < 0.05$*), and that (in line with H2c) ideologically extreme (GAL or TAN) politicians are more negative than moderate politicians ($p < 0.05$* for both comparisons). The interaction coefficients for increasing sentiment divides between male/female and extreme/moderate politicians after the invasion are also (in line with H3) in the expected direction, but not statistically significant at the 5% level.

In sum, the sentiment and heterogeneity analyses reveal two trends: (1) communication about Russia-Ukraine topics became significantly more negative following the Russian invasion, much more so than communication about other topics, even though it started from a more negative baseline. (2) Those at the extreme ends of the political spectrum and men, who were already more negative than moderates

Table 6.2 Regression analyses for H1-H3

	Russia-Ukraine Topic (H1)	Sentiment (H2a)	Sentiment (H2b)	Sentiment (H2c)	Sentiment (H3)	Sentiment (H3)
(Intercept)	0.04*** (0.00)	0.12*** (0.01)	– 0.00 (0.01)	0.00 (0.02)	0.02 (0.02)	0.03 (0.02)
After Invasion	0.13*** (0.01)				– 0.03 (0.02)	– 0.03 (0.02)
Russia-Ukraine Topic		– 0.15*** (0.01)				
Male			– 0.04* (0.02)		– 0.03 (0.02)	
GAL				– 0.04* (0.02)		– 0.01 (0.01)
TAN				– 0.06** (0.02)		– 0.05 (0.03)
Male * After					−0.02 (0.02)	
GAL * After						−0.04 (0.03)
TAN * After						−0.02 (0.02)
Num. obs	512666	512666	55991	49298	55991	49298
R^2	0.05	0.01	0.00	0.00	0.00	0.00
Adj. R^2	0.05	0.01	0.00	0.00	0.00	0.00

***$p < 0.001$; **$p < 0.01$; *$p < 0.05$

Note Standard errors are clustered at the politician level

and women, began to grow more negative after the invasion, further widening the gap between moderate and radical politicians. These findings indicate an increase in polarization in political communication due to the Russian invasion of Ukraine.

However, when combining insights from the topic models with those from sentiment analyses, we see that those who are more moderate in their discussion of the Russia-Ukraine war (i.e., members of centrist parties and those with neutral GALTAN scores) tend to talk about the topic more on average. This shows that the more polarizing voices in the debate are not necessarily the dominant ones, except for the men. They are more negative in their Russia-Ukraine political communication before the invasion, discuss the topic more often than women, and become even more negative to a greater degree than women after the invasion.

6.7 Discussion and Conclusion

Do catastrophic events lead to polarization on social media? And do political elites exploit these sudden crises to boost their visability? To answer these questions, we analyzed the reactions of MEPs and EU Commissioners on Twitter/X to the Russian invasion of Ukraine on February 24, 2022. We compiled and machine-translated an original dataset of all MEPs and Commissioner tweets between October 13, 2021, and July 8, 2022 (Total N = 520.871), and enriched this data with a comprehensive set of individual-level covariates covering various political and sociodemographic groups.

Our hypotheses regarding attention-grabbing political communication during crises, sentiments expressed on social media, and the impact of a crisis on polarization among different social and political groups inform our design. For the attention hypothesis, we analyzed a BERTopic model to map the frequency of topics over time. The sentiment and polarization hypotheses were tested with the VADER sentiment analyzer, which we used to compare different sentiments between topics, within topics over time, and within topics across sociopolitical strata.

We found, consistent with our expectations and similar to others (Mainych et al. 2023), that politicians immediately concentrated their attention on the war in most Twitter posts, making this conflict the central issue of Spring 2022. In the weeks following the invasion (and even in the days before it), no other topic received nearly as much attention as the war in Ukraine.

Sentiment in conflict-related communication was consistently more negative than in other topics, and this difference in sentiment grew following the full-scale invasion. As hypothesized, male and ideologically extreme politicians expressed significantly more negative emotions than female and moderate politicians. However, contrary to our expectations, politicians from countries geographically closer to Ukraine were not systematically more negative than those from more distant countries. Spatial borders are becoming less meaningful for European politicians given the scope of Russia's military attack.

Polarization grew as the pre-war gap in sentiments widened between more negative men and extreme politicians on one side, and more positive women and moderate politicians on the other after the Russian invasion.

Since our findings are based on a single case, their scope is limited. Future research should expand the database to include different events, various politician samples, and multiple social media platforms, ideally combining observational and (quasi-) experimental methods to establish causality and external validity.

Still, our results provide compelling empirical evidence that European political elites are emotionally triggered by external shocks like the Russia-Ukraine war. They utilize negative emotions especially at the end of the ideological spectrum, thereby activating extreme views and contributing to polarization on social networks. While emotions directly influence behavior, we also show that they do not last long. After 100 days of war, politicians have mostly returned to normal. Thus, political polarization is a volatile and malleable phenomenon (Axelrod et al. 2021; Macy et al. 2021). However, in times of poly-crises (Tooze 2022), constantly new events may sustain the exceptional emotional state.

References

H. Allcott, L. Braghieri, S. Eichmeyer, M. Gentzkow, The welfare effects of social media. Amer. Econ. Rev. **110**(3), 629–676 (2020). https://doi.org/10.1257/aer.20190658

S.D. Arora, G.P. Singh, A. Chakraborty, M. Maity, Polarization and social media: a systematic review and research agenda. Technol. Forecast. Soc. Change **183,** 121942 (2022). https://doi.org/10.1016/j.techfore.2022.121942

R. Axelrod, J.J. Daymude, S. Forrest, Preventing extreme polarization of political attitudes. Proc. Natl. Acad. Sci. **118**(50), e2102139118 (2021). https://doi.org/10.1073/pnas.2102139118

N. Baccouri, Deep translator: a flexible free and unlimited python tool to translate between different languages in a simple way using multiple translators [Requires Python >=3.7, <4.0] (2020) Retrieved 29 Sep 2025, from https://pypi.org/project/deep-translator/

C.A. Bail, L.P. Argyle, T.W. Brown, J.P. Bumpus, H. Chen, M.B.F. Hunzaker, J. Lee, M. Mann, F. Merhout, A. Volfovsky, Exposure to opposing views on social media can increase political polarization. Proc. Natl. Acad. Sci. **115**(37), 9216–9221 (2018). https://doi.org/10.1073/pnas.1804840115

E. Bakshy, S. Messing, L.A. Adamic, Exposure to ideologically diverse news and opinion on Facebook. Science **348**(6239), 1130–1132 (2015). https://doi.org/10.1126/science.aaa1160

A. Banks, E. Calvo, D. Karol, S. Telhami, #PolarizedFeeds: three experiments on polarization, framing, and social media. The Int. J. Press/politics **26**(3), 609–634 (2021). https://doi.org/10.1177/1940161220940964

W.J. Brady, K. McLoughlin, T.N. Doan, M.J. Crocket, How social learning amplifies moral outrage expression in online social networks. Sci. Ad. **7**(33), eabe5641 (2021). https://doi.org/10.1126/sciadv.abe5641

V.L. Brescoll, E.L. Uhlmann, Can an angry woman get ahead?: Status conferral, gender, and expression of emotion in the workplace. Psychol. Sci. **19**(3), 268–275 (2008). https://doi.org/10.1111/j.1467-9280.2008.02079.x

J. Chueri, P. Törnberg, Did Russia's invasion of Ukraine unite Europe? cohesion and divisions of the European parliament on twitter. Political Res. Exchange **6**(1), 2299121 (2024). https://doi.org/10.1080/2474736X.2023.2299121

M. Cinelli, G. De Francisci Morales, A. Galeazzi, W. Quattrociocchi, M. Starnini, The echo chamber effect on social media. Proc. Natl. Acad. Sci. **118**(9), e2023301118 (2021). https://doi.org/10.1073/pnas.2023301118

J.N. Druckman, S. Klar, Y. Krupnikov, M. Levendusky, J.B. Ryan, Affective polarization, local contexts and public opinion in America. Nat. Hum. Behav. **5**(1), 28–38 (2020). https://doi.org/10.1038/s41562-020-01012-5

Economist Intelligence Unit, Economist intelligence unit (2023), economist intelligence unit (2021) via gapminder—processed by our world in data. "Democracy" (2023). (Last Accessed 12 Feb 2022)

European Parliament, *Members of the European Parliament* (2022). Retrieved 1 July 2022, from https://www.europarl.europa.eu/meps/en/home

E.J. Finkel, C.A. Bail, M. Cikara, P.H. Ditto, S. Iyengar, S. Klar, L. Mason, M.C. McGrath, B. Nyhan, D.G. Rand, L.J. Skitka, J.A. Tucker, J.J. Van Bavel, C.S. Wang, J.N. Druckman, Political sectarianism in America. Science **370**(6516), 533–536 (2020). https://doi.org/10.1126/science.abe1715

M. Funke, M. Schularick, C. Trebesch, Going to extremes: politics after financial crises, 1870–2014. Eur. Econ. Rev. **88**, 227–260 (2016). https://doi.org/10.1016/j.euroecorev.2016.03.006

M.H. Graham, M.W. Svolik, Democracy in America? partisanship, polarization, and the robustness of support for democracy in the United States. Amer. Polit. Sci. Rev. **114**(2), 392–409 (2020). https://doi.org/10.1017/S0003055420000052

J. Green, J. Edgerton, D. Naftel, K. Shoub, S.J. Cranmer, Elusive consensus: polarization in elite communication on the covid-19 pandemic. Sci. Adv. **6**(28), eabc2717 (2020). https://doi.org/10.1126/sciadv.abc2717

M. Grootendorst, BERTopic: neural topic modeling with a class-based TF-IDF procedure [Publisher: arXiv Version Number: 1] (2022). https://doi.org/10.48550/ARXIV.2203.05794

S. Guriev, E. Papaioannou, The political economy of populism. J. Econ. Literat. **60**(3), 753–832 (2022). https://doi.org/10.1257/jel.20201595

S. Haggard, R. Kaufman, *Backsliding: Democratic Regress in the Contemporary World*, 1st edn. (Cambridge University Press, 2021). https://doi.org/10.1017/9781108957809

E. Harris, S. Rathje, C.E. Robertson, J.J.V. Bavel, The role of media in political polarization| the SPIR framework of social media and polarization: exploring the role of selection, platform design, incentives, and real-world context. Int. J. Commun. **17**(0), 20 (2023). Retrieved 31 Aug 2023, from https://ijoc.org/index.php/ijoc/article/view/19014

C. Hutto, E. Gilbert, VADER: a parsimonious rule-based model for sentiment analysis of social media text. in *Proceedings of the International AAAI Conference on Web and Social Media*, vol. 8(1) (2014), pp. 216–225. https://doi.org/10.1609/icwsm.v8i1.14550

S. Iyengar, Y. Lelkes, M. Levendusky, N. Malhotra, S.J. Westwood, The origins and consequences of affective polarization in the united states. Annu. Rev. Polit. Sci. **22**(1), 129–146 (2019). https://doi.org/10.1146/annurev-polisci-051117-073034

S. Jolly, R. Bakker, L. Hooghe, G. Marks, J. Polk, J. Rovny, M. Steenbergen, M. A. Vachudova, Chapel hill expert survey trend file, 1999–2019. Electoral Stud. **75,** 102420 (2022). Retrieved 1 Oct 2025, from https://doi.org/10.1016/j.electstud.2021

J. Kingzette, J.N. Druckman, S. Klar, Y. Krupnikov, M. Levendusky, J.B. Ryan, How affective polarization undermines support for democratic norms. Public Opin. Q. **85**(2), 663–677 (2021). https://doi.org/10.1093/poq/nfab029

S. Kinkartz, I. Manteufel, T. Wills, G.-C. Grün, J. Järviniemi, Age and gender balance of the 2019 incoming European parliament (2019). DW 2 July 2019. https://github.com/dw-data/mep-sociodemographics?tab=readme-ov-file

D. Kreiss, S.C. McGregor, A review and provocation: on polarization and platforms. New Media & Soc. **26**(1), 556–579 (2024). https://doi.org/10.1177/14614448231161880

E. Kubin, C. Von Sikorski, The role of (social) media in political polarization: a systematic review. Ann. Int. Commun. Assoc. **45**(3), 188–206 (2021). https://doi.org/10.1080/23808985.2021.1976070

M.S. Levendusky, Americans, not partisans: Can priming American national identity reduce affective polarization? The J. Politics **80**(1), 59–70 (2018). https://doi.org/10.1086/693987
S.A. Levin, H.V. Milner, C. Perrings, The dynamics of political polarization. Proc. Natl. Acad. Sci. **118**(50), e2116950118 (2021). https://doi.org/10.1073/pnas.2116950118
P. Lorenz-Spreen, L. Oswald, S. Lewandowsky, R. Hertwig, A systematic review of worldwide causal and correlational evidence on digital media and democracy. Nat. Hum. Behav. **7**(1), 74–101 (2022). https://doi.org/10.1038/s41562-022-01460-1
M.W. Macy, M. Ma, D.R. Tabin, J. Gao, B.K. Szymanski, Polarization and tipping points. Proc. Natl. Acad. Sci. **118**(50), e2102144118 (2021). https://doi.org/10.1073/pnas.2102144118
S. Mainych, A. Bulhakova, V. Vysotksa, *Cluster Analysis of Discussions Change Dynamics on Twitter About War in Ukraine.* Colins (2) 2023. CEUR Workshop proceedings, vol. 3396, paper 39 (2023). https://ceur-ws.org/Vol-3396/paper39.pdf
S. Mau, T. Lux, L. Westheuser, *Triggerpunkte. Konsens und Konflikt in der Gegenwartsgesellschaft.* (Suhrkamp, 2023)
V. Mechkova, S.L. Wilson, Norms and rage: gender and social media in the 2018 U.S. mid-term elections. Electoral Stud. **69**, 102268 (2021). https://doi.org/10.1016/j.electstud.2020.102268
OED, Oxford English dictionary (2023). Retrieved 15 Feb 2024, from https://www.oed.com/dictionary/polarization_n?tab=meaning_and_use&show-all-quotations=true#41606736
E. Pariser, *The Filter Bubble: What the Internet is Hiding From You.* (Penguin UK, 2011)
S.C. Phillips, J. Uyheng, K.M. Carley, A high-dimensional approach to measuring online polarization. J. Computat. Soc. Sci. **6**(2), 1147–1178 (2023). https://doi.org/10.1007/s42001-023-00227-6
S. Rathje, J.J. Van Bavel, S. Van der Linden, Out-group animosity drives engagement on social media. Proc. Natl. Acad. Sci. **118**(26), e2024292118 (2021). https://doi.org/10.1073/pnas.2024292118
A.-M. Renner, L. Masch, Emotional woman—Rational man? gender stereotypical emotional expressivity of German politicians in news broadcasts. Communications **44**(1), 81–103 (2019). https://doi.org/10.1515/commun-2017-0048
A. Schedler, Rethinking political polarization. Political Sci. Quarter. **138**(3), 335–359 (2023). https://doi.org/10.1093/psquar/qqad038
C.R. Sunstein, *Hashtag republic* (Princeton University Press, 2001)
C.R. Sunstein, *#Republic: Divided Democracy in the Age of Social Media.* (Princeton University Press, 2018). https://doi.org/10.1515/9781400890521
M. Svozil, A. Gronow, P. Ocelík, Climate polarization on czech social media after trump's announcement to withdraw the US from the Paris agreement. Environ. Commun. **19**(4), 749–765 (2025). https://doi.org/10.1080/17524032.2025.2456230
A. Tooze, Welcome to the world of polycrisis (2022). Financial Times. Retrieved 15 Feb 2022, from https://www.ft.com/content/498398e7-11b1-494b-9cd3-6d669dc3de33
R. Traister, *Good and Mad: The Revolutionary Power of Women's Anger* (Simon & Schuster, 2018)
J. Tucker, A. Guess, P. Barbera, C. Vaccari, A. Siegel, S. Sanovich, D. Stukal, B. Nyhan, Social media, political polarization, and political disinformation: a review of the scientific literature. (2018, Mar 19). SSRN 3144139. https://doi.org/10.2139/ssrn.3144139
M. Weber, D. Grunow, Y. Chen, S. Eger, Social solidarity with Ukrainian and Syrian refugees in the twitter discourse. A comparison between 2015 and 2022. Europ. Soc. **26**(2), 346–373 (2024). https://doi.org/10.1080/14616696.2023.2275604
S.W. Webster, B. Albertson, Emotion and politics: noncognitive psychological biases in public opinion. Annu. Rev. Polit. Sci. **25**(1), 401–418 (2022). https://doi.org/10.1146/annurev-polisci-051120-105353
S.J. Westwood, E. Peterson, The inseparability of race and partisanship in the United States. Polit. Behav. **44**(3), 1125–1147 (2022). https://doi.org/10.1007/s11109-020-09648-9
A.E. Wilson, V.A. Parker, M. Feinberg, Polarization in the contemporary political and media landscape. Current Opinion Behav. Sci. **34**(SI), 223–228 (2020). https://doi.org/10.1016/j.cobeha.2020.07.005

E. Zhuravskaya, M. Petrova, R. Enikolopov, Political effects of the internet and social media. ed. by P. Aghion, H. Rey, Annual Rev. Econ. **12** 415–438 (2020). https://doi.org/10.1146/annurev-economics-081919-050239

Chapter 7
Linguistic Polarization in Minority Representation: Analyzing Parliamentary Speeches in Germany and the UK (1980–2021)

Younghyun Lee, Florencia Piñeyrúa, Christian S. Czymara, and Maximilian Weber

Abstract Political polarization shapes how minority issues are discussed in public and parliamentary discourse, with implications for representation and policy. We examine the representation of migration and sexual minorities in all parliamentary speeches across Germany and the United Kingdom from 1980 to 2021. In particular, we ask: (1) How parties in both countries contributed to shifts in the overall *salience* of the two minority issues, (2) how language use differs between party groups and the two minority issues (*average linguistic differences*), and (3) how has this evolved over time (*linguistic polarization*). To this end, we employ natural language processing techniques on all political speeches in both parliaments during this period and roughly 143,000 speech parts in total. The results show that speeches on both issues increased notably over time for all parties in both countries. Moreover, relative frequency analyses reveal that linguistic polarization concerning the terminology used by political parties has intensified over the years. In both countries, right-leaning parties emphasized economic and security aspects more when discussing migration, whereas left-leaning parties focused more on normative and rights-based issues. Regarding sexual minorities, the rhetoric of left parties more often included terms relating to equality or discrimination, while right parties more often referred to aspects of marriage and morals. In sum, our research shows that left

Y. Lee (✉)
University of Illinois, Urbana-Champaign, Illinois, USA
e-mail: yl78@illinois.edu

F. Piñeyrúa
National Council for Scientific and Technical Research, National University of San Martín, Buenos Aires, Argentina

C. S. Czymara
Netherlands Interdisciplinary Demographic Institute, The Hague, The Netherlands

M. Weber
University Mainz, Mainz, Germany

M. A. Keijzer et al. (eds.), *Computational Social Science of Social Cohesion and Polarization*, Computational Social Sciences,
https://doi.org/10.1007/978-3-032-01373-6_7

and right parties strongly differ in their language use when debating minorities and that linguistic polarization intensifies over time.

Keywords Migration · Sexuality · Parliament speeches · Political polarization · Linguistic polarization · Text-as-data · Political rhetoric · Minority politics

7.1 Introduction

Political polarization refers to the degree to which opinions on issues are increasingly opposed and how such opposition grows over time (DiMaggio et al. 1996; Rekker 2021). It is a process that is generated between two or more groups in contexts of interaction, whether real or imaginary (Kessler et al. 2020) and has attracted the attention of researchers because its effects are usually closely related to the aspects and actions of individuals and societies. Thus, the ability to assess and quantify shifts in political ideology and polarization holds paramount importance for researchers, stakeholders, and the broader public (Caravaca et al. 2022). An increase in political polarization also polarizes public opinion in the most politically committed groups with strong party identification (DiMaggio et al. 1996; Evans 2003; Abramowitz and Saunders 2008; Fiorina et al. 2008). Research on polarization is structured around the questions of whether polarized debates are a social phenomenon produced by elites (Hunter and Wolfe 2006) or also by the public (Abramowitz and Saunders 2008) and about the extent of polarization in the mass public (Baldassarri and Bearman 2007).

Political polarization can have an even more significant impact on public opinion, especially on minority issues, which are often emotionally and ideologically charged due to their underrepresentation. Debates surrounding immigration and LGBTQ + rights, for instance, lie at the heart of partisan divides and are particularly vulnerable to polarizing rhetoric (Dijk 1997). When polarization is heightened, the rhetoric of political elites tends to become more charged and divisive (Quirk 2011), which can amplify existing prejudices among the public or, conversely, mobilize support for minority rights. For example, when political elites discuss immigration-related issues, they can shape attitudes toward immigration (Bohman 2011; Flores 2018; Schmidt-Catran and Czymara 2023) and increase far-right voting (May and Czymara 2024). For sexual minorities (i.e., individuals identifying as lesbian, gay, bisexual, transgender, or queer), depending on the prevailing political rhetoric and legislative measures enacted, such laws may serve as a catalyst for heightened persecution of sexual minorities or, conversely, ensure their access to rights as minorities (Thränhardt 1995). In addition, by focusing on specific issues, political parties can express their core identities, which are not necessarily directly related to the issues themselves. Thus, the way political elites discuss minority issues stands as a central concern in the realm of democratic governance, holding profound implications for the political climate in an increasingly diverse society. Studying these issues allows us to trace how political parties differentiate themselves, mobilize their bases, and reinforce distinct ideological positions over time.

This paper analyzes how migrants and sexual minorities issues are discussed and represented in parliamentary debates in two European democracies, Germany and the United Kingdom (UK), spanning the period from 1980 to 2021. We specifically focus on the representation of migrants and sexual minorities, two groups of minorities that are similar in facing marginalization and discrimination, yet differ significantly in the specific challenges and the progression of their rights development. In particular, we explore a specific kind of political polarization in minority representation, which is *linguistic polarization*. In the context of this study, we define linguistic polarization as an increasing difference in the language used by political parties when referring to the minority representation of these two groups. Linguistic polarization can be understood as part of political polarization more broadly, such as affective (Gidron et al. 2020) or attitudinal (Schmidt-Catran and Czymara 2023) polarization. However, linguistic polarization is not equal to these phenomena. That is, linguistic polarization refers specifically to semantic differences rather than differences in sentiment or emotion. While these aspects can overlap, since some words carry more positive or negative valence, they remain distinct. Politicians, for instance, may use different terms for the same concept while holding similar positions on the issue. Analyzing linguistic polarization specifically is important because language shapes public perception and can signal division even in the absence of diverging attitudes.

Our study is based on all parliamentary debates in Germany and the UK. While previous research on elite discourses concerning minority groups based on parliamentary speeches mostly focused on single-country cases (Beese et al. 2022; Card et al. 2022), we aim to advance the understanding by examining the language employed by political elites when discussing minority groups in a comparative framework, focusing on two distinct cases. Our paper examines the entire corpus of more than four decades of parliamentary discourse on migration and sexual minorities in the two countries. In line with theoretical expectations, our results show that *linguistic polarization concerning the terminology used by political parties has intensified over the years, with discussions on migration primarily focusing on economic aspects, whereas those on sexual minorities concentrate on normative issues. This contrast also reflects underlying differences in how these groups are positioned within the political community: immigrants, often perceived as outsiders, are subject to more polarized discourse, while discussions of sexual minorities tend to be framed within debates about rights and values.* Our paper explores the emergence and evolution of political discourses on minorities, thereby contributing to a deeper understanding of the political representation within contemporary democratic societies.

We begin with a timeline of significant events in the history of minority rights, which is divided into two main areas of interest: migration and sexual minority rights, specifically in Germany and the United Kingdom. Subsequently, the theory and expectations section addresses the conceptual foundations and theoretical expectations. This is followed by the data and methods section, which explains how the data were collected and analyzed. Subsequently, we show the empirical results and discuss them in relation to our theoretical expectations in the discussion. Finally, we present the study's limitations and suggestions for future research.

7.2 Timeline of Major Events in Minority Rights History

Minorities are a group of people who are relatively marginalized and disadvantaged in society compared to members of a dominant social group. While there have always been minority groups in every society, the level of recognition and salience has been context-dependent and has changed over time.

7.3 Migration

The end of World War II marked a period of significant labor shortages in many European countries, driven by the need to rebuild economies and infrastructure devastated by the war. Both the United Kingdom and Germany attempted to address this shortage by encouraging international migration for employment purposes. As a result, during the post-war period, there was a notable increase in the number of immigrants in both countries, significantly influencing their demographic compositions and labor markets.

7.3.1 Germany

Immigration to West Germany increased during the 1960s following an agreement between the Federal Republic of Germany and Turkey, which brought in "guest workers" to address temporary labor shortages (Triadafilopoulos and Schönwälder 2006). Over time, this temporary arrangement led to long-term immigration (Ellermann 2015). From the early 1980s until approximately 1988, there was no considerable political interest in immigration and the social integration of immigrants in Germany (Münz 2003a, b). This has changed considerably since 1989. The political debate on the consequences of immigration was primarily a result of the major changes occurring in Central and Eastern Europe, the impact on large migration flows from these territories, the subsequent integration of these countries into the European Union, and the potential implications of this on East–West migration flows (Münz 2003a, b). Despite growing diversity in the country, Germany maintained an exclusionary national identity until the 1990s (Kurthen 1995). During the period 2000–2004, attempts to draft new immigration regulations have dominated the intellectual and political discourse on immigration and immigrant integration. Following four years of intense political debate, the Immigration Act[1] was approved in July 2004, which

[1] The complete text of the law under the official title "Gesetz zur Steuerung und Begrenzung der Zuwanderung und zur Regelung des Aufenthalts und der Integration von Unionsbürgern und Ausländern" dated July 30, 2004, is available on the website of the Ministry of the Interior: http://www.bmi.bund.de

regulates aspects of asylum and refugee and immigration focused on the labor market (Kleiner 2004a, b).

Immigration again peaked in late 2015 when Germany received an unprecedented number of asylum applications, surpassing all other EU countries (Burmann and Valeyatheepillay 2017). Debates about Germany's handling of the refugee influx intensified further after refugees were linked to sexual assaults in Germany on New Year's Eve in 2015/16 (Czymara and Schmidt-Catran 2017). These events were also accompanied by an increase in anti-refugee violence (Jäckle and König 2019) and the Alternative für Deutschland (AfD), a right-wing party advocating for stricter immigration laws, emerged as the third-largest party in the 2017 federal election and has maintained a presence in the parliament since then (Arzheimer and Berning 2019; Mushaben 2020).

In 2020, Germany was the second most significant international migration destination, hosting nearly 16 million international migrants, representing 17% of its total population (McAuliffe and Triandafyllidou 2021). This influx included a diverse group of newcomers, comprising both refugees and highly skilled workers, each contributing to the country's demographic and economic landscape. According to a recent report by the International Organization for Migration (IOM) between 2015 and 2020 the number of immigrants in the country increased by almost 5 million (McAuliffe and Triandafyllidou 2021). The most numerous groups came from Poland, Turkey, the Russian Federation, Kazakhstan, and the Syrian Arab Republic (McAuliffe and Triandafyllidou 2021). Furthermore, in 2020, Germany continued to harbor the largest population of refugees and asylum seekers in Europe, ranking fifth among the world's leading refugee-hosting nations. Notably, there was a considerable arrival of refugees from Ukraine, initially driven by Russia's attack in 2014 and intensified significantly after Russia's full-scale invasion in February 2022, leading to a sharp increase in refugee numbers (Weber et al. 2023).

Simultaneously, Germany has actively recruited highly skilled workers to address labor and skill shortages within its economy. According to the German Federal Employment Agency, the country reported 1.73 million vacant jobs, prompting the implementation of the new Skilled Immigration Act aimed at simplifying the entry and integration of skilled workers from abroad (Romaniec 2024). This underscores Germany's complex approach to managing both humanitarian responsibilities and economic necessities, marking it as a focal point of migration-related issues in Europe.

7.3.2 United Kingdom

The election of Margaret Thatcher as Prime Minister in 1979 marked the beginning of an era of severe immigration restrictions and measures against irregular migration (Layton-Henry and Wilpert 2003). From 1980 onwards, intense workplace raids were conducted to detect irregular workers, and they began to be excluded from social and medical benefits (Social Security Act, 1980; Couper and Santamaria

1984). Additionally, in 1981, with the passage of the British Nationality Act, rules for acquiring nationality were changed for children of foreigners born in the UK, and visas were established for nationals of countries exporting the highest number of irregular migrants and asylum seekers. In 1987, the Immigration (Carriers' Liability) Act introduced fines for airlines transporting individuals without proper documentation. This law received considerable criticism as it significantly affected refugees' right to seek asylum and allowed the UK to effectively restrict or evade its international obligations. In 1988, a new immigration law came into effect, which amended some parts of the 1971 law while still adhering to its overall framework. The Immigration Act of 1988 removed benefits that citizens of the New Commonwealth still retained.[2]

In 1993, the Asylum and Immigration Appeals Act came into force, revising the asylum procedure and granting extensive powers to the government to administer it to prevent fraudulent applications and, therefore, irregular immigration by these individuals. For example, it reduced the government's obligations to provide housing for asylum seekers and established transit visas. In 1996, the Asylum and Immigration Act established significant measures to control irregular migration. This legislation, for the first time, classified the employment of irregular workers and imposed severe punishment fines. It also facilitated the arrest without a court order of suspects of irregular migrants and increased penalties for irregular entry and assistance in remaining irregularly in the country.

In 2004, nationals of the A8 countries (Poland, Lithuania, Estonia, Latvia, Slovenia, Slovakia, Hungary, and the Czech Republic) were granted free movement, and a worker registration scheme was introduced. The entry and work rights for immigrants from the European Community (EC), which had been in effect since the United Kingdom's accession to the EC in 1973, underwent modification on December 31, 2020, when free movement between the United Kingdom and the European Union ended with the completion of Brexit. On January 1, 2021, the United Kingdom implemented a points-based immigration system, which places emphasis on skills and talent rather than the country of origin of individuals.

Similar to Germany, the United Kingdom stands as one of the primary international immigration destinations. According to recent data from the IOM, in 2020, it held the fourth position among the main destination countries, hosting 9 million international migrants, accounting for 13.1% of its total population (McAuliffe and Triandafyllidou 2021). Notably, immigrant populations from India, Poland, and Pakistan are among the largest in the country. Additionally, in 2020, the United Kingdom ranked fourth among European countries with the highest total number of refugees and asylum seekers (McAuliffe and Triandafyllidou 2021). The issue of immigrants and refugees remains salient, with tens of thousands of refugees having crossed

[2] For example, the right to residency was exclusively granted to citizens of the United Kingdom and those from former colonies who had resided in the country for five or more years. All other foreigners were required to apply for special permits to live, work, or settle, which did not authorize permanent residency or family reunification.

the English Channel in small boats. The situation has polarized the government on how to address the dangerous crossing and combat human trafficking effectively.

7.4 Sexual Minorities

The majority of reforms about the decriminalization of homosexuality were enacted through legislative measures in Germany and the United Kingdom. An important moment occurred with the issuance of the Wolfenden Committee report in 1957, which led England and Wales to adopt its recommendations by amending the Sexual Offenses Act in 1967, thereby decriminalizing consensual homosexual practices between adults in private settings. On June 25, 1969, the West German parliament also took significant action by amending the penal code two years later to decriminalize homosexuality for adults aged 21 and above. It is important to note, however, that both countries maintained a higher age of consent for homosexual acts in comparison to heterosexual acts during this period.

7.4.1 Germany

During the 1980s and 1990s, Germany witnessed notable advancements in legal recognition and rights for sexual minorities. In 1987, the East German Supreme Court declared that "homosexual individuals are not excluded from the socialist community, and their civil rights are guaranteed to them as to all others". This ruling prompted a relaxation of the provisions outlined in the Penal Code and a harmonization of the age of consent for homosexual and heterosexual activities less than a year before the fall of the Berlin Wall.

The reunification of East and West Germany on October 3, 1990, marked an important moment in the nation's history, leading to the harmonization of laws regarding homosexuality. In 1990, several of the newly established federal states, including Brandenburg and Saxony, formulated constitutions that explicitly prohibited discrimination based on sexual orientation. On May 31, 1994, after 123 years in force, Article 175 of the German Penal Code was repealed, thereby equalizing the age of sexual consent for both homosexual and heterosexual individuals at 16 years. Concurrently, in the same year, the prohibition on military service for homosexual individuals was lifted.

Germany continued to progress in sexual minority rights with the introduction of registered partnerships for same-sex couples on August 1, 2001. This legal change granted same-sex couples some of the rights and obligations of marriage, including inheritance, alimony, and health insurance benefits. Further advancements occurred on January 1, 2005, when adoption rights were granted to same-sex couples, allowing them to become parents legally. On June 30 2017, same-sex couples were granted full marital and adoption rights. Just a few months later, on October 1, 2017, same-sex marriage was officially legalized, ensuring equal marriage rights for all. Finally, on May 7, 2020, Germany took steps to protect minors by initiating a ban on conversion therapy, a practice aimed at changing an individual's sexual orientation or gender identity.

7.4.2 United Kingdom

The pioneers of sexual minority rights in the United Kingdom were England and Wales, which legalized homosexuality in 1967 under the Sexual Offences Act 1967. Subsequently, in Scotland, homosexual acts were decriminalized by the Criminal Justice (Scotland) Act 1980, which took effect on February 1, 1981. A year later, Northern Ireland also legalized homosexuality. However, a setback in sexual minority rights occurred during the 1980s. Protests and campaigns were organized to advocate for more restrictive legislation, prompted by controversy surrounding a book available in public school libraries in London, which some argued promoted homosexuality among teenagers. Consequently, in 1988, the British Parliament introduced an amendment to Section 28 of the Local Government Act, prohibiting the deliberate promotion of homosexuality by any local government authority and the endorsement of homosexuality acceptance in any publicly funded school.

In line with the German case, the onset of the twenty-first century saw the implementation of several legislative measures aimed at ensuring equal rights within British law. In 2000, legislation was enacted to establish an equal age of consent for both homosexual and heterosexual relationships. Subsequently, in 2004, the Sexual Offences Act 2003 came into force, removing all references to homosexuality from the 1967 law, thereby eliminating the requirement for strict privacy and no longer delineating differences in the sexual orientation of participants in any given activity. Additionally, the Criminal Justice Act 2003 designated hostility based on sexual orientation as an aggravating factor in any offense. In November 2004, legislation regarding civil unions for same-sex couples was ratified. In October 2007, the English government announced plans for the introduction of an amendment to the penal code to criminalize hate speech based on sexual orientation. Furthermore, in 2008, rights pertaining to same-sex parenting were formally recognized. Same-sex marriage was introduced in England and Wales in July 2013 and in Scotland in December 2014, marking a significant milestone in the pursuit of equal rights. This legislation also facilitated the recognition of same-sex marriage in Northern Ireland in 2020, following an extensive process of advocacy and political deliberation.

Although both Germany and the United Kingdom experienced developments in migration and sexual minority rights, key differences lie in their institutional and historical contexts. On the one hand, the institutional gap between Germany's multi-party system and the UK's (mainly) two-party structure. On the other hand, Germany's history is strongly shaped by labor migration and post-war integration policies, while the UK's colonial legacy influences how diversity, citizenship, and identity are discussed. Similarly, recent legal changes regarding sexual minority rights in Germany were influenced by the reunification and the repeal of Section 175 in 1994. Whereas in the UK, political debates continue to reflect the historical impact of Section 28 in 1988. These differences help contextualize how minority issues entered political agendas and set the stage for understanding country-specific dynamics in political discourse.

7.5 Theory and Expectations

As demonstrated in the previous section, minority rights have been expanded gradually, often sparking major debates between majority and minority groups, as well as among political camps. In this section, we aim to place our study in the literature of minority rights and party politics, focusing on ideological differences in how left- and right-leaning parties frame these issues and how these differences intensify over time.

Minority rights are closely tied to liberalism (Will Kymlicka and Rubio Marín 1999), and their political prominence has evolved alongside human rights advancements promoted by international organizations (Kymlicka 2007). The issues of minority rights started to receive more attention in the political arena, particularly from 1980 to 1990s with the multiculturalism debates and the breakup of the former Yugoslavia and the former Soviet Union (Pejic 1997), which created large migration streams to Western Europe as well as an increasing number of declarations, resolutions, reports, and treaties to strengthen the international legal protection of minorities (Wippman 1997). We conceptualize salience not merely as an outcome but as a precursor to partisan engagement and polarization. As minority issues become more visible in political discourse, parties are compelled to respond—often in divergent ways. Thus, understanding this trend is foundational to explaining the patterns that follow. As a result of these transformations, we expect that:

- Expectation 1: Minority issues are addressed more frequently over time in parliamentary debates in both countries.

7.5.1 *Partisan Differences in Framing Minority Issues*

As minority issues have become increasingly prominent in political debates, parties have had to engage with them more frequently. However, rather than fostering consensus, this growing salience has reinforced partisan divides in how these issues are framed. Political parties do not simply differ in how often they address minority rights; they also employ distinct rhetorical strategies, reflecting ideological divisions over issues of inclusion, national identity, and economic impact. These differences in framing are especially pronounced between left- and right-wing parties. Broadly, left-wing and liberal parties have historically been the primary advocates for expanding minority rights, aligning with ideological commitments to individual liberty, equality and diversity (Magni and Reynolds 2023). Accordingly, we expect left-wing parties to be more responsive to minority views and identities, framing them through normative appeals to inclusion and rights.

In contrast, right-wing parties are, by nature, more interested in preserving the status quo, which, arguably, can go hand in hand with the interest of the majority. Right-wing political parties have been stricter on immigration than their leftist opponents, tending to emphasize issues such as national security, cultural cohesion, and economic burden (Shehaj et al. 2021), while left-wing parties tend to become "the defender of immigration and multiculturalism" (Dancygier and Margalit 2020). This implies that conservative parties will focus more on the majority perspective when addressing minority-related issues. Relevant to our study, we expect that rhetoric revolving around economic aspects is more likely used by the political right, while the political left should use normative aspects more often. Due to the politicization of both issues, we expect that the difference between parties in both aspects should increase over time.

- Expectation 2a: Parties on the right use more terms related to traditional norms when discussing minorities.
- Expectation 2b: Parties on the left use more terms related to inclusion when discussing minorities.

7.5.2 *Differences Between Migration and Sexual Minority Issues*

While both migrants and sexual minorities are framed as "minorities" in political discourse, their political potential differs due to their divergent access to electoral participation and institutional representation. They differ in two key aspects: (1) how their rights were dealt with in society and (2) their status as native citizens. These distinctions should also shape how political parties engage with the two groups and influence the degree of politicization and polarization surrounding each issue.

First, political representation and party responsiveness differ significantly between these groups. Democracy induces governments to be responsive to the preferences of the voters and the goal of political parties is to represent these people (Stokes 1999). Political parties are rooted in social cleavages and their goals are to translate the demands of the populace into policy and aggregate the demands of their voters (Ford and Jennings 2020; Lipset and Rokkan 1967). Past research shows that the increasing visibility and legal recognition of LGBT families has prompted institutional changes and greater social legitimacy, particularly through the recognition of parenting rights and family diversity (Moore and Stambolis-Ruhstorfer 2013). In parallel, cross-national studies show that public attitudes and policy responsiveness toward LGBTQ issues have evolved as these groups gained visibility, legal recognition, and political voice through democratic channels (Adamczyk and Liao 2019).

In addition, groups with voting rights and established civil society networks—such as sexual minorities—are more likely to be addressed in inclusive rhetoric (Brown et al. 2024), whereas non-citizen migrants are often politically disregarded. Unlike sexual minorities who usually have voting rights, the lack of political rights and formal representation mechanisms often renders non-citizen migrants less visible within political agendas compared to enfranchised minorities. This puts the two minorities differently in the political landscape. While sexual minorities are voters in national politics, immigrants do not have voting rights unless they are naturalized. In that sense, sexual minorities are situated within the political community, whereas immigrants are outside of the community.

Second, the historical framing and public perception of these two groups differ. As we mentioned in the previous section, both Germany and the UK have begun to adopt immigrants to overcome the shortage of labor after World War II. While the rights of immigrants have been expanded over time with the development of human rights, the immigration issue was mainly driven by "realistic" reasons, to solve some of the economic challenges the countries were facing. In addition, adopting immigrants is closely related to their welfare policy and taxation, which leads countries to approach the issue more realistically. This is different from sexual minority rights where the issue of sexual minority rights is more related to adopting values that some view as incompatible with the existing social norms. In addition, the issue of migration is often more securitized beyond everyday politics, whereas sexual minority issues are more related to ideological and political struggles (Unlu and Kotonen 2024).

Moreover, political parties in Europe have become increasingly responsive to public opinion on immigration (Dassonneville et al. 2024), making it a highly politicized and electorally salient issue (Alonso and Fonseca 2012; Grande et al. 2019). By contrast, advances in sexual minority rights have typically resulted from long-term normative shifts, rather than direct voter pressure. Taken together, these dynamics suggest that migration issues are more frequently discussed in parliament due to their centrality to economic, demographic, and political concerns. In addition to partisan divisions, we consider how the nature of the minority group—citizen-based or not—shapes party rhetoric. We therefore expect that:

- Expectation 3: Migration is a more salient issue than sexual minorities in parliamentary debates in both countries.

7.5.3 The Dynamics of Language Use Over Time: Linguistic Polarization

However, the increased salience of these issues can also lead to increasingly different rhetoric between the political camps and their view of these issues. Given the ideological differences between left/liberal and right/conservative parties, it is likely that these two groups also differ in their language use, and that this difference in language gets stronger over time (Card et al. 2022). That is, left and right parties are likely to increasingly use different terms when talking about the same issues (Jensen et al. 2012). We refer to this tendency as *linguistic polarization*. Generally, linguistic polarization may stem from two mechanisms, which are different but not mutually exclusive. First, it can reflect increasing distance in political party positions, with language mirroring deeper divides along party lines. Second, language itself may become a strategic tool and, thus, language use can become more polarized over time as a strategic process reinforcing group boundaries and signaling differentiation, even when underlying positions remain stable, manifesting more in rhetorical style than in actual policy stances or actions. While we acknowledge that this relationship can be reciprocal, we emphasize salience as a primary driver that compels parties to respond and differentiate rhetorically. Moreover, linguistic polarization may not only be a consequence of issue salience but may also contribute to it: differences in how parties frame and discuss an issue can increase public attention and perceived controversy, thereby reinforcing its salience and potentially deepening polarization. In any case, the increasing importance of minority issues should likely be reflected in the terms left and right parties use when discussing these issues. This should be a pattern that generalizes across contexts and should thus be the case for both Germany and the UK.

- Expectation 4a: Linguistic polarization of minority issues in political speeches increases over time.

While linguistic polarization is expected to rise across all minority issues, we also anticipate variation in its intensity depending on the particular issue. Specifically, migration debates are likely to generate more pronounced polarization than those concerning sexual minority rights. As discussed above, migration is more frequently framed in exclusionary, securitized, and strategic terms, particularly by right-wing and populist parties. These actors emphasize threats to cultural identity, economic burden, and national sovereignty, while left-wing parties tend to adopt normative, rights-based, and inclusionary language. The fact that two groups have different political statuses implies that political parties have different approaches to the groups. The issues of sexual minorities were more related to them being discriminated against and underrepresented in politics (Magni and Reynolds 2021, 2023) and to their limited rights and to expanding the rights. On the contrary, immigrants do not have voting rights and are hardly considered ingroup members or "us" in terms of national identity, which is an important part of defining a political community. Even though immigrants raise their voices, political parties often do not have enough incentives to take their demands into account. Instead, the debates on immigration can be more politicized when political elites use the issue to attract voters, whether through anti-immigration rhetorics or through granting more rights to minority groups including immigrants. The recent success of anti-immigrant populist parties has been attributed to the idea of us versus them, as a form of identity politics, to explicitly exclude immigrants from the political community (Mudde 2007; Noury and Roland 2020). The populist parties have argued that politics should be an expression of the general will of the people, which excludes immigrants. This shows that, unlike sexual minorities, the issue of immigrants was mobilized by political elites. Thus, at the elite level, we could assume that immigration is a more politicized issue than sexual minorities. The result is a sharper linguistic divide between party camps.

In contrast, while sexual minority rights also provoke disagreement, they are less frequently tied to national security or existential threat narratives, and are less often used as a central mobilizing issue by parties—especially on the right. Thus, we expect the linguistic divergence between left and right to be more muted in discussions of sexual minorities compared to migration.

- Expectation 4b: Linguistic polarization between left and right parties is higher for migration than for sexual minorities issues.

7.6 Data and Methods

7.6.1 Data

We use a data set of all parliamentary speeches in Germany and the UK. For Germany, we draw upon data from the PolMine Project (version 2.0.0) provided by Blaette (2023). For the UK, the data comes from the Hansard Speeches (version 3.1.0) corpus provided by Odell (2021). Both sources provide all speeches given in the respective parliament, the *Bundestag* and the *House of Commons*, from January 1980 to September 2021. We used the data from each parliament and used Python and R to perform the analysis. All code is available at https://github.com/czymara/min-rep-parl-speech.

To identify relevant speeches, we used four sets of keywords (one for each issue and country) taken from prior research, web searches, and ChatGPT. To have a meaningful comparison, we decided to keep the migration and sexual minorities keywords as similar as possible between Germany and the UK. The full list of keywords can be found in Appendix A. We ensured the reliability of these keyword sets through manual annotation of random samples. The manual validation also revealed that using full speeches as the unit of analysis is too broad. This issue was particularly pronounced with longer speeches,[3] where keywords were present but the overarching speech content diverged significantly from the targeted issues. To address this, we split each speech into tri-sentence segments, enabling a more granular analysis by examining keyword presence within these concise units. We refer to this unit of analysis as *speech parts*. This refined method allowed for the precise tuning of our keywords with minimal adjustments—for instance, isolating “gay” as a standalone term—resulting in a reduction of false positives to below 10 percent in each case. This keyword-driven strategy, thus, proved highly effective, consistently isolating relevant segments of speeches across both countries. This worked particularly well for the sexual minorities issues, where almost all selected texts were relevant in both

[3] The average speech length (in characters) of the random samples is: Migration Germany: 6,059, Migration UK: 3,238, Sexual minorities DE: 5,033, Sexual minorities UK: 3,018.

countries.[4] For immigration-related issues, this approach resulted in 63,558 speech parts for Germany and 67,939 speech parts for the UK. For issues relating to sexual minorities, the keywords yielded 4,592 speech parts for Germany and 6,988 speech parts for the UK. These speech parts are the basis of all following analyses and treated as four data sets. Figures 7.5, 7.6, 7.7 and 7.8 in the appendix show the trends in the total number of speech parts about migration and sexual minorities by party in Germany and the UK, respectively.

7.6.2 Method

The main goals of this research are to examine (1) the *salience* of minority-related issues, (2), the *average linguistic differences* in word use between parties, and (3) their *linguistic polarization* over time. The salience is measured by the frequency of speech parts that contain issues-related keywords. The level of linguistic differences and of linguistic polarization are measured by applying relative frequency analysis. For the salience analysis, we present the frequency of the extracted tri-sentence segments about a specific issue per date and party.[5] The relative frequency analysis, in contrast, depicts words that are relatively more often used by one group compared to another group, in our case left- and right-leaning parties (see below). This analysis is conducted using the *quanteda R* package (Benoit et al. 2018) and follows a bag-of-words approach. To explore how language use differs between political parties, we analyze the frequency of individual words across party groups. For each word, we calculate a Chi-squared statistics, also known as *keyness*, which indicates how strongly a word is associated with either political side. Words with higher values are used significantly more often by one group than would be expected by chance. This is calculated by comparing the observed frequency of each word in one party group to its expected frequency under the assumption of equal usage across groups. The greater the difference between observed and expected counts, the higher the keyness score. To capture how these linguistic patterns evolve over time, we conduct the relative frequency analysis separately for each year, allowing us to track changes in language use across the observed time span. We use the signed version of the Chi-squared statistic to indicate the direction of association. If a word is more frequent in the left-leaning group than overall expected, the score is positive; if it is relatively more frequent in the right-leaning group, the score is negative. Before performing the relative frequency analysis, we used the following pre-processing steps: lemmatization, removal of numbers, symbols, and stop-words.

[4] The false positive rates are: Migration Germany: 9%, Migration UK: 8%, Sex minorities DE: 0%, Sex min UK: 2%.

[5] Salience is measured as the frequency of speech parts (tri-sentence segments) on a given issue. While the share of speech parts on an issue relative to all speech parts would provide a more precise estimate of salience, we rely on raw counts due to the computational demands of segmenting the full corpus of all speeches into tri-sentence segments.

In the German political landscape, the left group includes the Social Democratic Party (SPD), the Left (Die Linke), and the Greens (Bündnis 90/Die Grünen). On the right side, the spectrum comprises the Christian Democratic Union (CDU) along with its Bavarian sister party, the Christian Social Union (CSU), the Alternative for Germany (AfD), and the Free Democratic Party (FDP). In the UK political landscape, the left group includes the Labour Party, and the Scottish National Party (SNP). On the right side, the spectrum comprises the Conservative Party, and the Liberal Democrats.

7.7 Results

In the following, we first present a descriptive overview of the *total* number of speech parts by party for each issue and country over time. We refer to this as *salience*. This allows us to assess our first expectation on the trends in the overall frequency of the two issues in the parliamentary debates in Germany and the UK.

Next, we inspect *average* differences in language use between parties by employing relative frequency analyses showing which terms were used more often by right vs. left parties to test our Expectations 2a and 2b on the terms related to norms being more frequently featured by right parties and terms related to inclusion more by left parties. This is a measure of *average linguistic difference*. We illustrate these average differences using word clouds.

Finally, we explore the time *trends* in these differences in word usage between the parties, which captures *linguistic polarization*, based on chi-squared values from relative frequency analyses to test our Expectations 4a and 4b, arguing that linguistic polarization generally increased over time, and is higher for migration than for sexual minorities issues.

We follow these three steps (salience, average linguistic difference, linguistic polarization), for each issue-country-combination, first presenting the results of the migration debate in Germany and the UK, followed by the discourse on sexual minorities in Germany and the UK.

(1) ***Discourse on Migration in the German Parliament***

As shown in the first plot of Fig. 7.1, migration has significantly increased as an issue in parliamentary speeches since the 2010s in Germany by all the major parties, with some considerable fluctuations. There was a minimal focus on migration before 1990, with three prominent surges in discourse occurring between 1992 and 1993, caused by the war in Yugoslavia and the related “Asylkompromiss”, between 2015 and 2016, caused by the war in Syria, and between 2018 and 2019. The upper panel of Fig. 7.1 further indicates that Germany’s two major parties, the center-conservative CDU/CSU and the social-democratic SPD, emerged as the primary drivers of migration discussions, with the AfD joining the conversation around 2018. Notably, parties maintained a relatively similar share of the overall number of speech parts on migration in Germany, except during the years 2015/16. The overall trend shows that immigration issues became more salient over time, with some peaks during the major events.

The second plot of Fig. 7.1 shows the terms that were used in these debates, with larger words being more often used in general, words at the top being more often used by left leaning parties, and words at the bottom more often by right leaning parties. We see that left and right parties differ in the way they refer to fleeing people. While left parties are more likely to use the term "Flüchtlinge" (refugees) or "Geflüchtete" (persons who fled), right parties more often use the word "Asylbewerber" (asylum seekers). Moreover, parties on the right are much more likely to use a security frame when talking about migration, using words such as "illegal" or "problem".

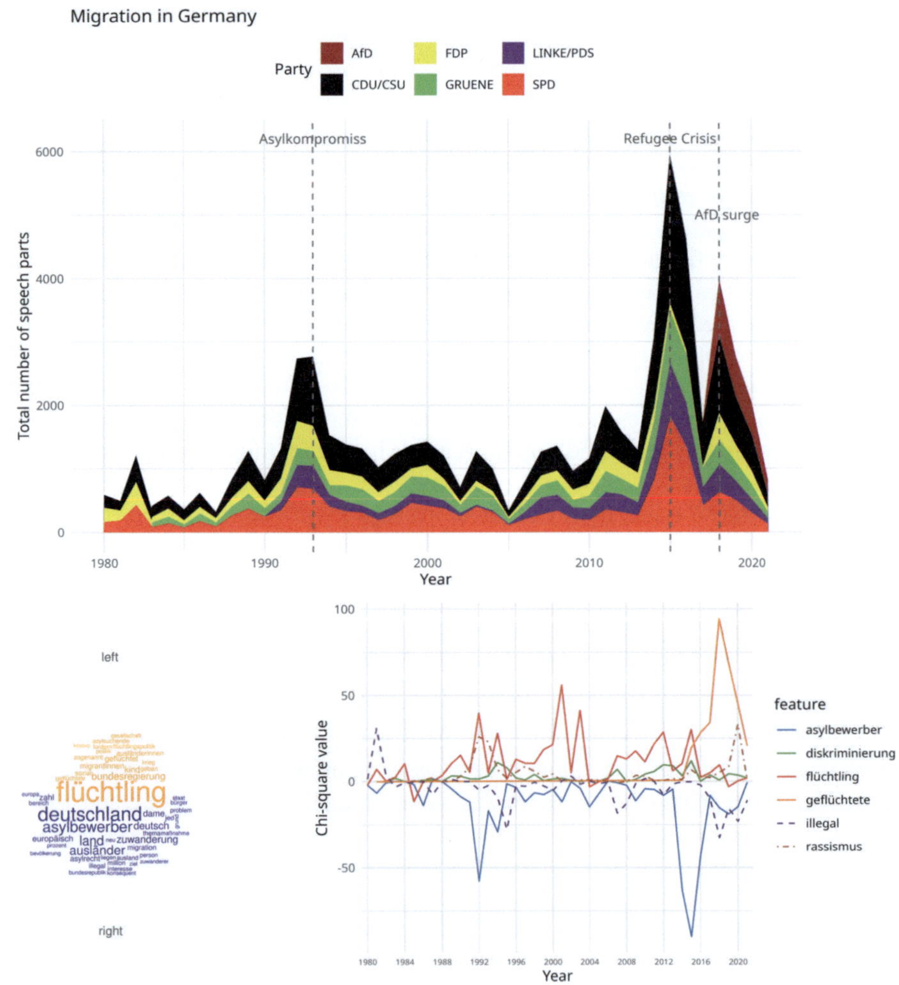

Fig. 7.1 Discourse on migration in political speeches in Germany

They also use language that suggests ingroup and outgroup dynamics, highlighting national identity and outsiders with terms like "Deutschland" (Germany), "Ausländer" (foreigner), and "Deutsch" (German). This language use may thus reinforce divisions between citizens and non-citizens.

The third plot of Fig. 7.1 shows that there is also fluctuation in the polarization in the usage of these words over time. The plot displays the Chi-squared (keyness) values for selected keywords related to migration, showing how strongly each word is associated with either left- or right-leaning parties over time. Positive values indicate that the term was used more frequently by left-leaning parties in a given year, while negative values reflect higher usage by right-leaning parties. We see that the difference in word usage occurs most often during the two peaks in refugee migration, in the early 1990s and after 2015. We also see that the left is more likely to address racism during times of high migration compared to the right. Interestingly, we also observe a shift in language use *within* left parties over time. While they referred to refugees primarily as "Flüchtlinge" (refugees) before 2015, they changed to predominantly use the term "Geflüchtete" (persons who fled) after. While the term "Flüchtlinge" is the traditional word for refugees, "Geflüchtete" is meant to emphasize the action of fleeing and is often used to highlight the agency of the individuals.

(2) ***Discourse on Migration in the UK Parliament***

Turning to the migration discourse in the UK, the first plot of Fig. 7.2 shows that, in contrast to Germany, migration issues have been consistently salient since the 1980s in the UK. Yet, we also observe an increase over time, which confirms our first expectation that the issue of immigration becomes more salient in both countries over time. This trend was predominantly led by the two major parties—the Conservative and the Labour Party, with prominent surges around the refugee inflow of 2015. However, if we look closely at the speeches by party, a clear shift is evident. Between 1999 and 2009, the Labour Party demonstrated a heightened focus on migration issues, surpassing the Conservative Party. This trend reversed since 2010, with the Conservative party taking a more prominent role in discussing migration, while Labour's attention relatively decreased during this period (See Appendix).

The second plot of Fig. 7.2 shows that, similar to Germany, the right-wing parties are more likely to use a security frame when discussing migration, by using terms such as "illegal", "deportation", "offender", or "control". Left-wing parties, on the other hand, were more likely to address issues of family migration, by using words such as "child", "family", or "woman". This is an aspect we did not observe for the German left-leaning parties talking about immigration.

The third plot of Fig. 7.3 displays that the polarization in word usage was again most pronounced during times of high migration in the early 1990s and after 2015. We see that, after 2016, left parties were much more likely to use the term "hostile" compared to right-wing parties, perhaps in the way they describe the discussion and current policies. Another interesting finding is that the use of the term refugee actually flipped over time: while right-wing parties were more likely to use the term refugee in the late 1980s than left parties, this changed completely after 2005, when

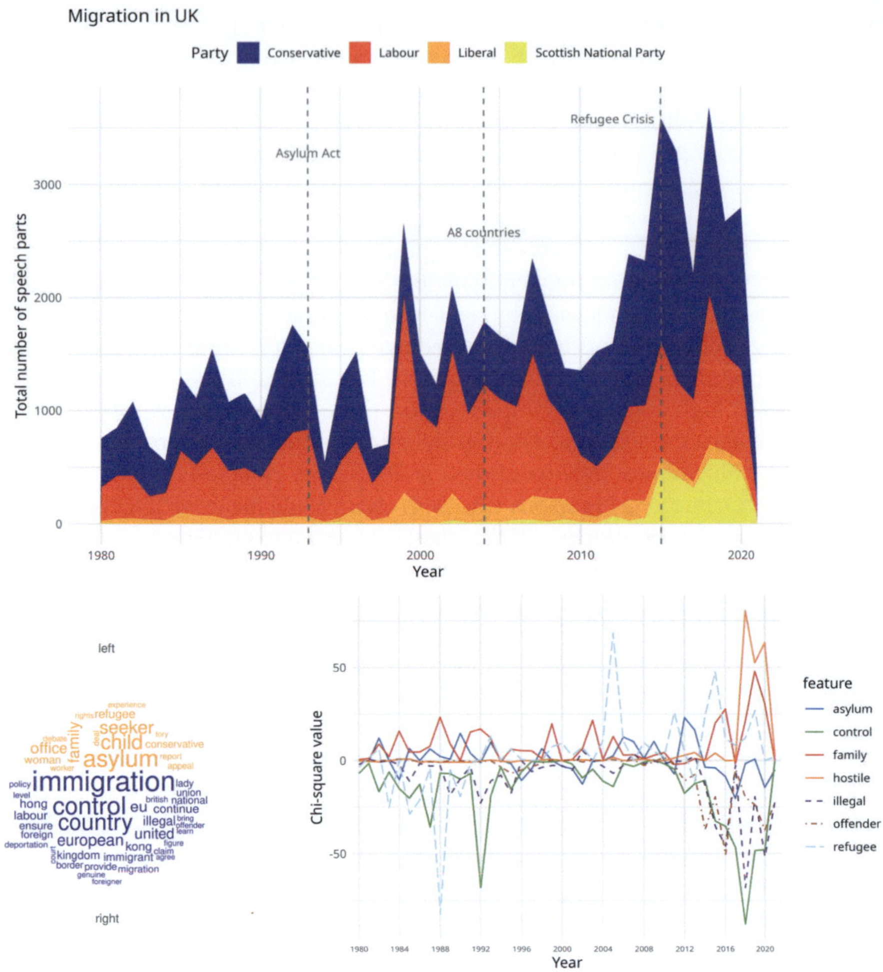

Fig. 7.2 Discourse on migration in political speeches in the UK

left parties were much more likely to use the word refugee as compared to right parties.

(3) ***Discourse on Sexual Minorities in the German Parliament***

In contrast to speeches on migration, issues relating to sexual minorities received comparatively less attention in political debates in Germany, marked by fluctuations in the number of speech parts in the first plot of Fig. 7.3. The issue gained limited attention until the early 2010s, with an exception at the beginning of the 2000s, when Germany introduced registered partnerships for same-sex couples. Notably, parties generally maintained a similar share of the overall number of speech parts on sexual minorities, except in 2017 when CDU/CSU placed a significantly higher focus on the

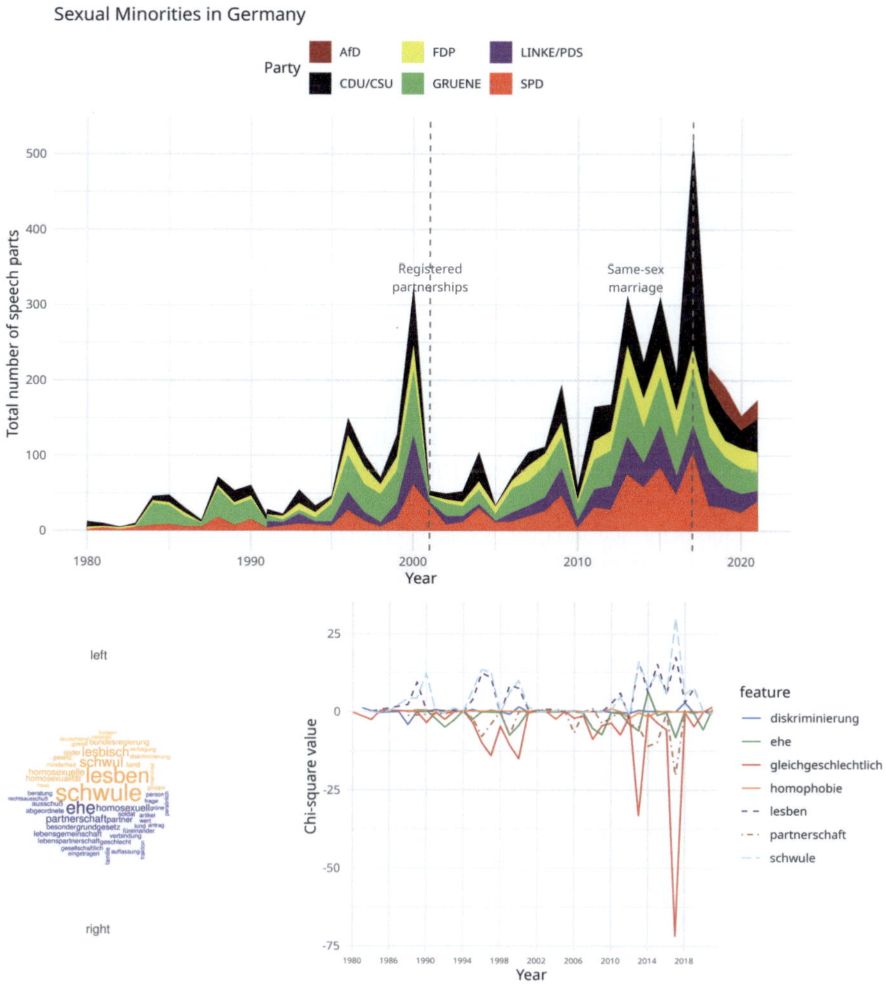

Fig. 7.3 Discourse on sexual minorities in political speeches in Germany. *Note* The word "gleichgeschlechtlich" could not be plotted in the word cloud but is among the most frequently used.

issue compared to other major parties. This is when the CDU/CSU remained in the government (forming a coalition with the SPD) after federal elections, and same-sex couples were granted full marital and adoption rights shortly after.

The word cloud in the second plot of Fig. 7.3 shows remarkable differences in the terms used by left and right parties when addressing issues related to sexual minorities. Left parties were more likely to address the identities of sexual minorities, by using the terms "schwul" (gay) or "lesbisch" (lesbian), but also their "Diskriminierung" (discrimination). In contrast, right parties primarily talk about traditional values such as "Familie" (family), "Ehe" (marriage), "Partnerschaft" or "Lebenspartnerschaft" (both meaning partnership), and "Lebensgemeinschaft" (cohabitation).

The third plot in Fig. 7.3 shows that, somewhat similar to the migration discourse, polarization in word use is strongest when the issue is salient, i.e. in times of big events or policy reforms. This is true for both the left's focus on identities and the right's focus on family values and marriage. Although the spikes in the third plot of Fig. 7.3 are strongest in the 2010s, this pattern was already in place in the 1990s.

(4) ***Discourse on Sexual Minorities in the UK Parliament***

Finally, Fig. 7.4 displays the sexual minorities discourse in the UK. Comparing the first plots of Figs. 7.3 and 7.4, the UK and Germany both exhibited a gradual increase in discussions related to sexual minorities. However, the issue of sexual minorities was notably more salient in the UK than in Germany, but there is also somewhat more fluctuation. What is interesting in the UK is that the two major parties consistently held similar shares of speeches since the 1980s, with five distinct instances of heated debates: around the mid-1980s, 2000, mid-2000s, and before and after 2015.

The word cloud in the second plot of Fig. 7.4 shows a remarkably similar pattern to the word cloud for Germany in Fig. 7.3: the left parties mostly address identity terms in the sexual minorities debate, such as "gay", "lesbian", "bisexual", "transsexual", or "transgender" (although the latter aspect did not play a larger role in Germany, even for the left parties). Left parties are also more likely to address "discrimination" and "homophobia". In contrast, the right parties mostly address the traditional values related to "marriage", "couple", or "moral". One unique aspect of the UK is the presence of terms related to the "navy" and the "military", or "armed" forces. This is due to the Merchant Shipping (Homosexual Conduct) Act 2017, which repealed sections of the Criminal Justice and Public Order Act 1994 that permitted the dismissal of merchant ship crew members for engaging in homosexual acts and was passed on 27 April 2017 (hence the use of the term "merchant" among right parties).

The trends of word use polarization in the third plot in Fig. 7.4 are somewhat less clear. While the spike in the use of words related to the Merchant Shipping Act among the right happened, as expected, in 2017, the polarization in other terms seems to fluctuate. It does appear, however, that word use became more polarized in recent years, during which issues related to sexual minorities were generally more salient in the parliament of the UK.

7.8 Discussion

Our frequency analysis of discourse on minority issues, specifically immigration and sexual minorities, in Germany and the UK have demonstrated a growing salience of these issues over time, aligning with our first expectation. Notably, the issue of immigration was discussed significantly more often than issues relating to sexual minorities, engaging a broader spectrum of political parties (Expectation 3). This

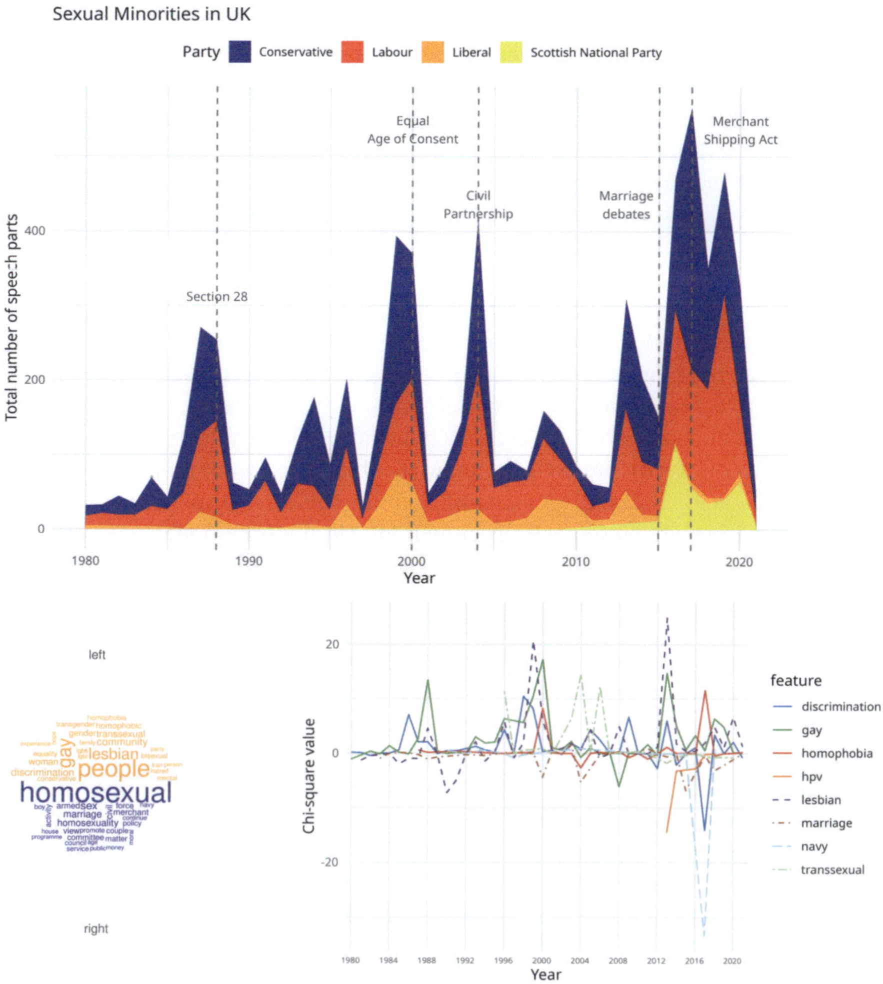

Fig. 7.4 Discourse on sexual minorities in political speeches in the UK

suggests that immigration has been one of the most salient political issues in Europe (Givens and Luedtke 2005; Noury and Roland 2020).

Our relative frequency analysis revealed an increasing linguistic polarization concerning these issues over time, with a notable rise in the average values of Chi-square for the four groups under study (Expectation 4a). This polarization suggests that as debates around immigration and sexual minorities become more frequent, the ideological divide in language choice between left- and right-wing parties also intensifies. Specifically, right-wing parties emphasize economic and security aspects, using terms like "provide," "illegal," "offender," and "border" when discussing migration. Meanwhile, left-wing parties focus on normative and rights-based terms such as "rights," "asylum seekers," "refugee," and "child". Regarding sexual minorities, left-wing rhetoric includes terms like "community," "discrimination," and "equality," while right-wing discussions often revolve around "marriage," "civil service," "money," and "public".

Moreover, in analyzing the language used by different political spectrums, it is evident that left parties consistently employ terminology more supportive of and associated with minority groups (Expectation 2b). For instance, in both Germany and the UK, left-wing discourse frequently includes terms such as "refugees," "child," "family," and "woman," emphasizing a humanitarian perspective focused on individual and familial aspects of immigrants. This highlights a pattern where left-wing parties prioritize minority well-being in their discourse. Conversely, right-wing parties in both countries adopt a lexicon centered around national identity and security concerns. Commonly used terms include "Germany" and "foreigners" in Germany, and "illegal", "deportation", and "control" in the UK, indicating a discourse that frames immigration primarily as a security issue rather than a humanitarian one. This finding is consistent with previous literature that has examined political speeches in the U.S. (Card et al. 2022), demonstrating that this pattern is somewhat common in countries experiencing an increase in immigrant and minority populations (Expectation 2a). We find similar patterns in discourses about sexual minorities. Left-wing parties tend to focus on the rights and issues of minorities, whereas right-wing parties often emphasize traditional values such as "marriage", and "moral". Typically, these discussions avoid direct mentions of sexual minority groups, using terms such as "gays", "lesbians", or "transgender". Linguistic polarization stems from the political values that different party groups care about, regardless of the specific issues, such as immigration and sexual minorities.

Migration, being discussed more frequently than sexual minority issues in both countries, shows stronger patterns of linguistic divergence between parties on average. One possible explanation is that issues with high political attention attract clearer ideological positioning, encouraging parties to differentiate their rhetorical strategies. The relationship between salience and linguistic polarization is illustrated most clearly in the German case. Our results show that major peaks in migration-related parliamentary discourse—particularly in the early 1990s and around 2015—coincide with sharp increases in linguistic polarization. These moments, linked to the Post-Yugoslav and Syrian refugee crises, triggered intensified debates between left and right parties, as evidenced by higher divergence in word use. In the UK, although salience of migration remained more stable over time, peaks in polarization also align with periods of intense debate, such as post-2015. Similarly, in the case of sexual minorities, polarization grew notably during key legislative events, such as the legalization of same-sex marriage in both countries. These findings suggest that polarization tends to rise not merely with overall salience, but during politicized moments that concentrate party attention and emphasize ideological differences. Therefore, the temporal overlap observed in our data supports the theoretical expectations.

While our findings show similar trends in both countries, institutional and historical specificities may help explain variations in the intensity and framing of linguistic polarization. On one hand, the institutional gap between Germany's multi-party system and the UK's two-party structure may shape the dynamics of political polarization. Coalition governments in Germany often require compromise, which can encourage more moderated discourse. In contrast, the UK's adversarial system tends to produce sharper rhetorical devices. On the other hand, national histories also influence how minorities are represented. Germany's migration debates are rooted in labor migration and economic integration, while the UK's colonial legacy shapes discourses of citizenship and diversity. A similar pattern emerges in the history of sexual minority rights. In Germany, the repeal of Section 175 in 1994 and reunification led to a more institutionalized focus on legal equality, with early inclusion of anti-discrimination clauses in regional constitutions. In the UK, however, the legacy of Section 28 in 1988, which banned the promotion of homosexuality in schools, still resonates in political discourse, especially among Conservative voices. These distinctions may help explain cross-national differences in language use and suggest that both institutional design and historical legacies are relevant factors in the evolution of linguistic polarization.

7.9 Conclusion

Based on all political speeches held in the parliaments of Germany and the United Kingdom in the period from 1980 to 2021, our study explored the differences in language use between left and right parties when debating issues related to immigration and sexual minorities. Using natural language processing, we show that both issues became much more salient over our investigated period. Deeper analyses reveal that left and right parties strongly differed in the terms they used when talking about the two issues. In parliamentary discussions on migration, right-leaning parties in both countries prioritize economic and security issues, while their left-leaning counterparts emphasize human rights and ethical considerations more often. Regarding sexual minorities, the discourse from the left often centered on issues of equality and discrimination, whereas the right was more concerned with moral and marital values. Importantly, the tendencies in the differences in language use clearly increased over time. Thus, linguistic polarization, which we defined as an increase in the differences in the usage of words over time between political parties, intensified over the years.

This study also has some limitations. The method we employed to analyze the parliamentary debate makes use of the so-called bag-of-words approach, while counting the occurrence of the words, we are not capturing the deeper semantic meanings of the sentences or the context in which these words are used. Additionally, the focus on keywords might miss less frequent but potentially significant expressions that signal emerging trends or shifts in attitude that are not yet predominant in the discourse. Given these constraints, future research could benefit from incorporating more advanced linguistic analyses that consider the context. Expanding the scope to include media representations or public opinion surveys could also provide a more comprehensive understanding of how these issues are discussed and perceived in society. Moreover, while our paper focuses on language, future research could explore how linguistic and other types of political polarization relate to each other. For example, it is likely that certain words carry a particular valence. For example, the German "Geflüchtete" (person who fled) has a more positive connotation than "Asylbewerber" (asylum seeker). Future research may want to examine these patterns more systematically to explore whether linguistic polarization aligns with shifts in policy positions or is a more autonomous dynamic. Finally, we focused on minority representation in Germany and the UK in the past 40 years, but future research may want to explore linguistic polarization with respect to other issues, contexts, or even larger time frames. While we do think minority representation with respect to immigration and sexual minorities is particularly relevant in the current political discourse, the concept of linguistic polarization is likely to apply to other political issues as well. Moreover, one might also go beyond the political sphere and examine linguistic polarization, for example, in newspaper articles or social media posts (Bail et al. 2018; Czymara and Gorodzeisky 2024). The increasing availability of such data sources to computational social scientists will increasingly allow us to explore such research questions.

These limitations notwithstanding, our study shows that language use in political speeches has polarized between left and right parties when discussing minority representations in both Germany and the UK. Given that political rhetoric can have a significant impact on public opinion, understanding how political elites refer to issues of minority representation is particularly important. This is particularly true for both immigration and the rights of sexual minorities, which are likely to be highly salient and vividly discussed issues in the coming years.

Appendix

(A) Keywords

- Migration (German): "Einwander", "Zuwander", "Migrant", "Migration", "Ausländer", "Flüchtling", "Geflüchtete", "Asyl", "Visum", "Abschieb", "Einbürgerung", "Aufenthaltsgenehmigung"
- Migration (English): "migrant", "migration", "foreigner", "refugee", "asylum", r"\bvisa\b", "deport", "naturalization", "residence permit"
- Sexuality (German): "schwul", "lesbisch", "homosexuell", "bisexuell", "Männer, die Sex mit Männern haben", "transgender", "transsex", "queer", "lgbt", "homophob", "gleichgeschlechtlich", "ehe für alle"
- Sexuality (English): r"\bgay\b", "lesbian", "homosexual", "bisexual", "men who have sex with men", "transgender", "transsex", "queer", "LGBT", "homophob", "same sex".

Number of Speech Parts on Migration by Party

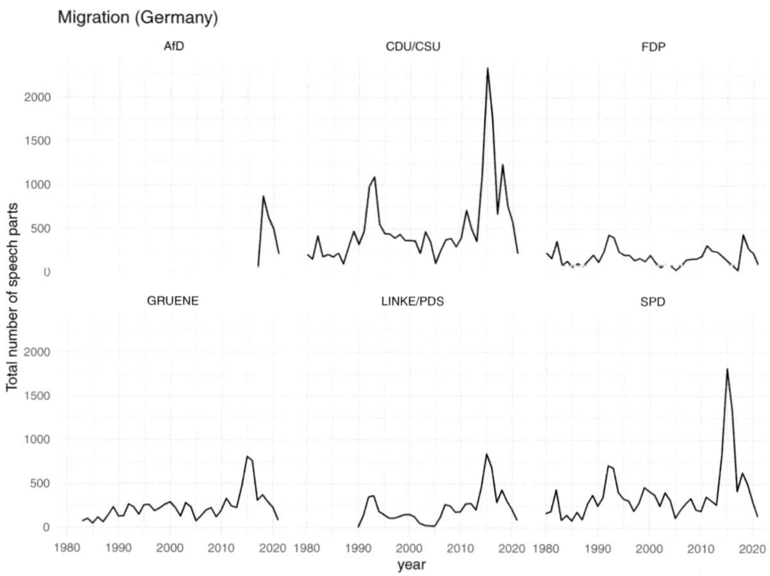

Fig. 7.5 Migration (Germany)

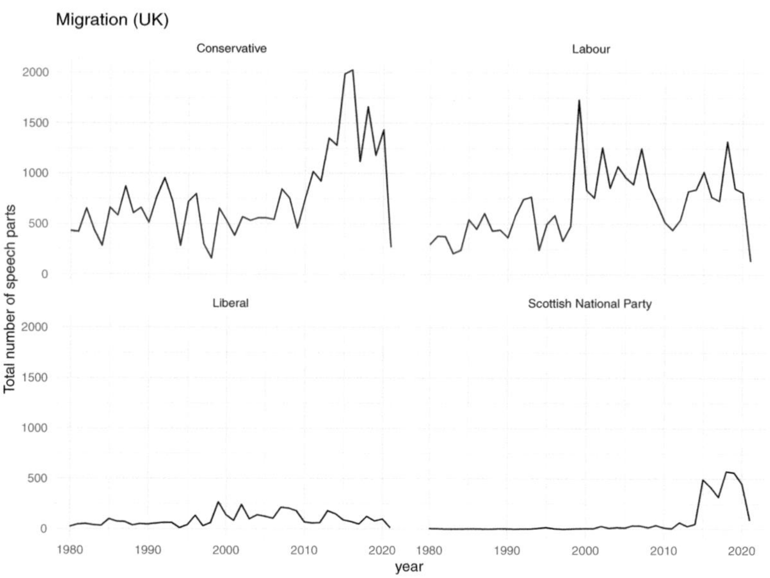

Fig. 7.6 Migration (UK)

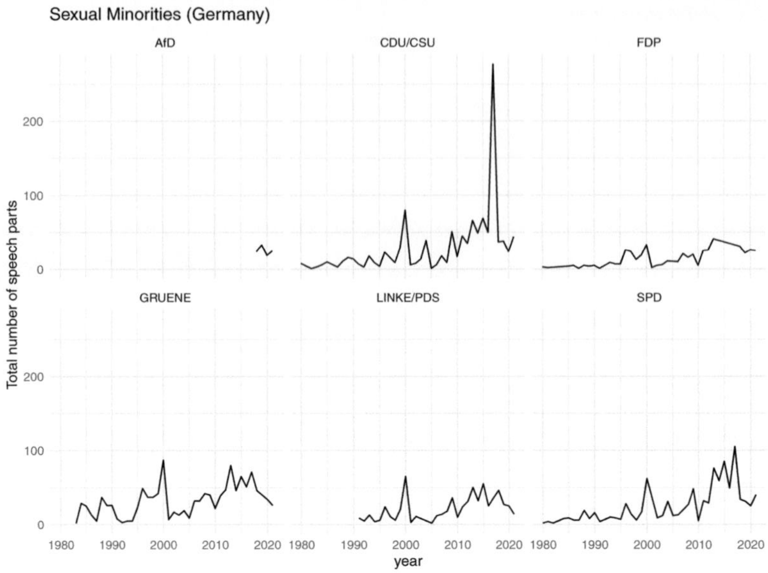

Fig. 7.7 Sexual minorities (Germany)

Number of Speech Parts on Sexual Minorities by Party

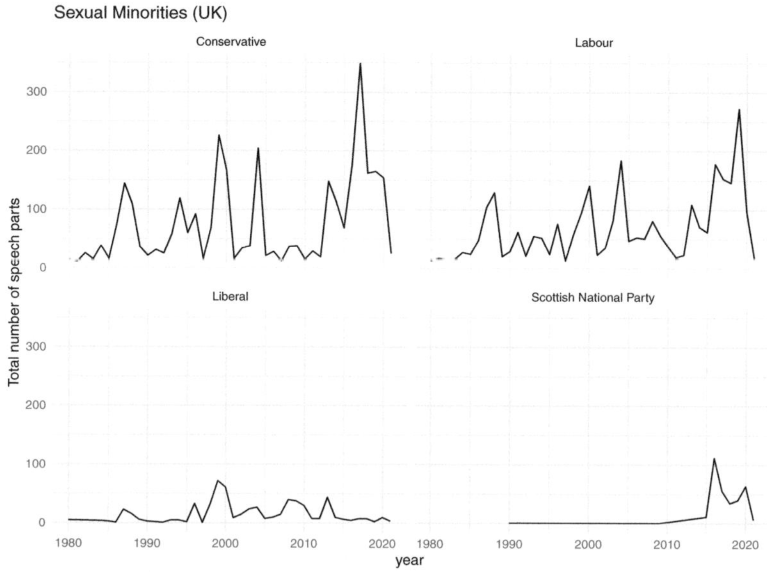

Fig. 7.8 Sexual minorities (UK)

References

A.I. Abramowitz, K.L. Saunders, Is polarization a myth? The J. Polit. **70**(2), 542–555 (2008). https://doi.org/10.1017/S0022381608080493

ACNUR, La protección internacional de las personas LGBTI: solicitudes de la condición de refugiado relacionadas con la orientación sexual y/o la identidad de género (2014). https://biblio.flacsoandes.edu.ec/libros/141549-opac

A. Adamczyk, Y.C. Liao, Examining public opinion about LGBTQ-related issues in the United States and across multiple nations. Ann. Rev. Sociol. **45**(1), 401–423 (2019). https://doi.org/10.1146/soc.2019.45.issue-1. https://doi.org/10.1146/annurev-soc-073018-022332

S. Alonso, S.C.D. Fonseca, Immigration, left and right. Party Polit. **18**(6), 865–884 (2012). https://doi.org/10.1177/1354068810393265

K. Arzheimer, C.C. Berning, How the Alternative for Germany (AfD) and their voters veered to the radical right, 2013–2017. Electoral Stud **60**, 102040. https://doi.org/10.1016/j.electstud.2019.04.004

C.A. Bail, L.P. Argyle, T.W. Brown, J.P. Bumpus, H. Chen, M.F. Hunzaker, J. Lee, M. Mann, F. Merhout, A. Volfovsky, Exposure to opposing views on social media can increase political polarization. Proc. Nat. Acad. Sci. **115**(37), 9216–9221 (2018). https://doi.org/10.1073/pnas.1804840115

D. Baldassarri, P. Bearman, Dynamics of political polarization. Am. Sociol. Rev. **72**(5), 784–811 (2007). https://doi.org/10.1177/000312240707200507

D. Beese, O. Pütz, S. Eger, FairGer: Using NLP to Measure Support for Women and Migrants in 155 Years of German Parliamentary Debates (2022). arXiv. http://arxiv.org/abs/2210.04359

K. Benoit, K. Watanabe, H. Wang, P. Nulty, A. Obeng, S. Müller, A. Matsuo, Quanteda: an R package for the quantitative analysis of textual data. J. Open Source Softw. **3**(30), 774 (2018). https://doi.org/10.21105/joss.00774

A. Blaette, PolMine Project (2023). http://polmine.github.io

A. Bohman, Articulated antipathies: political influence on anti-immigrant attitudes. Int. J. Comp. Sociol. **52**(6), 457–477 (2011). https://doi.org/10.1177/0020715211428182

M. Bondi, Scott. n.d. Keyness in Texts. Scl.41 (John Benjamins Publishing Company, 2024). Accessed 13 May 2024. https://benjamins.com/catalog/scl.41

N.E. Brown, C.J. Clark, A.M. Mahoney, O. Siow, M.G. Strawbridge, Intersectional identity and representative politics. Polit. Gend. **20**(3), 727–733 (2024). https://doi.org/10.1017/S1743923X24000199

M. Burmann, M. Valeyatheepillay, Asylum recognition rates in the top 5 EU Countries. CESifo DICE Rep. **15**(2), 48–50 (2017)

F. Caravaca, J. González-Cabañas, Á. Cuevas, R. Cuevas, Estimating ideology and polarization in European countries using Facebook data. EPJ Data Sci. **11**(1), 56 (2022). https://doi.org/10.1140/epjds/s13688-022-00367-1

D. Card, S. Chang, C. Becker, J. Mendelsohn, R. Voigt, L. Boustan, R. Abramitzky, D. Jurafsky, Computational analysis of 140 years of US political speeches reveals more positive but increasingly polarized framing of immigration. Proc. Natl. Acad. Sci. **119**(31), e2120510119 (2022). https://doi.org/10.1073/pnas.2120510119

K. Couper, U. Santamaria, An elusive concept: the changing definition of illegal immigrant in the practice of immigration control in the United Kingdom. Int. Migr. Rev **18**(3), 437–452 (1984)

C.S. Czymara, A. Gorodzeisky, Hostility on Twitter in the aftermath of terror attacks. J. Comput. Soc. Sci. **7**(2), 1305–13257 (2024). https://doi.org/10.1007/s42001-024-00272-9

C.S. Czymara, A.W. Schmidt-Catran, Refugees unwelcome? Changes in the public acceptance of immigrants and refugees in Germany in the course of Europe's 'immigration crisis'. Eur. Sociol. Rev. **33**(6), 735–751 (2017). https://doi.org/10.1093/esr/jcx071

R. Dancygier, Y. Margalit, The evolution of the immigration debate: evidence from a new dataset of party positions over the last half-century. Comp. Pol. Stud. **53**(5), 734–774 (2020). https://doi.org/10.1177/0010414019858936

R. Dassonneville, N. Fréchet, A. Jabbour, B. Ferland, J. Homola, Party responsiveness over time: from left-right to issue-specific dimensions. Party Polit. **31**(4), 751–760 (2025). https://doi.org/10.1177/13540688241245065

T.A.V. Dijk, Political Discourse and Racism: Describing Others in Western Parliaments (1997)

P. DiMaggio, J. Evans, B. Bryson, Have American's social attitudes become more polarized? Am. J. Sociol. **102**(3), 690–755 (1996)

A. Ellermann, Do policy legacies matter? Past and present guest worker recruitment in Germany. J. Ethn. Migrat. Stud. **41**(8), 1235–1253 (2015). https://doi.org/10.1080/1369183X.2014.984667

J.H. Evans, Have Americans' attitudes become more polarized?—An update. Soc. Sci. Q. **84**(1), 71–90 (2003)

R.D. Flores, Can elites shape public attitudes toward immigrants?: Evidence from the 2016 US presidential election. Soc. Forces **96**(4), 1649–1690 (2018). https://doi.org/10.1093/sf/soy001

M.P. Fiorina, S.A. Abrams, J.C. Pope, Polarization in the American public: misconceptions and misreadings. The J. Polit. **70**(2), 556–560 (2008). https://doi.org/10.1017/S002238160808050X

R. Ford, W. Jennings, The changing cleavage politics of Western Europe. Annu. Rev. Polit. Sci. **23**(1), 295–314 (2020). https://doi.org/10.1146/annurev-polisci-052217-104957

N. Gidron, J. Adams, W. Horne, *American Affective Polarization in Comparative Perspective* (Cambridge University Press, 2020)

E. Grande, T. Schwarzbözl, M. Fatke, Politicizing immigration in Western Europe. J. Eur. Publ. Policy **26**(10), 1444–1463 (2019). https://doi.org/10.1080/13501763.2018.1531909

J.D. Hunter, A. Wolfe, *Is There a Culture War? A Dialogue on Values and American Public Life.* ed. by E.J. Dionne, M. Cromartie (Brookings Institution Press, 2006). https://www.jstor.org/stable/10.7864/j.ctt6wpfn4

S. Jäckle, P.D. König, Drei Jahre Anschläge auf Flüchtlinge in Deutschland—welche Faktoren erklären ihre räumliche und zeitliche Verteilung? Three years of attacks against refugees in Germany—which factors explain the spatial and temporal distribution? KZfSS Kölner Zeitschrift

für Soziologie und Sozialpsychologie **71**(4), 623–649. https://doi.org/10.1007/s11577-019-00639-1
J. Jensen, E. Kaplan, S. Naidu, L. Wilse-Samson, Political polarization and the dynamics of political language: evidence from 130 Years of Partisan speech. Brookings Papers on Econ. Activity **43**(2 (Fall)), 1–81 (2012)
G. Kessler, B. Focas, J.M.O. de Zárate, E. Feuerstein, The 'Divergents' in a Polarized scenario: an exploratory study on the 'Non-Polarized' in controversies about crime news on argentine television. Revista SAAP **14**(2) (2020). https://doi.org/10.46468/rsaap.14.2.A3. [Original in Spanish]
D. Kleiner, The new German immigration law: history and details. Migraciones: J. Univer. Institut. Migrat. Stud. **16**, 227–236 (2004)
H. Kurthen, Germany at the crossroads: national identity and the challenges of immigration. Int. Migr. Rev. **29**(4), 914–938 (1995)
W. Kymlicka, The internationalization of minority rights. Int. J. Constitutional Law **6**(1), 1–32 (2007). https://doi.org/10.1093/icon/mom032
W. Kymlicka, R.R. Marín, Liberalism and minority rights. an interview. Ratio Juris **12**(2), 133–152 (1999). https://doi.org/10.1111/1467-9337.00116
Z. Layton-Henry, C. Wilpert eds,.*Challenging Racism in Britain and Germany.* Migration, Minorities, and Citizenship (New York, Palgrave Macmillan, 2003)
S.M. Lipset, S. Rokkan, Cleavage structures, party systems, and voter alignments (1967)
G. Magni, A. Reynolds, Voter preferences and the political underrepresentation of minority groups: lesbian, gay, and transgender candidates in advanced democracies. J. Polit. **83**(4), 1199–1215 (2021). https://doi.org/10.1086/712142
G. Magni, A. Reynolds, Why Europe's right embraces gay rights. J. Democr. **34**, 50–64 (2023). https://doi.org/10.1353/jod.2023.0003
A.C. May, C.S. Czymara, Careless whisper: political elite discourses activate national identities for far-right voting preferences. Nations Nationalism **30**(1), 90–109 (2024). https://doi.org/10.1111/nana.12985
McAuliffe and Triandafyllidou, World Migration Report 2022 [EN/SW]—World | ReliefWeb (2021). 1 Dec 2021. https://reliefweb.int/report/world/world-migration-report-2022
M.R. Moore, M. Stambolis-Ruhstorfer, LGBT sexuality and families at the start of the twenty-first century. Ann. Rev. Sociol. **39**, 491–507 (2013). https://doi.org/10.1146/annurev-soc-071312-145643
C. Mudde, *Populist Radical Right Parties in Europe.* 1st ed. (Cambridge University Press, 2007). https://doi.org/10.1017/CBO9780511492037
R. Münz, Germany and its immigrants. Migraciones: J. Univer. Institute for Migrat. Stud. **14**, 7–42 (2003). [Original in Spanish]
J.M. Mushaben, A spectre haunting Europe. German Polit. Soc. **38**(1), 7–29 (2020). https://doi.org/10.3167/gps.2020.380102
A. Noury, G. Roland, Identity politics and populism in Europe. Annu. Rev. Polit. Sci. **23**(1), 421–439 (2020). https://doi.org/10.1146/annurev-polisci-050718-033542
E. Odell, Hansard speeches 1979-2021: version 3.1.0 (Version V 3.1.0) [Data set]. Zenodo (2021). https://doi.org/10.5281/zenodo.4843485
J. Pejic, Minority rights in international law. Hum. Rights Q. **19**(3), 666–685 (1997). https://doi.org/10.1353/hrq.1997.0032
P.J. Quirk, Polarized populism: masses, elites, and partisan conflict. The Forum **9**(1), 0000102202154088841428 (2011). https://doi.org/10.2202/1540-8884.1428
R. Rekker, The nature and origins of political polarization over science. Public Underst. Sci. **30**(4), 352–368 (2021). https://doi.org/10.1177/0963662521989193
R. Romaniec, Germany: would-be migrant workers worried by growing racism (2024). Dw.Com. 2024. https://www.dw.com/en/germany-would-be-migrant-workers-worried-by-growing-racism/a-68095799

A.W. Schmidt-Catran, C.S. Czymara, Political elite discourses polarize attitudes toward immigration along ideological lines. A comparative longitudinal analysis of Europe in the twenty-first century. J. Ethn. Migrat. Stud. **49**(1), 85–109 (2023). https://doi.org/10.1080/1369183X.2022.2132222
A. Shehaj, A.J. Shin, R. Inglehart, Immigration and right-wing populism: an origin story. Party Politics **27**(2), 282–293 (2021). https://doi.org/10.1177/1354068819849888
Social Security Act, n.d., Social security act 1980. Text. Statute Law Database (1980). Accessed 14 May 2024. https://www.legislation.gov.uk/ukpga/1980/30/contents
S.C. Stokes, Political parties and democracy. Annual Rev. Polit. Sci. **26** (1999)
M. Stubbs, Three concepts of keywords. in *Keyness in Texts*, ed. by M. Bondi, M. Scott Studies in Corpus Linguistics (John Benjamins Publishing Company, 2010), pp. 21–42. https://doi.org/10.1075/scl.41.03stu
D. Thränhardt, The political uses of xenophobia in England, France and Germany. Party Politics **1**(3), 323–345 (1995). https://doi.org/10.1177/1354068895001003002
T. Triadafilopoulos, K. Schönwälder, How the federal republic became an immigration country: norms, politics and the failure of west Germany's guest worker system. German Polit. Soc. **24**, 1–19 (2006). https://doi.org/10.3167/104503006780441629
A. Unlu, T. Kotonen, Online polarization and identity politics: an analysis of Facebook discourse on Muslim and LGBTQ+ communities in Finland. Scand. Polit. Stud. **47**(2), 199–231 (2024). https://doi.org/10.1111/1467-9477.12270
M. Weber, D. Grunow, Y. Chen, S. Eger, Social solidarity with Ukrainian and Syrian refugees in the Twitter discourse. a comparison between 2015 and 2022. Europ. Societ. **0**(0), 1–28 (2023). https://doi.org/10.1080/14616696.2023.2275604
D. Wippman, The evolution and implementation of minority rights. FORDHAM Law Rev. **66** (1997)

Chapter 8
Emergence of Master Frame: A Semantic Network Analysis of News Framing of the LGBTQ Rights Movement in the United States (1960s–2010s)

Weijun Yuan

Abstract Framing is important for political communication, as it shapes how the public perceives political issues. Current studies of political framing rely on scholarly hindsight and interpretation, and typically focus on frames produced by a single actor or a small, homogeneous group. This chapter traces the dynamics of a wide range of frames associated with 59 organizations within the LGBTQ rights movement in the United States. It examines 5942 news headlines about the LGBTQ rights movement in four major U.S. newspapers over six decades. Using semantic networks, this study captures the structure of political frames and accounts for transient news framings of LGBTQ issues. It provides a dynamic analysis of when and how news framings of the LGBTQ rights movement converge to a dominant master frame. The results show that dichotomous master frames emerged during the early stage of the movement. While a master frame of gay "rights" rose to dominance in the 1980s and persisted into the 1990s, "same-sex marriage" emerged as the most dominant frame in the 2000s. These two inclusive and legitimate master frames become prominent as the activists and journalists attempted to address a broad audience. However, the rise of "same-sex marriage" was not driven by the most established groups or those with the most media coverage, but by organizations focused on family and children—whom the media viewed as having strong moral relevance to "marriage."

Keywords Social movements · LGBTQ movement · Newspaper · Framing · Semantic networks

W. Yuan (✉)
University of Chicago, Chicago, USA
e-mail: weijuny@uchicago.edu

M. A. Keijzer et al. (eds.), *Computational Social Science of Social Cohesion and Polarization*, Computational Social Sciences,
https://doi.org/10.1007/978-3-032-01373-6_8

8.1 Introduction

Framing plays a critical role in political communication. It shapes how people interpret, evaluate, and respond to political issues. Through framing, political actors define problems, identify their sources, suggest solutions, strategies, and tactics, and provide a rationale for action. By highlighting certain aspects of an issue while downplaying others, framing provides a lens through which individuals understand what is at stake, who is responsible, and what actions are appropriate. It helps organize complex information, align audiences with particular values or ideologies, and mobilize support for policy or collective action (Snow et al. 1986).

Classical studies on political framings focus on communication between elites and the masses, examining how elites shape public preferences (Lewis 2001; Chong and Druckman 2007; Druckman and Nelson 2003). In studying social movements, scholars have adopted a similar approach. They view social movement organizations and activist leaders as effective "recruiters" who convert bystanders into active participants through framing political issues at stake (Benford and Snow 2000; McVeigh et al. 2004; Evans 1997).

In identifying the frames developed by political actors, current studies typically rely on scholarly hindsight and subjective interpretation to identify a limited number of articulated frames (McCaffrey and Keys 2000; Koopmans and Duyvendak 1995; Swart 1995; Meyer and Whittier 1994; Snow et al. 1986). This approach allows for scrutinies of the most prominent frames that gain broad resonance, the most articulated frames that attract media attention, or to "master frames"—those broad, unifying narratives that transcend individual groups or movements (Benford 2013). It presumes that movement actors are strategic and well-informed—they generate well-articulated and effective frames. Although this assumption may be valid for politicians' statements, it likely overstates the communicative capacity of social movement organizations and activists. In contrast, many frames within a social movement's discourse are ambiguous and transient. Some of them only *become* prominent over time. To capture these dynamics of framing, we need to move away beyond retrospective analysis and instead trace the processes through which discursive frames are constructed, transmitted, and diffused.

Furthermore, current studies have been focused on frames developed by a single actor or a small group of similar actors, typically the most established organization or actors that received the most media attention. While this approach allows for in-depth analysis of key movement actors, less prominent or marginal actors may also shape the discourse in news media (Bail 2012). Through analyzing a more inclusive set of actors and frames, we could understand how frames evolve: how they spread and gain resonance, and how different frames conflict with or reinforce one another. These gaps call for a theory of framing dynamics and systematic empirical testing to better understand who drives what frames under what conditions.

Computational text analysis and semantic analysis methods enable us to empirically capture and analyze the dynamics of framing. This chapter focuses on the news framing of the LGBTQ rights movement in the United States. By analyzing 5942 newspaper headlines published over six decades in four major U.S. newspapers, this study captures a wide range of transient and unsettled frames within the LGBTQ rights movement. Using semantic network analysis and principal component analysis, it provides a descriptive analysis of how dominant master frames emerge in the news and change over time. The results show that dichotomous master frames about "discrimination" and "acceptance," "minority" and "society", "militancy" and "plea," and "backer" and "objector" emerged during the early stage of the movement. While a dominant master frame of gay "rights" emerged in the 1980s and persisted into the 1990s, "same-sex marriage" emerged as the most dominant frame in the 2000s. These inclusive and legitimate master frames become prominent as the activists and journalists address a broad audience. However, the rise of "same-sex marriage" as a prominent frame was not driven by the most established groups or those with the most media coverage, but by organizations focused on family and children—whom the media viewed as having strong moral relevance to "marriage."

8.2 When and How Does a Master Frame Emerge in the News?

When and how does a master frame emerge in the news? A "master frame" refers to a central organizing principle or narrative in the context of social movements. Master frames unify diverse groups and individuals by providing a common language or set of concepts that resonate with the audience. They are particularly important in social movement theory where they mobilize a broader constituency by making different grievances comprehensible and actionable under a *dominant* and *unifying* framework (Benford 2013). For example, in environmental activism, the master frame of *sustainability* can unify various specific movement issues such as climate change, anti-pollution, and wildlife conservation. By adopting this overarching frame, different groups can align their specific struggles and initiatives with a broader, more powerful narrative that appeals to a larger audience and is more likely to influence public opinion and policy. This has found to be the case in formal settings of political communication. In analyzing an archive of speeches from presidential debates between 1960 and 2004, Doerfel and Connaughton (2009) find that a centralized master frame provides an "anchor" that helps the audience understand complex political issues, making it more likely to garner broad support.

8.2.1 News Norms and Dichotomous Frames in Early Stage of a Movement

News media, as important communicators of political issues, craft or amplify certain frames, while downplaying others to shape public understanding (Gitlin 2003;

Gamson and Modigliani 1989; Vliegenthart and Walgrave 2012). When it comes to covering social movements, a prominent frame in news articles often emerges, as journalists rely on familiar narrative scripts and professional news values (Gans 1979; Tuchman 1978; Amenta and Caren 2022). In making sense of fast-moving and complex events, reporters gravitate toward well-known archetypes—such as peaceful protesters versus violent disruptors, or grassroots activists versus powerful elites—that offer coherent and emotional appeal to the audience (Bail 2012; Krebs 2015). These framing efforts help audience quickly interpret who the heroes, victims, and villains are. At the same time, standard news values—such as a preference for conflict, drama, individual stories, and balanced report—shape which elements of a movement get mentioned and emphasized in a news story (Gans 1979; Smith 2019). As a result, stories that highlight dramatic confrontations, suffering individuals, or striking moral decisions are more likely to be told, while more mundane aspects of organizing may be overlooked in the news. Over time, these patterns can reinforce a dominant interpretation of the movement across outlets, which solidify a master frame about a movement.

One of such examples is the news framing of the Occupy Wall Street movement. By introducing "the 99% versus the 1%," journalists recast economic inequality as a conflict between the vast majority of ordinary people and a small group of wealthy elite. This master frame resonated beyond the protesters and journalists in Manhattan. It appeared in media coverage of related movements across Europe, Latin America, and Asia (Kingsley and Gabbatt 2011). By simplifying a complex economic critique into a moral struggle, the frame traveled easily and shaped the public discourse about inequality long after the encampments ended.

Given the journalist norms and values, we expect to see a dichonomous master frame—one that organized interpretation around binary oppositions. Specifically, in the semantic network of political framings, we expect to see a cohesive core featuring two nodes with high centrality, and they each connects with a cluster of terms. The two clusters of terms are semantically coherent within themselves, yet contradictory to one another.

Such dichotomous master frames are more likely to emerge during the early stage of a movement because this is the moment when meaning is still fluid and contested. Journalists, under pressure to quickly make sense of unfolding events, are more likely to default to familiar news routines and cultural schemas and rely on moral contrasts and dramatic oppositions (Jacobs and Townsley 2011). These dichotomies provide narrative clarity and emotional resonance for audiences.

Moreover, because early coverage tends to set the tone for subsequent public understanding of the movement issues, media outlets are particularly influential at this moment. They are more likely to contrast the movement issue against pre-existing frames or dominant cultural scripts—especially when official sources (e.g., police, politicians) dominate early news narratives (Tuchman 1978; Entman 2002; Hallin 1986), which often lead reporters to structure coverage around competing sides.

Hypothesis 1: *Dichotomous master frames are more likely to emerge during the early stage of a movement.*

8.2.2 *Inclusive and Legitimate Frames Before Outsider Audience*

Master frames are more likely to emerge and be adopted across movements when there is a need to resonate broadly beyond the movement's core constituency (Benford 2013). As movements grow and seek broader support, they tend to craft more inclusive and legitimate master frames to engage outsider audiences. To reach those beyond the core activist base, movements must adopt frames that are morally compelling and culturally resonant. When frames reflect mainstream values, media are more likely to treat them as legitimate. This increases the chance that the frames will be amplified and spread across multiple news outlets (Koopmans and Olzak 2004). On the other hand, when addressing outsider audience, journalist tend to amplify master frames that are legible to a broader public. One of such examples is the Arab Spring, when protests erupted across countries like Tunisia, Egypt, Libya, and Syria—each with distinct political contexts and demands. Yet international media quickly adopted the master frame of a "pro-democracy uprising," which emphasized a shared struggle against authoritarianism and for civil liberties. This frame helped global audiences make sense of disparate events as part of a larger regional wave, even though the movements themselves differed in goals and outcomes.

Hypothesis 2: *Master frames are more likely to emerge when journalists and activists seek to address a broad outsider audience.*

8.2.3 *Influence of Large and Established Organizations*

Frames initiated by large, established organizations are expected to be amplified by the media. Organizations with established reputations, ties to elites, and professional infrastructure are better positioned to set the agenda (Gamson and Wolfsfeld 1993; Ryan 1991; McAdam et al. 1996). Furthermore, large organizations have more resources—media relations staff, public relations strategies, and pre-existing relationships with reporters—which allows them to craft messages that align with journalistic values and norms. Master frames developed by large and established organizations, therefore, are more likely to shape how issues are defined and depicted in the news (Amenta and Caren 2022).

However, it is worth noting that frames from large organizations may still be ignored if they lack newsworthiness. Recent studies have shown that established and media-savvy organization can be viewed as inauthentic—comparing with grassroots organizations and spontaneous participants (Polletta et al. 2021). This perceived lack of authenticity can limit their ability to resonate with audiences or attract sympathetic journalists (Bob 2005; Polletta 2006; Tufekci 2017). The influence of large and established organizations in a movement, therefore, warrants further empirical investigation.

Hypothesis 3: *Master frames are more likely to be associated with large and established organizations.*

8.3 The Case: LGBTQ Rights Movement

In the United States, the LGBTQ Rights Movement can date back to the early twentieth century. It gained significant momentum in the 1950s with the founding of pioneering organizations like the Mattachine Society in 1950 by Communist organizer Harry Hay in Los Angeles. The name of the society originates from a medieval French society of masked players, Société Mattachine, and represents the "masking" of homosexuality. The Society is dedicated to promoting equal civil rights for gay people. It adopted the organizational structure of the Communist Party and the members remained anonymous (D'Emilio 1983). Another early organization, the Daughters of Bilitis, was established in 1955, inspired by Pierre Louÿs's erotic lesbian poetry, *Chansons de Bilitis*. While these two prominent organizations were active in the 1950s' "Homophile Movement," they did not gain national newspaper coverage until August 9, 1963. This very first news article in the *Washington Post* (Goshko 1963), reports on a congressional hearing that discussed a bill aimed at limiting the activities of the Mattachine Society and similar "heterosexual organizations". Titled *'Morality' Talk Slows Sex Hearing*, the article focuses on the debate over "legal constitutionality and public morality" of "homosexual" issues among the members of the House District Subcommittee.

The LGBTQ Rights Movement in the United States provides an ideal case for studying news framing because it bring together a diverse range of organizations and its goals and tactics have changed over six decades. Initially, the movement focused on issues like repealing sodomy laws and challenging bans on gay bars. Over time, its focus expanded to include combating the HIV/AIDS epidemic, funding AIDS research, advocating for non-discriminatory employment policies, publicizing hate crime data, ending the military service ban for gay men and women, and promoting same-sex marriage. Analyzing the news coverage of the LGBTQ rights movement allows us to understand which activist claims have received attention in mainstream media.

Second, the LGBTQ rights movement is led by several prominent national organizations. Unlike grassroots organizations engaged in local civic engagement, LGBTQ rights groups are more like advocacy groups, seeking to influence policies and promote cultural changes at the national level. Unlike disruptive groups engaged in non-institutionalized activism, LGBTQ rights organizations primarily advance their claims through institutional channels. This approach likely increases their legitimacy in the eyes of mainstream media, leading to more substantive coverage of their demands (Amenta and Caren 2022). As a result, how newspaper frames the broader movement largely depends on how they report these organizational claims. The LGBTQ rights movement thus offer a valuable case for studying how the news media treat different organizations and their demands.

8.4 Data and Methods

The data for testing these hypotheses come from the *ProQuest Historical Newspapers* database. This news archive database contains published articles in 72 national and local newspapers in the United States and Canada, some dating to the late eighteenth century. I sampled articles on the LGBTQ rights movement in the United States using the organization list from Amenta and Caren's Political Organizations in News (PONs) project (2012). An article was included in the sample if it mentions any of the 59 LGBTQ organizations or advocacy groups in its headline or full text. The list includes only organizations specifically dedicated to LGBTQ issues, excluding allies or groups with a hybrid identity. For example, while the American Civil Liberties Union (ACLU) has a long history of supporting gay and lesbian rights through its Lesbian and Gay Rights Project since 1985, it was not included in the sample. Excluding such hybrid or ally organizations helps identify LGBTQ-specific coverage and reduces noise for NLP-based analyses. This approach is unlikely to bias the results, as these organizations often collaborate with major LGBTQ groups that are co-mentioned in the same articles. For instance, ACLU often partners with Lambda Legal to support gay and lesbian rights through the courts, and such collaborations are captured in articles that mention Lambda Legal, which are included in my sample.

The ProQuest search yields 5942 articles from the *New York Times*, *Washington Post*, *Wall Street Journal*, and *Los Angeles Times* between 1960 and 2018. My analysis focuses on the headlines of these articles. Analyzing headlines rather than full article texts is not only methodologically more feasible but also analytically more appropriate for identifying dominant frames. Headlines are crafted to summarize and emphasize the central message; they encapsulate the important information and significantly influence their audience. On one hand, headlines convey key messages to readers. They foreground the dominant frame that journalists believe will seize the attention or readers. Furthermore, headlines are more likely to reflect editorial judgement and the position of the news agency, unlike the text of the article that may be more balanced. On the other hand, headlines provide the first impression of the article. They shape readers' expectations and influence how they engage with the text. Ecker et al. (2014) found that respondents in an experiment primarily recalled details that aligned with the headline. Headlines not only guide subsequent information processing but also bias readers toward a particular interpretation. Most readers scan headlines more than they read full articles, and headlines thus shape initial interpretation. By framing the issue in a specific way, a headline can shape the readers' cognition, making it difficult for them to revise initial perceptions later on.

All headlines in the sample were retrieved from the ProQuest Historical Newspapers archive. The corpus consists of a total of 478,432 terms. The average and median word counts per headline are 12.73 and 10, respectively, with minimal repetition of words. The terms used to construct semantic networks of political framings only include nouns. I used CoreNLP part-of-speech tagging tools to isolate nouns. Then I removed stopwords and applied stemming to reduce words to their root forms. I also manually identified and processed key bi-grams and multi-word expressions—such as "White House" and "don't ask," which refers to the "Don't Ask, Don't Tell" (DADT) policy.

This research employs a network approach to political communication and framing. Inspired by Carley's mental model (Carley and Palmquist 1991; Diesner and Carley 2008; Corman et al. 2002), it use text networks to bridge language and cognition. By representing texts as semantic networks, this study empirically visualizes and analyzes how communicators evoke concepts and make meanings. It examines a diversity of frames and the degree of consensus among communicators and their audiences.

Semantic networks are constructed based on word occurrences within each headline. Nodes in the network represent terms, and an undirected edge is established between two nodes if their corresponding terms co-occur in the same headline. These edges are weighted according to the frequency of the terms' co-occurrence. A political frame is captured by a set of concepts that are interrelated, such that the meaning of each concept is comprehensible within the context of other concepts. In this way, frames can be identified as labeled induced subgraphs within the concept network. The analysis starts with a descriptive review of the framings about the LGBTQ rights movement in the United States.

Then to analyze the driver of the emergence of the "same-sex marriage" master frame, I use network Principal Component Analysis (PCA) to compare the frames associated with different social movement organizations. To that end, I sampled 139 frequently mentioned terms in the headlines that appear in the corpus at least 20 times. Using these terms as nodes, I constructed semantic networks for the nine top organizations, each mentioned in over 80 news articles. These include the Human Rights Campaign (817 articles), Lambda Legal Defense Fund (618 articles), National Gay and Lesbian Task Force (484 articles), Log Cabin Federation (292 articles), Gay and Lesbian Alliance Against Defamation (241 articles), Parents, Families, and Friends of Lesbians and Gay (217 articles), Queer Nation (180 articles), Children of Lesbians and gay Everywhere (112 articles), and Gay and Lesbian Victory Fund (82 articles).

In comparing the semantic graphs of different organizations, I started by generating a graph covariance matrix $\boldsymbol{C}$ for the semantic graphs of different organizations $G_1, \ldots, G_9$. Then the eigendecomposition of $\boldsymbol{C} = \mathbf{W}\Lambda\mathbf{W}^{\mathrm{T}}$ allows for specifying the loading, $\mathbf{W}_{ij}$ of G_i on the jth principal component. The method helps reduce the dimensionality by generating the covariance between the adjacency matrices of the graphs and identifying dimensions with the most variance (Butts and Carley 2001).

8.5 Results

8.5.1 LGBTQ Rights Movement in the News: Trend Over Time

Figure 8.1 presents the news coverage of the LGBTQ Rights Movement in the *New York Times*, Washington Post, *Wall Street Journal*, and *Los Angeles Times*. Initially low in the 1960s, coverage saw a modest increase in the late 1960s and early 1970s. The increase coincides with the 1969 Stonewall Riots. This critical event occurred when police raided the Stonewall Inn, a gay bar in New York City's Greenwich Village. On June 28, 1970, the first anniversary of the riots, thousands marched in Manhattan. Later the activists institutionalized the pride parade as a commemoration of the Stonewall Riots (Armstrong and Crage 2006).

As shown in Fig. 8.1, the newspaper coverage surged during the 1980s and the early 1990s. This period saw the establishment of prominent national organizations such as the Human Rights Campaign and Gay and Lesbian Alliance Against Defamation (GLAAD), which garnered extensive media attention. During the 1980s, the LGBTQ rights movement began to achieve institutional policy rewards, and gay activists increasingly aligned with the Democratic Party. Notably in 1980, the Democratic Party expanded its anti-discrimination platform to include a clause on sexual orientation.

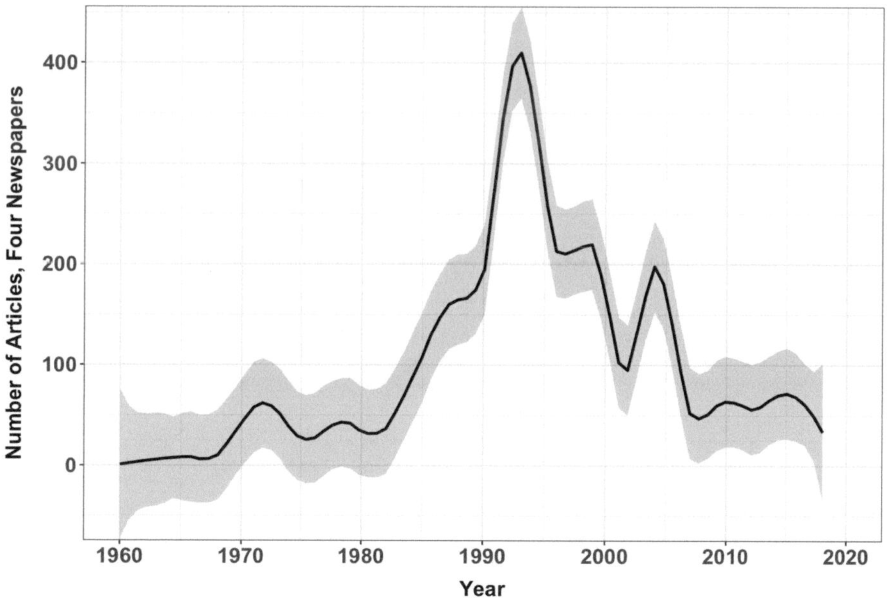

Fig. 8.1 News coverage of the LGBTQ rights movement in the United States in *New York Times, Washington Post*, *Wall Street Journal*, and *Los Angeles Times*

The number of articles peaked in 1993 with 544 articles, then experienced a sharp decline in the late 1990s and early 2000s. Coverage revived in 2004, which coincides with an increase in court rulings related to same-sex marriage and civil unions.

8.5.2 *Terms in the News Headlines*

Concepts constitute framings. How did concepts in newspaper headlines evolve between 1960 and 2018? The bump chart in Fig. 8.2 shows the most frequently used terms across six decades and how their rankings changed over time. As indicated by the blue lines, only 5 out of the 29 most frequent terms (each appeared more than twice) consistently ranked in the top across all six periods: "group," "bill," "rights," "ban," and "rule." All other terms fell out of the top rankings. Of the 28 most frequent terms listed in the 2010 wave, three were new: "transgender," "don't ask," and "Trump," marked by red dots. The remaining 25 top terms from the 2010 wave ascended to prominence between 1970 and 2010. For instance, "court" and "law" first appeared in the 1970s and gained prominence in the 1980s, while "same-sex" and "marriage" became salient in the 2000s. The bump chart reveals significant shifts in the concepts associated with LGBTQ rights/issues, particularly during the 1990s and early 2000s—an unsettled period when many terms shifted in ranking.

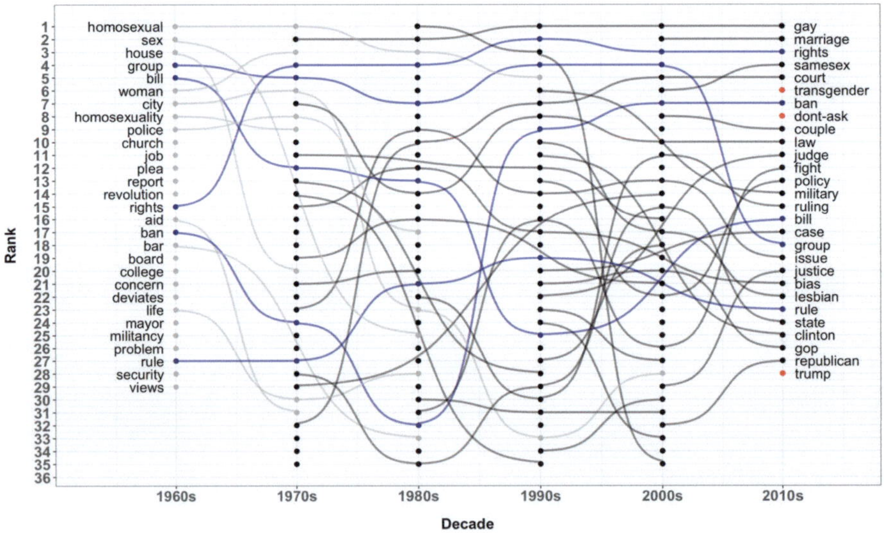

Fig. 8.2 The most frequent terms about the LGBTQ rights movement that appear in the newspaper headlines (1960s–2010s). *Note* blue nodes and lines highlight the five most frequent terms that consistently ranked among the top across all six periods. Red nodes denote the three terms that rise to the top list in the 2010 wave: "transgender," "don't ask," and "Trump"

8.5.3 The Emergence of Dichotomous and Inclusive Master Frames

The structure of political framing is operationalized using semantic networks, which are constructed using terms from newspaper headlines. The nodes of the semantic networks are the terms, and the edges represents co-occurrences of these terms in the same headline. These edges are weighted by the frequency of co-occurrence. Figure 8.3 displays the aggregated semantic networks for each of the six decades. Consistently central terms like "gay" and "homosexual/homosexuality" have been excluded from the analysis. For each graph, I included approximately 150 terms that were most frequently mentioned in the news during that period. Specifically, in the 1960s, 1970s, 1980s, 2000s, and 2010s, terms included appeared at least twice in the corpus. In the 1990s, a period marked by a significant larger volume of text, terms needed to appear at least seven times in the corpus to be included in the graph.

In the 1960s, the connection between terms in the semantic networks was relatively weak, with most ties appearing only once. Eliminating ties with a weight of 1 result in numerous isolated concepts. Notable exceptions include strong associations between "house" and "bill," "life" and "city," "rights" and "minority", and "militancy" and "job." Given that coverage of the LGBTQ movements was just beginning during the 1960s, the framing of these issues was still in its formative stages.

We expected the master frame that emerges during the early stage of a movement to manifest a structure of contradictions—one that organizes interpretation around binary oppositions and provides narrative clarity and emotional resonance for audiences (Hypothesis 1). The semantic network of news framings during the 1960s shows a structure of two well-connected clusters, representing two master frames focusing on two different issues: (1) "homosexuals" fighting back against being fired or barred from public service jobs and (2) the resistance to Internal Revenue Service (IRS) classification of gay rights organizations as "unjustified associations. Within each of these cohesive cores, we can identify a few sets of binary contradictions at the center: "discrimination" and "acceptance," "minority" and "society", "militancy" and "plea," and "backer" and "objector." These initial framings about the LGBTQ rights movement align well with the news value for dramatic conflicts, newsworthy disruptions, and balanced report.

The semantic network for the 1970s, on the contrary, forms a multi-core structure, with "protest," "activist," "rights," and "city" at the center of each core. Yet at the same time, "city," "vote," "rights," "council," and "bill" form a clique. The clique captures the frame of "homosexual bill" and "rights." The bill was debated at the New York City Council, which aimed to prohibit discrimination against gay people in housing, employment, and public accommodations. At this stage, "rights" had not yet emerged as a master frame. References to "heterosexual" rights remained limited to narrow legislative contexts, and the debates had not expanded beyond the local level or mobilized broader support from LGBTQ communities nationwide. Moreover, it is notable that in the 1970s, "parade" and "pride" are at the periphery of the semantic network. Although activists celebrated the Stonewall Riots and argued that the pride

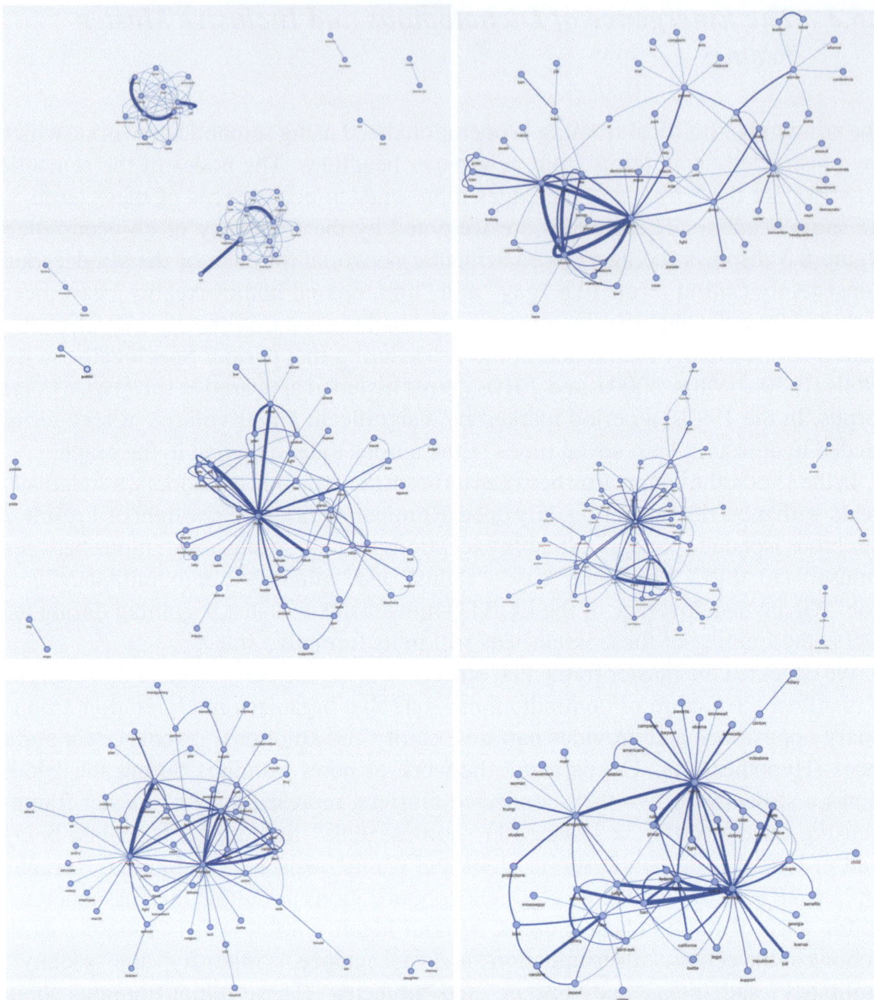

Fig. 8.3 Semantic networks of newspaper headlines (the 1960s–2010s). **a** Semantic networks of newspaper headlines in the 1960s. **b** Semantic networks of newspaper headlines in the 1970s. **c** Semantic networks of newspaper headlines in the 1980s. **d** Semantic networks of newspaper headlines in the 1990s. **e** Semantic networks of newspaper headlines in the 2000s. **f** Semantic networks of newspaper headlines in the 2010s. *Note*: "gay" and "homosexual/homosexuality" are removed from the corpus for constructing semantic networks

parade fueled the movement; mainstream news media appear to overlook this event during the 1970s (Armstrong and Crage 2006).

The 1980s semantic network shows a one-core structure with the unifying concept "rights" at the very center. "Rights" begins to take shape as a master frame, as evidenced by growing number and generality of co-occuring concepts. Terms such as "activist," "issue," "bill," "group," and "court" are all directly linked to "rights," thereby expanding and reinforcing its meaning. In the 1990s, the core structure around "rights" persisted, with sustained ties to terms like "court," "ban," "activist," "fight," and "group." New additions to the core included "military," "lesbian" and "AIDS." Notably, "lesbian," connected directly to "rights" for the first time, moving from its earlier peripheral link to "woman." "AIDS" emerged as a prominent issue, framed both as a public health crisis—linked with "patient," "test," and "health"—and a gay rights issue—connected to "fight," "activist," and "case." The term "military" is tied to "suit," "service," "rule," "president," and "compromise," reflecting debates over the "Don't ask, Don't tell" policy.

The emergence of the "rights" master frame coincides with a sharp rise in news coverage of the LGBTQ movement beginning in the 1980s and peaking in the 1990s (See Fig. 8.1). This period marked a turning point: the movement gained increased visibility and political recognition, partly due to the passage of policies that granted legitimacy to LGBTQ issues and helped elevate LGBTQ concerns into the mainstream political discourse (D'Emilio 2000; Bernstein 2005). At the same time, the movement broadened its coalition, forging alliances with civil rights groups, feminist organizations, and public health advocates (Tarrow 1998; Gamson 1995; Rimmerman 2002). These partnerships expanded the movement's reach and encouraged activists to craft more inclusive and resonate frames aimed at a broader audience. As a result, the "rights" frame became central—not only to unify diverse groups within the movement but also for the journalists to communicate legitimacy, and moral urgency to the wider public.

In the 2000s, the semantic network once again diverges, organizing around four master frames: "rights," "(activist) group," "court," and "marriage." "Marriage," previously a peripheral term in the 1990s semantic network, becomes central—appearing 178 times in 1137 headlines—emerging as the most frequently mentioned term. This prominence continues into the 2010s, where "marriage," "rights," and "law/court" are located at the core of the semantic network structure. Notably, the term "transgender" rose to prominence in the 2010s, which forms a new cluster with terms such as "movement," "lesbian," "student," "woman," "man," and "Trump." However, these associations appear weak, and the framing of transgender issues tends to be transient and largely reactive to political events. For example, during the 2016 presidential campaign, Donald Trump's comments on LGBTQ issues, such as his stance on unisex bathrooms, led the *New York Times* to describe him as "far more accepting of sexual minorities" than other GOP leaders (Haberman 2016).

As the semantic networks of newspaper headlines show, in the early stage of the LGBTQ rights movement, journalists tended to adopt dichotomous master frames shaped by established news norms and values. This finding coincides with what we expect in Hypothesis 1. As the movement proliferated, new master frames centered on "rights" and "same-sex marriage" emerged. This shift reflects changes in the movement's cycle and audience. With increased media attention, government responses, and broader coalition, both activists and journalists faced the need to speak to a wider public. In this context, the movement became more likely to craft inclusive and legitimate master frame to address outsider audiences, and journalists were more inclined to adopt such frames. These dynamics align with the expectation of Hypothesis 2: inclusive master frames are likely to arise when the movement address a broad outsider audience.

8.5.4 Who Drove the Rise of the "Same-Sex Marriage" Master Frame?

Which organizations have driven the rise of "same-sex marriage" as a new master frame? This section focuses on the process through which "same-sex marriage" emerged as a master frame between 1990 and 2005. Figure 8.4 shows the PCA biplot for semantic networks (loaded on the first two components. The variance explained by these components is 0.495 $\left(\boldsymbol{\Lambda}_{jj}/\sum_i \boldsymbol{\Lambda}_{ii}\right)$. The PCA results reveal two distinct clusters of organizations, suggesting that the political frames (subgraphs) associated with these two groups are unlikely to co-occur. One cluster includes Queer Nation, Lambda Legal, and Parents, Family, and Friends of Lesbian and Gay. The other includes Children of Lesbians and Gay Everywhere, Gay and Lesbian Alliance Against Defamation (GLAAD), Gay and Lesbian Victory Fund, the National Gay and Lesbian Task Force, Log Cabin Federation, and Human Rights Campaign. The overall aggregated semantic network structure aligns more closely with the second group.

PCA analysis of unweighted adjacency matrices yields similar results. As shown in Fig. 8.5, Queer Nation, Lambda Legal, and Parents, Family, and Friends of

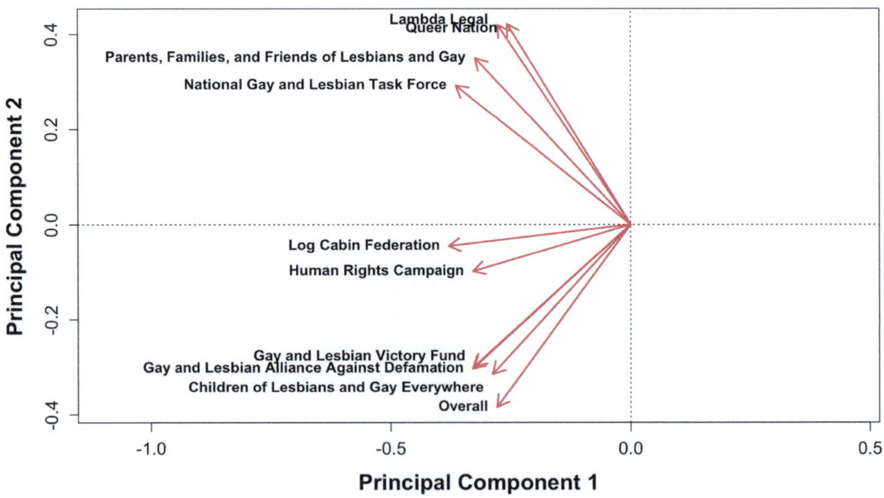

Fig. 8.4 PCA biplot of semantic networks associated with the nine most covered organizations (weighted matrices). *Note* Semantic network edges are weighted according to the frequency of the terms' co-occurrence

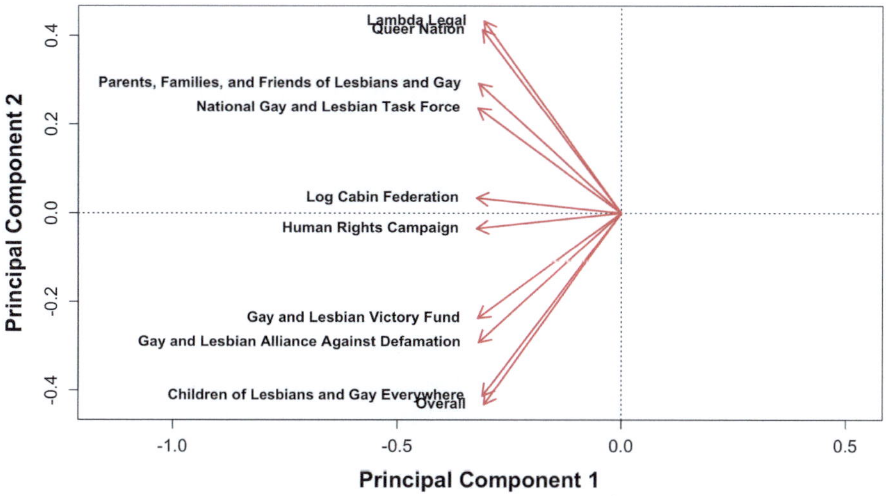

Fig. 8.5 PCA biplot of semantic networks associated with the nine most covered organizations (unweighted matrices). *Note* Semantic network edges are unweighted. An edge exists between two terms if they co-occur at least once

Lesbian and Gay form a cluster, separate from the cluster consisting of Gay and Lesbian Victory Fund, Gay and Lesbian Alliance Against Defamation, and Children of Lesbians and Gay Everywhere. Again, the overall pattern graph aligns more closely with the latter group of organizations.

The PCA results suggest that the most influential frames are not those associated with established, large, or prominent organizations, such as the National Gay and Lesbian Task Force. This finding does not support Hypothesis 3, which expects master frames developed by large and established organizations to be more likely to attract media attention. In contrast, despite receiving the least news coverage among the selected organizations, the frames in the articles about the Children of Lesbians and Gays Everywhere and the Gay and Lesbian Victory Fund align most closely with the overall news framing of the LGBTQ rights movement. This organization, founded by individuals with same-sex parents, is linked to the "same-sex marriage" frame. However, the organization's primary activities are more related to civic actions supporting children of gay parents, rather than leading initiatives on same-sex marriage. Their association with the "same-sex marriage" master frame is likely to stem from the media's perception of them direct stake in the issue. To the mainstream media, children represent the most directly affected group when it comes to matters of "marriage," which is traditionally viewed as the foundation of a nuclear family. In contrast, another family-related organization, Family, and Friends of Lesbian and Gay, are not associated with the same-sex marriage frame in the news as much. Instead, their news coverage emphasizes "support" through narratives of "fight," "battle," and "rights."

8.6 Discussion

This chapter provides a descriptive analysis of the dynamics of framing around the LGBTQ rights movement in the United States in four national newspapers from the 1960s to the 2010s. By analyzing the semantic networks of news headlines, it traces how the structure of master frames evolved over time. Network Principal Component Analysis (PCA) results reveal the role of activist groups in driving certain frames in the news. Results from semantic analysis and network PCA shows that newspaper framing shifts over time—sometimes coalescing around an inclusive and unifying master frame, and at other times remaining fragmented and unsettled. During the early stage of the movement, dichotomous master frames are more likely to emerge because journalists tend to default to familiar scripts, moral contrasts, balanced report, and newsworthiness of conflicts to quickly make sense of events. Furthermore, with increased media attention, government responses, and broader coalition, unifying master frames are more likely to emerge, as both activists and journalists face the need to address a wider public. And yet, we also find that a master frame is not always initiated by the largest or most established activist groups, nor by the most covered organizations in the news. Instead, it can be driven by marginal organizations that mainstream media perceived as morally relevant to the issue at hand.

This study explores the structure and dynamics of political framings over six decades. The decade-long time slices used in this analysis may be too wide to capture rapid frame shifts. Further studies are needed to focus on periods when significant shifts occurred. Furthermore, the results suggest a divergence in the news frames associated with different social movement organizations. However, it is still too soon to conclude that specific organizations directly crafted, reinforced, or drove the formation of certain frames. On the one hand, the word choice in the headlines can be significantly different from the framing of the organizations in the body of the article. On the other hand, the framing in the headlines may differ significantly from the organization's own narratives. The frames used by activists and those adopted by the media exist within a competitive discursive field, with both aiming to influence cultural change. Future studies would benefit from analyzing framings in both news media and activists' own accounts to better understand how they shape one another.

In studying the framing process related to the LGBTQ rights movement, it would be beneficial to also consider celebrities as influential communicators. Celebrities significantly impact how the media and activists discuss LGBTQ issues. For instance, openly gay politicians and entertainers launched "come out of the closet" campaigns and encourage gay individuals to run for political office. Similarly, when former Vice President of the United States, Dick Cheney publicly supported his lesbian daughter, discussions about same-sex marriage began to intersect with conservative family values (Cheney 2006).

Moreover, the current sample excluded organizations that cut across movement boundaries and yet shaped the public discourse about LGBTQ rights. These may include ACT-UP (AIDS Coalition to Unleash Power), Human Rights Watch, and the ACLU. Such "hybrid" organizations are expected to be more innovative in creating frames and tactics (Heaney and Rojas 2014) and are more frequently cited by mainstream media (Wang and Soule 2016). Excluding these organizations from the sample might have led to fewer frames being captured, especially in the early stages of the movement, when LGBTQ-specific organizations had yet to be established. Future research could examine the role of hybrid organizations in driving the media attention to certain master frames, although compiling and validating a comprehensive list of such groups across multiple decades may pose a methodological challenge.

The current semantic networks are constructed based on word co-occurrences within news headlines. While this approach captures the relationships between key concepts, it misses details such as word order and the valence of relations, which are important for understanding framing. Future studies may consider rule-based syntactic approaches to extract the subject-predicate-object triplets from each sentence (Van Atteveldt et al. 2006; Rusu et al. 2007). This allows us to distinguish relationships such "A attacks B" from "B attacks A," a crucial distinction since framing often involves identifying a cause and targeting an object. Furthermore, the predicate usually conveys the valence of the relationship. For instance, verbs like "seek," "facilitate," and "promote," indicate positive ties, while "rebuff," "protest," and "blame," suggest a negative relationship between the subject and the object. Such nuances are critical for differentiating frames, although this approach entails complicities involved in the data processing and validation.

Computational and network approaches have advanced our ability to manipulate granular text data, map structures of meaning, and trace the evolution of political framing. These methods open new possibilities for studying how political frames emerge and change over time, but they also pose challenges for validation, inference, and interpretation. Thoughtful analytical and validation strategies based on domain knowledge are essential for accurate interpretations and meaningful conclusions.

References

E. Amenta, N. Caren, *Rough Draft of History* (Princeton University Press, 2022)

E. Amenta, N. Caren, J.E. Stobaugh, Political reform and the historical trajectories of U.S. social movements in the twentieth century. Soc. Forces **90**, 1073–1100 (2012)

E.A. Armstrong, S.M. Crage, Movements and memory: the making of the stonewall myth. Am. Sociol. Rev. **71**(5), 724–751 (2006). https://doi.org/10.1177/000312240607100502

C.A. Bail, The fringe effect: civil society organizations and the evolution of media discourse about Islam since the September 11th attacks. Am. Sociol. Rev. **77**(6), 855–879 (2012)

R.D. Benford, D.A. Snow, Framing processes and social movements: an overview and assessment. Ann. Rev. Sociol. **26**, 611–639 (2000)

R.D. Benford, Master frame, in *The Wiley-Blackwell Encyclopedia of Social and Political Movements*, ed. by D. Snow, D.D. Porta, B. Klandermans, D. McAdam (Wiley-Blackwell, Hoboken, New Jersey, 2013)

M. Bernstein, Liberalism and social movement success: the case of the United States sodomy laws. Mob. Int. Q.**10**(2), 145–160 (2005)

C. Bob, *The Marketing of Rebellion: Insurgents, Media, and International Activism* (Cambridge University Press, Cambridge, 2005)

C.T. Butts, K.M. Carley, Multivariate methods for interstructural analysis. CASOS Working Paper, Carnegie Mellon University, 2001

K.M. Carley, M. Palmquist, Extracting, representing, and analyzing mental models. Soc. Forces **70**(3), 601–636 (1991)

M. Cheney, *Now it's My Turn: A Daughter's Chronicle of Political Life* (Simon and Schuster, 2006)

D. Chong, J. Druckman, Framing public opinion in competitive democracies. Am. Polit. Sci. Rev. **101**(4), 637–655 (2007). https://doi.org/10.1017/S0003055407070554

S.R. Corman, T. Kuhn, R.D. McPhee, K.J. Dooley, Studying complex discursive systems: centering resonance analysis of communication. Hum. Commun. Res. **28**(2), 157–206 (2002)

J. D'Emilio, *Sexual Politics, Sexual Communities: The Making of a Homosexual Minority in the United States, 1940–1970* (The University of Chicago Press. Library of Congress General Collections, Chicago, 1983)

J. D'Emilio, Cycles of change, questions of strategy: the gay and lesbian movement after fifty years. In *The Politics of Gay Rights*, ed. by C. Rimmerman, K.D. Wald, C. Wilcox (eds.) (University of Chicago Press, Chicago, 2000)

J. Diesner, K.M. Carley, Conditional random fields for entity extraction and ontological text coding. J. Comput. Math. Organ. Theory. **14**(3), 248–262 (2008). https://doi.org/10.1007/s10588-008-9029-z

M.L Doerfel, L. Connaughton, Semantic networks and competition: election year winners and losers in U.S. televised presidential debates, 1960–2004. J. Am. Soc. Inf. Sci. Technol. **60**(1), 201–218 (2009)

J.N. Druckman, K.R. Nelson, Framing and deliberation. Am. J. Polit. Sci. **47**(Oct), 728–744 (2003)

U.K.H. Ecker, S. Lewandowsky, E.P. Chang, R. Pillai, The effects of subtle misinformation in news headlines. J. Exp. Psychol. Appl. **20**(4), 323–335 (2014). https://doi.org/10.1037/xap0000028

R. Entman, Framing: towards clarification of a fractured paradigm, in *McQuail's Reader in Mass Communication Theory*, ed. by D. McQuail, pp. 390–397 (2002)

J.H. Evans, Multi-organizational fields and social movement organization frame content: the religious fro-choice movement. Sociol. Inq. **67**(4), 451–469 (1997)

J. Gamson, Must identity movements self-destruct? a queer dilemma. Soc. Probl. **42**(3), 390–407 (1995)

W.A. Gamson, A. Modigliani, Media discourse and public opinion on nuclear power: a constructionist approach. Am. J. Sociol. **95**(1), 1–37 (1989)

W.A. Gamson, G. Wolfsfeld, Movements and media as interacting systems. Ann. Am. Acad. Pol. Soc. Sci. **528**, 114–125 (1993)

H. Gans, *Deciding What's News: A Study of CBS Evening News, NBC Nightly News, Newsweek, and Time* (Pantheon Books, New York, 1979)

T. Gitlin, in *The Whole World is Watching: Mass Media in the Making and Unmaking of the New Left* (University of California Press, 2003)

J.M. Goshko, 'Morality' Talk Slows Sex Hearing: Law Requires Permit Dowdy Cites Other Curbs Will try To Draft Bill. The Washington Post. 09 Aug 1963: C2 (1963)

J. Grimmer, B. Stewart, Text as data: the promise and pitfalls of automatic content analysis methods for political texts. Polit. Anal. **21**(3), 267–297 (2013). https://doi.org/10.1093/pan/mps028

M. Haberman, Trump Flouts G.O.P. Dogma on Gay Issues. New York Times. 23 Apr 2016: A.1 (2016)

D.C. Hallin, *The "Uncensored War:" The Media and Vietnam* (Cambridge University Press, New York, 1986)

M.T. Heaney, F. Rojas, Hybrid activism: social movement mobilization in a multimovement environment. Am. J. Sociol. **119**(4), 1047–1103 (2014). https://doi.org/10.1086/674897

R. Jacobs, E. Townsley, *The Space of Opinion: Media Intellectuals and the Public Sphere* (Oxford University Press, New York, 2011)

P. Kingsley, A. Gabbatt, Occupy: we are the world. The Guardian. 30 Nov 2011

R. Koopmans, J.W. Duyvendak, The political construction of the nuclear energy issue and its impact on the mobilization of anti-nuclear movements in western Europe. Soc. Probl. **42**(2), 235–251 (1995)

R. Koopmans, S. Olzak, Discursive opportunities and the evolution of right-wing violence in Germany. Am. J. Sociol. **110**(1), 198–230 (2004)

R.R. Krebs, in *Narrative and the Making of US National Security*, vol. 138. (Cambridge University Press, New York, 2015)

K. Krippendorff, in *Content Analysis An Introduction to Its Methodology* (SAGE Publications, New York, 2012(1980))

J. Lewis, in *Constructing Public Opinion: How Political Elites Do What They Like and Why We Seem to Go along with It* (Columbia University Press, 2001)

D. McAdam, J.D. McCarthy, M.N. Zald, *Comparative perspectives on social movements: Political opportunities, Mobilizing Structures, and Cultural Framings* (Cambridge University Press, New York, 1996)

D. McCaffrey, J. Keys, Competitive framing processes in the abortion debate: polarization-vilification, frame saving, and frame debunking. Sociol. Q. **41**(1), 41–61 (2000)

R. McVeigh, D.J. Myers, D. Sikkink, Corn, Klansmen, and Coolidge: structure and framing in social movements. Soc. Forces **83**(2), 653–690 (2004)

D.S. Meyer, N. Whittier, Social movement spillover. Soc. Probl. **41**(2), 277–298 (1994)

F. Polletta, in *It Was Like a Fever: Storytelling in Protest and Politics* (University of Chicago Press, 2006)

F. Polletta, T. DoCarmo, K.M. Ward, J. Callahan, Personal storytelling in professionalized social movements. Mobilization: Int. Q. **26**(1), 65–86 (2021). https://doi.org/10.17813/1086-671X-26-1-65

C.A. Rimmerman, in *From Identity to Politics: The Lesbian and Gay Movements in the United States* (Temple University Press, 2002)

D. Rusu, L. Dali, B. Fortuna, M. Grobelnik, D. Mladenic, Triplet extraction from sentences, in *Proceedings of the 10th International Multiconference Information Society-IS* (2007), pp. 8–12

C. Ryan, *Prime Time Activism: Media Strategies for Grassroots Organizing* (South End Press, Boston, MA, 1991)

P. Smith, in *Why War? The Cultural Logic of Iraq, The Gulf War, and Suez* (University of Chicago Press, 2019)

D.A. Snow, E.B. Rochford, S.K. Worden, R.D. Benford, Frame alignment processes, micromobilization, and movement participation. Am. Sociol. Rev. **51**(4), 464–481 (1986). https://doi.org/10.2307/2095581

W.J. Swart, The league of nations and the Irish question: master frames, cycles of protest, and "master frame alignment." Sociol. Q. **36**(3), 465–481 (1995)

S. Tarrow, in *Power in Movement: Social Movements and Contentious Politics* (Cambridge University Press, New York, 1998)

G. Tuchman, *Making News: A Study in the Construction of Reality* (Free Press, New York, 1978)

Z. Tufekci, in *Twitter and Tear Gas: The Power and Fragility of Networked Protest* (Yale University Press, 2017)

W. Van Atteveldt, J. Kleinnijenhuis, K. Carley, RCADF: Towards a relational content analysis standard. Presentated at the International Communication Association (ICA), Dresden (2006)

R. Vliegenthart, S. Walgrave, The interdependency of mass media and social movements, *The Sage Handbook of Political Communication*, ed. by in M. Scammell, H.A. Semetko (2012), pp. 387–398

D.J. Wang, S.A. Soule, Tactical innovation in social movements: the effects of peripheral and multi-issue protest. Am. Sociol. Rev. **81**(3), 517–548 (2016). https://doi.org/10.1177/0003122416644414

Part III
Agent-Based Modeling

Chapter 9
Understanding Mutual Social Influence When People Prefer Coherent Beliefs

Bruce Edmonds, Peter Steiglechner, Jan Lorenz, František Kalvas, and Marlene C. L. Batzke

Abstract Humans tend to accept beliefs that are coherent with their other beliefs and reject those that do not fit with them. As a result of this, different people might arrive at different belief structures and the consequences of this on societal belief patterns are not known. In this chapter we show one way to induce possible 'coherence structures' for groups of people from survey data and then set them going, influencing each other, within a computer simulation of individual agents. Of course, people do not perfectly adhere to coherence strategy but are amenable to all sorts of other influences. In the simulation, these other influences are represented as randomness that affects whether to accept or reject beliefs. The simulation shows that the degree to which agents act randomly (rather than based on coherence) is critical to the outcomes. Low levels of randomness (i.e., strong strive for coherence) result in agents converging on more extreme beliefs. With high levels of randomness (i.e., weak striving for coherence) the simulated agents converge on moderate beliefs. It is with some intermediate adherence to coherence that the resulting spread of beliefs looks more like what we observe in the real world—spread out or polarised in some beliefs but converged in

B. Edmonds
UiT The Arctic University of Norway, Tromsø, Norway

B. Edmonds (✉)
The Centre for Policy Modelling, Manchester, UK
e-mail: bruce@edmonds.name

Umeå University, Umeå, Sweden

P. Steiglechner · J. Lorenz
Constructor University, Bremen, Germany

P. Steiglechner
Leibniz Centre for Tropical Marine Research (ZMT), Bremen, Germany

Complexity Science Hub, Vienna, Austria

F. Kalvas
University of West Bohemia, Pilsen, Czech Republic

M. C. L. Batzke
Royal Holloway, University of London, London, UK

M. A. Keijzer et al. (eds.), *Computational Social Science of Social Cohesion and Polarization*, Computational Social Sciences,
https://doi.org/10.1007/978-3-032-01373-6_9

others. The approach is illustrated using data from the European Social Survey about attitudes in five dimensions.

Keywords Cognitive coherence · Social influence · Agent-based simulation · Diversity · Polarisation · Data-driven

9.1 Motivation

Cognitive coherence or consistency is the idea that an individual's beliefs tend to be coherent with each other. So, to give some examples:

- if one likes to drive a petrol car then one might be more likely to think the dangers of climate change are exaggerated,
- if one is against COVID vaccination then one is probably also against other measures suggested by authorities, such as the wearing of masks,
- if one believes that a minimum wage is a good thing, then one might also believe that some kind of universal health insurance/provision is good.

Thus, by and large, an individual's beliefs, opinions, or attitudes do not contradict each other, either in terms of their detailed implications or their broader associations. This goes beyond strict logical consistency (e.g. that beliefs about climate change determine beliefs towards climate policies) but is more related to "emergent" coherence (e.g. questions of identity). Thus, for example, most people do not have some right-wing beliefs and some left-wing ones but tend to be at some point on the left–right political spectrum in a recognisable manner, and beliefs, opinions and attitudes may all cohere with each other in non-obvious ways (DellaPosta et al. 2015). For this reason, we will use the broader term "coherence" rather than "consistency" here, with consistency being a particular and specific form of coherence. In the following, we will use the term belief more broadly to capture opinions, attitudes and beliefs together, although there might be differences in how coherence between these elements could be represented (discussed later).

This need for coherence has been described as a universal motive and a psychological need (Festinger 1957; Heider 1946, 1958), or, to put it another way, people seek to increase their coherence (Thagard 2000). Incoherence between cognitive elements, such as between two beliefs, creates a feeling of dissonance (Festinger 1957), which has been described as a psychologically uncomfortable state that people tend to avoid or seek to alleviate using a variety of strategies (e.g., by changing some of them, Harmon-Jones and Harmon-Jones 2007).

These tendencies can be particularly powerful in conjunction with those associated with social identity. The beliefs central to our identity are particularly resistant to change (because they are part of a whole system of beliefs, all mutually coherent), so these tend to form a coherent and stable context for less fixed beliefs. Hence, for modelling purposes, we try to divide people into groups that share the same relationships between beliefs, which we call their shared "cognitive model". Individuals with a shared cognitive model do not need to agree on the beliefs; they just need to agree on how they perceive the coherence of beliefs. Hence, the cognitive model defines what is considered coherent and what not.

In the illustration of this approach described in this chapter, we derived these groups (each with a distinct "cognitive model") empirically, where all the intensities of different dimensions of belief of individuals in the same group are correlated in the same way. We also assume that an individual's beliefs tend to change in order to improve the internal coherence of its beliefs. In this chapter we focus on two processes for such change: social influence and self-reflection. Humans are inherently social animals, highly influenced by their social surroundings and so may accept the suggested beliefs of others that they interact with. This adds to the beliefs an agent has (or intensifies their degree of belief). At the same time, they possess the "distinctly human" capability to reflect upon their own beliefs in a process that favours discrepancy reduction (Bandura 2001b)—this may result in the dropping of an existing belief (or reduces their degree of belief towards zero).

9.2 The General Approach

In this section we describe the general approach, before illustrating this with a particular implementation in the next section. The key idea here is to initialise the cognitive models in an agent-based model (ABM) using data, so that there is *not* one cognitive model for all agents, but a set of models—one for each subgroup of agents. Agents sharing a cognitive model will not necessarily hold the same beliefs but they will share the logic of what constitutes coherence and dissonance. The goal here is to do this in a way that can represent a population of survey respondents. These cognitive models are then used in a simulation to determine how the agents learn, interact, and behave. What is important for us is to explore the way that these agents might interact. This approach involves the following stages.

1. Choose a theoretical framework concerning the relevant cognitive processes of individuals, preferably one which has some empirical support.
2. Find some suitable data about individuals; select from this and prepare it.
3. Use the framework and the data to simultaneously infer:
    (a) A partition of the individuals into subsets.
    (b) A cognitive model for each sub-set.
4. Implement these subsets and corresponding cognitive models in an ABM.
5. Run the ABM and analyse the results.

This extends the idea of data-driven ABM (e.g. Dean and George 2000, Kennedy et al. 2007, Hassan et al. 2010) where (for example) the state of agents or the environment might be inferred from data, to also specifying aspects of their learning and decision-making processes. Clearly, there are lots of different ways of implementing such a project—we will only demonstrate one possibility in this chapter.

The motivation here is (a) to move towards a more data-driven approach to initialising a set of interacting agents and (b) to move away from generic approaches where all agents are endowed with basically the same cognitive model and towards one that is more tailored to reflect some more of the dynamic diversity that we observe. We hypothesise that such a move is important in order to better understand how both a group-based convergence of views but also an intra-group divergence of views can develop and co-exist.

9.3 An Exemplar of the Approach

In this chapter we illustrate the above approach in a relatively simple manner, using the strength of attitudes from a survey as the target beliefs. In this exemplar, we implement two processes of belief change in our simulation model: social influence and self-reflection. Both are assumed to work towards improving an individual's internal belief coherence. In this, how internal belief coherence is defined will depend on two things: (1) the "cognitive model" that is shared with the other individuals in the group (which can be thought of as implicitly standing all the other beliefs of those agents that result in the group being similar minded) and (2) their foreground beliefs that are explicitly represented as intensities of agreement and disagreement in different belief dimensions.

We describe the approach we used in this proof-of-concept exemplar in more detail below, but summarise our principal choices we made next.

1. The framework we chose was that of "belief coherence"—suggesting that individuals accept their beliefs based upon their coherence with their other beliefs—and "social influence"—suggesting that, besides self-reflection, social interaction can trigger belief change subject to coherence. Within this framework, the particular model of belief coherence we used was that of correlation between different belief intensities.
2. For data, we used the German sample of the 2019 European Social Survey, using the responses to five items in the survey representing different political attitudes.
3. To infer the groups and their cognitive models we used Correlational Class Analysis (CCA).
4. The ABM including the different correlation models for sub-groups and the initial belief intensities on each issue was implemented both in NetLogo and Python.
5. The results are described below.

We now describe this exemplar and its analysis in some more detail. Even more detail and with more extensive analysis is in another paper that is under review. However, our aim here is to give an idea of the approach rather than a comprehensive account.

9.3.1 Data Analysis

To empirically derive different cognitive models and the sub-groups that these belong to, we used the German sample of the 2019 European Social Survey (ESS ERIC 2021). From the survey data we selected five items measuring political attitudes: regarding homosexuals' rights (*freehms*), support for the European Union (*euftf*), the role of the government in reducing inequality (*gincdif*), immigration (*impcntr*) and political orientation (*lrscale*). For example, the question for the item euftf is: "Now thinking about the European Union, some say European unification should go further. Others say it has already gone too far. Using this card, what number on the scale [from 0 to 10] best describes your position?". We chose those items that distinctly measured political attitudes (see Table 9.1 for more details). We transformed these to a common scale to indicate agreement; towards homosexuals' rights, support for the EU, governmental efforts to reduce inequality, immigration, and being positioned in the 'right' side of the political spectrum.

We use the German subset of the 9th wave of the ESS survey (ESS ERIC 2021) collected between 2018 and 2019. There are, in total, 2358 participants. We removed those with any invalid data or "Don't know" answers leaving a total of 2203 valid

Table 9.1 Selected questions from the ESS 9 questionnaire that define the five belief dimensions

Key	Topic	Question	Original scale
euftf	European Union: European unification go further or gone too far	Question: Now thinking about the European Union, some say European unification should go further. Others say it has already gone too far. Using this card, what number on the scale best describes your position?	0–10
freehms	Gays and lesbians free to live life as they wish	Using this card, please say to what extent you agree or disagree with each of the following statements. Gay men and lesbians should be free to live their own life as they wish	1–5 inverted
gincdif	Government should reduce differences in income levels	Using this card, please say to what extent you agree or disagree with each of the following statements. The government should take measures to reduce differences in income levels	1–5 inverted
lrscale	Placement on left right scale	In politics people sometimes talk of 'left' and 'right'. Using this card, where would you place yourself on this scale, where 0 means the left and 10 means the right?	0–10
impcntr	Allow many/few immigrants from poorer countries outside Europe	[Now, using this card, to what extent do you think Germany should allow] people from the poorer countries outside Europe [to come and live here]?	1–4 inverted

participant replies. Note that we inverted the scale for three of the five dimensions: freehms, gincdif, and impcntr, such that a higher score means the participant supported "more EU unification" (euftf), "more freedom for homosexuals" (freehms), "more government measures to reduce income inequality" (gincdif), and "more immigration from poor countries" as well as located themselves "more on the 'right' in the political spectrum" (lrscale). Each of the questions have different Likert-type scales, so we rescaled the responses of each item separately to values between -1 to 1 using linear translation, where a value of 1 corresponds to the highest value possible. We interpreted these values as corresponding to the strength of beliefs to the individuals who filled out the survey.

9.3.2 Deriving Cognitive Models and Group Membership from the Data Using Correlational Class Analysis

Correlational Class Analysis (CCA hereafter; Boutyline 2017) was applied to deduce different simple cognitive models and corresponding sub-groups from the data. CCA is a methodology for identifying groups of data individuals that share similar correlational schemas. We do not go into the details of the algorithm here (see Newman 2006, for a detailed description) but in outline: a pair-wise measure of similarity between individuals is determined by the correlation between their belief intensities, and then an algorithm of modularity-maximisation is applied returning a partition of the individuals into a certain number of groups. What this does is to simultaneously find a partition of the data into subgroups, and a correlation between the intensities of beliefs within each subgroup (with the strongest correlations and the fewest number of subgroups). Thus, the intensities of beliefs within each subgroup might not be similar but the correlations between them are. For example, people with entirely right-wing beliefs may interpret coherence very similar to people with entirely left-wing beliefs—they might share a subjective 'logic' of belief systems.

There is a single parameter for this process—a significance level—that determines which correlations are considered in the analysis, but here we set this to zero, resulting in all correlations being considered and hence got a smaller number of groups (three in this example). These three groups had 562, 601, and 1040 respondents. This simple case is sufficient to illustrate all of our basic points.

9.3.3 Differences in Inferred "Cognitive Models" of Each Group

In the following, we describe the cognitive models of the three groups arising from the CCA grouping. In this simple exemplar this is merely a fixed correlation matrix for each group, defined by the correlations between the intensities of belief in all five belief dimensions over all agents in that group. Thus, the most coherent set of belief intensities for an individual is if these correlate perfectly according to this matrix. This allows for several different possibilities of coherence pattern to be encoded, albeit only those using linear relationships between them. Thus patterns such as: "belief in dimension X is correlated with that in dimension Y and Z", "belief in dimension X is anti-correlated with that in dimension Y" or "belief in dimension X is uncorrelated with that in dimension T". This is a simplistic way of modelling belief coherence but has the advantage that it can be easily inferred from a set of data using CCA.

To illustrate the differences between those groups, we also analyse the dominant political parties that members of the groups voted for. The three groups identified are now described.

Group 1. The cognitive model of group 1 (n = 1040) is defined by associating support of homosexual rights positively with support of immigration and the EU. Supporting homosexual rights is also associated with being left-wing and endorsing governmental action regarding inequality. Group 1 is composed of people that voted disproportionately for the Green Party (and the Social Democrat Party).

Group 2. In the cognitive model of group 2 (n = 601), supporting homosexual rights is related to being positioned on the 'right' side of the political spectrum and against governmental action regarding inequality. Supporting governmental action regarding inequality is in turn related to opposition to immigration from poorer countries. Group 2 is composed of people that voted disproportionately for the Conservative Party (with considerable proportions who voted for the right-wing party, the AfD, and the liberal party, the FDP).

Group 3. The cognitive model of group 3 (n = 562) is described by associating the support of homosexual rights with being in favour of governmental action regarding inequality and being against further European unification. Opposition to further European unification is in turn associated with being left-wing and in opposition to immigration from poor countries. Group 3 comprises voters from all parties (with similar proportions as in the overall population) demonstrating a diverse range of political affiliations.

9.3.4 *The Simulation*

We now present an agent-based model (ABM), which simulates the belief dynamics of a society of individual human beings. The model was implemented in NetLogo (Wilensky 1999) version 6.3.0 as well as a version in Python version 3.9. Readers less interested in the model may jump to Section "Summary, Initialisation and Experiments", where we summarise the most important aspects of the model and outline the simulation experiments.

9.3.4.1 Agent Characteristics

In this simulation we have $N = 2203$ agents, where each agent represents one participant in the survey data, as described above. Agents each have five values, each corresponding to the extent that they agree with [value 1], disagree with [− 1] or are indifferent to the five belief dimensions in the survey data. Agents are initialised with the values for these in each of the data points of the survey.

9.3.4.2 Measuring Belief Coherence Using the CCA Correlation Matrices

The cognitive "model" of an agent in the simulation is simply the correlation matrix of the survey data inferred from the subset of participants that contains that agent. The sign of each matrix element at position {a, b} indicates whether beliefs *a* and *b* should be correlated (positive sign) or anti-correlated (negative sign) for that. The magnitude of the matrix element at *{a, b}* indicates how important this correlation is to the agent's evaluation of a set of beliefs. If the element is 0 the agent perceives belief items *a* and *b* as fully independent. The idea is that this matrix captures some of the connection between its belief intensities, a connection shared with group the agent belongs to. Given this, the coherence of a set of beliefs, x, is $1/2 \cdot x^T \cdot (R - I) \cdot x$. Intuitively this is the extent to which that set is correlated according to the groups correlation matrix, R. This is quite a simplistic way of calculating belief coherence, but it illustrates the general idea and is sufficient for the illustration of the idea.

9.3.4.3 Belief Change Through Social Influence and Self-reflection

Social Influence

In each time step, each agent engages in social interaction with another agent with some probability. We distribute the agents randomly in a sparse small-world social network (Watts and Strogatz 1998) and restrict social interactions only to those agents with a direct link between them (which means that the interaction network is independent of the CCA group membership).

Each simulation time click, each agent does the following:

1. Selects one of the other agents that it is linked at random.
2. Selects one of the belief dimensions of the other agent randomly.
3. The number representing the intensity of the selected belief and the belief dimension is presented to the original agent.
4. The original agent then calculates the coherence of its belief set if it adopted this presented belief and compares it with the coherence of its current belief set.
5. The belief of the original agent in that dimension is altered towards the direction of the suggested belief with a certain rate (a parameter), that depends logistically on the coherence difference calculated in step (4). This logistic curve is

parameterised by a parameter, *k*, so it is sharper with high k and flatter with low k (so k determines the strength of the coherence process as compared to noise in accepting and adopting new beliefs—a low *k* means it is mostly noise).

Self-Reflection

Besides social interactions, an agent's belief on a topic *m* can also change through self-reflection. This process also occurs with some probability in each time step after a potential social interaction (step 2–5). Self-reflection follows the same principle as social interaction, but the suggested belief on the focal topic, *m*, is not the belief of a neighbouring agent (as in step 3 above), but a random fluctuation of the agent's prior belief (drawn from a zero-mean normal distribution and truncated such that the suggested belief remains within the bounds of the belief space, + 1 or − 1). The intensity of the belief is more likely to change if the change increases the coherence of the belief set.

9.3.5 The ABM: Summary, Initialisation and Experiments

Let us emphasise the most important aspects of our model again: Agents update their beliefs noisily following social and asocial influences driven towards increased coherence. The parameter *k* determines how important coherence is to the agents by controlling the amount of determinism/randomness in this belief update process. If agents do not care whether their beliefs are coherent with each other (given their cognitive model), meaning $k = 0$, they decide randomly whether to incorporate social/asocial influences. But if agents care a lot about the coherence of their beliefs (e.g. for $k = 100$) they only adapt to social interaction or self-reflection when this adaptation would increase the internal coherence of their set of beliefs, and consequently they reject all influences that do not increase coherence.

We initialise the model as follows. Each agent represents one of the $N = 2203$ participants in the German sample for the ESS 9 survey (ESS ERIC 2021) and we endow each agent with an initial set of beliefs at time $t = 0$ according to the participant's answer in the survey. We also endow each agent with a cognitive model corresponding to its group membership: the correlation matrix derived using the CCA algorithm as described above.

The crucial aspect in this study is that agents have particular preferences for which combinations of beliefs they find coherent or incoherent, which is represented by their cognitive model, but different agents may have different cognitive models and thus different perspectives on coherence of a given belief.

Below, we first illustrate the dynamics in a couple of single runs of the simulation comparing the cases with and without coherence pressure.

9.3.5.1 Illustrating the Simulation Dynamics, Showing the Impact of Coherence

First, we just give some illustrative outcomes from a single run of the simulation to give a flavour of its dynamics, in Fig. 9.1 using the groups and correlation matrices form the CCA algorithm—showing the effect of the pressure towards coherence.

Panel (A) in Fig. 9.1 shows the agent beliefs on different topics at the start of the simulation, with each dot representing an individual. The colours of the dots indicate which 3-CCA group it would be in. The different beliefs range along the y-axis, with the intensity value of the belief for each individual shown on the y-axis, from 1 (completely agree) to − 1 (completely disagree). The options available to respondents in the survey have been mapped onto [− 1, 1] and restrict the initial range of values (which appears as lines composed of many dots).

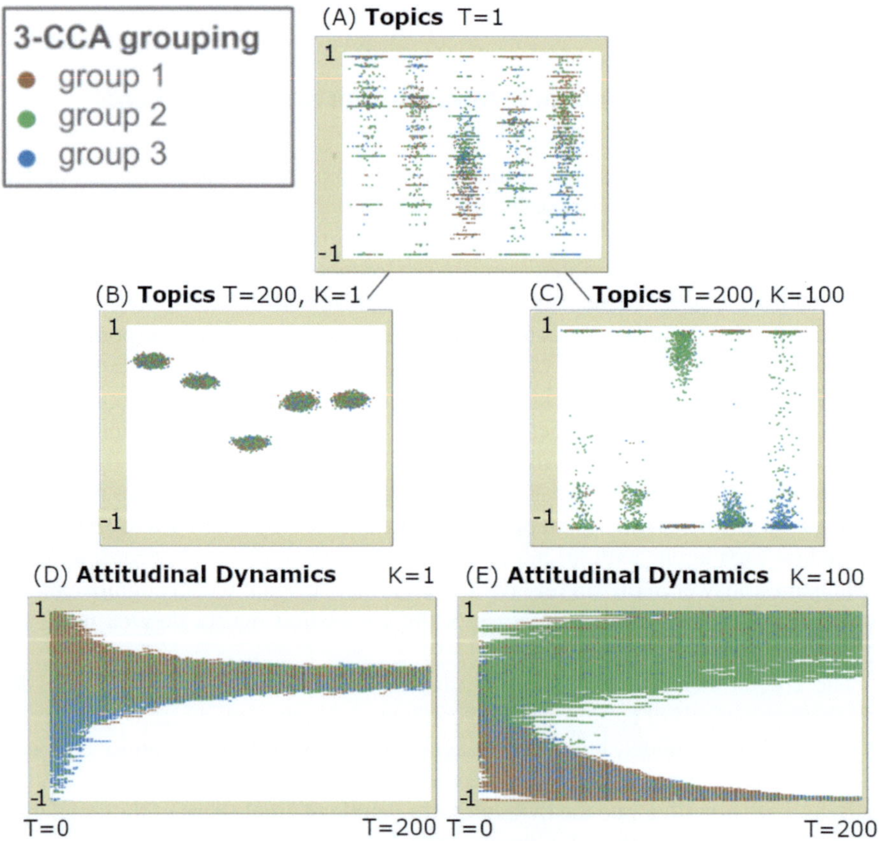

Fig. 9.1 Some illustrative simulation results (left—with low *k* so coherence plays almost no part: A→B→D, right—with high k so coherence dominates the dynamics: A→C→E)

Figure 9.1 (B and C) illustrate the belief distributions after 200 time steps with low coherence pressure (panel B, k = 1) and with high coherence pressure (panel C, k = 100). These illustrate extreme cases, and it is likely that real humans lie somewhere in between. We see in the low coherence case (left) that all belief values for all groups have now clustered around the same values, which is not surprising as the differing cognitive models for each group have no impact (the belief change processes being dominated by randomness). In the high coherence case (right) the belief values for agents have shifted to the extremes but differently for different groups.

The bottom two panels in Fig. 9.1 show the dynamics over time for the same two cases for one particular topic. On the left, with low coherence, although each group might start with different beliefs (shown by the distribution along the y-axis) they converge to the same values over time. On the right, with a high coherence pressure, different groups each converge to different final values. There is convergence within the group, but a divergence between groups.

9.3.5.2 The Belief Distributions at the End of a Simulation Run with High Coherence—The 3-Group Case

Figure 9.2 shows the final distribution of beliefs (at $t = 200$) among the agents split into the three groups (left, middle and right) in the example simulation with a high importance of coherence, $k = 100$. The model produces nearly full consensus among the agents in group 1 (left panel). The model, however, also produces within-group diversity on certain topics (e.g. immigration, *impcntr)* among the agents in group 2 and fosters between-group diversity (e.g. on (dis-)approving the EU, *euftf*).

Agents in the simulation tend to move in the direction of maximal coherence, when k is high. But this can mean different things. In group 1, for example, the beliefs of nearly all agents in a group converge to the same corner in the belief space that maximises the group's coherence. However, the agents remain moderate about some beliefs in certain groups, for example, group 3 has a moderate stance on immigration (*impcntr*). This is plausible since the cognitive model of this group suggests that coherence is largely independent of beliefs about immigration. To what extent within-group and between-group diversity arise depends non-trivially on the grouping and the importance of coherence (determined by the parameter k).

9.4 The Impact of Coherence in the 1-Group and 3-Group Cases Over Many Runs

We now compare two setups with different groupings of agents to show the impact of the grouping with different levels of coherence pressure (from k = 1 to 100) looking at the final distribution of belief intensities for each group. The setups are:

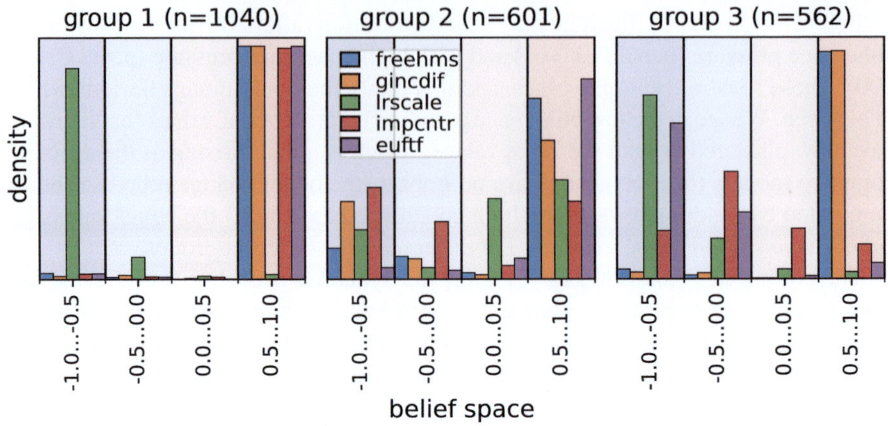

Fig. 9.2 Final distribution of agent beliefs in each group in the example simulation with the three CCA groups, with $k = 100$. The colours denote the five different topics. The belief space, $[-1, 1]$, is binned into four categories (strong disagreement, disagreement, agreement, strong agreement). For instance, group 1 is quite consensual about all topics with a nearly unanimous stance on all topics and left wing. Group 2 is largely split for most topics, but with some level of common support for the EU (*euftf*) and homosexual rights (*freehms*). Beliefs in Group 3 are quite diverse on topics such as immigration (*impcntr*), but nearly unanimous on homosexual rights (*freehms*) and governmental action regarding inequality (*gincdif*), but mostly left-wing (*lrscale*) and against the EU (*euftf*)

- "*Exp* (1)". No grouping at all, i.e. all agents are in the same group and so have the same cognitive model (represented by the correlations calculated over all agents. This experiment represents our baseline assumption.
- "*Exp* (2)". The three groups derived using the CCA algorithm as described above. This experiment is our main test scenario.

Figure 9.3 presents a more detailed analysis of the simulation results as k varies, comparing the 1-group and the 3-group cases. In particular, it shows the mean group beliefs (and the standard deviation) at time $t = 200$ of the five belief items over different importance of coherence k for the experiment without grouping (panels A1–A5) and with the 3 grouping (panels B1–B5).

In the experiment without grouping, a high importance of coherence, $k = 100$, causes the agents to adopt, on average, a strongly negative value on the political orientation (*lrscale*)–implying a left orientation (solid line in Fig. 9.3A3), but there is strong diversity among the agents on this item (coloured area). Similarly, the society converges to quite extreme levels of support for LGBTQI + rights (Fig. 9.3A1), government involvement in reducing income inequality (4A2), immigration from poorer countries (4A4), and EU integration (4A5).

In the experiment with the 3 groups the dynamics are more diverse. For low values of k, all groups tend to follow the majority consensus belief. With increasing k, this consensus belief moves further away from a moderate centre. If k is sufficiently large, there is both between-group and within-group disagreement on most topics and groups. But there are substantial differences in this general pattern between the

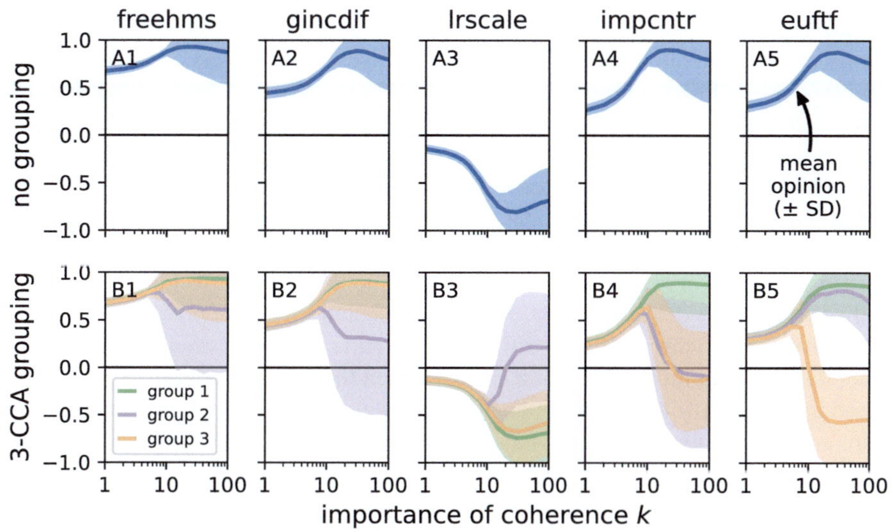

Fig. 9.3 Mean beliefs (and standard deviation) for Experiment 1 (top) without grouping and these outcomes from Experiment 2 (bottom) with 3 groups for each of the five topics (1–5, shown from left to right). Each panel shows the mean and standard deviation of the outcomes of many simulations starting from the same initial conditions, but with varying k (from $k = 1$ on the left to $k = 100$ on right within each panel). When coherence is not important (low k), the agents reach a consensus within and between groups. As coherence becomes more important (higher k), the mean beliefs (solid lines) of the groups polarise—between-group polarisation—and some groups can split internally, shown by an increase in the standard deviation of the groups' beliefs in each dimension (coloured areas)—within-group polarisation

groups and between the five belief items. For instance, group 1 deviates from the others in terms of immigration (*impcntr*), group 3 on the EU (*euftf*) and group 2 on the other items, but the groups are themselves split. Notably, the threshold of k at which groups start to polarise from others and split internally (see, for instance, the green line in Fig. 9.3B1) varies between groups and belief items.

To summarise, the partitioning of individuals into groups with shared cognitive models allowed particular groups to deviate from the others (when the coherence mechanism is strong) leading to more complex patterns of within- and between-group diversity. These patterns can be triggered following small increases in the importance of the coherence k if the cognitive models differ.

9.5 Discussion

Whilst the described work was intended as a proof-of-concept—illustrating an approach that we think will be productive—it does show that: (a) it is possible to move towards a more data-driven approach in terms of specifying aspects of the cognitive models of agents within simulations, (b) that such an approach does significantly change the outcomes in terms of how a diversity of beliefs could be socially preserved while those within groups can still remain cohesive, and (c) that within-group convergence is quite sensitive to the importance of coherence (while group here refers to a subset of agents sharing a cognitive model). Also we hope it shows the potential of this approach in terms of application and extension.

Individuals perceive the political world from a subjective viewpoint and often apply subjective cognitive models, which causes them to experience coherence differently and respond in distinct ways to outside influences. This aspect has been rarely studied using (data-driven) models. We have presented such an approach, using CCA to identify groups with shared cognitive models, and comparing simulation results of coherence-seeking individuals for a case in which they share a cognitive model and a case in which they hold distinct cognitive models. In our model, individuals may share a cognitive model even if they hold very distinct beliefs. Two individuals—for example, one with "right-wing" beliefs about migration and economic policies, and one with "left-wing" beliefs on both topics—may both feel coherent, because they share the same cognitive model; a third person with mixed "left"/"right" beliefs may feel coherent only if she holds a different cognitive model that deviates from the left–right scheme. Ideological pressures may be one possible explanation for the alignment of cognitive models between antagonistic groups, but in this study we are agnostic as to how the individuals have come to share cognitive models. Empirical data on how coherence perception differs within a population, would be useful to validate the model.

In our model, coherence drives two kinds of outcome: between-group and within-group diversity. This is particularly true if coherence means something different for the individuals because their cognitive models differ. If coherence is unimportant to individuals, a consensus emerges. The more coherence plays a role (so that cognitive models differ), the more diversity manifests within and between groups of agents with the same cognitive model. Interestingly, we find that the model exhibits non-linear behaviour: a small increase in the importance of coherence can cause a sudden shift from consensus to pronounced diversity, but this threshold varies among different groups.

Our model emphasises the need for agent-based simulation by showing that probabilistic coherence maximisation in a social structure does not necessarily lead to the obvious outcomes (just becoming more extreme in the average direction that a group started with in terms of its belief values). Some results, such as the differential emergence of within-group diversity and between-group diversity, are path-dependent phenomena and thus non-trivial to understand from an equilibrium analysis. Moreover, our approach demonstrates how agent-based simulation allows studying the dynamic interrelations of psychological/cognitive micro-level processes and social/political macro-level patterns of beliefs – a link that is understudied.

One aspect of our model is that extremeness can increase belief coherence. If two beliefs are correlated, extreme support for both is more coherent than moderate support for both. We believe—in line with other modelling studies (Dalege et al. 2023)—that this might be a reasonable assumption given that more extreme beliefs are less ambiguous and, thus, reinforce consistency. Nevertheless, it is also psychologically plausible that there are individuals that experience strong coherence by maintaining neutral or moderate beliefs. Whether this is a quality of real-world coherence or due to other mechanisms that favours extremeness of beliefs, remains to be further investigated.

There are many directions that a further development of this approach could take. Independent validation is currently lacking—it would be good to compare the results of such models in cases where there is a series of relatively fine-grained snapshots of the development of beliefs over time, to see if this approach results in the right kind of dynamics and check the overall resulting distributions were in the right ball-park. The kind of cognitive model here is simplistic and this might be made more sophisticated to reflect the kinds of coherence patterns humans apply. For example, we are not distinguishing between beliefs, attitudes, and opinions, although the cognitive model that connects might have interesting structures. Lastly, it is assumed that each individual keeps the same cognitive model over time. There is currently no possibility of changes in group membership or dynamics in the cognitive models.

9.6 Conclusion

Here we described a more empirically driven approach to specifying the cognitive models of agents in an ABM. This results in different *types* of agents, each of which are based upon a different cognitive model. Of course, in the example instantiation of the general approach shown, we have only taken a modest step towards inferring different 'cognitive models' for different groups, represented by the correlation matrix for the group beliefs.

We have shown one way of realising this goal, but freely admit there are many other possible variants. We have shown that this makes a difference—that the outcomes from this, more diverse, approach are significantly different from one where there is a single cognitive model for all. We believe that this direction for developing research is a productive one, and is one that has not been explored.

The difference this approach makes is a matter of degree, the correlation matrix we use could be thought of as a property of the agents interpreted by the coherence framework, but that is true for any "cognitive model" as any algorithm can be encoded as a property (as Turing showed with his Universal Turing Machine in 1933). However, the described approach represents a shift towards inferring the agent cognitive process from data, and thus can be situated within a wider trend towards data-driven rather than theory-driven methods, KIDS vs KISS (Edmonds and Moss 2005).

Acknowledgements The collaboration was initiated at the BIGSSS Summer School in Computational Social Science on Social Cohesion 2022 in Groningen (Netherlands) (https://bigssscss.janlo.de/schools-2018-2023/social-cohesion-2022-groningen/) funded by the Volkswagen Foundation. JL and PS acknowledge support from a grant by Deutsche Forschungsgemeinschaft (DFG—German Research Foundation, No. 396901899) for the project "ToRealSim—Towards realistic models of social influence". BE acknowledges support from a grant by ESRC No. ES/S015159/1 also for ToRealSim. PS acknowledges support from the Deutsche Forschungsgemeinschaft (DFG—German Research Foundation) though the project SEATRAC (project number 423711127) as part of the Priority Programme 1889: Regional Sea Level Change and Society (Sea Level). MB acknowledges the support of the ZumWert project funded by the University of Kassel in their profile building initiative. FK acknowledges the institutional support of the University of West Bohemia in Pilsen.

References

A. Bandura, Social cognitive theory of mass communication. Media Psychol. **3**(3), 265–299 (2001). https://doi.org/10.1207/S1532785XMEP0303_03

A. Boutyline, Improving the measurement of shared cultural schemas with correlational class analysis: theory and method. Sociol. Sci. **4**(15), 353–393 (2017). https://doi.org/10.15195/v4.a15

J. Dalege, M. Galesic, H. Olsson, Networks of beliefs: an integrative theory of individual- and social-level belief dynamics. OSF Preprints (2023). https://doi.org/10.31219/osf.io/368jz

J.S. Dean, J. G. George, Understanding Anasazi culture change through agent-based modeling, in *Dynamics in Human and Primate Societies: Agent-Based Modeling of Social and Spatial Processes* ed. by T.A Kohler, G.J. Gumerman (Oxford Academic, 2000), pp. 179–206. https://doi.org/10.1093/oso/9780195131673.003.0013

D. DellaPosta, Y. Shi, M. Macy, Why do liberals drink lattes? Am. J. Sociol. **120**(5), 1473–1511 (2015). https://doi.org/10.1086/681254

B. Edmonds, S. Moss, From KISS to KIDS—an 'anti-simplistic' modelling approach, in *Multi Agent Based Simulation 2004, Lecture Notes in Artificial Intelligence*, vol. 3415, ed. by P. Davidsson et al. (Springer, Berlin, 2005), pp. 130–144. http://cfpm.org/cpmrep132.html

ESS ERIC (2001)

European Social Survey European Research Infrastructure (ESS ERIC), ESS9—integrated file, edition 3.1. Sikt—Norwegian Agency for Shared Services in Education and Research (2021). https://doi.org/10.21338/ESS9E03_1

L. Festinger, A theory of cognitive dissonance. (Stanford University Press, 1957)

E. Harmon-Jones, C. Harmon-Jones, Cognitive dissonance theory after 50 years of development. Zeitschrift Für Sozialpsychologie **38**(1), 7–16 (2007)

S. Hassan, J. Pavón, L. Antunes, N. Gilbert, Injecting data into agent-based simulation, in *Simulating Interacting Agents and Social Phenomena: The Second World Congress* (Springer, Japan, 2010), pp. 177–191. https://doi.org/10.1007/978-4-431-99781-8_13

F. Heider, Attitudes and cognitive organization. J. Psychol. **21**, 107–112 (1946)

F. Heider, *The Psychology of Interpersonal Relations* (Wiley, New York, 1958)

C. Kennedy, G. Theodoropoulos, V. Sorge, E> Ferrari, P. Lee, C. Skelcher, AIMSS: An architecture for data driven simulations in the social sciences, in *Computational Science—ICCS 2007. ICCS 2007. Lecture Notes in Computer Science*, vol. 4487, ed. by Y. Shi, G.D. van Albada, J. Dongarra, P.M.A. Sloot (Springer, Berlin, Heidelberg, 2007). https://doi.org/10.1007/978-3-540-72584-8_144

M.E.J. Newman, Modularity and community structure in networks. Proc. Natl. Acad. Sci. **103**(23), 8577–8582 (2006). https://doi.org/10.1073/pnas.0601602103

P. Thagard, Coherence in thought and action. The MIT Press (2000). https://doi.org/10.7551/mitpress/1900.001.0001

A.M. Turing, On computable numbers, with an application to the Entscheidungsproblem. Proc. London Math. Soc. **2**(42), 230–265 (1936)

D.J. Watts, S.H. Strogatz, Collective dynamics of "small-world" networks'. Nature **393**(6684), 440–442 (1998). Available at: https://doi.org/10.1038/30918

U. Wilensky, NetLogo (Center for Connected Learning and Computer-Based Modeling, Northwestern University. Evanston, IL, 1999). http://ccl.northwestern.edu/netlogo/

Chapter 10
An Investigation into the Causal Mechanism of Political Opinion Dynamics: A Model of Hierarchical Coarse-Graining with Community-Bounded Social Influence

Valeria Widler, Barbara Kamińska, André C. R. Martins, and Ivan Puga-Gonzalez

Abstract Polarization is an emergent outcome of political opinion dynamics, yet the causal processes linking individual-level opinion updates to collective consensus remain poorly understood. To address this, we conceptualize political discourse as hierarchical coarse-graining where individual-level opinions are compressed and aggregated into group- and system-level representations. In this framework, upward causation refers to individual updates influencing group-level opinion, while downward causation captures how dominant collective views shape individual opinion updating. Using the Continuous Opinions and Discrete Actions (CODA) model, we simulate Bayesian belief updating, social identity–driven information integration, and migration between identity groups to capture coarse-graining across micro-, meso-, and macroscales. Our results show that connectivity between identity groups shapes overall opinion dynamics, producing three distinct regimes: independent (local convergence), parallel (rapid local and global convergence), and iterative (slow global convergence). In the iterative regime, low connectivity fosters transient diversity, reflecting a more informed consensus. Across all regimes, time-scale separation gives rise to downward causation that ultimately drives agents toward consensus. Critically, any coherent connectivity between identity groups leads to downward

V. Widler (✉)
Modeling and Simulation of Complex Processes, Zuse Institute Berlin, Berlin, Germany
e-mail: valeria.widler@gmx.de

B. Kamińska
Faculty of Management, Wroclaw University of Science and Technology, Wroclaw, Poland

A. C. R. Martins
Escola de Artes, Ciências e Humanidades, Universidade de São Paulo (EACH-USP), São Paulo, Brazil

I. Puga-Gonzalez
Center for Modelling Social Systems, Norwegian Research Center (NORCE), Kristiansand, Norway

M. A. Keijzer et al. (eds.), *Computational Social Science of Social Cohesion and Polarization*, Computational Social Sciences,
https://doi.org/10.1007/978-3-032-01373-6_10

causation. These findings highlight the key role of downward causation, identity group structure, and inter-group connectivity in shaping the dynamics underlying polarized political discourse.

Keywords Political opinion dynamics · Downward causation · Identity groups · Hierarchical coarse-graining · Collective computation

10.1 Introduction

Political discourse in many established democracies has become increasingly dysfunctional (Borbáth et al. 2023). Conflicts over immigration, cultural issues and international cooperation have superseded the classic left-right economic cleavage, consolidating what is often referred to as a "cultural cleavage" (Borbáth et al. 2023; Dalton and Berning 2022; Enke et al. 2023). This restructuring of the issue landscape is characterized by increasingly extreme and consistently opposed positions between opinion groups, a phenonemonon known as polarization. The ideological polarization is often accompanied by affective polarization, with increased hostility, distrust, and negative feelings toward opinion outgroup members, even among those whose policy positions might not be substantially dissimilar. Constructive political discourse depends on the integration of diverse perspectives into shared understandings or consensus (Jost et al. 2022; Törnberg 2022). Yet, affective polarization can undermine this process by reducing cross-cutting interactions and reinforcing in-group cohesion, ultimately impeding integrative discourse and consensus on a widening range of issues (Hobolt et al. 2021; Iyengar and Westwood 2015; Iyengar et al. 2019).

Research on the causes of increasing dysfunction in political discourse often centers on changes in the communication architecture induced by the internet (Barberá 2020; Böhmelt et al. 2020; Ohme 2020). These innovations have fundamentally altered connectivity, a network property that shapes who interacts with whom, how often, and with what influence weight. However, the mechanisms through which these connectivity changes affect political discourse remain incompletely understood. We propose to investigate the bidirectional causal mechanism underlying information integration in political opinion dynamics and their role in the emergence of collective consensus through an agent-based model. We conceptualize public discourse as a collective sense-making process that aggregates inferences of individuals into a unitary perception by way of hierarchical coarse-graining. By implementing likely bottom-up mechanisms of human collectives in an agent-based model, we seek to investigate the emergence of the top-down mechanism of downward causation. We then go on to test how higher-level connectivity, patterns of interaction and influence between aggregated units, impacts the dynamics and the achievement of a consensus.

How can we model public discourse? Human societies are embedded in environments of immense complexity. Survival depends on the computation of predictions that reduce the uncertainty in the environment, informing collective action and a unitary perception of the world. Flack (Flack 2017a) coined the term 'endogenous coarse-graining' for this process of collective sense-making in natural systems. Generally, coarse-graining is the lowering of the resolution of a system's information across scales at minimal loss of information. A system's microscopic information is compressed or smoothed over and abstracted, but along a functional dimension. It serves as an effective way to understand a system for the purpose of prediction and intervention (Liao et al. 2019). We take the perspective that human societies employ endogenous coarse-graining to construct a collective perception of the environment. Consequently, political opinion formation is a collective computation where individuals process information about the environment (accumulation phase) and these inferences are aggregated into a collective perception through opinion exchanges within and across local communities (consensus phase) (Flack 2017a). We are interested in the consensus mechanism that regulates the hierarchical coarse-graining of opinions across scales via upward and downward causation into a unitary joint opinion (Harte et al. 2024).

Since systems in nature process information with constrained computational capacity, they integrate information on the basis of heuristics (Gigerenzer et al. 2011), making the simplification an approximation rather than a direct translation of the environmental inferences (Flack 2017a). Subsequently, how the mechanism clusters information across scales, can be beneficial to the collective estimation or a source of bias (Flack 2017a; Smaldino et al. 2017). Research in epistemological studies on decision-making in heterogeneous groups suggests that a transient diversity of opinions, an intermediate rise in diversity of opinions before convergence, indicates a more informed consensus, whereas herding (i.e. a quick convergence to a global consensus) signifies a time efficient, however less informed consensus (Smaldino et al. 2022).

At the microlevel, where bottom-up mechanisms drive information integration, social learning strategies (SLS), such as preferential integration of social information from individuals sharing the same social identity, modulate the flow of information (Abrams and Hogg 1990; Smaldino et al. 2017; Hämäläinen et al. 2023; Laland 2004; Hawkins et al. 2023), acting as a gatekeeping criterion for information integration based on similarity (Steiglechner et al. 2024). When shared local identities act as the social influence heuristic, the society is essentially partitioned into 'epistemic communities' (Albarracin et al. 2022) wherein information is integrated freely, leading to an alignment of beliefs, preferences, and behaviors. Between these communities information integration is impeded, since based on this mechanism alone no opinions should be integrated by a sender from a different epistemic community. Higher-level connectivity is thus facilitated by other means. One possibility are types of noise that act on the social interaction at different points, e.g. 'selectivity noise' (Steiglechner et al. 2024), where social information that a social learning strategy would typically ignore is included nonetheless every so often.

We model how people simplify and integrate information using Bayesian inference within the Continuous Opinions and Discrete Actions (CODA) model (Martins 2008). In this model, individuals hold internal beliefs about different choices regarding a specific issue and express the one they consider most likely to be correct, i.e., its preferred choice. They share this preferred choice with others in one-on-one exchanges. The extent to which someone adjusts their beliefs in response to another's preferred choice depends on whether they belong to the same epistemic community (represented by a label). If they share a label, they integrate information, if they are from different groups, the influence varies–ranging from being ignored to slightly affecting the receiver's belief. When agents receive enough input favoring a different choice, their preferred choice changes. They may also switch communities by dropping their current label and adopting a new one, allowing preferred choices to spread between groups. By adjusting how often agents switch communities, we can observe how different levels of cross-community connectivity influence the coarse-graining process, shaping how individual preferred choices evolve from the micro level into collective patterns at the macro level.

Using this model, we investigate our research questions: What is the causal mechanism, including both upward and downward causation, that leads to consensus in choices? How does higher-level connectivity affect this mechanism? How does the mechanism relate to polarization? To address these questions, we measure whether preferred choices among agents and communities align or diverge over time. We use the term components to refer to units of information processing, such as individual agents and local communities, that are aggregated to form coarse-grained information at the next hierarchical scale, i.e., the local and global community, respectively. Alignment refers to the increasing convergence of preferred choices among components at a given scale. A global consensus is reached when alignment emerges both within local communities and across the global community.

We systematically varied all model parameters within specified ranges to evaluate their influence on the dynamic outcomes of information integration (e.g., local and global convergence, diversity indices). We found that the probability of dropping the label (PDL) is the dominant factor determining system dynamics and regime transitions, while other parameters, such as the number of labels, issues, choices, 'ignoring on/off', strength-of-influence, and multi-issue-discourse, primarily modulate the critical PDL thresholds. Our findings reveal that varying levels of inter-group connectivity (PDL) give rise to three distinct information integration regimes:

- Independent Information Integration Regime: When inter-group connectivity (migration) is absent, agents reach local alignment, but no global information aggregation occurs. Information is coarse-grained only at the local level.
- Parallel Information Integration Regime: At high inter-group connectivity, local and global alignment happen simultaneously, leading to rapid global consensus (local and global alignment) in a single phase. This corresponds to herding–a fast but less informed consensus process (Smaldino et al. 2017).
- Iterative Information Integration Regime: At low levels of inter-group connectivity, information integration occurs in three phases (I:local alignment, II: global alignment, III: local alignment), with slow but informed convergence that gives rise to a transient diversity (Smaldino et al. 2022).

These results highlight how simple social heuristics can interact with network dynamics to produce complex, multi-level political phenomena. The discovered bidirectional causal mechanism suggests that polarization may arise from a disturbance in higher-level information integration that disrupts the emergence of downward causation necessary to reach consensus. Further development of this model could offer new perspectives on the forces that contribute to democratic erosion, the reinforcement of ideological bubbles, and strategies to encourage more functional public discourse.

10.2 Background

Collective decisions in democratic societies emerge from the aggregation of individual judgments regarding which actions governments should prioritize to promote social welfare (Lorenz and Neumann 2018). Like adaptive biological systems, human societies consist of semi-independent individuals, whose interactions result in ordered behavior at aggregate higher levels (Flack 2017b). In political discourse, this manifests as consensus emerging from diverse perspectives on societal issues. As a complex adaptive system, the mechanism underlying democratic discourse likely exhibits bidirectional cross-scale causation where micro- and macroscale dynamics are 'entwined' (Harte et al. 2024). Understanding these dynamics requires considering both bottom-up mechanisms and top-down causal influences. However, recent work notes that the dynamics of multilevel systems are often analyzed without explicitly modeling downward causation (Harte et al. 2024).

The theory of collective computation (Flack 2017a, b; Daniels et al. 2016; Brush et al. 2013) proposes that individuals act as information processors, coarse-graining environmental information into models during an accumulation phase (Flack 2017a). In a second, the consensus phase, individual models are hierarchically coarse-grained into a collective perception, a process termed 'endogenous coarse-graining' (Flack 2017a). This coarse-grained process reduces uncertainty over fast microscopic behavior, producing a lower-resolution variable of the state of the system (Daniels et al. 2016; Harte et al. 2024). When coarse-grained models stabilize across individuals, a coherent aggregate scale emerges, allowing a slower state variable to form. This time-scale separation of the micro- and the higher-level serves as a stable 'social environment', enabling individuals to tune their behaviors to collective patterns (Flack 2017a). As a result, the coarse-grained aggregate exerts downward causation, reducing entropy and creating order, ultimately leading to convergence.

Downward causation suggests that higher-level components (e.g., communities), can constrain the future of all lower-level components (e.g., individuals) (Flack 2017a; Santos 2024). Tuning occurs when individuals identify regularities in coarse-grained variables and adapt their estimates accordingly. When tuning is partial or imprecise, agent estimates diverge, a phenomenon called Apparent Downward Causation or weak emergence (Flack 2017a). In contrast, Effective Downward Causation or strong emergence occurs when individuals' estimates cohere, leading to perfect tuning and convergence in the sampling environment (Flack 2017a).

Effective downward causation occurs when:

- Aggregate properties predict the future state of lower level components in the system
- Aggregate properties are stable and exhibit time-scale separation from the level below
- All components tune to the same aggregate properties
- Increasing convergence of components' estimates of aggregate properties
- Convergence comes with an increase in mutual information between the level exerting downward causation and the level below

(Flack 2017a)

Using this framework of "coarse-graining as a downward causation mechanism" (Flack 2017a), we can quantify top-down causal influence in our model to analyze its role in system dynamics. For the remainder of the paper we use 'downward causation' to refer specifically to 'effective downward causation'.

To understand the bottom-up mechanism, we need to understand how human groups implement endogenous coarse-graining. First, detailed information is coarse-grained at the microlevel. In a hierarchically coarse-graining system, this coarse-grained information is further abstracted into aggregate variables across scales, forming a hierarchy where components at one level are grouped into higher-level state variables, simplifying the description of the system as we go up the scale. Upward causation occurs when interactions at the lower lead to changes in higher-level components (Mediano et al. 2022). In the context of opinion dynamics, upward causation describes how the information integration mechanism at the microlevel influences the coarse-grained state variable at the higher level, in this case, the distribution of opinions in a group.

Coarse-graining is advantageous because the aggregation of microlevel data into the macro level representation, with what Flack terms "slow variable construction" (Flack 2017a), can detect subtle or slow-changing patterns in the environment. In contrast, rapid aggregation of information (fast variable construction) may smooth over microdata too quickly, risking loss of relevant information. Coarse-graining improves the signal-to-noise ratio, offering a time- and energy-efficient way to build an effective theory of the world that allows prediction and intervention without requiring detailed knowledge of causal origins (Flack 2017a). Another benefit is the reduction of uncertainty, as the system converges on a single coarse-grained model. How noise is smoothed across and within scales affects how faithfully the macrolevel reflects the original system. In natural systems, this smoothing is often guided by heuristics that prioritize efficiency over accuracy (Flack 2017a). To define a bottom-up mechanism for political opinion dynamics, we explore simple heuristic mechanisms that might underlie this coarse-graining.

For the microlevel coarse-graining mechanism, we adopt a Bayesian inference perspective, where beliefs are represented as probabilistic states. We use a variant of the Continuous Opinions Discrete Actions (CODA) model (Martins 2008), where choices represent the possible hypotheses on an issue, and their input frequencies, encode expected probabilities. This forms an agent's choice distribution for a given issue, informing it on the plausibility of a choice. The relative entropy of the distribution reflects uncertainty: high entropy indicates maximum uncertainty (equal evidence across choices), while low entropy reflects certainty and convergence on a single choice. The 'preferred choice' is the one with the highest frequency and this is the agent's current opinion that is communicated to others. An expressed opinion is coarse-grained, as it condenses the agent's past social interactions into a single output. The recipient does not access the full interaction history, rather, they infer the sender's position from the expressed opinion alone.

Another key element of the micromechanism is how agents select sources of information for incorporation into their internal model of the world. While people differ along many dimensions, such as gender, age, or socioeconomic situation, social identity theory and self-categorization theory (Tajfel and Turner 1979; Abrams and Hogg 1990) suggest that individuals rely on a subjective social frame of reference dividing the social world into social categories of similarity and difference. This process results in in- and outgroups, shaping patterns of social influence, ingroup conformity and outgroup differentiation (Abrams and Hogg 1990; Smaldino and Velilla 2025). While there are other heuristics, like authority or expertise, that can activate social influence, a person's social identity remains a primary social frame of reference and has been shown to play a key role in political opinion formation (Abrams and Hogg 1990). Ingroups can be viewed as 'epistemic communities', a local sense-making environment where information is trusted and shared, creating shared mental models, preferences and codes of conduct (Albarracin et al. 2022). These communities create relatively stable social environments (Flack 2017a) and reflect the multi-scale nature of human social organization, where strong local interactions give way to weaker ones across increasing social distance, from kin to stranger (Ramos-Fernandez et al. 2020). Additionally, affective polarization has been linked to social identity processes, particularly those driven by perceived inter-group dynamics (Barberá 2020; You and Lee 2024).

To reflect this self-categorization into ingroups of social influence, we extend the CODA model by introducing 'labels': identity markers that determine whether an interaction leads to information integration. To enable information sharing across communities, we implement noise into the social influence heuristic (Steiglechner et al. 2024) via a probability of migrating between labels, representing the assimilation of individuals into another epistemic community.

In this model, we implemented two bottom-up mechanisms: the shift in preferred choice of an agent and the probability of agents switching their label. From these two sources of change emerge the regimes and phases observed in the simulations. The coarse-grained output, the preferred choice, becomes the input for the higher scale (Fig. 10.1). Due to the hierarchical clustering of components in our model, a change in preferred choice of an agent shifts the composition of the preferred choice distribution within the label which may in turn accumulate and produce a shift in the label's preferred choice and thus a change in the global distribution in a hierarchical chain of upward causation.

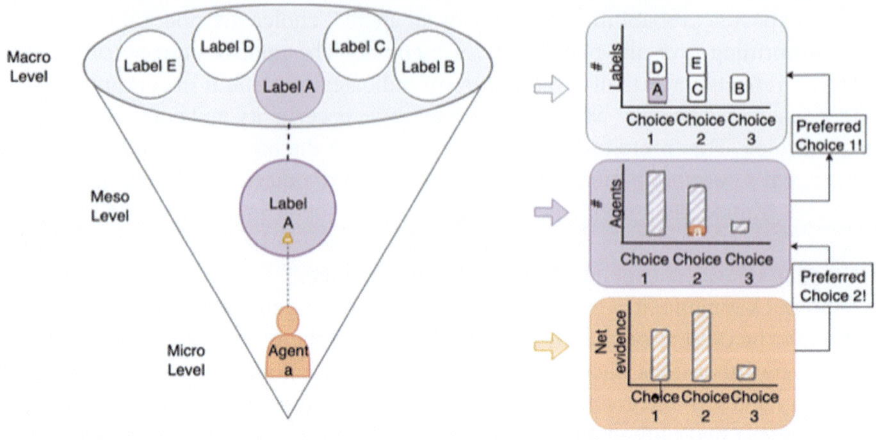

Fig. 10.1 The hierarchical coarse-graining of preferred choices from agent to global level is shown on the left, while the process of upward causation in the hierarchical coarse-graining scheme is shown on the right

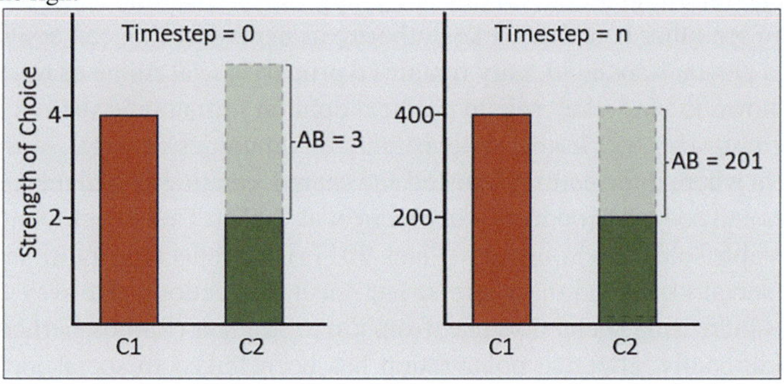

Fig. 10.2 Activation barrier (AB) At initialization, the agent's internal choice distribution consists of six units of information (left panel), the AB is low. As time goes by, the agent integrates information and the AB becomes higher. C1-C2 represent choice 1 and 2 respectively

The shift in preferred choice, i.e. upward causation, occurs when the amount of evidence favoring a divergent choice overtakes the current one. We term this threshold the activation barrier (AB). While our notion of the activation barrier (AB) arises from the logic of our model, it is conceptually anchored in the energy barrier concept in complex systems. In statistical physics and nonlinear dynamical systems, transitions between stable states require overcoming an energy barrier, which determines the likelihood of state change (Strogatz 2001). Similarly, here, the AB represents the cumulative divergent social input required for an agent to change its preferred choice. A larger activation barrier requires a greater accumulation of social inputs, which in turn means an increase in the number of interactions, and therefore timesteps, required before an agent can change their preferred choice.

In our model, the AB is dynamic and increases as a function of time: the more information is stored in the agent's choice distribution, the larger the sum of inputs needed to overcome the AB due to the fixed size of the input over the simulation run, reducing its impact on the agent's distribution. Figure 10.2 illustrates how the AB increases from 3 at $t = 0$ to 201 at $t = n$. We refer to the sum of inputs between preferred choice changes as the input term. A second aspect of the activation barrier is linked to relative entropy. Agents with strong evidence for one choice and little for others are certain, making them more resistant to change. In contrast, agents with more evenly distributed choice strengths (high relative entropy) have higher uncertainty and lower activation barriers. The AB at the local community level is given by the activation barrier of agents in that community, i.e. their level of stubbornness, and the relative entropy of the distribution. The global AB is defined by the label's AB and its level of relative entropy, with high relative entropy signifying a high AB and v.v.

We hypothesize that when agents' internal distributions are increasing in infor mation content, and when they are increasing in certainty, the AB rises, lengthening the time required for preferred choice change to occur. This stabilization reinforces time-scale separation, making higher-level distributions progressively more resistant to changes at lower levels. These ideas in combination with Flack's indicators for downward causation form the basis for our analysis of the emergent causal mechanism.

Since this paper focuses on the consensus phase of collective computation, we concentrate on tuning, the process by which agents estimate regularities in the social environment, i.e. the coarse-grained variable (Flack 2017a). Here, the social environment is defined as the distribution of choices within the agent's local community. At any point during the simulation, an agent's model represents its current estimation of that distribution, shaped by past interactions. To isolate the intrinsic mechanism of information integration, we start the simulation with a uniform distribution of choices. This maximum entropy condition minimizes the influence of prior information, allowing the dynamics to emerge primarily from the model's structure and interactions (Yuan et al. 2024).

By implementing a bottom up mechanism at the microlevel and tracking the hierarchical transmission of information via upward causation, our goal is to identify the emergent downward causal influence of the collective computation using Flack's (Flack 2017a) indicators for downward causation outlined in this section. Because the terminology for describing the evolution of distributions is sparse, we define key concepts for clarity. Alignment is defined as the convergence on a single preferred choice within a given scale, for example, when all agents within a label share the same majority choice (local alignment) or when all labels converge on the same preferred choice (global alignment). Misalignment, conversely, refers to the persistence of diverse preferred choices within a distribution. Global consensus is achieved only when both local and global alignments are realized, meaning all agents across all labels share the same choice.

In summary, our theoretical framework suggests that opinion formation and consensus-building are driven by hierarchical coarse-graining mechanisms, where microlevel interactions shape local and global distributions through upward causation, and after stability and time-scale separation emerge, the respective higher-level distribution exerts downward causation on the level below. Understanding how different levels of connectivity influence these dynamics is essential to understand political discourse higher-level outcomes such as polarization. To systematically explore these mechanisms, we implement an agent-based model that captures the interplay between individual learning, epistemic communities, and hierarchical opinion integration. The following section outlines the structure of our model, its key parameters, and the methodological approach used to analyze the emergent dynamics.

10.3 Methods

10.3.1 Model Overview

The model is written in Python v 3.11.5. Here we present a brief description, a full ODD+D protocol can be found as Supporting Information (Kamińska 2025).

The model simulates an artificial society inhabited by 2500 human agents who have a set of independent issues, varying from 2 to 10. Each issue represents a specific problem or topic the agents face, and for each issue, agents evaluate a set of choices, varying from 2 to 10. Agent holds an internal belief about which choice is the best solution for a given issue i.e., the preferred choice. This belief is represented by a vector of choice strengths (Fig. 10.3), where each value corresponds to the agent's estimation of how strongly each choice is the best solution. The preferred choice is the one with the highest choice strength, which is communicated to others during interactions (Fig. 10.3).

To simplify the model, choice strengths are updated using a Bayesian inference process. To reduce computational complexity, the probabilities are transformed into the log-odds domain. This change allows the use of a simple additive rule, enabling efficient calculation of the strength of each choice while preserving probabilistic

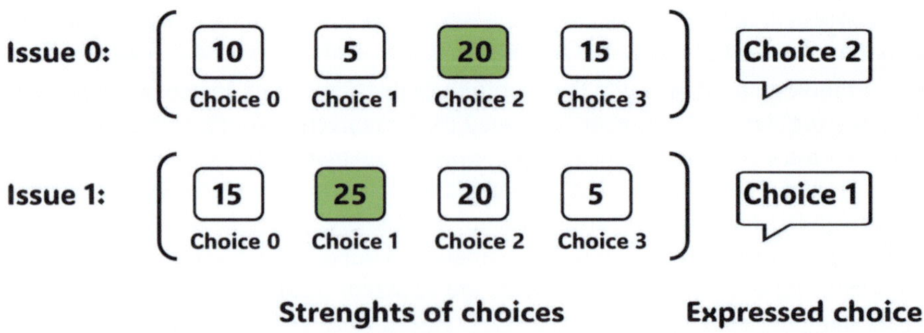

Fig. 10.3 Graphical representation of agents' choices on issues agents evaluate the strength of each choice and express the one with the highest strength

reasoning. Agents thus hold a numerical vector per issue, where values represent the strength of the choice. Further, agents also belong to a label. The label value ranges from none (no label) to 1, …, *number_of_labels* in the system. Labels influence the frequency and trustworthiness of interactions: agents trust and interact more frequently with those sharing the same label. Every time step, agents may drop their current label with probability *prob-dropping-label* or adopt a new one with probability *prob-adopting-a-label* (Fig. 10.4).

At initialization the parameters are set as outlined in Table 10.1. The rationale for these choices is as follows: Probability of dropping label (*prob-dropping-label*): values higher than 0.01 lead to rapid consensus across labels. We explored the 0 to 0.005 range as it preserves diverse dynamics. Although these values seem small, they result in a steady flow of individuals changing labels every time step (e.g., at 0.005,

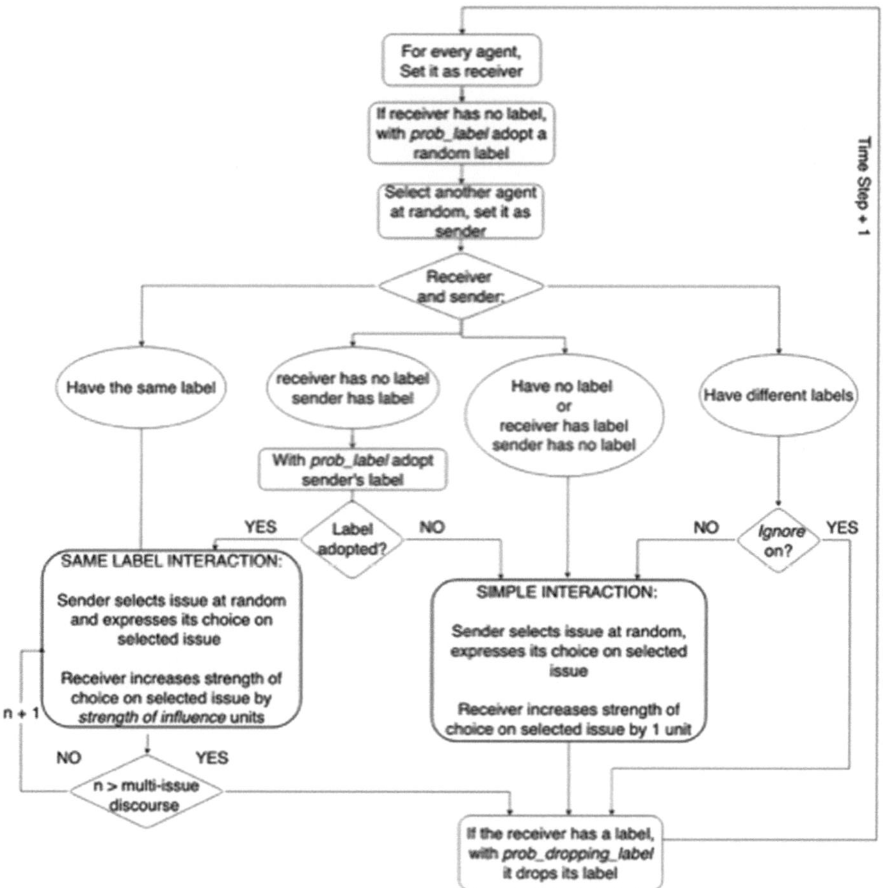

Fig. 10.4 Flow diagram representing algorithm of the interactions between agents. Note that whether ignoring is ON or OFF is a parameter of simulation (fixed for given run)

Table 10.1 Model parameters and their explored values.

Parameter	Values explored	Description
Pop-size	2500	Number of agents in the model
Num-labels	[2,6,10]	Number of labels in the system
Num-issues	[1,5,10]	Number of issues (problems or topics) that agents face
Num-choices	[2,5,10]	Number of potential choices (solutions) for each issue
Multi-issue discourse	[1,5,20]	Number of issues discussed during a single interaction with same-label agents
Strength-of-influence	[1,5,20]	Degree of influence that agents with the same label exert on each other
Ignoring	[on/off]	Whether agents ignore the choices expressed by agents from a different label
Prob-dropping-label	[0.000, 0.0001, 0.0005, 0.0010, 0.0050, 0.0100]	Probability that an agent drops its current label
Prob-adopting-a-label	0.1	Probability that an agent without a label adopts a new label

$\sim$ 12 individuals switch labels per time step in a population of 2500). The range for number of labels and issues was chosen to ensure manageable, interpretable outcomes and computational efficiency. Higher values affect the speed of the dynamics but do not yield qualitative differences. Number of choices per issue: A maximum of 10 choices was selected to approximate the cognitive limit for an average individual. Multi-issue discourse and strength of influence: These parameters represent minimum, medium, and extreme influence levels and were set arbitrarily to explore diverse scenarios. Probability of adopting a label: Fixed to simplify the exploration of other variables, as varying it would primarily affect the speed of dynamics rather than qualitative outcomes. Population size: Fixed at 2500 for computational efficiency.

The simulation starts with agents randomly assigning low initial choice strengths drawn from a uniform distribution [0,3]) for all choices and selecting a random label. Thereafter, the simulation starts and at each time step, individuals hold a dyadic interaction where they exchange preferred choices on multiple issues and update their beliefs accordingly (Fig. 10.4).

10.3.2 Interactions

Every time step, each agent selects another agent at random to interact with. Thus, every agent can always potentially interact with every other in the model. In this sense, the model represents a fully connected network. Once an interaction partner is selected, the active agent becomes the receiver and the randomly selected partner the sender. The sender picks an issue at random and communicates its preferred choice for that issue to the receiver. The preferred choice is the one with the highest strength. If two or more choices have the same strength, one of these is selected at random. Thus, while the strength of choices can vary in magnitude, the receiver only observes the sender's preferred choice. (Fig. 10.3).

The outcomes of these interactions differ depending on the labels held by the sender and receiver. There are four possible combinations of sender-receiver labels, grouped into two interaction types: simple interactions and same-label interactions. For clarity, the interaction process is summarized in a flow diagram (Fig. 10.4).

Simple interactions. Simple interactions occur when the sender and receiver have no label, only one of them has a label, or both have different labels but the receiver does not ignore the sender (*ignoring* is off, Fig. 10.4). In these interactions, the sender communicates its preferred choice and the receiver updates the strength associated with observed choice by adding +1. For example, if a sender, holding a different label than the receiver, communicates choice B as its preferred choice on an issue, the receiver increases the strength of choice B by +1, provided that *ignoring* is off. Conversely, if *ignoring* is on, the receiver disregards the sender's input.

Same-label interactions. In interactions when both agents share the same label, the sender has greater influence on the receiver. The *strength-of-influence* parameter determines the degree of this influence. Upon observing the sender's preferred choice, the receiver updates its internal representation of the issue by increasing the strength associated with the observe choice by *strength-of-influence* units. Further, the *multi-issue discourse* parameter determines the number of issues discussed during the interaction. Consequently, the sender may express its preferred choice for one or more issues during each interaction (Fig. 10.4). For example, if *multi-issue discourse* is set to 3, the sender shares its preferred choices for three randomly selected issues, and the receiver updates the strengths for all three according to *strength-of-influence* (Fig. 10.4).

10.3.3 Simulations, Data Collection and Analyses

We explored the parameter space outlined in Table 10.1. For each parameter combination, we ran 10 simulations. Here, we present results where multi-issue discourse and strength-of-influence were fixed at 20, while prob-dropping-label was restricted to 0, 0.0001, and 0.01. This selection was made to illustrate the model's key dynamics more clearly, as these parameters primarily influence the speed at which the system reaches stability but do not introduce qualitative differences in the model's dynamics. For a detailed presentation of all parameter combinations, see the Supporting Information (Kamińska 2025).

During the simulations every 200 time steps we collected for all agents' labels and current opinion distribution. With the data collected, we calculate two indexes that help us describe the state of the system: the Cosine index and the Shannon-Wiener

(SW) diversity index. These two indexes focus on two key aspects of the system: the alignment of choices within groups sharing the same label (SW index) and the diversity of choices across labels (Cosine index). Both, the SW diversity index and the Simpson index, are valid measures of diversity within a given community. The fact that there is a logarithm in the SW index formula makes it more sensitive to minorities. In the case of our model it allows us to more accurately determine when the unanimity among agents holding the same label is broken (when there are agents expressing choices different than the majority).

The SW index assesses how similar the choices are among agents holding the same label. For each label and each issue, we take the frequencies of choices and calculate the SW diversity index, which is defined as the entropy normalized by the logarithm of the number of possible choices, so it ranges between [0, 1]. A value of 0 indicates unanimous agreement within a label on a given issue (label alignment), while a value of 1 suggests a uniform distribution of choices (label misalignment). For the sake of clarity in our visual representations, we present the SW diversity index averaged over issues and labels. The mathematical formula to calculate the SW index is presented in Eq. 10.1:

$$\text{Shannon-Wiener Index} = \frac{1}{n_{\text{labels}} \cdot n_{\text{issues}}} \sum_{l=1}^{n_{\text{labels}}} \sum_{i=1}^{n_{\text{issues}}} \left(\sum_{c=1}^{n_{\text{choices}}} p_{c,i,l} \ln p_{c,i,l} \right) \tag{10.1}$$

where $p_{c,i,l}$ denotes the current frequency that an agent holding label l expresses choice c regarding issue i . To measure the likeness between choices of agents from two different labels on a specific issue, we examine the distribution of agent support for each possible choice within both groups. Then, we calculate cosine similarity between resultant vectors representing frequencies of choices. A similarity score of 1 denotes identical vectors (global alignment), while 0 means that they are orthogonal (global misalignment). Subsequently, we compute the average similarity across issues and all possible pairwise comparisons. The mathematical formula to calculate the Cosine similarity index is presented in Eq. 10.2:

$$\text{Cosine index} = \frac{1}{n_{\text{issues}}} \sum_{i=1}^{n_{\text{issues}}} \frac{1}{2n_{\text{labels}}(n_{\text{labels}}-1)} \sum_{l_1=1}^{n_{\text{labels}}} \sum_{l_2=l_1+1}^{n_{\text{labels}}} \left(\frac{\sum_{c=1}^{n_{\text{choices}}} P_{c,i,l_1} \cdot P_{c,i,l_2}}{\sum_{c=1}^{n_{\text{choices}}} \sqrt{P_{c,i,l_1}^2} \sum_{c=1}^{n_{\text{choices}}} \sqrt{P_{c,i,l_2}^2}} \right) \tag{10.2}$$

where $p_{c,i,l}$ is defined as in Eq. 10.1.

10.4 Results

We conducted multiple simulations across a broad range of parameter settings (Table tab:parameters) to examine the dynamics produced by our model of political opinion dynamics, which is grounded in hierarchical coarse-graining and community-bounded social influence. The results indicate that the model robustly generates large-scale patterns of information integration and alignment within and across labels. Notably, the parameter space segregates into three distinct regimes of information integration, predominantly modulated by the degree of higher-level connectivity. These regimes are distinguished by differences in the evolution of alignment and misalignment within labels, as measured by the Shannon-Wiener diversity index, and at the global level, as measured by cosine similarity. As discussed in Sect. 10.3.3, we focus on a narrower parameter range that remains qualitatively consistent with these regimes to illustrate our findings.

10.4.1 Regimes of Information Integration

Our results reveal three distinct regimes of information integration, determined by the probability of label switching (prob-dropping-label, PDL) as well as 'ignoring' off. Each regime exhibits a unique pattern of choice integration both within and across labels, influencing the system's progression toward local and global consensus. Below, we provide a detailed description of each regime. To enhance clarity and coherence, we have restructured the results and discussion sections. Consequently, Figs. 10.5 and 10.6 contain examples that do not strictly correspond to the regimes they describe. Each section will explicitly clarify these instances.

10.4.1.1 Independent Information Integration Regime

When *prob-dropping-label* (PDL) equals 0, no individual switches across labels, leading to a rapid alignment of choices within the label but no integration across labels. In this case the diversity of choices within labels decreases (SW index quickly drops close to zero), indicating convergence of choices within labels (Fig. 10.5b). Further interactions do not lead to any choice changes after timestep ~500, indicating equilibrium. After timestep 0, the diversity across labels is high (Cosine of ~1), increases until timestep ~400 (Cosine index drops) and remains at a stable level (Fig. 10.5a). As a result, the system reaches a rapid steady state, where labels maintain distinct and isolated choices, forming persistent informational silos that prevent global convergence. We refer to this as the independent information integration regime, where no information flows between labels, leading to global misalignment

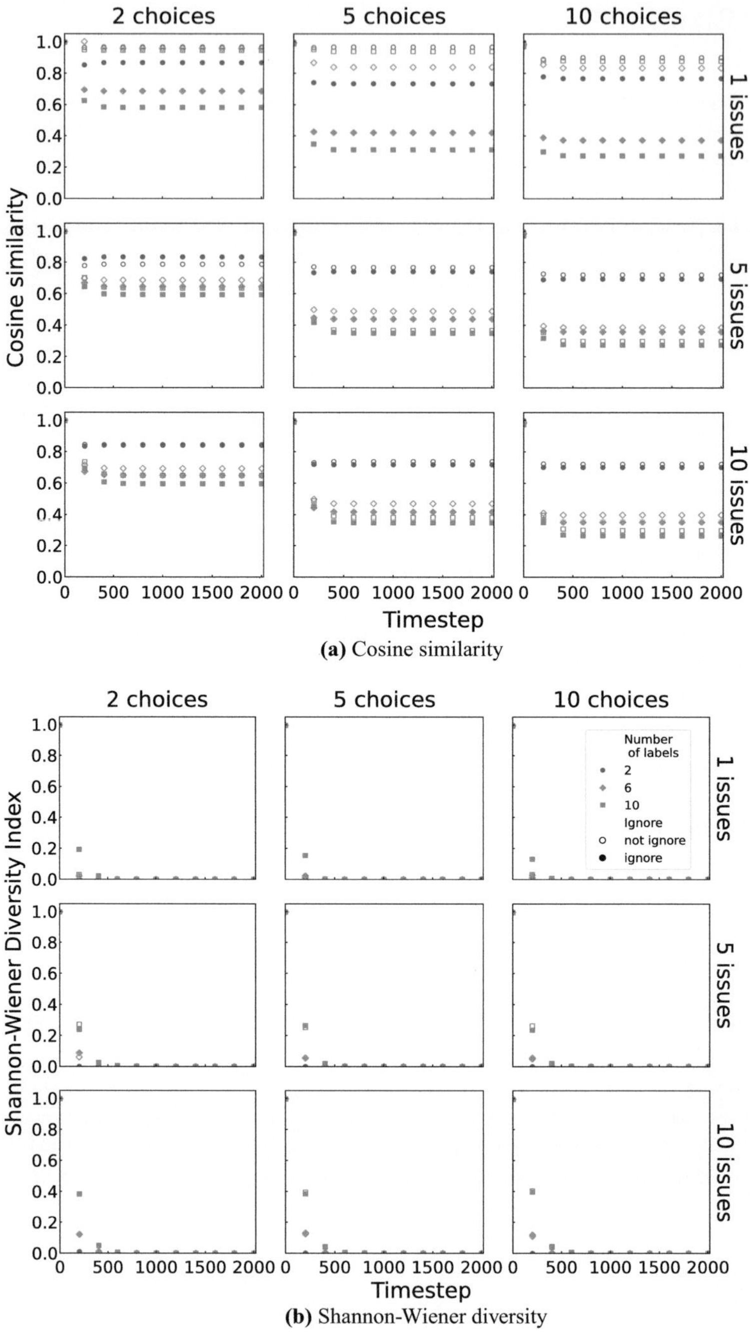

(a) Cosine similarity

(b) Shannon-Wiener diversity

Fig. 10.5 Independent information integration regime (part 1), Independent information integration regime (part 2), Results shown are means of 10 simulations per parameter set. PDL = 0; Strength of influence = 20; multi-issue discourse = 20; and ignore is ON or OFF (filled and hollow points). 2, 6, or 10 labels (color and shape-coded points); 1, 5, and 10 issues (rows); and 2, 5 or 10 choices (columns)

but label alignment (Fig. 10.5). While the figure is intended to illustrate the independent regime, it includes some settings where ignoring is off, that do not align with this regime.

10.4.1.2 Parallel Information Integration Regime

When PDL is sufficiently high ($\sim$ 0.001, depending on the exact configuration of issues, labels, choices, SoI and MID), agents switch labels more frequently. In this regime, the Cosine index starts completely aligned and quickly drops, indicating divergence, from which point, on the Cosine index increases until global alignment is reached (timestep ~500). Within labels, we can observe a convergence of agents' preferred choices, however at a slower rate than global alignment, reaching local alignment for all parameter settings between timestep ~1000 to ~2000 (Fig. 10.6b). The fact that global alignment precedes label alignment suggests that agents are integrating information globally at such a rate that an initial divergence between labels is eliminated before alignment within labels is reached. Because global and local alignment are reached in the same phase, we refer to this as the parallel information integration regime. The high variance in label alignment trajectories (Fig. 10.6b), illustrates that the PDL of 0.01 in combination with various parameters produces dynamics that border on the iterative information integration regime (see below). In the case of two labels and ignoring on for all parameter settings, as well as ignoring off for 5 and 10 issues (Fig. 10.6b), we can see transient increases in diversity after initial local alignment, corresponding more closely to an iterative regime.

10.4.1.3 Iterative Information Integration Regime

In the independent and parallel regimes, a final steady state is reached relatively quickly, within 500–2000 timesteps (Figs. 10.5–10.6). These regimes show rapid increases in alignment, either within labels only (independent regime), or at both global and local levels (parallel regime). A different regime emerges under intermediate levels of PDL ($0 < \text{PDL} < \sim 0.005$, depending on the exact configuration of issues, labels, choices, SoI and MID), where rapid and temporary local alignment is followed by an increase in divergence of preferred choices within labels until a 'transient diversity', i.e. temporary misalignment, within labels is reached. The evolution of this regime is clearly illustrated in Fig. 10.7b. At first, the SW index drops rapidly, indicating aligning preferred choices within labels. A high Cosine index (Fig. 10.7a) shows that this state of local alignment coincides with global misalignment. This is followed by a temporary increase of divergence at label level. The Cosine index seems to show that global alignment is reached while labels are once more internally misaligned (Fig. 10.7b). Equilibrium is reached only after ~10,000 timesteps, making it considerably longer than the parallel regime.

The SW index shows that the iterative regime gives rise to transient diversity at the local level and has three phases: local alignment, local divergence/global alignment

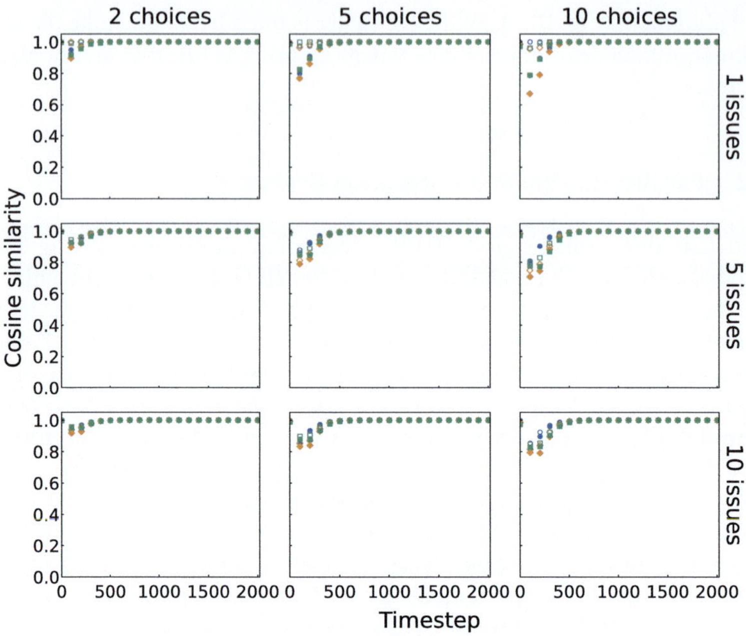

(a) Cosine similarity

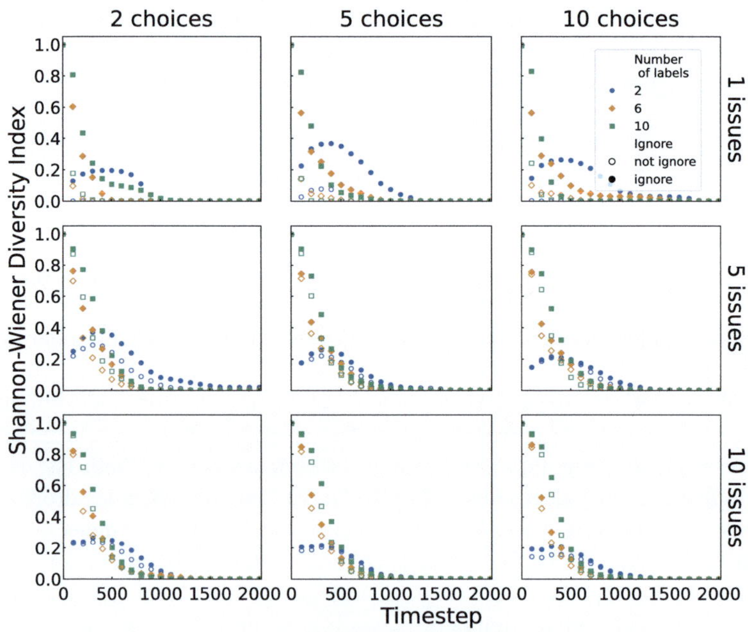

(b) Shannon-Wiener diversity

Fig. 10.6 Parallel information integration regime (part 1), Parallel information integration regime (part 2). Results shown are means of 10 simulations per parameter set. PDL = 0.01; Strength of influence = 20; multi-issue discourse = 20; and ignore is ON or OFF (filled and hollow points). 2, 6, or 10 labels (color and shape-coded points); 1, 5, and 10 issues; and 2 or 10 choices (columns)

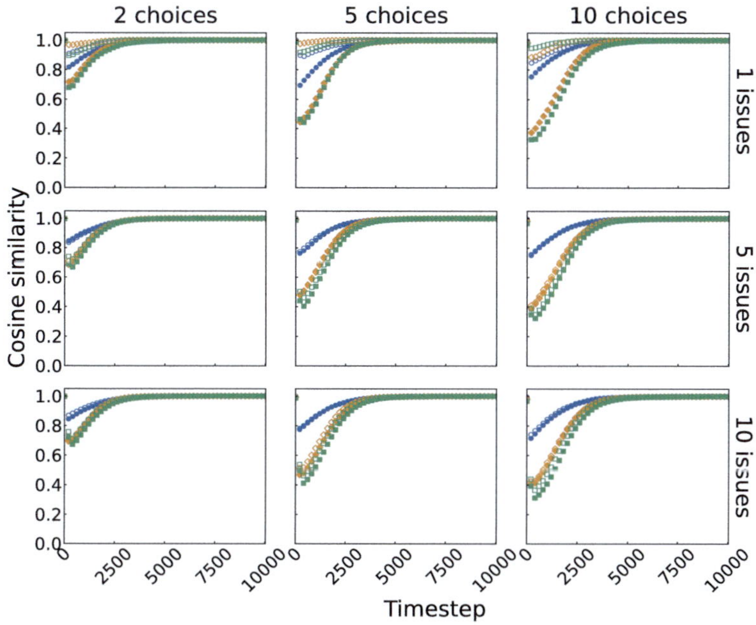

(a) Cosine similarity

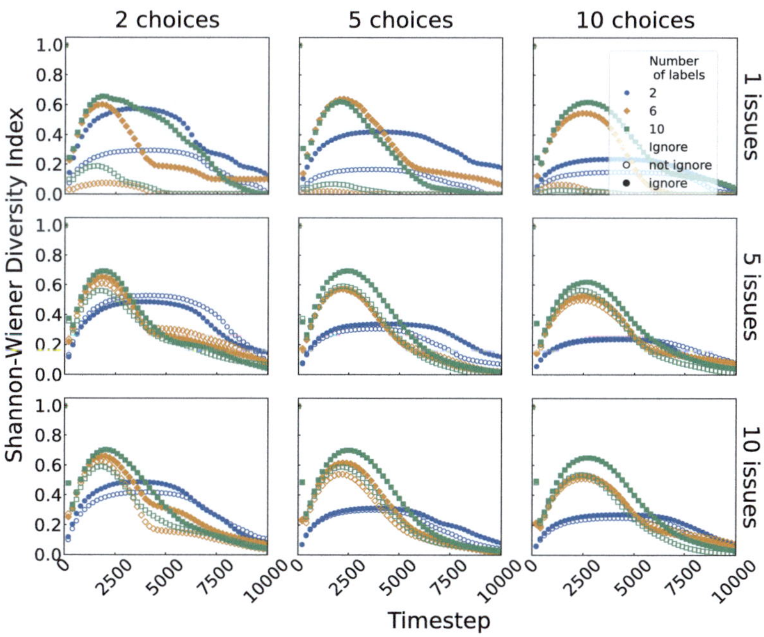

(b) Shannon-Wiener diversity

Fig. 10.7 Iterative information integration regime (part 1), Iterative information integration regime (part 2). Results shown are means of 10 simulations per parameter set. PDL = 0.001; Strength of influence = 20; multi-issue discourse = 20; and ignore is ON or OFF (filled and hollow points). 2, 6, or 10 labels (color and shape-coded points); 1, 5, and 10 issues; and 2 or 10 choices (columns)

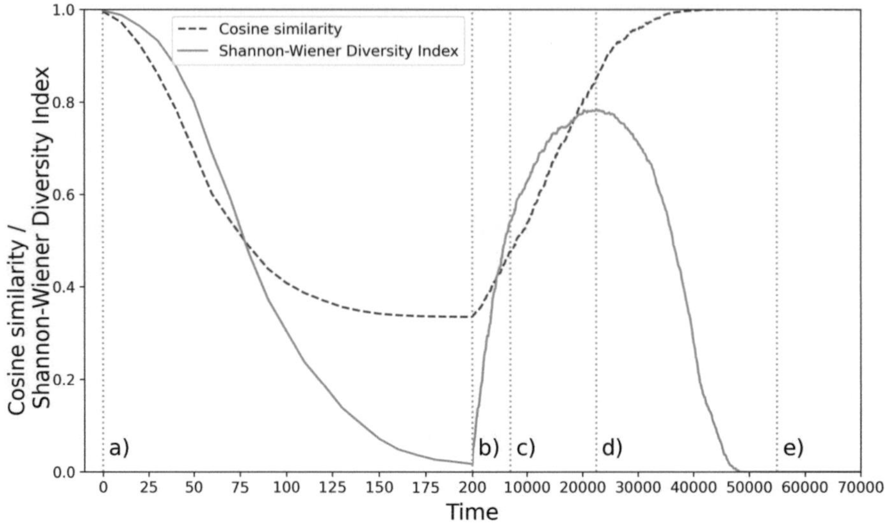

Fig. 10.8 Iterative information integration regime. The time-scale (x-axis) is adjusted to show the decrease of relative entropy in Phase I in more detail. PDL = 0.0001; Strength of influence = 20; multi-issue discourse = 20; and ignore is ON; 8 labels; 1 issue; and 5 choices. Different timepoints are depicted by the dashed vertical lines. Point a = 0, b= 200, c = ~7,000; d= ~22,400; and e = ~55,000 timesteps

and local alignment. We refer to this as the iterative information integration regime because the initial alignment within labels gives rise to a global misalignment, starting a separate information integration between higher-level components (the labels) until global alignment is achieved. In the next section, we focus on the phases of a specific instance of the iterative regime and analyze the underlying causation (Figs. 10.8, 10.9,and 10.10). However, note that the patterns described below are qualitatively consistent across simulations with an iterative information integration regime.

10.4.2 Analysis of Hierarchical Causation in the Iterative Regime

In order to understand what ultimately leads to the information integration phases and regimes we have observed, we employ the previously defined indicators for upward and downward causation to a simulation run of the iterative regime. In addition, we rely on the activation barrier concept, as defined in the background, to support our analysis. To identify the different phases and track the alignment or misalignment of the distributions, we plotted the SW index and Cosine index of an iterative regime simulation run.

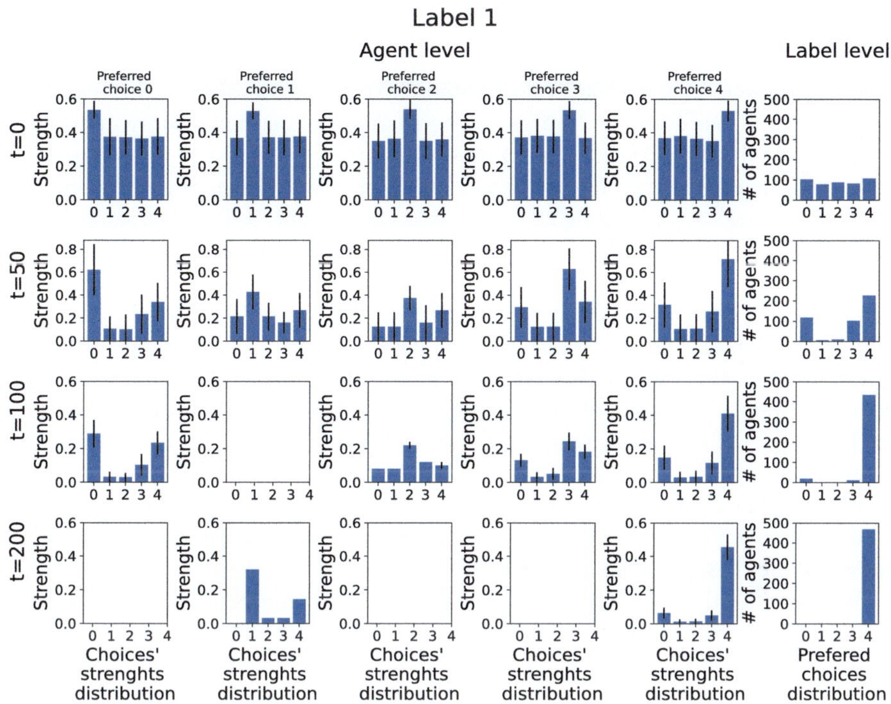

Fig. 10.9 Distributions of choices' strengths at the agent level and label choice distributions of Label 1 at different time points (rows) during Phase I. In the agent-level panel, columns represent agents preferring a given choice, bar plots show the average strength of choices, and error bars indicate standard deviation. Blank plots indicate that no agents preferred the given choice. The label-level panel (last column on the right) presents bar plots depicting the number of agents preferring each choice at different time points. PDL = 0.0001; Strength of influence = 20; multi-issue discourse = 20; and ignore is ON; 8 labels; 1 issue; and 5 choices

We further mapped the distributions of preferred choice for each level (agent, label, global) in all the phases of the iterative regime to identify changes in activation barriers, downward causation and alignment. Figure 10.9, outlines the distributions at the agent and label level for label 1. Columns 1–5 show the choices' strength distribution for agents preferring choice 0–4 (columns) at different time points (rows). The last column to the right shows the label's distribution of agents with a given preferred choice at different timesteps.

10.4.2.1 Phase I: Local Alignment

At timestep 0, the activation barrier to preferred choice change is low (Fig. 10.9). The SW index is highest (Fig. 10.8, point a), due to the normal distribution at initialization. After interactions begin, at timestep 50, we can see that all choices are still preferred by at least one agent in the label (last column, row 2 in Fig. 10.9). The relative entropy among choices is decreased and the activation barrier goes up from 2 at timestep 0, to ~500 at timestep 50 and ~10000 at timestep 200 (see y-axis values at different time steps in Fig. 10.9). The label preferred choice distribution increasingly converges: By timestep 50, choice 1 and 2 are almost eliminated; by timestep 100, choice 1 is eliminated and agent's preferring choices 0, 2, or 3 are on the verge of switching preferred choice; by timestep 200, it is clear that the agents will converge on choice 4. This corresponds to point b in Fig. 10.8. We can see that the preferred choice distribution stabilizes around timestep 50 (consolidating around preferred choice 4) which triggers downward causation leading all agents to converge on choice 4. The rate at which agents change their preferred choice shows a sharp decline after ~10 timesteps (Fig. 46 in the supporting information (Kamińska 2025), the local level becomes time-scale separated. Hence, the preferred choice at timestep 50 predicts the future state of the agents at timestep 200, and the mutual information between the label and the agents increases. All agents tune to the same social environment given by the model design that restricts information integration to the local community for all members of a label. All of Flack's (Flack 2017a) outlined criteria for downward causation are thus observable in phase I.

We argue that the time-scale separation and stability of the local distribution results in local downward causation because it changes the inputs to agents. It increases the precision of the input term in depicting the local distribution across agents, producing coherent output in the direction of the locally preferred choice. We believe this is a consequence of the increased amount of samples needed until agents can change their preferred choice due to the activation barrier (Fig. 10.9). A perfectly accurate coarse-grained estimation of the higher-level distribution can only result in that local choice. If an agent were to sample everyone else in their community before their preferred choice changes, and in the amount of time they are doing so the distribution remains roughly the same, the input term would have to be highly accurate in conveying the real local distribution, which is what agents are estimating (Flack 2017a). This would lead the agent to change its state to the preferred choice of the label. The more agents become accurate in their estimation, the smaller the pool of possible outcomes, making agents in the label converge on the locally preferred choice. Therefore, an activation barrier, increasing evenly in agents of a local community and globally, can be thought of as increasing the accuracy of the input term that serves as the measurement of the local distribution for each agent. In a nutshell, the local distribution—due to a high level of accuracy of the distribution of inputs until opinion change in measuring the local distribution—causes (downward causation) the output (agent upward causation) and in turn the agents' preferred choice aligns with that of the local distribution. As can be seen in Fig. 10.10, $ts = 200$, the iterative regime gives rise to global misalignment after phase I. At higher levels of PDL, the parallel information integration of the global distribution can lead to global alignment before local alignment (parallel regime). Since all communities tune to the same global distribution, the stabilization of the global level with local alignment and remaining global misalignment activates downward causation.

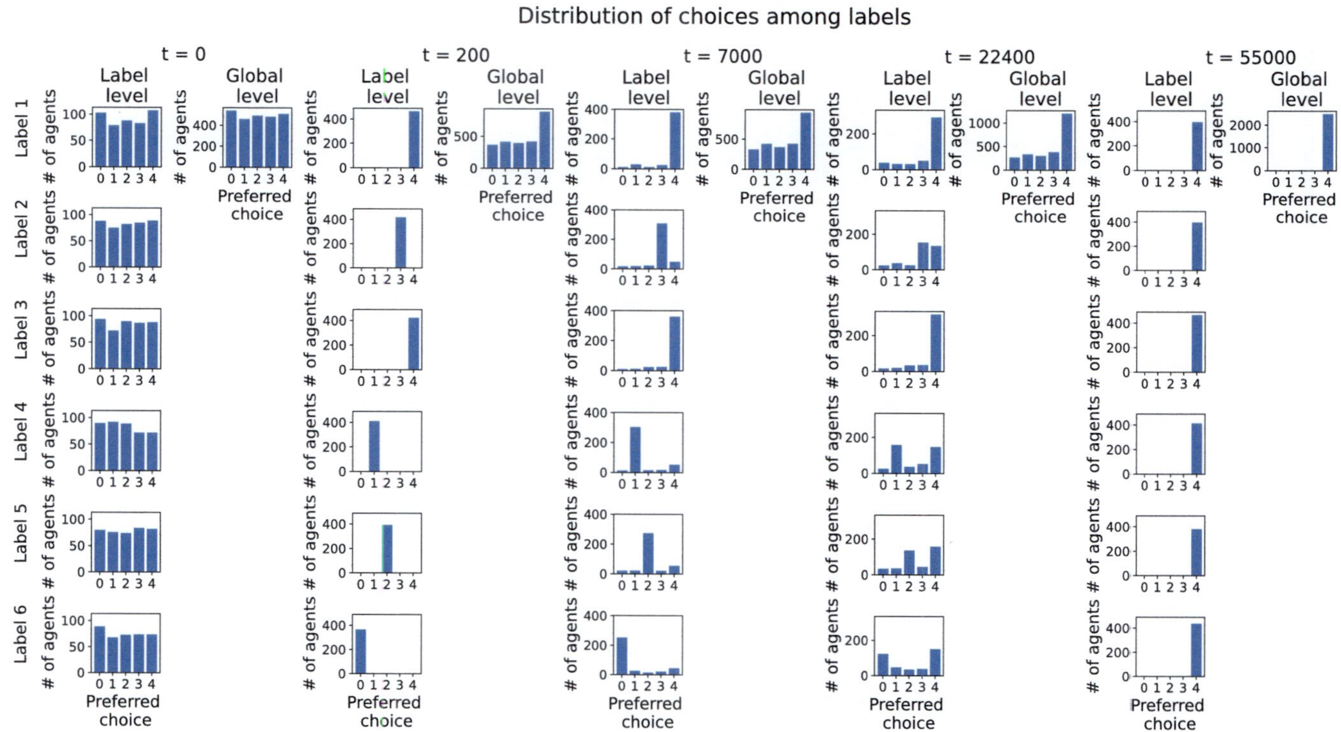

Fig. 10.10 Preferred choice distributions at the label and global level at different time points during stage I-III. Rows represent different labels and histograms represent the number of agents preferring a given choice at the label or global level. PDL = 0.0001; Strength of influence = 20; multi-issue discourse = 20; and ignore is ON; 8 labels; 1 issue; and 5 choices

10.4.2.2 Phase II: Global Alignment

Figure 10.10 outlines the preferred choice distribution at the label and global level at different time points during the simulation. At the beginning of phase II (point b in Fig. 10.8 and $t = 200$ in Fig. 10.10), the labels are internally aligned, but there is global misalignment, even though there appears to be a preference towards choice 4. At this point, two labels (1 and 2) are aligned with the global choice but all others prefer a different choice. These four divergent labels (2, 4–6) switch or start switching to choice 4 around timestep 22,400, point d in Fig. 10.8. Like in phase I, the switching of preferred choices is asynchronous and divergence at the global level decreases one label at a time. Note that the preferred choice at the global level remains unchanged from timestep 200 on until the end of phase III, and in phase II the global distribution undergoes only marginal changes, whereas labels diverge in their preferred choice distribution till timestep 22,400 (point d in Fig. 10.8, end of phase II). We can identify global downward causation because the global distribution, that becomes stable at point b (Fig. 10.8), compels labels to align their preferred choices with the global preference (choice 4) at point d (Fig. 10.8), resulting in marked global alignment.

During this phase, agents are sampling and reinforcing the preferred choice of their label (local downward causation), contributing to the increase in the agent's activation barrier, while also sampling the choices of migrating agents (global downward causation), likely diverging from the label's preferred choice. We argue it is this moving of agents with high activation barriers (stubborn and high in certainty) across labels that increases the diversity of preferred choices within labels and ultimately aligns labels with the global distribution. The stability of the global distribution stems from the fact that it is constituted of labels, and the only source of change in the global distribution comes from labels changing their preferred choice (label upward causation). In phase II, labels themselves have a high activation barrier (stubborn agents and highly aligned distribution) but compared to the global distribution they are more reactive to the information input. Diverging agents from other labels keep coming in, and eventually, the divergent information crosses, first, the agents' activation barrier and then, the label's activation barrier to preferred choice change. Therefore, the label tunes to the global opinion distribution and not the other way around. However, slowly, since the ratio between label and non-label agents at every timestep is tipped in favor of the label. The outcome of phase II is global alignment of preferred choice and label misalignment. Global and local downward causation are aligned, having the same preferred choice, and as a result the local distribution is not subject to further divergence.

10.4.2.3 Phase III: Local Alignment

In our example, this phase occurs between timestep 22,400 (point d, Fig. 10.8) and 55,000 (point e, Fig. 10.8). The alignment of the local and global social environment (due to global alignment from the previous phase) signifies that the agents, again, coherently tune to the same local distribution and stable preferred choice, mirroring the conditions of local alignment during phase I. In phase III, agents increasingly converge in their estimates of the label's probability distribution until local alignment, signifying consensus of all agents in all labels with the coarse-grained preferred choice 4 (Fig. 10.10, t = 55,000). At this point, the system is in equilibrium: every encountered agent agrees on the preferred choice (local and global alignment) and the continued interactions cease to cause preferred choice changes, only serving to increase agents' activation barriers.

10.4.2.4 Hierarchical Coarse-Graining Mechanism with Regimes

The causal analysis, combined with our previous observations, can be abstracted into an algorithmic mechanism illustrated in Fig. 10.11. In Phase I, the system transitions from initial local and global misalignment to either complete alignment (the parallel regime), solely local alignment (the independent regime), or, under higher-level connectivity, global misalignment initiates a second phase of the iterative regime. In Phase II, the diversity of preferred choices across labels converges toward a single global preference (Outcome II, Fig. 10.11), which in turn disrupts local alignment (Outcome I, Fig. 10.11). Finally, Phase III starts with local misalignment and ends with local alignment (Outcome I, Fig. 10.11), which in combination with the global alignment yields global consensus, thereby fulfilling the end condition of the iterative regime.

10.5 Discussion

Our paper addresses the gap in our understanding of what causal mechanism of information integration leads to the emergence of consensus in political opinion dynamics and polarization, a dysfunction of the information integration mechanism. In combining an understanding of political opinion dynamics with a hierarchical coarse-graining mechanism, we were able to trace the emergence of downward causation, higher levels of organization and consensus in a multilevel mechanism. A realistic account of such a causal mechanism is necessary to inform further research and policy interventions that can successfully curb polarization. Hierarchical causation helps explain how individual opinions aggregate into collective beliefs (upward causation) and how those collective beliefs, once stabilized, shape future individual opinions and alignment (downward causation). In this section, we examine the broader implications of our model results in the context of polarization.

Our results show that social influence based on shared social identity alone confines information integration to the local community (independent regime). The implementation of noise, simulating higher-level information integration between local communities, leads to consensus at any value of label switching probability. A low value of probability leads to an iterative regime that is distinguished by a transient diversity before global consensus. The iterative regime has the additional phases

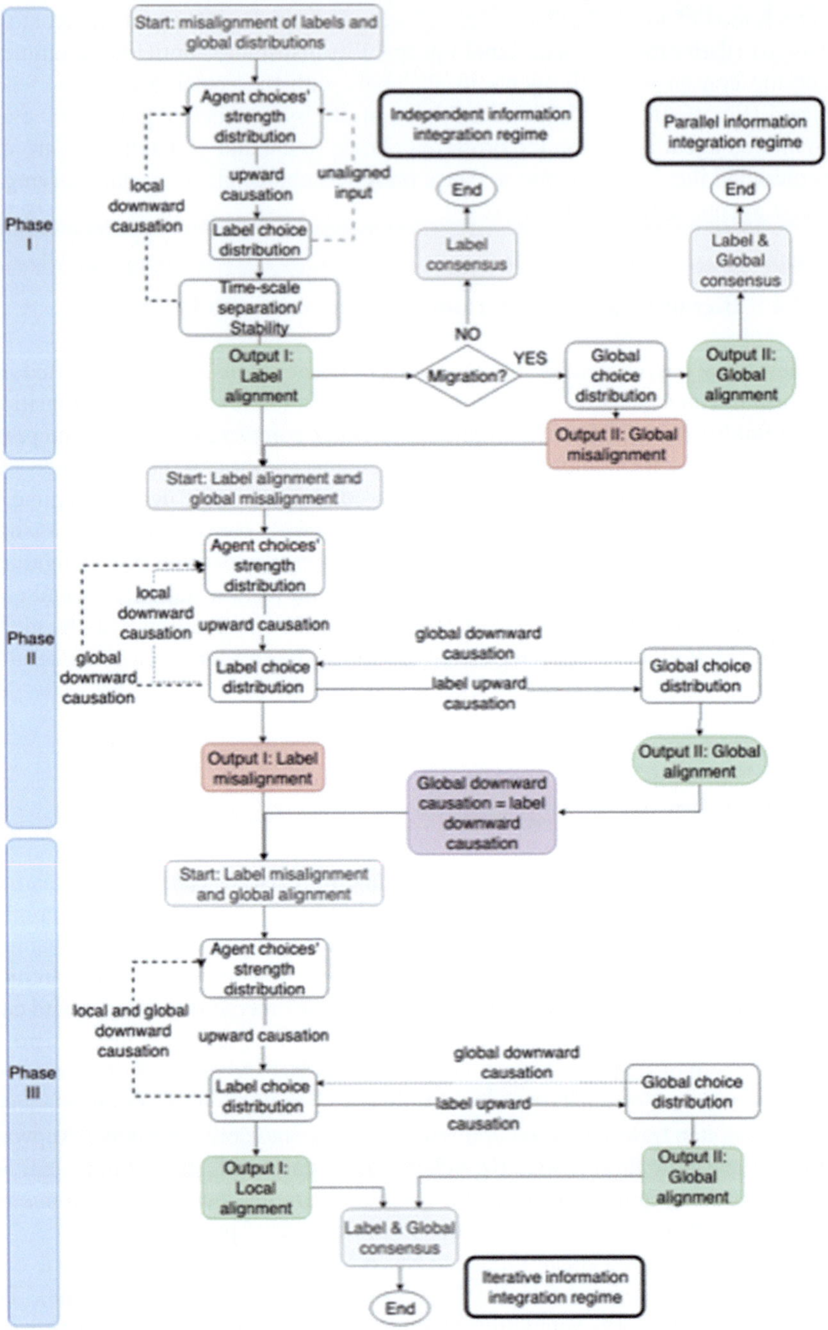

Fig. 10.11 Hierarchical coarse-graining mechanism with regimes. Phases start with the output of the previous one: local and/or global misalignment, activated downward causation; green: alignment, red: misalignment; process ends when all misalignment in the social environment is resolved

of global alignment (phase II) and local alignment (phase III) and is substantially longer than the other regimes. This might be universally beneficial for democratic functioning since overall more information contributes to the final slowly constructed variable (Smaldino et al. 2022; Flack 2017a) and point to a general benefit of a low degree of higher-level connectivity. A higher value of switching probability leads to a parallel information integration regime with a rapid, and nearly simultaneous local and global alignment. The parallel regime exhibits fast variable construction, which seems to respond to 'herding' (Smaldino et al. 2017). Public discourse is commonly understood as the discussion of diverse points of view on a given issue at the global societal level, with opinions characterized by some degree of certainty about one's perspective before agreement. Therefore, the iterative information integration regime which includes a phase II of high personal certainty and diversity of points of view, corresponds most closely to public discourse in democracies.

Downward causation in our model arises dynamically from emergent time-scale separation. It first comes about in phase I between micro- and meso level due to the increasing barrier to opinion change. At the end of phase I, when labels are fully aligned and the activation barrier to preferred choice change at the local level is high, the global distribution becomes consolidated. Time-scale separation stabilizes the distributions, providing coherent and accurate input to components at the lower scale. Agents start to converge when their estimates of the local choice distribution start to align, i.e. tuning becomes increasingly coherent across agents (Flack 2017), and the number of agents with the most popular choice of that label starts to increase. In a nutshell, the causation needs to become "circular" (Fuchs 2020), where the higher-level distribution that exerts downward causation becomes itself affected by its effect on agents changing their choice, which in turn converges the higher-level distribution itself. Fittingly, Fuchs calls circular causation "downward/upward causation or global-to-local/local-to-global causality" (Fuchs 2020). By thinking about what real world phenomena could intervene in the emergence of circular causation, we can hypothesize what might cause democratic societies to struggle with coming to consensus. Since information connectivity in democratic societies beyond local communities is high, the independent regime can be ruled out. An inability to come to global consensus thus indicates a failure to complete coarse-graining by not meeting the emergent conditions for local or global downward causation. The discovered mechanism of our model can give insight into how ideological polarization, which is a disagreement on policy positions, and affective polarization, ingroup favoritism and outgroup disdain, may arise in democratic societies.

According to (Hobolt et al. 2024), polarized societies exhibit political conflict that "solidifies and political identities crystallize into polarized groups" (Hobolt et al. 2024). Further, affectively polarized societies show high homogeneity within the polarizing communities and sustained disagreement and disdain between them (Bednar 2021; Törnberg 2022). This is akin to locally aligned groups interacting but maintaining their preferred choice nonetheless, sustaining a situation of global misalignment. A common explanation ascribed to continued disagreement and hostility between opinion groups is the idea of echo chambers, or social environments with homogenous opinion distributions, that confirm each other's point of view (Barberá

2020; Hobolt et al. 2024). In the iterative regime, after phase I, most members of labels have converged on a single choice which they keep reinforcing in interactions. Agents are stubborn and high in certainty, so the activation barrier is high. The label at this point can be compared to an echo chamber, in that choices are homogeneous and interactions continuously amplify the shared choice. Interestingly, even while agents within labels keep confirming their choice, the inter-community information integration from migrating agents inevitably leads to the divergence of preferred choices within the label and the alignment of labels over time, conflicting with the ascribed role of an echo chamber in entrenching ingroup views. In fact, the temporary creation of a locally aligned social environment is positive in our model, in that it is the precondition for global time-scale separation and thus global downward causation. What allows for the local alignment pressure exerted by local downward causation to be overcome, is the *global* downward causation that emerges when a stable and time-scale separated global distribution transmits information to all local communities equally. It is important to note that by design local communities in our model tune to the same global distribution that real-life political opinion dynamics might not.

Applied to the echo chamber phenomenon, this would signify that any exposure and integration of information that comes from a more stable (i.e. a higher-level distribution with time-scale separation) source will lead to information integration and alignment across communities, if the information source is the same for all local communities comprised in the higher-level distribution. This suggests that what matters is not only, as previously thought, the similarity of the input of community members (Hobolt et al. 2024) but also the input the community receives from the wider social network it is embedded in. More specifically, the input distribution all local communities are tuning to should possess the same majority or preferred choice and as in our model, time-scale separated from the level below, such that global downward causation can emerge and produce alignment across communities around that global preferred choice. What might affect time-scale separation and coherence of preferred choice of the inputs into local communities in democratic societies?

In our model, higher-level connectivity, i.e. the flow of information between communities, is implemented as a type of noise on the social influence heuristic that affects communities equally. The global distribution that consists of the communities and their preferred choices provides the same reference frame for each community. A source of incoherence of inputs might arise from the rejection of a particular community's opinion by another or when a local community rejects a certain opinion or choice. However, this only prevents global alignment when the ignored portion of the global distribution shifts the global preferred choice from the perspective of the ignoring local community, leading this particular community to align with their perceived global majority choice distinct from the other communities. This is possible when the communities are not equal in size and the ignored one tips the majority. When the criterion for ignoring is the choice itself, then all communities favoring that choice are ignored. This necessarily means that the ignored opinion is the majority opinion to produce a shift and therefore prevent alignment of that community with the actual global preferred choice. Other pathways for communities to perceive a different global preferred choice would be a categorical rejection of the majority or through the mediating information architecture.

In 21st century democratic societies, people do not only talk to their ingroup to reduce their uncertainty about an issue. They also consult sources of information that are broadcast from the top-down, such as TV shows, the radio, the newspaper or the internet that transmit the opinions of experts, politicians and the general public. The trust an individual has in the information source allows information from beyond the local community to influence them. When these globally accessible sources of information are trusted by all local communities, we can postulate that they are embedded in a fairly coherent information environment. Conversely, a source of incoherence would arise from community-based differences in what constitutes a trustworthy source of information, which agrees with findings that trust in media is highly polarized in the U.S. (Törnberg 2022). Further, research into the connection between misinformation and affective polarization provides evidence that people who are affectively polarized trust information that is aligned with their ingroup and distrust information that is aligned with the outgroup (Jenke 2023).

The finding that incoherent inputs across agents and communities hinder global consensus in political opinion dynamics aligns with Durkheim's observation that consensus on opinions and values requires social cohesion, which emerges from individuals' exposure to highly similar social influences (Durkheim 1982). Political theory on social cohesion states that social conflict is an inherent feature of a healthy society as long as lines of division are overlapping, i.e. social groups might be allied or opposed, depending on the issue, creating a plural and cross-cutting tapestry of political conflict (Coser 1956; Törnberg 2022). The theory of 'partisan sorting' argues that affective polarization is related to a process of aligning such cross-cutting social, cultural and ideological divides into two opposed mega-identities along partisan lines (Törnberg 2022). According to Törnberg (Törnberg 2022) sorting is driven by non-local interactions in digital media that expose individuals to a wide range of political opinions and attached social identities that they agree and disagree with. He argues that this exposure amplifies perceived differences with outgroups and similarities within ingroups, restructuring how individuals categorize themselves and others within the social landscape. This realignment of social influence and cross-cutting divisions converges into a singular salient identity, the political dimension, leading to a breakdown of cross-cutting global social cohesion, isolating information flows to the political identity across an expanding range of issues (Törnberg 2022).

A second implication of the discovered coarse-graining mechanism for affective polarization emerges in phase I, when local downward causation must develop to achieve initial local alignment. When agents have non-local inputs in this first phase, the conditions for local downward causation may not emerge. Depending on the amount of online versus real-life interaction and the degree of individualization of information input into the community, the requirement of coherent tuning to the same aggregate distribution and preferred choice might be violated. An incoherent input across the local community might thus block downward causation and local alignment from arising, resulting in individuals aligned with non-local communities.

This relates directly to Törnbergs (Törnberg 2022) finding that non-local interactions impact feelings of similarity and difference, potentially leading to new overarching social identities as ingroup markers.

While our model provides valuable insights into the mechanisms of information integration and consensus formation, several limitations should be acknowledged. First, the conclusions would benefit from empirical validation and a more rigorous mathematical analysis to better understand system stability and convergence. Second, the model currently represents a closed system with homogeneous interaction patterns shaped by singular identities, omitting potential asymmetries and external influences (e.g., media or institutional contexts). Future research should incorporate diverse mechanisms of cross-community information flow, including top-down sources, varying trust parameters and multiple identities, to more accurately capture the complexities of political opinion formation.

10.6 Conclusion

With this model, we investigated a bidirectional mechanism of political opinion dynamics in democratic societies and how it might be affected by changes in intergroup connectivity. We found that hierarchical coarse-graining and community-bounded social influence with a probability of inter-community migration of agents can lead to the emergence of downward causation, revealing the complete upward and downward causal mechanism leading to consensus in our model as well as three regimes of information integration. The iterative regime, with a small degree of higher-level connectivity gives rise to transient diversity and prolonged time until consensus. This allows for slow variable construction which increases the fidelity of the constructed coarse-grained variable to complex and slow-changing systems (Flack 2017a; Smaldino et al. 2022). When the migration of agents between communities has a higher probability, information integration across labels happens parallel to local information integration and quickly leads to global alignment before local alignment, preventing a transient diversity from arising.

Through this lens, polarization can be understood as a society's inability to coarse-grain to the macrolevel with locally diverging perceptions of issues along group lines. In a network like the one here, where information integration occurs within epistemic ingroups, any coherent information integration between communities leads to global consensus via the emergence of global downward causation. An explanation for polarization may therefore involve incoherence of tuning at the higher level that produces alignment within but misalignment across groups. Overall, the discovery of the causal mechanism behind the opinion dynamics in our model, including both upward and downward causation, can further the formulation of research on the causes of, and interventions for dysfunctions of political discourse.

References

D. Abrams, M.A. Hogg, Social identification, self-categorization and social influence. Eur. Rev. Soc. Psychol. **1**(1), 195–228 (1990)

M. Albarracin, D. Demekas, M.J.D. Ramstead, C. Heins, Epistemic communities under active inference. Entropy **24**(4), 476 (2022)

P. Barberá, Social media, echo chambers, and political polarization, in *Social Media and Democracy*. ed. by N. Persily, J.A. Tucker (Cambridge University Press, 2020), pp.34–55

J. Bednar, Polarization, diversity, and democratic robustness. *Proceedings of the National Academy of Sciences of the United States of America*, vol. 118(50) (2021)

E. Borbáth, S. Hutter, A. Leininger, Cleavage politics, polarization and participation in western Europe. West Eur. Polit. **46**(4), 631–651 (2023)

E.R. Brush, D.C. Krakauer, J.C. Flack, A family of algorithms for computing consensus about node state from network data. PLoS Comput. Biol. **9**(7), e1003109 (2013)

T. Böhmelt, K. Gavras, N.B. Weidmann, Social media and political polarization: a systematic review of the literature. Annu. Rev. Polit. Sci. **23**, 351–367 (2020)

L. Coser, *The Functions of Social Conflict* (The Free Press, New York, NY, 1956)

R.J. Dalton, C.C. Berning, Ideological polarization and far-right parties in Europe, in *Rechtspopulismus in Deutschland*. ed. by J.L. Cordovil, G. Santos, D. Vecchi (Springer, 2022)

B.C. Daniels, C.J. Ellison, D.C. Krakauer, J.C. Flack, Quantifying collectivity. Curr. Opin. Neurobiol. **37**, 106–113 (2016)

E. Durkheim, *The Rules of Sociological Method* (The Free Press, New York, 1982)

B. Enke, R. Rodriguez-Padilla, F. Zimmermann, Moral universalism and the structure of ideology. Rev. Econ. Stud. **90**(4), 1934–1962 (2023)

J.C. Flack, Coarse-graining as a downward causation mechanism. Philosophical Trans. Royal Soc. A: Mathemat. Phys. Eng. Sci. **375**(2109), 20160338 (2017)

J.C. Flack, Life's information hierarchy, in *From Matter to Life: Information and Causality*. ed. by P. Davies, S.R. Walker (Cambridge University Press, 2017), pp.283–309

T. Fuchs, The circularity of the embodied mind. Front. Psychol. **11**, 1707 (2020)

G. Gigerenzer, R. Hertwig, T. Pachur, *Heuristics: The Foundations of Adaptive Behavior* (Oxford University Press, Oxford, UK, 2011)

J. Harte, M. Brush, K. Umemura, P. Muralikrishnan, E.A. Newman, Dynamical theory of complex systems with two-way micro–macro causation. Proc. Natl. Acad. Sci. **121**(50), e2408676121 (2024)

R. D. Hawkins, A. M. Berdahl, A. Pentland, J. B. Tenenbaum, N. D. Goodman, P. M. Krafft, Flexible social inference facilitates targeted social learning when rewards are not observable. Nature Human Behav. (2023)

S.B. Hobolt, K. Lawall, J. Tilley, The polarizing effect of partisan echo chambers. Amer. Polit. Sci. Rev. **118**(3), 1464–1479 (2024)

S.B. Hobolt, T.J. Leeper, J. Tilley, Divided by the vote: affective polarization in the wake of the Brexit referendum. British J. Polit. Sci. **51**(4), 1476–1493 (2021)

R. Hämäläinen, M.H. Kajanus, J.T. Forsman, S.M. Kivelä, J.-T. Seppänen, O.J. Loukola, Ecological and evolutionary consequences of selective interspecific information use. Ecol. Lett. **26**(4), 490–503 (2023)

S. Iyengar, Y. Lelkes, M. Levendusky, N. Malhotra, S.J. Westwood, The origins and consequences of affective polarization in the united states. Annu. Rev. Polit. Sci. **22**, 129–146 (2019)

S. Iyengar, S.J. Westwood, Fear and loathing across party lines: new evidence on group polarization. Amer. J. Polit. Sci. **59**(3), 690–707 (2015)

L. Jenke, Affective polarization and misinformation belief. in *Political Behavior* (Advance Online Publication, 2023), pp. 1–60

J.T. Jost, D. Baldassarri, J.N. Druckman, Cognitive–motivational mechanisms of political polarization in social-communicative contexts. Nature Rev. Psychol. **1**(10), 560–576 (2022)

B. Kamińska, Coda model with labelling (2025)

K.N. Laland, Social learning strategies. Learn. Behav. **32**(1), 4–14 (2004)

L. Liao, Z. Jia, Y. Deng, Coarse-graining method based on hierarchical clustering on complex networks. Commun. Netw. **11**, 21–34 (2019)

J. Lorenz, M. Neumann, Opinion dynamics and collective decisions. Adv. Complex Syst. **21**(6–7), 1802002 (2018)

A.C.R. Martins, Continuous opinions and discrete actions in opinion dynamics problems. Int. J. Mod. Phys. C **19**(4), 617–624 (2008)

P.A.M. Mediano, F.E. Rosas, A.I. Luppi, H.J. Jensen, A.K. Seth, A.B. Barrett, R.L. Carhart-Harris, D. Bor, Greater than the parts: a review of information decomposition and causal emergence. Phil. Trans. R. Soc. A **380**(2227), 20210246 (2022)

B.D. Ohme, The effects of social media use on political participation, political knowledge, and political polarization: a meta-analysis. Polit. Commun. **37**(2), 251–274 (2020)

G. Ramos-Fernandez, S.E. Smith Aguilar, D.C. Krakauer, J.C. Flack, Collective computation in animal fission-fusion dynamics. Front. Robot. AI **7**, 90 (2020)

G. Santos, Emergence, downward causation, and interlevel integrative explanations. *New Mechanism. History, Philosophy and Theory of the Life Sciences*, ed. by J. Cordovil, G. Santos, D. Vecchi, vol. 35 (Springer, 2024), pp. 12

P.E. Smaldino, M. Janssen, V. Hillis, J. Bednar, Adoption as a social marker: innovation diffusion with outgroup aversion. J. Math. Sociol. **41**(1), 26–45 (2017)

P. E. Smaldino, C. J. Moser, A. Pérez Velilla, M. Werling, Maintaining transient diversity is a general principle for improving collective problem solving (2022). PsyArXiv

P.E. Smaldino, A.P. Velilla, The evolution of similarity-biased social learning. Evolut. Human Sci. **7**, e4 (2025)

P. Steiglechner, M. A.Keijzer, P. E. Smaldino, D. Moser, A. Merico, Noise and opinion dynamics: how ambiguity promotes pro-majority consensus in the presence of confirmation bias. Royal Soc. Open Sci. **11**, Article 231071 (2024)

S.H. Strogatz, Exploring complex networks. Nature **410**(6825), 268–276 (2001)

H. Tajfel, J. Turner, The social identity theory of intergroup behaviour, in *Psychology of Intergroup Relations*. ed. by S. Worchel, W.G. Austin (Brooks/Cole Publishing Company, Monterey (CA), 1979), pp.7–24

P. Törnberg, How digital media drive affective polarization through partisan sorting. Proc. Natl. Acad. Sci. U.S.A. **119**(42), e2207159119 (2022)

Z. T. You, S. W. S. Lee, Explanations of and interventions against affective polarization cannot afford to ignore the power of ingroup norm perception. PNAS Nexus **3**(10) (2024)

B. Yuan, J. Zhang, A. Lyu, J. Wu, Z. Wang, M. Yang, K. Liu, M. Mou, P. Cui, Emergence and causality in complex systems: a survey of causal emergence and related quantitative studies. Entropy **26**(2), 108 (2024)

Chapter 11
Modeling Social Cohesion: The Influence of Memory and Learning in Simulated Networks

Yara Khaluf, Bernd Wurpts, Till Hovestadt, Nikolas Zöller, and Gert Jan Hofstede

Abstract This study explores group cohesion on the base of social exchange theory, focusing on the dynamics within groups as influenced by memory and learning mechanisms. Using agent-based modeling, we examine how these factors affect individual and group-level cohesion. Specifically, we model the average time agents spend in groups (duration of individual membership), the duration of group existence (aggregate cohesion), and overall agent satisfaction under three conditions: No Memory, Memory, and Memory+Learning, across two network structures: Fully Connected (FC) and Preferential Attachment (PA). Our model incorporates dynamic cultural adaptation and reciprocal exchanges to simulate realistic social dynamics. Dynamic cultural adaptation in our model refers to the evolving behaviors of agents as they adjust their individualism and preferences based on past interactions and group experiences. We find that memory of past interactions enhances group cohesion and stability, while learning introduces new dynamics that influence group persistence.

The original version of the chapter has been revised. A correction to this chapter can be found at https://doi.org/10.1007/978-3-032-01373-6_13

Y. Khaluf (✉) · G. J. Hofstede
Vrije Universiteit Amsterdam, Amsterdam, Netherlands
e-mail: y.khaluf@vu.nl

G. J. Hofstede
e-mail: gertjan.hofstede@wur.nl

B. Wurpts
Independent Researcher, Lucerne, Switzerland
e-mail: bernd.wurpts@gmail.com

T. Hovestadt
Nuffield College, University of Oxford, Oxford, UK
e-mail: till.hovestadt@nuffield.ox.ac.uk

N. Zöller
Max Planck Institute for Human Development, Berlin, Germany
e-mail: zoeller@mpib-berlin.mpg.de

M. A. Keijzer et al. (eds.), *Computational Social Science of Social Cohesion and Polarization*, Computational Social Sciences,
https://doi.org/10.1007/978-3-032-01373-6_11

11.1 Introduction

Understanding social exchange processes is key to comprehending how groups maintain stability and how members derive satisfaction from their affiliations. In this study, we hypothesize that individuals' satisfaction with group membership directly contributes to group stability. Our aim is to explore the mechanisms that foster strong, enduring groups and identify the conditions under which individuals feel most connected and satisfied.

This study explores group cohesion through the lens of social exchange theory, focusing on the dynamics within groups as influenced by memory and learning mechanisms. Memory in this model refers to the agents' ability to store and recall past interactions and feedback, which influences their decision-making in future group interactions. In real societies, individuals regularly engage in various groups—such as workplaces, sports teams, or community organizations—where social cohesion is essential for maintaining collaboration and achieving common goals. Social cohesion, as modeled here, mirrors real-life social behavior where individuals derive satisfaction from positive interactions within their groups (Markovsky and Lawler 1994). Social exchange theory helps explain these dynamics by positing that individuals are motivated to stay in groups based on the rewards and status they receive through their social interactions. In our model, memory and learning mechanisms play a central role, allowing agents to adapt their behavior based on prior interactions and evolving group norms. This mirrors real-world scenarios in which individuals assess their past experiences to make more informed decisions about whether to maintain their group membership. Individualism, a key variable in our model, captures how agents prioritize their personal preferences over group norms, influencing their likelihood to stay in or leave a group. Thus, the model reflects real-world group dynamics where memory, learning, and individualism all contribute to the stability and cohesion of social groups.

Using agent-based modeling, we investigate how dependencies—the reliance on others for status—and interactions within groups affect group cohesion. Previous research has highlighted the role of dependencies in influencing power and status differences within groups (Molm 1994). These dependencies create a framework within which group dynamics operate, shaping how individuals interact and form bonds. We examine how memory—defined as the retention of past feedback from interactions, and learning, where agents adjust their behavior based on past interactions and evolving group norms akin to reinforcement learning—influences individual and group-level cohesion. Specifically, we model the average time agents (i.e., group members) spend in groups as a measure of individual membership, the duration of group existence as a measure of aggregate group cohesion, and the overall satisfaction of agents. The analysis is conducted under three conditions: No Memory, Memory, and Memory+Learning, across two network structures: Fully Connected (FC) and Preferential Attachment (PA) (Barabási and Albert 1999; Steyvers and Tenenbaum 2005).

Hofstede and Liu (2020) present the GRASP WORLD model, which is one of the studies that comes closest to our model. However, our model differs in fundamental aspects. While GRASP WORLD had culture as an unchanging attribute of agents, we modeled culture as a preexisting attribute that is subsequently updated after interactions, where agents staying longer in a group adapt to group norms over time. Additionally, GRASP WORLD models fully connected worlds without explicit links, whereas our model incorporates preferential attachment networks, which we argue provides a more realistic assumption than fully connected networks.

Other related models include the work on the cultural impact on social cohesion, which examines how cultural events and interactions influence social cohesion, such as those explored by Janssen and Jager (2002). However, their work primarily focuses on technological diffusion and the role of social networks in the spread of innovations, whereas our model incorporates dynamic memory and learning mechanisms to investigate how these cognitive processes influence group stability and individual satisfaction. Another work is Epstein and Axtell (1996), where the authors explore social dynamics from the bottom up, emphasizing the aggregation of individual actions into social outcomes. While they focus on simulating broad societal patterns, such as wealth distribution and population dynamics, our model is more specific, targeting the micro-level interactions related to social cohesion. In Gilbert and Troitzsch (2005), the authors investigate the dynamics of economic and social behavior, highlighting the importance of empirical calibration of agent-based models.

Our model extends these frameworks by specifically focusing on the dynamic adaptation of cultural attributes through memory and learning mechanisms, and by exploring the impacts within different network structures. This approach aims to provide a deeper understanding of how group cohesion and member satisfaction evolve under varying conditions of memory and learning.

11.2 Background in Social Exchange Theory

In this study, we draw on exchange theory. Following Markovsky and Lawler (1994), we consider social cohesion as a range of forces that motivate individuals to stay in a group and as a determinant of social solidarity. Both, cohesion, and solidarity, are outcomes of individual level phenomena such as emotions, but emotions are also themselves caused by social interactions (Scherke 2024).

Our study was initially motivated by Kemper's Kemper (1978) classic approach to emotions, which focuses on social structural positions and social interaction. Aiming for a general theory, Kemper claimed that status-power-relations determine which emotions are experienced. While the theory considers both status and power, we limit the present study to one dimension to begin with. The following analyses capture status conferral in social interactions. It is assumed that group loyalty or commitment results from satisfaction, which comes from positive feedback through sufficient status conferral. Individuals have a certain belief about the status they deserve and if the status conferred upon them is smaller, they become dissatisfied. Receiving too little status in a group might negatively impact an individuals' emotions and lead to the decision to leave and join another group. As the fundamental unit is status conferral, which is a valued resource in social interaction, the classical Kemperian perspective is consistent with the broader exchange theory, particularly in social-psychological approaches (Neuhofer et al. 2016).

In social exchange theory, the focus is on the relationships among individuals and the benefits and costs involved in forming and maintaining these relationships (Emerson 1972a, b). Emerson's theory uses learning theory as its micro-foundation, assuming that individuals aim to maximize positive outcomes and minimize negative ones. The theory does not specify what individuals value, allowing for a broad application across different contexts. When two individuals exchange resources, they form a transaction. Repeated transactions can lead to the formation of exchange relations, which may connect to create larger exchange networks, but only if these transactions are positively received by the agents. In our model, exchange networks exist regardless of the nature of the interactions—whether positive or negative. These networks can influence the frequency and value of exchanges, with positive connections increasing exchanges and negative ones decreasing them (Emerson 1972b; Molm 1997).

Four general forms of exchange are distinguished: productive, negotiated, reciprocal, and generalized exchange. Productive exchange involves collaboration between multiple parties to create a shared outcome, emphasizing group-based cooperation. Negotiated exchange is typically dyadic, where two parties explicitly agree on terms, such as contracts or deals, though it can involve more parties in complex situations. Reciprocal exchange usually occurs between two individuals in a dyadic manner, where one party gives with the expectation of receiving something back over time, without immediate negotiation. In contrast, generalized exchange involves larger social networks, where benefits are exchanged indirectly within a group, with no expectation of direct reciprocity from the same individual, fostering broader community engagement (Cook and Rice 2003).

Our proposed model primarily uses reciprocal exchange, where agents perform acts that benefit others in their group, such as conferring status. This approach allows us to simulate realistic social dynamics where agents' decisions to stay or leave a group are influenced by the benefits they receive from their interactions with other group members.

Furthermore, exchange theory posits that individuals commit to relationships because staying reduces uncertainty. In repeated exchanges, individuals learn about each other's behavior, increasing predictability and trust, which incentivizes maintaining the relationship (Molm 1994). Emerson highlighted that the cohesion of a relationship is influenced by the mutual dependence of individuals, where dependence refers to the degree to which individuals derive value from the relationship (Molm 1997). In our model, dependence could be interpreted as agents deriving satisfaction from interactions, though the model abstracts away from specific dependencies in favor of a more general satisfaction-driven decision-making process.

Lawler and Yoon (1993) introduced the theory of relational cohesion, which asserts that positive emotions from interactions lead to stronger commitments to the group. Positive feelings generated from exchanges can make groups intrinsically valuable to individuals, fostering group cohesion. This is particularly evident in multi-actor settings where collaborative tasks generate positive emotions, enhancing person-to-group ties and commitment (Lawler et al. Lawler, Thye and Yoon (2000)).

Our model incorporates these principles by allowing agents to update their satisfaction and individualism based on their interactions, reflecting the dynamic adaptation of their commitment to the group over time. By simulating these processes, our model provides insights into how group cohesion and member satisfaction evolve in response to varying conditions of memory and learning.

11.3 Model

In this study, we develop an agent-based model using NetLogo[1] to explore group formation and dissolution when derived by agents' satisfaction within their current group. Agent's satisfaction is influenced by the status conferral it received from its group members and hence by the agent's experiences within the group. Status conferral refers to the act of assigning value to an interaction partner based on their perceived worth. Conceptually, it reflects a social evaluation mechanism: agents attribute significance to others' presence or actions. This value can take various forms—such as recognition, respect, influence, or prestige—depending on the cultural norms. In our model, this conferral of status acts as a social reward. When agents consistently receive high status from others, they experience increased satisfaction, which in turn strengthens their motivation to remain in the group.

During each interaction, agents engage in a two-part process: status conferral and feedback reception. The first step is status conferral, where one agent (the sender) evaluates the other (the receiver) based on the receiver's status and the collective status of their group. The status conferral is calculated through the lens of the sender's individualism and group status—i.e., the average of the individual statuses of all current group members. Specifically, higher individualism makes the sender prioritize the individual status of the receiver, while lower individualism places more weight on the collective status of the receiver's group. A small random component is also added to introduce variability.

In the second step, the receiving agent compares the status conferral they received with their expected status conferral, which is a similar calculation but based on their own status and group status. The difference between the expected and actual status conferral determines the feedback. If the received status conferral is lower than expected (beyond a certain tolerance), the receiver gives negative feedback (-1); otherwise, they give positive feedback ($+1$).

This feedback is stored in the feedback memory of the sender and is used in subsequent decisions, such as whether to stay in or leave the group. Both status conferral and feedback reception influence agent satisfaction, which is then computed

---

[1] View the OSF project at https://doi.org/10.17605/OSF.IO/U5TSF.

by weighting the feedback over time, with more recent feedback given higher weight. Each simulation tick follows a fixed sequence of agent actions (see Fig. 11.1) that model social interaction and group restructuring.

At initialization, agents are assigned to groups of varying sizes. During each tick, agents search for potential interaction partners (mates) within their immediate network neighborhood (e.g., all group members in a fully connected setup). If no partner is found (e.g., in the case of solitary agents), the agent is flagged for group exit and prompted to seek or form a new group. At the end of each tick, agents process the outcomes of the interaction (e.g., satisfaction), decide whether to remain in their group, and possibly restructure the social configuration by joining or forming a new group. This is also when traits like satisfaction and memory are updated.

Table 11.1 presents the agent's main attributes as designed in the proposed model, whereas Table 11.2 presents the simulation phases over its timeline.

Memory plays a critical role in this model. It is used as a Feedback Memory to store previous feedbacks that an agent has received during interactions. This memory allows for a cumulative effect on the agent's behavior and satisfaction, which in turn affects its decision-making process, such as whether to stay in or leave its group. To emphasize more recent feedback, a range of weights is assigned to each feedback entry. This weight increases linearly, giving more recent feedback a higher weight compared to older feedback. The sum of the weighted positive feedback values is calculated to get a total positive feedback score, and the agent's satisfaction is computed by dividing the summed weighted positive feedback by the normalization factor. This gives a satisfaction value that reflects the agent's overall experience, weighted by the recency of feedback.

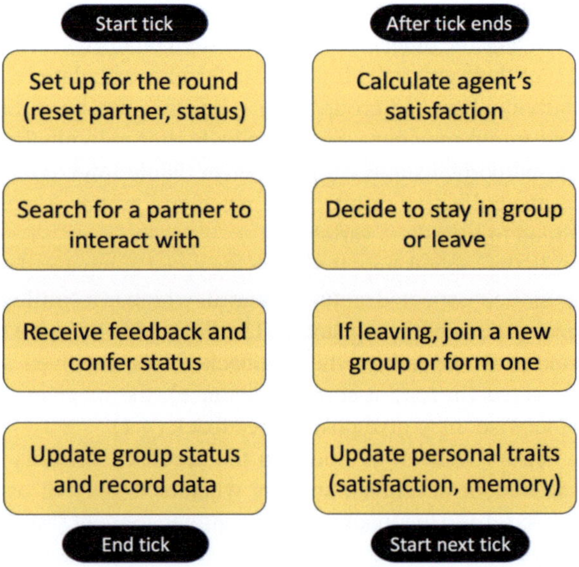

Fig. 11.1 This diagram shows the sequence of actions agents take during each tick, including resetting variables, interacting with group members, updating satisfaction, and deciding whether to stay in or leave the group

Table 11.1 Summary of agent's attributes: ranges and initial settings

Variable	Description	Range	Initial setting
Individualism	Degree to which an agent prioritizes self over group	0.0–1.0	Random normal (mean = 0.5, std = 0.1)
Status	Agent's initial status within group	0.0–1.0	Random normal (mean = 0.5, std = 0.1)
Memory length	Number of time steps agent remembers feedback	1–10	5
Group size	Initial number of agents per group	1–100	Randomly assigned
Satisfaction	Agent's cumulative satisfaction	−1.0 to 1.0	Computed based on feedback interactions
Leave-group flag	Indicates whether agent decides to leave group	True/false	False

Table 11.2 Simulation timeline

Phase	Description
Initialization	Agents are randomly assigned to groups and given initial values for individualism and status
Interaction phase	Agents interact with group members, exchange feedback, and confer status
Satisfaction phase	Agents calculate satisfaction based on feedback stored in memory
Decision phase	Agents decide whether to stay in their current group or leave based on satisfaction and individualism
Group restructuring	Agents that leave either join other groups or form new ones, and group status is updated
Recording phase	The simulation records agent data including satisfaction, group membership, and changes

When agents switch groups, our model can handle their feedback memory in two different ways. In one option, the agent's feedback memory is retained, allowing the agent to carry over past experiences that continue to influence the agent's decisions in their new environment. Alternatively, if the memory reset feature is activated, the agent's feedback memory is cleared allowing the agent to start fresh, without any influence from past interactions, enabling them to evaluate the new group independently of previous experiences.

Besides agent's memory, agent's learning is another key component offered by the model to enable agents to update their cultural dimensions based on their current group—here the model uses only one cultural dimension which is individualism. This update of the agent's individualism influences how agents interact in the future, as individualism affects how they confer status to others and how they perceive the feedback received. The learning process affects satisfaction indirectly. As agents adjust their individualism, their expectations and responses to feedback change. This, in turn, influences the cumulative feedback stored in their Feedback Memory. When computing satisfaction, the model uses this adjusted individualism to weigh the feedback received in previous interactions.

Agents decide to leave or stay in a group based on their cumulative satisfaction. The decision is probabilistic and takes into account their level of individualism. More individualistic agents are more likely to leave, even if their satisfaction is positive, while more collectivist agents may stay longer in the group even with declining satisfaction. In the "no memory" condition, agents do not base their decision on cumulative feedback. Instead, they change groups based on immediate interactions. After a negative interaction, they are more likely to leave their group and look for a new group to join. In the "memory" condition, agents accumulate feedback over time, and their decision-making incorporates both recent and older interactions.

Finally, the model studies group cohesion under different network structures—i.e. fully connected and preferential attachment. The Preferential Attachment (PA) network used in the model was generated using the Barabási–Albert algorithm (Barabási and Albert 1999; Barabási 2016), which creates a scale-free network by preferentially linking new nodes to existing nodes with higher connectivity. This results in a hierarchical structure with hubs that play a central role in group dynamics. The link density was set at 0.15, ensuring that each new node is more likely to connect to an existing hub, leading to stable group formations over time.

During the setup phase, the model initializes the network structure based on the specified type. This network structure determines the pool of potential mates (interaction partners) for each agent. For example, in a fully connected network, agents can interact with any agent, while in preferential attachment the probability to interact with hubs is much higher than the probability to interact with non-hub agents. Since the agent's satisfaction is computed based on the feedback received from interactions, the network structure indirectly affects satisfaction.

11.4 Results and Discussions

We model group cohesion both as a function of members staying in the group (duration of individual membership), as well as existence of the group (aggregate cohesion of the group). To quantitatively assess these dynamics, we focus on the following metrics: the average time agents spend in groups, group existence, and agent satisfaction, each of which provides insight into the system's behavior.

The average time agents spend in groups is computed by tracking the time each agent spends in their current group. When an agent leaves a group, the time spent in that group is recorded, and the average across all agents and simulations is calculated. This metric captures the stability of group membership from the individual's perspective.

The group existence metric, on the other hand, reflects how long a group persists over the course of the simulation. A group is considered to exist as long as it has at least one member. Group existence is calculated from the time a group forms (i.e., when it first has members) until the moment it disbands (i.e., when all its members leave).

Finally, agent satisfaction measures how content agents are within their current group. Satisfaction is calculated based on the feedback agents receive from their interactions with group members, with feedback weighted more heavily toward recent interactions. This rolling satisfaction score reflects an agent's cumulative experience in their group and influences decisions to leave or stay. Satisfaction is averaged across agents and simulations to assess overall contentment in different conditions, with lower variance suggesting higher group cohesion, while greater fluctuations may indicate instability or dissatisfaction within groups.

The above-mentioned metrics are evaluated under three different conditions: No Memory, Memory, and Memory+Learning. The analysis was conducted separately for two network structures: Fully Connected (FC) and Preferential Attachment (PA). In the FC network, agents in the No Memory condition spent the least amount of time in groups, indicating frequent group changes or short-lived groups. When memory was introduced, agents spent more time in groups, suggesting that memory helps maintain group cohesion. In the Memory+Learning condition, the average time in groups was slightly lower than with Memory alone but still significantly higher than in the No Memory condition. This difference can be attributed to the role of learning, which introduces a layer of adaptability to the agents' behavior. When learning is introduced, agents adjust their individualism based on the feedback they receive from interactions, allowing them to evolve their preferences over time. Unlike in the No Memory condition, where agents react immediately to negative feedback, learning enables agents to consider their past experiences and make more deliberate decisions. As a result, agents may switch groups not solely due to dissatisfaction but also as they evolve in their preferences over time. This adaptability leads to slower, but more meaningful rather than impulsive group changes, as agents balance both individual needs and group dynamics.

The average group existence time in the FC network was highest in the No Memory condition, with a high variance indicating that while some groups disbanded quickly, others lasted considerably longer. This unexpected result could be due to the highly interconnected nature of the FC network, where the lack of memory causes some groups to persist due to random stabilization factors. When memory was introduced, the average group existence time decreased. The Memory and Memory+Learning conditions showed almost the same values for average group existence time, suggesting that learning doesn't improve this dynamic.

In the PA network, the dynamics were influenced by the network's structure. The preferential attachment mechanism inherently creates a few highly connected nodes, which can impact group dynamics differently compared to a fully connected network. Agents in the No Memory condition again spent the least amount of time in groups, with frequent group changes. Memory led to more stable and longer group interactions, while learning induced a slightly lower time spent in group than with Memory alone but still significantly higher than in the No Memory.

The average group existence time in the PA network showed an interesting pattern. Both the No Memory and Memory conditions resulted in similar existence times, indicating that the presence of memory alone did not significantly alter the stability of groups. However, when learning was introduced along with memory (Memory+Learning), there was a significant increase in the average group existence time. This suggests that learning mechanisms, combined with memory, allow agents to adapt more gradually to group dynamics, leading to more persistent group structures. This is particularly in PA networks because agents' decisions are influenced by a few key nodes, leading to more deliberate, network-wide changes. In contrast, the FC network's uniformity diffuses this influence, making group changes more frequent

Agent satisfaction in both network structures remained relatively consistent across all three conditions. This indicates that the overall contentment of agents is not significantly influenced by memory and learning, regardless of the network structure. This is plausible as dissatisfied agents leave their groups and generate satisfaction from new interactions while satisfied members stay in their groups. Ultimately, agents find an optimum satisfaction.

In both the FC and the PA network structures, the average group status remained relatively consistent across all three conditions (Figs. 11.2 and 11.3). This suggests

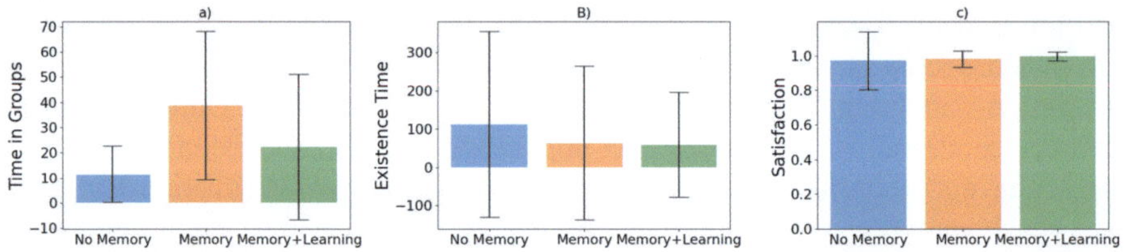

Fig. 11.2 Analysis of group dynamics under three conditions: no memory, memory, and memory+learning in a FC network. **a** Average time agents spend in groups. **b** Average group existence time. **c** Average satisfaction of agents

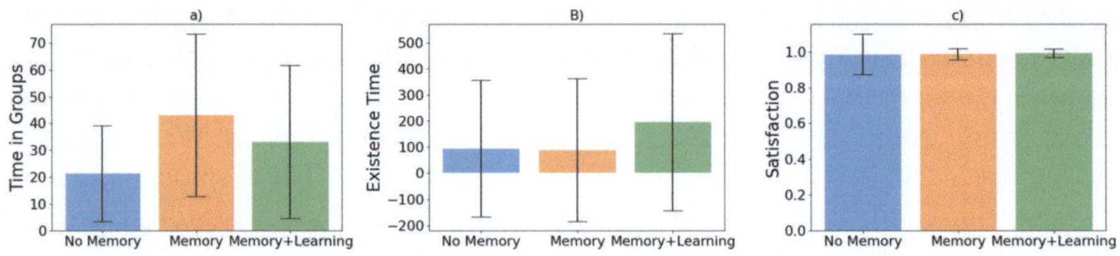

Fig. 11.3 Analysis of group dynamics under three conditions: no memory, memory, and memory+learning in a preferential attachment (PA) network. **a** Average time agents spend in groups. **b** Average group existence time. **c** Average satisfaction of agents

that the presence of memory and learning mechanisms does not significantly affect the overall status of the groups.

For average group size (Figs. 11.4 and 11.5), also for both network structures, the No Memory condition resulted in a moderately sized group with substantial variability. Introducing memory led to a larger average group size with increased variability, indicating that memory allows for the formation of larger groups but also introduces instability—i.e., fluctuating group sizes. However, when learning was combined with memory, the average group size decreased slightly compared to the memory-only condition, and the variability reduced. This suggests that learning helps stabilize group sizes by mitigating some of the fluctuations introduced by memory.

Finally, the average group sizes in the PA network are generally larger than those in the FC network, highlighting the influence of the network structure on group formation dynamics.

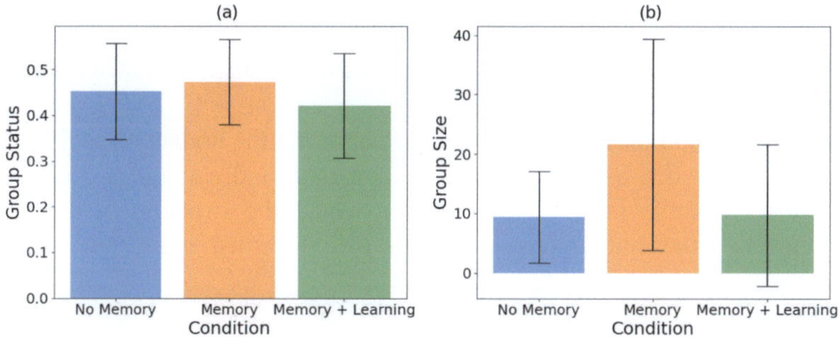

Fig. 11.4 Analysis of group dynamics in a fully connected (FC) network under three conditions: no memory, memory, and memory+learning. **a** Average group status. **b** Average group size

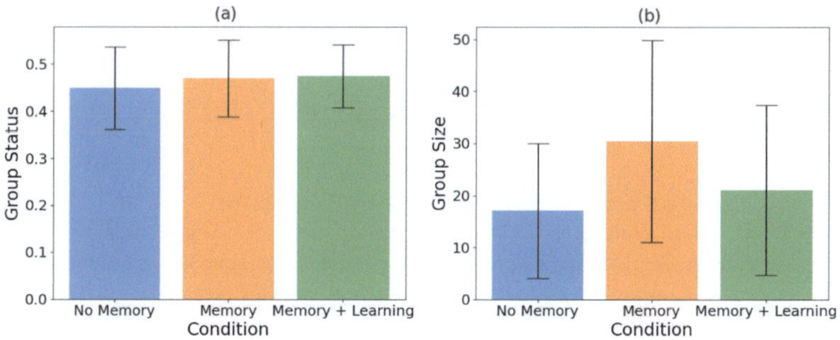

Fig. 11.5 Analysis of group dynamics in a Preferential Attachment (PA) network under three conditions: no memory, memory, and memory+learning. **a** Average group status. **b** Average group size

11.5 Conclusion

Our study employs an agent-based model to explore the dynamics of group cohesion through the principles of social exchange theory, focusing on the effects of memory and learning within different network structures. Our model extends the studies by Lawler and Yoon (1993, 1996, 1998) to the context of groups. We show that group cohesion emerges from the cumulative effect of sustained positive interactions. In particular, our results reveal that memory increases the duration of individual membership within groups due to the accumulation of past positive feedback—its effect on group-level stability varies depending on the network structure. Group existence time decreases in Fully Connected (FC) networks when memory is present, but it increases in Preferential Attachment (PA) networks. Learning on the other side, introduces new dynamics that can lead to group changes but still maintains higher cohesion compared to the absence of memory. We furthermore show that fully connected groups exist for shorter periods than in preferential attachment networks. These results provide significant contributions to social exchange theory, offering insights into how memory and learning mechanisms shape group dynamics and stability.

Future work could extend our model by integrating the update of additional cultural dimensions, such as power distance, alongside individualism. Additionally, incorporating dynamic network interactions, where the structure of the network evolves based on the interactions and relationships formed, could provide a more comprehensive understanding of group cohesion.

Acknowledgements and Funding Bernd Wurpts is grateful for financial support from the University of Lucerne Faculty of Humanities and Social Sciences Dean's Office.
Till Hovestadt was funded by a grant by the Deutsche Forschungsgemeinschaft (grant number 462521224).

References

A.-L. Barabási, *Network Science* (Cambridge University Press, 2016)

A.-L. Barabási, R. Albert, Emergence of scaling in random networks. Science **286**(5439), 509–512 (1999)

K.S. Cook, E. Rice, Social exchange theory, in *Handbook of Social Psychology*. ed. by J. Delamater (Springer, Boston, MA, 2003), pp.53–76

R.M. Emerson, Exchange theory, part I: A psychological basis for social exchange. Sociol. Theor. Progr. **2**, 38–57 (1972a)

R.M. Emerson, Exchange theory, part II: Exchange relations and networks. Sociol. Theor. Progr. **2**, 58–87 (1972b)

J.M. Epstein, R. Axtell, *Growing Artificial Societies: Social Science from the Bottom Up* (MIT Press, 1996)

N. Gilbert, K.G. Troitzsch, *Simulation for the Social Scientist* (McGraw-Hill Education, 2005)

G.J. Hofstede, C. Liu, To stay or not to stay? artificial sociality in grasp world, in *Advances in Social Simulation* (Springer, 2020), pp. 217–231

M. Janssen, W. Jager, Stimulating diffusion of technological innovations. Adv. Complex Syst. **4**(3), 323–347 (2002)

T.D. Kemper, *A Social Interactional Theory of Emotions* (Wiley, 1978)

E.J. Lawler, S.R. Thye, J. Yoon, Emotion and group cohesion in productive exchange. Am. J. Sociol. **106**(3), 616–657 (2000)

E.J. Lawler, J. Yoon, Power and the emergence of commitment behavior in negotiated exchange, *American Sociological Review* (1993), pp. 465–481

E.J. Lawler, J. Yoon, Commitment in exchange relations: test of a theory of relational cohesion, *American Sociological Review* (1996), pp. 89–108

E.J. Lawler, J. Yoon, Network structure and emotion in exchange relations. *American Sociological Review* (1998), pp. 871–894

B. Markovsky, E.J. Lawler, A new theory of group solidarity, in *Advances in Group Processes* (JAI Press, 1994), vol. 11, pp. 113–137

L.D. Molm, Dependence and risk: transforming the structure of social exchange. Soc. Psychol. Quarter. **57**(3), 163–176 (1994)

L.D. Molm, *Coercive Power in Social Exchange* (Cambridge University Press, 1997)

S. Neuhofer, I. Reindl, B. Kittel, Social exchange networks: a review of experimental studies. Connections **36**, 34–51 (2016)

K. Scherke, *Emotionssoziologie, Transcript* (2024)

M. Steyvers, J.B. Tenenbaum, The large-scale structure of semantic networks: statistical analyses and a model of semantic growth. Cogn. Sci. **29**(1), 41–78 (2005)

Epilogue

Chapter 12
From Summer Schools to Research Incubators in Computational Social Science and Beyond

Jan Lorenz

Abstract This chapter describes academic events called "Summer School and Research Incubator". They combine a lecture program with group project work, where lecturers and fellows collaborate on publication projects under a joint topical and methodological umbrella. This chapter reflects the experience of organizing five such events. It summarizes their benefits and the particular purposes of facilitating early academic independence, qualifying and enriching interdisciplinary research, and disseminating innovative research methods and topics.

Keywords Research incubator · Science organization · Graduate schools · Scientific dissemination · Methods training · Computational social science

12.1 Research Incubators

In 2016, VolkswagenStiftung published a call for "Summer Schools in Computational Social Science" with an emphasis on collaboration between social scientists and computational scientists. Together with colleagues mostly from Constructor University (at that time under the name Jacobs University), I was awarded a grant for a series of three schools with a concept called the "Summer School and Research Incubator". The grant was for three schools, each with a thematic focus. In 2018, the school was on *Conflicts*, 2019 on *Migration*, and (after the pandemic break) 2022 on *Social Cohesion*. In 2023, we held another school on the *Democratic Debate* with remaining funds. In 2024, a new initiative organized a similar school on *Wealth Data*

J. Lorenz (✉)
Bremen International Graduate School of Social Sciences, Constructor University, Bremen, Germany
e-mail: jlorenz@constructor.university

M. A. Keijzer et al. (eds.), *Computational Social Science of Social Cohesion and Polarization*, Computational Social Sciences,
https://doi.org/10.1007/978-3-032-01373-6_12

Science,[1] and in 2025 a group around a former fellow and former experts organized a Spring School on *Perceptions of Wealth Inequality*.[2]

The innovative aspect of these schools is the *Research Incubator*[3] component. This short note outlines this concept and provides its benefits for fellows,[4] experts,[5] organizers, funding agencies, and science itself.

Summer Schools and Research Incubators are academic events similar to classic summer schools for graduate students, which

- last for typically two weeks (ten working days),
- have 35–55 participants, split into fellows and experts, and
- have a typical summer school program with lectures, hands-on workshops, and keynotes, but only for less than half of the working time.

However, the time not spent on lectures is reserved

- for work on scientific projects where teams of 1–2 experts and 2–5 fellows work together on a project with the aim of a joint scientific publication, and
- for a smaller degree for coordination and round tables to discuss current matters of the school's topic.

The participants (experts and fellows) for these summer schools and research incubators were usually found in a two-round application process. First, a "Call for Experts and Project Leaders" was published, where interested researchers could propose projects with a title, methods, data, and project description on the topic of the school. Experts could also apply just with their topical or methods expertise. From the pool of applications, the organizers selected seven to ten projects for the school, each typically led by two experts, one with topical and one with methods expertise. In some cases, the organizers matched experts who did not know each other before and coordinated the project concept.

The second round was the selection of fellows in a normal call for applications. Applicants had to prioritize three projects of their choice. Participants were selected after review by organizers and experts. That way, experts could also watch out for applicants fitting their projects. The organizers made the final selection and assignment of fellows to projects. An ideal project team was composed of two experts and three to four participants. That means a team of five to six researchers worked on a joint publication.

[1] This school partnered with the University of Cape Town for a hybrid two-location campus. Organizing this, it also became a Winter School in South Africa.

[2] The first five schools' website is http://wedsss.janlo.de, the spring school's website is https://dariatisch.github.io/SPINE.

[3] The term "research incubator" is also used for other formats like funding schemes for longer-term but smaller projects or scientific institutions. Here, the term is used for short-term events breeding and fledging out smaller-scale collaborative scientific projects.

[4] A *fellow* is a non-expert participant. *Participant* is used for all individuals participating on site.

[5] An *expert* is a participant who leads a project and gives a lecture.

During the school, preferences for publication in a disciplinary journal or a joint publication outlet were discussed, and editorial teams of volunteers were formed when possible. The results were different. Two times the organizers, together with motivated experts, went for applying for an edited volume in Springer's *Book Series Computational Social Science* resulting in *Computational Conflict Research*,[6] (Deutschmann et al. 2020b) and *Computational Social Science of Social Cohesion and Polarization* [7] where this chapter is part of. Once, a team managed to get a special issue in the *Journal of Ethnic and Migration Studies*.[8] Around 75% of the project teams continued their work after the school to a successful publication, some independently, typically in disciplinary journals.[9] The projects from the latest schools are still ongoing. However, the organizers of SPINE 2025 have already acquired the editorship of a Special Issue on "Perceptions of Wealth Inequality" in the journal *Historical Social Research*.

12.2 Feedback

Participants' feedback on the research incubator concept was mostly very positive. The author received a few reflections from participants, which build the core content for this section.

Some aspects mentioned are similar to interdisciplinary conferences, scientific workshops, and traditional summer schools without incubators. Like international contacts:

> The international dimension of this interdisciplinary space enriches cultural exchange, allowing for the internationalization of knowledge—whether through the study objects, comparative perspectives, bibliography, or networking with colleagues from around the world.

Networking with colleagues is another typical aspect.

> Furthermore, it expanded my network of contacts and allowed me to meet people with whom I later reconnected at other events around the world.

It can be assumed that the intense collaborative work makes the establishment of long-standing contacts even more likely than conference contacts. Of course, an important aspect is the learning:

---

[6] With contributions of Asgharpourmasouleh et al. (2020), Brandenberger (2020), Cremaschi et al. (2020), Deutschmann et al. (2020a), Duffy et al. (2020), Gleditsch (2020), Hajdinjak et al. (2020), Kelling and Lin (2020), Kohne et al. (2020), Maerz and Puschmann (2020) and Salvi et al. (2020)

[7] With contributions of Boehnke et al. (2025), Bojanowski et al. (2025), Keijzer et al. (2025), Warncke et al. (2025), Brockmann et al. (2025), Lee et al. (2025), Yuan (2025), Edmonds et al. (2025), Widler et al. (2025), and Khaluf et al. (2025)

[8] With contributions of Czymara et al. (2023),Drouhot et al. (2023); Hoffmann Pham and Luengo-Oroz (2023); Kelling and Monroe (2023); Leal and Harder (2023); Pettrachin et al. (2023) and Zuccotti et al. (2023).

[9] For example, contributions from Oswald et al. (2020) and Ponizovskiy et al. (2020)

> As for the summer school participation, as a PhD student in sociology with a focus on qualitative methods, my participation in the school was a profoundly enriching experience. I sought to enhance my computational skills, which I had primarily developed independently, and the school provided an ideal setting for this growth.

More importantly, there was also feedback more specific to the incubator setup:

> Participating in a research incubator transformed my understanding of practical and theoretical knowledge, helping me to perceive them as an integrated and inseparable unit. [...] I learned how to manage time and material resources within a project, as well as how to coordinate work in a virtual environment with colleagues across different time zones.

> One aspect I found particularly valuable was the opportunity to dedicate two weeks exclusively to working on a project. This level of focus, which is uncommon in my academic experience, enabled me to lay the foundation for long-term projects.

> Participating in these incubators has been one of the most enriching experiences of my graduate studies. Not only did it broaden my academic horizons, but it also helped me to visualize and pursue my short- and medium-term goals.

> Moreover, these incubators serve as interdisciplinary spaces where a common language is developed, facilitating dialogue across different disciplines.

> This diversity broadened my understanding of interdisciplinary research and allowed me to appreciate the various methodologies that different academic fields bring to the table. Collaborating with my team highlighted the value of diverse perspectives in enhancing the research process.

> A key takeaway was recognizing the time-intensive nature of tasks that may initially appear simple. I recall a senior researcher in our team spending an entire day on what was meant to be a quick demonstration, which taught me the importance of patience and a meticulous approach.

Going beyond summer schools and conferences, the benefits for participants relate to the experience of doing actual interdisciplinary research. Thereby, participants learn project management and collaborative work, learn to pursue longer projects, and value interdisciplinary perspectives. It often takes more interaction than a conference presentation and chat to see the value through all the quirks and blind spots of other disciplines. The intensity of the interactions in these research incubators is particularly well suited to do that.

12.3 Research Incubators Compared to Other Summer Schools

In the last few years, many summer schools on Computational Social Science have appeared e.g. organized by GESIS Leibniz Institute for Social Sciences in Cologne, Germany on Computational Social Science methods (funded by money raised through the same call), a recently established Lake Como school, the BEHAVE summer school series focused on agent-based models, and most notably the *Summer Institutes in Computational Social Science* (SICSS) (https://sicss.io). Founded in 2017, these events have quickly developed into a franchise-like system with several events spread all over the world every year. The distinguishing features of research incubators compared to the institutes and other schools are that research incubators have a substantive topical focus, while the institutes focus on methods of computational social science. In addition, research projects are even more central in research incubators. In the research incubators, usually, all projects were already defined by the project leaders before the schools and fellows were assigned to one of their preferred projects upon admission. In the SICSSS institutes, project groups are typically built ad hoc after the lecture program and are often not guided by experts.

12.4 Benefits and Outlook

The feedback shows that there are some specific benefits of the research incubator concept. I summarize the benefits from my organizer's point of view for different groups.

Fellows benefit on their way to becoming independent researchers. They engage in an interdisciplinary research project independently of their supervisor and core research group; however, projects are often not too far away from their core research topic because of the topical focus of the particular research incubator. In my opinion, the incubator experience is superior to both, traditional summer school for methods training and normal scientific conferences. The lecture program and the diversity of about eight projects provide an additional overview of recent topical and methodological developments besides the narrower focus of the own project. The deep engagement in actual research provides more solid connections to other researchers than the typical talk at conferences. Of course, this is not to abolish summer schools and conferences. I want to make the point that a research incubator is more likely to be a foundational experience in becoming part of the research community.

Experts have a dual role in the research incubator: They lead the research project (usually together with a fellow expert) and they provide the lectures and hands-on workshops for all participants on the topics and research methods they are experts in. In contrast to lectures of traditional summer schools, the research incubator lecture program tends to be condensed and short inputs, and not full-fledged classes. Guiding a project gives experts the chance to pursue a publication project with talented junior researchers. This is particularly useful for early-stage researchers for building and broadening not only their visibility (which conferences and summer school lecturing also do) but also their network of scientific collaborators. For researchers developing new methods, this is an ideal testbed. The only risk is that the assigned team of junior researchers may turn out not to be as functional as expected. Our experience was that finding experts was the biggest challenge. Two weeks is a long time commitment, and the benefits may not be immediately visible. However, those experts who ultimately apply typically see the benefit and appreciate it.

Organizing a research incubator may be slightly more work than organizing a traditional summer school or a small workshop, because of the double selection process for experts and fellows and the coordination effort for project and lecture program composition. The benefit is the opportunity to leave a mark in a particular research field, much more practical than by only connecting people, through conducting topical events for all participants, and leading a joint publication project.

I also see a benefit for *research funding organizations*. Funding a high-level research incubator may cost a bit more than funding a high-level scientific workshop (because of the longer time), but documented research output in publications is much higher, probably even higher than actual research projects with funded doctoral and postdoctoral positions, which cost even more.

Finally, in my opinion, the *scientific community* benefits from such events because they create more productive and positive exchanges on excellent research and good research practice than the highly competitive and sometimes hostile peer-review system. They can also serve as events of scientific dissemination of larger research projects, when partners of the research project design spin-off projects of their core research projects.

Summarizing, research incubators are ideal for

- inter- and transdisciplinary topics because researchers with different backgrounds practically work together through the whole research cycle,
- linking innovative researchers (as experts) with talented and ambitious graduate students and early postdocs (as fellows), and
- scientific dissemination of new methodological approaches,

also beyond computational social science.

Acknowledgements The research incubator summer school concept could only be realized due to substantial funding from VolkswagenStiftung. I am thankful to Florencia Piñeyrua, Alzira Minikeeva, Daniel Mayerhoffer, and Marijn Keijzer for their substantial feedback.

References

A. Asgharpourmasouleh, M. Fattahzadeh, D. Mayerhoffer, J. Lorenz, On the fate of protests: dynamics of social activation and topic selection online and in the streets, in *Computational Conflict Research*. ed. by E. Deutschmann, J. Lorenz, L.G. Nardin, D. Natalini, A.F.X. Wilhelm (Springer International Publishing, Cham, 2020), pp.141–164

K. Boehnke, K. Unzicker, G. Dragolov, C. Hartz, R. Arant, Social cohesion and its development in germany before, during, and after covid-19: the bertelsmann social cohesion radar (Chapter 2), in *Computational Social Science of Social Cohesion and Polarization*, ed. by M. Keijzer, J. Lorenz, M. Bojanowski (Springer, Berlin, 2025)

M. Bojanowski, A. Loseva, P. Schuler, S. Boeller, M.J. Lubbers, Simulating an empirically informed population network of core discussion ties (Chapter 3), in *Computational Social Science of Social Cohesion and Polarization*, ed. by M. Keijzer, J. Lorenz, M. Bojanowski (Springer, Berlin, 2025)

L. Brandenberger, Interdependencies in conflict dynamics: analyzing endogenous patterns in conflict event data using relational event models, in *Computational Conflict Research*. ed. by E. Deutschmann, J. Lorenz, L.G. Nardin, D. Natalini, A.F.X. Wilhelm (Springer International Publishing, Cham, 2020), pp.67–80

H. Brockmann, W. Drews, P. Fierro Zamorra, J. Frese, D. Triana, Elites and polarisation: a text and sentiment analytical approach on the dynamics of polarized political discourses during times of crises (Chapter 6), in *Computational Social Science of Social Cohesion and Polarization*, ed. by M. Keijzer, J. Lorenz, M. Bojanowski (Springer, Berlin, 2025)

S. Cremaschi, B. Kirdemir, J. Masullo, A.R. Pah, N. Payette, R. Yarlagadda, Do Non-state armed groups influence each other in attack timing and frequency? Generating, analyzing, and comparing empirical data and simulation, in *Computational Conflict Research*. ed. by E. Deutschmann, J. Lorenz, L.G. Nardin, D. Natalini, A.F.X. Wilhelm (Springer International Publishing, Cham, 2020), pp.167–182

C.S. Czymara, S. Dochow-Sondershaus, L.G. Drouhot, M. Simsek, C. Spörlein, Catalyst of hate? Ethnic insulting on YouTube in the aftermath of terror attacks in France, Germany and the United Kingdom 2014–2017. J. Ethn. Migrat. Stud. **49**(2), 535–553 (2023)

E. Deutschmann, J. Lorenz, L.G. Nardin, Advancing conflict research through computational approaches, in *Computational Conflict Research*. ed. by E. Deutschmann, J. Lorenz, L.G. Nardin, D. Natalini, A.F.X. Wilhelm (Springer International Publishing, Cham, 2020), pp.1–19

E. Deutschmann, J. Lorenz, L.G. Nardin, D. Natalini, A.F.X. Wilhelm (eds.), *Computational Conflict Research* (Computational Social Sciences. Springer International Publishing, Cham, 2020)

L.G. Drouhot, E. Deutschmann, C.V. Zuccotti, E. Zagheni, Computational approaches to migration and integration research: promises and challenges. J. Ethn. Migrat. Stud. **49**(2), 389–407 (2023)

F. Duffy, K.C. Klosek, L.G. Nardin, G. Wagner, Rebel group protection rackets: simulating the effects of economic support on civil war violence, in *Computational Conflict Research*. ed. by E. Deutschmann, J. Lorenz, L.G. Nardin, D. Natalini, A.F.X. Wilhelm (Springer International Publishing, Cham, 2020), pp.225–251

B. Edmonds, P. Steiglechner, J. Lorenz, F. Kalvas, M.C.L. Batzke, Understanding mutual social influence when people prefer coherent beliefs (Chapter 9), in *Computational Social Science of Social Cohesion and Polarization*, ed. by M. Keijzer, J. Lorenz, M. Bojanowski (Springer, Berlin, 2025)

K.S. Gleditsch, Advances in data on conflict and dissent, in *Computational Conflict Research*. ed. by E. Deutschmann, J. Lorenz, L.G. Nardin, D. Natalini, A.F.X. Wilhelm (Springer International Publishing, Cham, 2020), pp.23–41

S. Hajdinjak, M.H. Morris, T. Amos, Migration policy framing in political discourse: evidence from Canada and the USA, in *Computational Conflict Research*. ed. by E. Deutschmann, J. Lorenz, L.G. Nardin, D. Natalini, A.F.X. Wilhelm (Springer International Publishing, Cham, 2020), pp.83–111

K. Hoffmann Pham, M. Luengo-Oroz, Predictive modelling of movements of refugees and internally displaced people: towards a computational framework. J. Ethn. Migrat. Stud. **49**(2), 408–444 (2023)

M.A. Keijzer, L. Erhard, Z. Kharazian, M. Lamba, The anatomy of rabbit holes: studying information segregation in youtube's recommendation graph (Chapter 4), in *Computational Social Science of Social Cohesion and Polarization*, ed. by M. Keijzer, J. Lorenz, M. Bojanowski (Springer, Berlin, 2025)

C. Kelling, Y. Lin, Analysis of Conflict Diffusion Over Continuous Space, in *Computational Conflict Research*. ed. by E. Deutschmann, J. Lorenz, L.G. Nardin, D. Natalini, A.F.X. Wilhelm (Springer International Publishing, Cham, 2020), pp.201–223

C. Kelling, B.L. Monroe, Analysing community reaction to refugees through text analysis of social media data. Journal of Ethnic and Migration Studies **49**(2), 492–534 (2023)

Y. Khaluf, T. Hovestadt, N. Zöller, B. Wurpts, G.J. Hofstede, Modeling social cohesion: the influence of memory and learning (Chapter 11), in *Computational Social Science of Social Cohesion and Polarization*, ed. by M. Keijzer, J. Lorenz, M. Bojanowski (Springer, Berlin, 2025)

J. Kohne, N. Gallagher, Z.M. Kirgil, R. Paolillo, L. Padmos, F. Karimi, The role of network structure and initial group norm distributions in norm conflict, in *Computational Conflict Research*. ed. by E. Deutschmann, J. Lorenz, L.G. Nardin, D. Natalini, A.F.X. Wilhelm (Springer International Publishing, Cham, 2020), pp.113–140

D.F. Leal, N.L. Harder, Migration networks and the intensity of global migration flows, 1990–2015. J. Ethn. Migrat. Stud. **49**(2), 445–464 (2023)

Y. Lee, F. Piñeyrúa, C.S. Czymara, M. Weber, Linguistic polarization in minority representation: analyzing parliamentary speeches in germany and the uk (1980–2021) (Chapter 7), in *Computational Social Science of Social Cohesion and Polarization*, ed. by M. Keijzer, J. Lorenz, M. Bojanowski (Springer, Berlin, 2025)

S.F. Maerz, C. Puschmann, Text as data for conflict research: a literature survey, in *Computational Conflict Research*. ed. by E. Deutschmann, J. Lorenz, L.G. Nardin, D. Natalini, A.F.X. Wilhelm (Springer International Publishing, Cham, 2020), pp.43–65

C. Oswald, M. Sauter, S. Weber, R. Williams, Under the roof of rebels: civilian targeting after territorial takeover in Sierra Leone. Int. Stud. Q. **64**(2), 295–305 (2020)

A. Pettrachin, L. Gabrielli, J. Kim, S. Ludwig-Dehm, S. Pötzschke, Did exposure to asylum seeking migration affect the electoral outcome of the 'Alternative für Deutschland' in Berlin? Evidence from the 2019 European elections. J. Ethn. Migrat. Stud. **49**(2), 576–600 (2023)

V. Ponizovskiy, M. Ardag, L. Grigoryan, R. Boyd, H. Dobewall, P. Holtz, Development and validation of the personal values dictionary: a theory-driven tool for investigating references to basic human values in text. Eur. J. Person. **34**(5), 885–902 (2020)

A. Salvi, M. Williamson, J. Draper, On the beaten path: violence against civilians and simulated conflict along road networks, in *Computational Conflict Research*. ed. by E. Deutschmann, J. Lorenz, L.G. Nardin, D. Natalini, A.F.X. Wilhelm (Springer International Publishing, Cham, 2020), pp.183–199

P. Warncke, Y. Chen, A. Speer, B. de Bruijn, A. Lüders, D. Carpentras, Resin: a new method to analyze socio-political attitude systems (Chapter 5), in *Computational Social Science of Social Cohesion and Polarization*, ed. by M. Keijzer, J. Lorenz, M. Bojanowski (Springer, Berlin, 2025)

V. Widler, B. Kamińska, A.C.R. Martins, I. Puga-Gonzalez, An investigation into the causal mechanism of political opinion dynamics: a model of hierarchical coarse-graining with community-bounded social influence (Chapter 10), in *Computational Social Science of Social Cohesion and Polarization*, ed. by M. Keijzer, J. Lorenz, M. Bojanowski (Springer, Berlin, 2025)

W. Yuan, Convergence in framing: A semantic network analysis of news coverage of the lgbtq movement in the united states (1960s–2010s) (Chapter 8), in *Computational Social Science of Social Cohesion and Polarization*, ed. by M. Keijzer, J. Lorenz, M. Bojanowski (Springer, Berlin, 2025)

C.V. Zuccotti, J. Lorenz, R. Paolillo, A. Rodríguez Sánchez, S. Serka, Exploring the dynamics of neighbourhood ethnic segregation with agent-based modelling: an empirical application to Bradford, UK. J. Ethn. Migrat. Stud. **49**(2), 554–575 (2023)

Correction to: Modeling Social Cohesion: The Influence of Memory and Learning in Simulated Networks

Yara Khaluf, Bernd Wurpts, Till Hovestadt, Nikolas Zöller, and Gert Jan Hofstede

Correction to:
Chapter 11 in: M. A. Keijzer et al. (eds.), *Computational Social Science of Social Cohesion and Polarization*, Computational Social Sciences, https://doi.org/10.1007/978-3-032-01373-6_11

The original version of the chapter has been revised. An acknowledgment section has been added. The chapter has been updated with these changes.

The updated version of this chapter can be found at
https://doi.org/10.1007/978-3-032-01373-6_11

M. A. Keijzer et al. (eds.), *Computational Social Science of Social Cohesion and Polarization*, Computational Social Sciences,
https://doi.org/10.1007/978-3-032-01373-6_13

MIX
Papier aus verantwortungsvollen Quellen
Paper from responsible sources
FSC® C105338

If you have any concerns about our products,
you can contact us on
ProductSafety@springernature.com

In case Publisher is established outside the EU,
the EU authorized representative is:
Springer Nature Customer Service Center GmbH
Europaplatz 3, 69115 Heidelberg, Germany

Printed by Libri Plureos GmbH
in Hamburg, Germany